GMIT
31/7/06

Gillian Watson is Senior Lecturer in Human Resource Management and currently Programme Leader for MA International Management at the University of Sunderland. She has been Programme Leader for the MSc Human Resource Management and the MSc Human Resource Development programmes and has management experience at senior level in an international business environment. She has conducted management development courses both in the UK and overseas. Her experience includes being a CIPD national examiner for Employee Development.

Kevin Gallagher is Senior Lecturer in Human Resource Management and currently Programme Leader for BA Applied Management at the University of Sunderland, and has managerial experience in the civil engineering and paper industries both in the UK and overseas. He has wide experience in teaching on CIPD and HRM programmes within business, project management, the NHS and call centres. He is a member of the Chartered Management Institute and the Higher Education Academy.

The CIPD would like to thank the following members of the CIPD Publishing Editorial Board for their help and advice:

- Pauline Dibben, Middlesex University Business School

- Edwina Hollings, Staffordshire University Business School

- Caroline Hook, Huddersfield University Business School

- Vincenza Priola, Wolverhampton Business School

- John Sinclair, Napier University Business School

The Chartered Institute of Personnel and Development is the leading publisher of books and reports for personnel and training professionals, students, and all those concerned with the effective management and development of people at work. For details of all our titles, please contact the publishing department:

tel 020 8612 6204

e-mail publish@cipd.co.uk

The catalogue of all CIPD titles can be viewed on the CIPD website:

www.cipd.co.uk/bookstore

Managing for Results

(based on *Managing Activities* by Michael Armstrong)

GILLIAN WATSON and
KEVIN GALLAGHER

Chartered Institute of Personnel and Development

Published by the Chartered Institute of Personnel and Development
151 The Broadway, London, SW19 1JQ

This edition published 2005
Reprinited 2006
First published 1999 as *Managing Activities*
Reprinted 1999, 2001, 2002, 2003 (twice)

Typeset by Fakenham Photosetting Ltd, Fakenham, Norfolk
Printed in Great Britain by The Cromwell Press, Trowbridge, Wiltshire

British Library Cataloguing in Publication Data
A catalogue of this publication is available from the British Library

ISBN 1-84398-014-2

Chartered Institute of Personnel and Development,
151 The Broadway, London, SW19 1JQ
Tel: 020 8612 6200
E-mail: cipd@cipd.co.uk   Website: www.cipd.co.uk
Incorporated by Royal Charter   Registered Charity No. 1079797

Permissions and Acknowledgements

Firstly, the authors would like to thank the following companies and individuals for giving their help, support, time and information. This has enabled us to formulate case studies and/or interesting comparison.

Dr R. Meredith Belbin, founder partner of Belbin Associates and honorary fellow of Henley Management College.

Barrie Watson, a member of Belbin Associates and Managing Director of CERT Consultancy and Training.

Pat Walton (After-Sales Manager), Berghaus Ltd.

Anna Pringle (HR Director), Microsoft Europe and Ireland.

Trish Stokoe (Director of CLDI), Centre for Learning Development and Innovation (Mental Health and Learning Disability Services), Tees and North-East Yorkshire NHS Trust.

Ian Green (Training Controller), Nissan Motor Manufacturing UK Ltd.

Although this book is a second edition the authors have significantly added to or adapted the models, diagrams and theories of other writers. We therefore have many individuals, companies and publishers to thank for giving us their kind permission to use their material, as acknowledged in the text where appropriate. Among these, however, we would like to express our particular gratitude to:

Belbin Associates, for use of Belbin materials

City & Guilds, for permission to reproduce the material in Table 15.2

Elsevier, for permission to reproduce material from *Organisational Behaviour and Human Performance*

John Wiley & Sons, Inc., for permission to reproduce Schein's model of organisational culture

Sage Publications, for permission to reproduce material the copyright of John Child

The CIPD, for extracts from *People Management*

The Regents of the University of California, for permission to reproduce material from the *California Management Review*

The University of Illinois Press, for permission to reproduce the Shannon and Weaver model of communication

We would also like to extend our personal thanks to Ruth Lake at CIPD Publishing for her invaluable support throughout this endeavour.

Contents

Figures

Tables

A note about the Exercises

Three types of exercises feature throughout the text:

- exercises that involve reading, especially the reading of case studies or recommended articles or chapters, often followed by questions on what has been read
- exercises that themselves pose questions for the reader to ponder over or critique
- exercises related to the reader's experience, particularly in the work situation.

The type is indicated at the top of each Exercise with a symbol, as shown below:

    chapter-based Exercise (analytical task or case study)

    an Exercise introducing a question to ponder over or to critique

    an experiential or work-related Exercise

Online support for CIPD students of Managing for Results

This book is supported by the CIPD website:

Access on-line student support at:
www.cipd.co.uk/sss

Included on the site is a sample CIPD exam paper for Managing for Results and accompanying Guidance Notes, written by the CIPD National Examiner.

Managing for Results reflects and complements the new CIPD Leadership and Management Standard. The Standard recognises that leaders and managers at all levels and in all sectors must have the relevant knowledge, understanding and skills to enable them to work effectively in their organisations.

The future presents many challenges and opportunities for the organisation and makes significant, often conflicting, demands upon managers in changing and uncertain circumstances. Aspects of managerial work are aligned with the organisational infrastructure that provides the bedrock of acceptable and necessary procedures and systems. However, managers also need to be leaders and visionaries; they must think and act to differentiate both their own and their organisation's performance so as to distinguish themselves from their competitors in terms of best practice and achieving results.

Achieving results is key in all sectors and, of course, it follows that a successful organisation will attract, engage and retain the 'best' employees. In the *Sunday Times* '100 Best Companies to Work For 2005' the message is clear: leadership and management continue to be the most highly rated factors by employees. In recent years, companies (such as Microsoft) that have been listed as being the best to work for have also outperformed – in some cases by two or three times – the FTSE top 100 in terms of growth and profit.

Gosling and Mintzberg (in J. Gosling and H. Mintzberg, 'The Education of Practice Managers', *M.I.T. Sloan Management Review*, 2004) remind us that 'management is a practice – it has to be appreciated through experience, in context'. This text enables the reader to do just that.

This book is for HR/ Management students and practising managers who themselves seek continuous improvement. It provides a convincing blend of established and contemporary research, theory and practice. We must continue to develop in all of these areas in an integrative fashion. This is why the excellent case studies and exercises in the text are important. They offer an opportunity to evaluate and contrast how ideas can be applied and with what degree of success. In line with the manager's role, the book is wide-ranging, drawing on a rich variety of sources and concluding each chapter with a focused summary of the main points for effective retention of the content.

Tina Stephens
CIPD Examiner, Managing for Results

This book considers the essential requirements of management, including the role of the manager and teamwork, the key concepts of managing the customer, quality and continuous improvement, and excellence and the management of change in today's uncertain organisational environment. The theme of communication runs throughout all elements. There is a definite emphasis upon self-development and the development of managers. It is written for both practising managers and management students, and is based upon current managerial thinking upon a range of – it must be said – quite diverse theories, concepts and practices. It draws upon elements from a variety of disciplines: organisational behaviour, quality, the management of change, operations management and learning development.

The book has been specifically written for those engaged in obtaining accreditation by the Chartered Institute of Personnel and Development, and in particular for those taking the Managing for Results module, as outlined in the new (CIPD) Management Standards, which draws upon recent developments of the sort outlined above. However, it will also be relevant to non-CIPD managers and students who wish to learn about Managing for Results in the modern workplace.

We have deliberately tried to make this a practical book but underpinned by relevant theory. Case studies and exercises are included to reflect good practice and to offer the reader food for thought as to the relevant issues and contingencies at work. A number of these case studies have emerged from interviews conducted in a range of high-profile international organisations operating from within the UK (Berghaus, Nissan, Microsoft) as well as the NHS.

RECENT TRENDS IN MANAGEMENT

In recent years there has been a general movement by both researchers and practitioners towards a deeper understanding of the factors which influence effective management and of how these factors interact to produce the desired results, whatever they may be. The realisation now is that a sole focus upon organisational profits and efficiency as goals or results is insufficient in itself, and that we also need to include consideration of the individual employee, teamwork, the customer, quality and change in much greater depth. For instance, customer satisfaction is something that many organisations now explicitly aspire to measure and improve. All of this requires the development of the management function; effective communication within this new environment is of paramount importance. New frameworks for managing and delivering quality have been developed and adopted throughout Europe and the United States with these considerations in mind, some of them using the term 'results'. Another concurrent thread has been a push towards the professionalisation of the management role – industry and government have been involved in breaking the role down into discrete elements linked to standards and performance criteria which then form the basis for managerial development.

Learning outcomes

Upon completion of this chapter the reader will:

- be able to identify the CIPD's definition of results as outlined in the Managing for Results module
- have an understanding of some of the business environmental factors under which the CIPD Leadership and Management Standards have been developed
- be aware of the importance of employees, customers and suppliers in achieving results
- be familiar with the terms 'infrastructure' and 'differentiators'
- be able to identify the links between desired results, management focus (CIPD) and managerial development, and appreciate how they are mapped out within the book.

WHAT DO WE MEAN BY 'RESULTS'?

Let us first consider the CIPD Leadership and Management Standard (2004) 'Managing for Results'. This is arranged under the following four broad headings and weightings:

- Management practice   40 per cent
- Delivering change   20 per cent
- Enhancing customer relations   20 per cent
- Enabling continuous improvement 20 per cent

This 'recipe' for achieving results is indicative of two criteria: the nature of the desired results, and the perceived balance of them in the overall results equation.

The nature of results

Let us consider each of the four broad headings in a little more detail:

- *Management practice* is concerned with operations within the infrastructure of the organisation under the existing status quo, and is directly related to the product or service being delivered.
- *Delivering change* acknowledges the need for organisations to be aware, plan for, and deliver change effectively in an uncertain environment. This will include internal change projects and responding to external changes.
- *Enhancing customer relations* puts the customer's importance into the results equation.
- *Enabling continuous improvement* advocates an emphasis upon striving for improved quality of product and service.

The perceived balance of results

The percentage figure against each of the areas is indicative of its relative weighting (according to the CIPD Standard). From a simplistic viewpoint this may be seen as a measure of the degree of effort and attention that the manager should associate with the managerial role. However, it is important to realise that the organisation needs all of them if managers are to be effective, and it is the 'whole being greater than the sum of the parts' that marks out the excellent organisation.

THE ENVIRONMENT IN WHICH THE CIPD STANDARD HAS BEEN DEVELOPED – A CONSIDERATION OF RECENT MANAGERIAL THINKING

Why is this background important?

As a professional body the CIPD both reflects and helps advance the latest management practice and managerial development. 'Managing for Results' is the product of various concepts and knowledge, research and techniques, analyses and experiences from leading sources, and is thus consistent with much of what is presently accepted as 'good practice'. In many ways it is the drawing together of these elements. It is thus appropriate to outline here briefly some of the seminal ideas that have contributed to or influenced the writing of the Standard and which form the background work to this book.

Employees, customers and suppliers

To achieve results today, organisations equally need to focus on 'employees, customers and suppliers' (Dalrymple and Drew, 2000). With customers' expectations comes the requirement to continually improve quality both of goods and services. The term that has entered management vocabulary is 'excellence'.

Excellence

Tom Peters used the term 'excellence' in the 1980s in his almost evangelical book *In Search of Excellence*, in which he analysed top-performing companies in the United States at the time. His examination of their success focused on eight types of virtues – for instance, being action-oriented, 'entrepreneurship' (innovation and risk-taking), being close to the customer, and 'productivity through people'. He produced a model he called the McKinsey '7–S Framework', which showed the inter-relationship between various organisational variables (strategy, organisational structure, management style, operational systems, people, corporate strengths or skills), which were all influenced by cultural 'shared' values. These ideas were very popular at the time and their influence is still felt today – although later commentators such as Gareth Morgan in *Images of Organization* were to question the extent to which organisations could control their culture.

The Baldridge model

Then in 1987 the Baldridge Criteria for Performance Excellence were launched by the United States government and set the scene for a range of excellence models. The Baldridge model currently identifies seven key areas (Bloisi *et al*, 2003) or drivers that determine an organisation's business results:

- leadership
- strategic planning
- customer and market focus
- measurement, analysis and knowledge management
- human resource focus
- process management
- excellence levels and trends.

The EFQM model

A recent foray (1990s and after) into the world of excellence is represented by the EFQM (European Foundation for Quality Management) Excellence model. The model provides a framework of 'enablers' and 'results' for organisations to consider if they wish to achieve excellence. (The Excellence model itself is considered later in this book.) The *results* on which the Excellence model centres are:

- customer satisfaction results
- people satisfaction results
- impact on society results, and
- key performance results.

[© 1999–2003 EFQM Excellence model. www.efqm.org]

In other words, results in the new 'excellence' world include not only the traditionally accepted results of output, revenue, profit, etc (under 'key performance results') but also the satisfaction of customers and staff. Additionally, the impact of the organisation on society (positive and negative) has been included. To achieve all of this the Excellence model's *enablers* must be brought into play:

- leadership
- strategy
- people management
- resources and partnerships, and
- processes.

[© 1999–2003 EFQM Excellence model. www.efqm.org]

Thus we may define 'results' in a broader sense than the classical theorists. By their nature, results are not always due to one or other of the enablers acting in isolation but may arise through the cumulative sum of two or more acting together.

The Balanced Scorecard

Kaplan and Norton (1996) introduced the Balanced Scorecard as a strategic management tool. The scorecard translates the vision and strategy of the organisation into four perspectives: financial, internal business, learning and growth, and customers. The organisation measures itself against all of these (as opposed to, say, the tendency to consider only the financial aspects of its business) and in so doing attempts to achieve a balance in which the development of both the organisation and its staff, as well as the focus on the customer, is brought into play. A full analysis of the Balanced Scorecard lies outside the scope of this book, but it is interesting to note the themes of organisation/staff development and customer which are very much at the heart of our discussions here.

The CIPD: infrastructure and differentiators

We also refer to the terms 'infrastructure' and 'differentiators' throughout this book. These terms have been adopted by the CIPD for the Managing for Results module.

Addressing this on behalf of the CIPD, Johns (2004) defines 'infrastructure' in terms of all those elements of an organisation's basic systems, procedures and *modi operandi* which are essential for the organisation to function healthily but which do not of themselves guarantee a successful organisation. In order to guarantee success the organisation needs not only good infrastructure but also a liberal smattering of the 'differentiators' – ie those additional factors which raise the organisation up above its competitors. To give an example, on the infrastructure level of leadership we can talk about 'giving direction to staff' as something that is absolutely essential for any task to be accomplished competently. However, at the differentiator level of leadership we can see that 'vision' goes beyond this: organisations which have the vision to see strategically and the ability to transmit that vision in terms of emotion and commitment are often those which stand head and shoulders above their rivals.

As Johns points out, the new CIPD Leadership and Management Standards are consistent with leading organisational specialists in drawing attention to these distinctions. Nicholas Carr, for instance, in an article written for the *Harvard Business Review* (May 2003) argued that computer hardware and software had progressed from being something that was competitively advantageous to what he terms a necessary part of the 'infrastructure' – that IT has joined history's other revolutionary technologies in this trend, and that it is no longer a differentiator.

Later in this book we will see how Gary Hamel in his bestseller *Competing for the Future* (1994) talks of 'competitor differentiation' – that which is uniquely different from the competition's services. To be one of a number of organisations offering the same competence is not to be uniquely differentiated.

THE PROFESSIONALISATION OF THE MANAGERIAL ROLE

MCI

Another important development has been the ongoing professionalisation of the managerial role. From the late 1980s there has been a commitment towards introducing the MCI (Management Charter Initiative) and associated standards with the aim of developing the managerial role and gaining general acceptance of national standards.

The CEML Report 2002 *Raising our Game*

The government set up CEML (the Centre for Excellence in Management and Leadership) in 2000. This group was set the task of investigating the state of management and leadership in the UK, and reported back with an analysis and recommendations for action in 2002 with the report *Managers and Leaders: Raising our Game*.

MSC

Following on from the MCI the government established the MSC (Management Standards Centre) which established National Occupational Standards for management. These laid out performance criteria, knowledge requirements and evidence for various elements of management and leadership. Candidates could be assessed against these standards while earning NVQs (National Vocational Qualifications). The National Occupational Standards have been influential in the determination of the Leadership and Management Standards of the CIPD, and thus for the Managing for Results module.

MANAGING FOR RESULTS: THE SCHEMA FOR THIS BOOK

The CIPD Standard's (2004) stated focus for Managing for Results is:

- providing direction
- gaining commitment
- facilitating change
- improving organisational performance
- satisfying customers (internal and external)
- maintaining quality
- continuous improvement.

Drawing together the Management focus of the CIPD Standards we can make links to the Desired results (defined here in terms of Excellence) and the necessary Managerial development and competencies required to achieve these results. This provides us with a broad schema for the book. Figure 1.1 shows how the various elements of the book interact.

Table 1.1 shows, for CIPD purposes, the mapping of individual chapters and the book schema against the requirements of the Managing for Results' four main headings of Management practice, Delivering change, Enhancing customer relations, and Enabling continuous improvement.

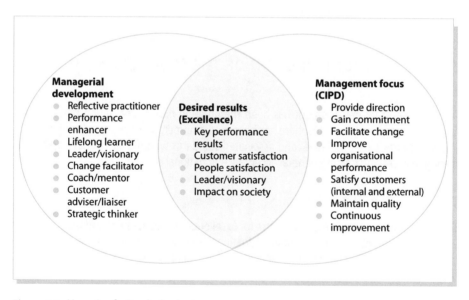

Figure 1.1 *Managing for Results: book schema*

Table 1.1 *Mapping this book's chapters against Managing for Results*

CIPD broad headings (Management Standards)	(CIPD-based) chapter headings in this book	Managerial development (book schema)	Desired results (book schema)	Management focus (CIPD) (book schema)
Management practice 40%	2 The role of the manager 3 How do we develop the role of the manager? 4 Communication: how we inter-relate 5 Communication: practical applications 6 Working with your manager 7 Teamworking 12 Health and safety at work 16 Future directions: managing change	Performance enhancer Reflective practitioner Lifelong learner Leader/ visionary Coach/ mentor	Key performance results (output, sales, profits, etc)	Improve organisational performance Provide direction
Delivering change 20%	10 The living organisation: culture 8 The organisational skeleton: strucutre 11 Power and politics 16 Future directions: managing change 9 Organisational communication	Strategic thinker Leader/ visionary Change facilitator	Key performance results Customer satisfaction People satisfaction Impact on society	Gain commitment Facilitate change
Enhancing customer relations 20%	15 Enhancing customer relations	Customer adviser/ liaiser	Customer satisfaction	Satisfying customers (internal and external)
Enabling continuous improvement 20%	13 Quality – differentiating for excellence 14 Continuous improvement	Reflective practitioner Change facilitator	Key performance results Customer satisfaction	Maintaining quality Continuous improvement

SUMMARY

This chapter has served to introduce the nature of Managing for Results.

It has emphasised the human side of the management requirements. It has also highlighted the key roles of the customer, the associated concept of quality, and the management of change.

It has also outlined the Managing for Results module as detailed in the CIPD's Standard for Leadership and Management, and then mapped out how the various areas are covered in this book

REFERENCES

BLOISI W., COOK C. W. and HUNSAKER P. L. (2003) *Management and Organisational Behaviour.* Maidenhead, McGraw-Hill.

CARR N. (2003) 'IT doesn't matter', *Harvard Business Review,* May, Vol. 81, Issue 5.

CEML (Council for Excellence in Management and Leadership)(2002) *Managers and Leaders: Raising our game.* Report.

CIPD Leadership and Management Standards 2004.

DALRYMPLE J. and DREW E. (2000) 'Quality: on the threshold or the brink?', *Total Quality Management,* Vol. 11, Nos 4, 5 and 6, S697–S703.

EFQM website (2004) http://efqm.org [accessed 23/6/04].

Government response to the report (May 2002) of the CEML (see above) as downloaded from http://dfes.gov.uk/ceml/ [accessed 7/5/04].

HAMEL G. and PRAHALAD C. K.(1994) *Competing for the Future.* Boston, MA, Harvard Business School Press.

JOHNS E. (2004) *CIPD Leadership and Management Standards.* London, CIPD.

KAPLAN R. S. and NORTON D. P. (1996) 'Using the Balanced Scorecard as a strategic management system', *Harvard Business Review,* January–February.

MANAGEMENT STANDARDS CENTRE, National Occupational Standards, as downloaded from http://managers.org.uk/msu2001/ [accessed 7/5/04].

MORGAN G. (1986) *Images of Organization.* London, Sage.

PETERS T. J. and WATERMAN R. H. (1982) *In Search of Excellence.* New York, Harper & Row.

INTRODUCTION

The usual place for management books to start their discussions of what management is about and what managers do is to take the reader back to the pioneering days of management theorists from the nineteenth and early twentieth centuries and then slowly bring them up to date – and in one sense that is what this chapter will do. However, we are also going to state from the outset what we believe are the essential ingredients that presently define successful management today. Recall the terms 'infrastructure' and 'differentiators' from the last chapter? These concepts will be used to assist our illustration of all of those factors that have to be taken into consideration for successful results in the workplace.

Although we may be introducing some 'old' models, it is important to realise that just because a managerial idea, concept or model is 'old' it is not necessarily obsolete. Occasionally we discard it, but just as often early work allows for more sophisticated theory to be built upon it. Although it may be an over-simplification, we might concur that much of today's necessary 'infrastructure' is built upon these traditional models, and that they occasionally supply pointers towards the differentiators. But a cautionary note here: we tend to think that the differentiators are a modern invention and therefore that all new management thinking is overwhelmingly differentiator-oriented. Take the term 'customer relations', for example – it cries out as a differentiator-loaded item with its ideas of putting the customer first. But without the necessary infrastructure in which to operate, including all of those necessary concepts of rules, procedures and systems, it could not exist. Probably the best way to think of what constitutes good management today is to accept that both infrastructure and differentiators are necessary in today's successful organisations – that infrastructure enables an organisation to operate efficiently and that differentiators allow it to be superior or truly effective.

Chapter layout

- In the first part of this chapter we consider elements that are associated largely with infrastructure – ie the concept of managerial functions of planning, organising, leading and controlling. The idea of compartmentalising management into various functions which described the manner in which management could be studied (no matter what the particular business) was one the early theorists such as Henri Fayol proposed. Much of what was proposed then is still relevant today.
- We then discuss Mintzberg's managerial roles. This gives a perspective more on what it feels like to be a manager in the hustle and bustle of everyday work and the roles that we, as managers, are asked to play. This too, is relevant to our discussion because it links with the next chapter on how we develop the managerial role.
- Finally, we reflect upon a range of theories that contribute to our discussion of what a manager's role actually entails.

On completing the chapter, the reader will:

- have a view as to what a manager is and what management is about
- be familiar with the traditional theories of management which emphasise order, structure and control
- be aware of more recent attempts to describe what managers do, based on empirical studies which indicate that rather than being ordered, structured and controlled, management tends to be fragmented, varied and governed to a large degree by events over which managers have little or no control.

Managerial work is fragmented, but the effective management of diverse activities still requires managers to exercise a number of skills in order to achieve their goals. In fact, these skills become even more important as a means of maintaining some order in what might otherwise be chaos.

On completing this chapter, the reader will understand and be able to explain the managerial skills concerned with:

- planning – planning and prioritising
- organising – organising work, directing (which includes the agreement of objectives)
- allocating tasks and delegating
- leading – leading, co-ordinating and implementing
- controlling – controlling work, including monitoring and evaluating.

The other basic skills given detailed consideration in succeeding chapters are how we develop the role of the manager (Chapter 3), practical aspects of communication (Chapter 5), and teamworking (Chapter 7).

THE TRADITIONAL CONCEPTS OF MANAGEMENT

Traditional writers on management set out to define the nature of managerial work in terms of basic universal elements. These were believed to provide a framework for the analysis and conduct of the managerial task.

Henri Fayol

The traditional framework was developed in 1916 by a pioneer writer on management, Henri Fayol, in his book *General and Industrial Management* (translated from French into English in 1949), who based it on an analysis of his experience as a practising manager.

He set out six industrial undertakings that he maintained are present in the workplace:

Technical activities	Production, manufacture, adaptation
Commercial activities	Buying, selling, exchange
Financial activities	Search for the optimum use of capital
Security activities	Protection of property and persons
Accounting activities	Stocktaking, balance sheet, cost, statistics
Managerial activities	Planning, organising, command, co-ordination and control

Source: Gallagher, Rose, McClelland, Reynolds and Tombs: *People in Organisations: An active learning approach*, Blackwell, Oxford, 1997

Fayol (1949) focused his attention on 'managerial activities' by postulating what he believed were a set of guidelines that worked in his managerial experience (Gallagher et al, 1997). Fayol went further and said that there were 14 'principles of management' that could enable managers to achieve the desired results and thereby gain success (see Table 2.1).

Table 2.1   Fayol's 14 principles of management

1	Division of work	The principle here was to produce more and better work with the same effort. It was believed that through focused experiences workers and managers became better at their jobs.
		It is … applied to … all work involving a more or less considerable number of people and demanding abilities of various types, and it results in specialisation of functions and separation of powers.
		(Fayol, 1949)
		Some disadvantages to this way of thinking particularly in today's organisations are:
		▪ boredom – automatic response ▪ loss of autonomy – management controls the operation ▪ stress – speed dictated by the line fatigue.
		(Gallagher et al, 1997)
2	Authority	Here Fayol (1949) recognises the necessity to have authority and discipline in the workplace: 'Application of sanction to acts of authority forms part of the conditions essential for good management.'
		However, a distinction must be made between formal and personal authority: Gallagher et al (1997) state that 'Personal authority is derived from intelligence, experience and ability; official [formal] authority from a position within the organisation's hierarchy.'
3	Discipline	Fayol (1949) describes discipline as obedience, application, energy, behaviour and outward marks of respect. Today, we work in a less formal environment than in Fayol's day and often see aspects of discipline more in terms of 'outward marks of respect' afforded to managers.
		There nonetheless remains a need for formal policy and procedure in regard to discipline as well as the need for signs of mutual respect – a respect that Gallagher et al (1997) describe as 'ultimately, obedience to what a successful outcome requires'.

Table 2.1 *continued*

4	Unity of command	Fayol disliked dual command of any type. He declared (Fayol, 1949): 'As soon as two superiors wield their authority over the same person or department, unease makes itself felt …' He would therefore have looked askance at contemporary organisations that follow a matrix structure (see Chapter 8). It is quite evident therefore that our present-day organisations do not follow the 'unity of command' principle in all circumstances. Whichever structure an organisation might choose to follow, it is nonetheless essential that roles do not become blurred and that a focused reporting structure is in place.
5	Unity of direction	In Fayol's terms (1949) this meant 'one head, one plan'. He saw the function of 'unity of direction' as uniting and co-ordinating activities towards organisational goals. Today we might describe it as working within the organisational aims or corporate mission statement which is designed to give direction and gain success for the organisation.
6	Subordination of individual interests to the general interests	The successful/result-oriented outcomes modern organisations seek, and their desire for success, are perhaps no different from in Fayol's time. It is still the case that fulfilling the organisations' needs prevails over meeting the individual or departmental needs. Fayol (1949, as quoted by Gallagher *et al*, 1997) suggests this can be brought about by: ▪ good examples from superiors ▪ seeking fair agreement as far as possible between conflicting interests ▪ instant supervision to ensure that individual interests are not taking priority.
7	Remuneration	Fayol (1949) described various methods of remuneration for the workforce: ▪ schemes for individuals and groups ▪ piece-time rates ▪ profit-sharing. He conceded, however, that no one method was perfect for all organisations. He went on to advocate that a principle of fairness should prevail – one of 'a fair day's pay for a fair day's work'.
8	Centralisation	Although an advocate of centralisation, Fayol recognised that in certain times de-centralisation was necessary. This, he maintained, was dependent on the situation, the circumstances and the size of the organisation. Arguably, Fayol was ahead of management thinking at the time, in that he was effectively endorsing contingency theories with the idea that 'control and management approaches should be varied according to particular tasks and personal involvement' (Gallagher *et al*, 1997).

Table 2.1 *continued*

9	Scalar chain	Here we refer to the hierarchical chain of authority and communication. Fayol (1949) highlighted the need for this 'chain' in order for 'unity of command' to be maintained. Problems are apparent, however, if we consider that:
		■ a message can be distorted at any link in the 'scalar chain'; this distortion can in turn change the meaning of the original message ■ distortion can occur when distance may be involved – eg one individual in the organisation is a significant physical distance from the other and there are limited opportunities to communicate ■ the data may become unnecessary or redundant for individuals within certain links of the chain – eg they do not need to know the information.
		Fayol suggested a horizontal link in the chain (a 'gangplank') so that communication could take place between people in different parts of the organisation.
10	Order	Fayol (1949) promoted an ordered work environment such that everything had a place in the organisation. This he applied both to people and property. Workshop and office equipment, for example, had to be housed in pre-designated areas, kept clean and tidy in a neat and ordered manner.
		People, he advocated, also needed a 'place' in the organisation. He believed that organisational charts were the key to help 'locate' people in their place in the organisation. The 'organisational chart' plays a large part in our organisational life today: it helps plan the strategic use of staff.
11	Equity	When describing this particular principle, Fayol (1949) returned to the notion of 'fairness'. This he distinguishes from any legal requirement or company policy and procedure. His advocacy of 'fairness' went beyond the legal aspect by suggesting that organisations show equity by managing within the 'spirit of the law'.
		Today we might see this as managing within diversity or from a moral stance within corporate social responsibility.

Table 2.1 *continued*

12	Stability of tenure of personnel	This Fayol (1949) expressed as the need for continuity in the manager's role and declared that it should be linked to 'security of tenure'. In fact he advocated that all workers should be managed under those principles. He also advanced the view that a 'mediocre' manager who stays with the firm helps the organisation more than a series of 'good' managers who leave in rapid succession.
		Training a manager is an expensive undertaking. Stability of tenure may therefore allow an organisation to gain value from its investment in the manager's development.
13	Initiative	Fayol's ideas (1949) are surprisingly close to contemporary thinking in regard to managers' taking the initiative and using their discretion. He suggested that everyone in the organisation be asked to contribute to plans and ideas. Fayol believed that enabling people to contributing in this way is 'one of the most powerful stimulants in human endeavour'. However, he also postulated a cautionary note: that it took confident managers to encourage the initiatives of subordinates.
14	Esprit de corps	Here, Fayol (1949) considered the need for harmony and teamwork, and threw scorn on a divide-and-rule policy. Gallagher *et al* (1997) suggest divide-and-rule to be evident when 'management deliberately encourages conflict between worker groups on a basis that a divided workforce will cause no trouble'. Fayol encouraged the positives aspects of togetherness. One we would acknowledge in contemporary management thinking is that an organisation should have a strong culture.

Adapted from Fayol (1949) and Gallagher, Rose, McClelland, Reynolds and Tombs (1997)

Describing managerial activities, as we have seen, Fayol (1949) suggested that

> **'All undertakings require planning, organising, command, co-ordination and control to function properly.'**

- *planning* – a good plan to contain unity, flexibility, continuity and precision. He also asserted that planning was difficult and required a high level of competence from managers.
- *organising* – 'To organise a business is to provide it with everything useful to its functioning: raw materials, tools, capital, personnel.'
- *command* – a term that (outside the military) is rarely used in contemporary management terminology – instead, we use the term 'leadership'. Fayol devised yet

another list of guidelines for managers who are required to exercise 'command'/ leadership. These are:

- to have a thorough knowledge of their personnel
- to eliminate the incompetent
- to be well versed in the agreements binding the business and its employees
- to set a good example
- to conduct periodical audits of the organisation and use summarised charts to further them
- to bring together their chief assistants by means of conferences at which unity of direction and focusing of effort are provided for
- to avoid becoming engrossed in detail
- to aim at making unity, initiative and loyalty prevail among the personnel.

All of these have resonance today as requirements of good leadership.

- *co-ordination* – 'To coordinate is to harmonise all the activities of a concern so as to facilitate its working, and its success.' Fayol believed that for co-ordination to be effective, it had to be positively encouraged. He advocated 'unity of direction', good communication and weekly meetings of department heads.
- *control* – arguably, Fayol saw control as the culmination of the five management activities. He stated that 'Control consists in verifying whether everything occurs in conformity with the plan adopted, the instructions issued and principles established.'

Luther Gullick

A later (1937) theorist of the classical school was Luther Gullick (1937), who expanded Fayol's concept into the acronym POSDCORB, which stands for:

- **P**lanning – working out in broad outline the things that need to be done and the methods for doing them to accomplish the purpose set for the enterprise
- **O**rganising – establishing the formal structure of an organisation through which work subdivisions are arranged, defined and co-ordinated for the whole enterprise
- **S**taffing – bringing in and training the staff and maintaining favourable conditions of work: the personnel function
- **D**irecting – making decisions and continuously embodying them in specific general orders and instruction, and serving as the leader of the enterprise
- **C**o-ordinating – inter-relating the various parts of the work – an all-important duty
- **R**eporting – keeping those to whom executives are responsible informed as to what is going on, which includes keeping oneself and one's subordinates informed through records, research and inspection
- **B**udgeting – financial planning, accounting and control.

A MODEL OF MANAGEMENT PROCESS

A framework to help us conceptualise the next part of this chapter is that of:

- planning
- organising
- leading
- controlling

as used for example by Stoner, Freeman and Gilbert (1995) in their model of management process. You will readily note the similarity of this framework to that of Fayol, above. This process suggests that managers, despite their level in an organisation or their competence, employ a range of connected activities in order to fulfil their aims and objectives. These authors consider that (Stoner, Freeman and Gilbert, 1995):

> **'Management is the process of planning, organising, leading and controlling the efforts of organisation members, and of using all other organisational resources to achieve stated organisational goals.'**

Planning

Planning is the process of deciding on a course of action, ensuring that the resources required to implement the action will be available, and scheduling the programme of work required to achieve a defined end-result.

Planning for results

The main activities are:

- objective-setting – deciding what has to be achieved over a certain timescale
- activity analysis – deciding what will have to be done in order to achieve the objective
- forecasting – assessing how much work will have to be done, how the workload might change, and how likely it is that any specialised or rush jobs that might have to be undertaken might also require a reassessment of the plan
- scheduling – determining the sequence and timescales of the operations and events required to produce results within the deadline: this involves deciding on priorities (prioritisation) – a key managerial activity
- resourcing – deciding how many and what sort of people will be required, and when; assessing demands for finance, facilities, materials and bought-in parts in terms of amounts, types, and when they must be available
- procedure planning – deciding how the work will be carried out
- setting targets and standards – for output, sales, times, quality, costs, and for any other aspects of work where performance and progress must be monitored and controlled
- setting up monitoring procedures – deciding on performance measures and instituting methods for monitoring and controlling performance and progress.

EXERCISE 2.1

1   Winston Churchill once said that 'It is wise to plan ahead but only as far as you can see.' What are the implications of this statement for managers?
2   It has been argued that there is nothing special about planning – it is only a matter of thinking systematically and using common sense. What is your analysis of this statement?

3   Managers have been known to say 'What's the point of planning? You're always overtaken by events.' What concerns do you have about this comment?

4   You have been put in charge of a project to commission and build a new warehouse on a 'green-field' site for a publishing company to store about 250,000 books and from which the company will distribute books to wholesalers and retailers on demand. Taking into account the bullet-list provided above, what are the initial steps you would take?

Prioritising

The prioritising of work involves deciding on the relative importance of a range of demands or tasks so that the order in which they are then undertaken can be determined. The fragmented nature of managerial work (as described in Chapter 1) and the sudden and often conflicting demands made on managers' time means that managers are constantly faced with decisions on when to do things. They may often find themselves in a situation where they have to cope with conflicting priorities. This can be stressful unless they adopt a systematic approach to prioritisation.

Prioritisation can be carried out in stages.

1   List all the things you have to do. These can be classified in three groups:
- regular duties, such as submitting a report, calling on customers, carrying out a performance review
- special requests from managers, colleagues, customers, clients, suppliers, etc, delivered orally, by telephone, letter, fax or email
- self-generated work, such as preparing proposals on an innovation.

2   Classify each item on the list according to
- the significance of the task to be done in terms of its impact on your work (and reputation) and on the results achieved by the organisation, your team or anyone else involved
- the importance of the person requesting the work or expecting you to deliver something: less significant tasks may well be put higher on the priority list if they are set by the chief executive or a key client
- the urgency of the tasks – deadlines, what will happen if it is not completed on time
- any scope there may be for extending deadlines, altering start and finish times and dates
- how long each task will take to complete, noting any required or imposed starting and completion times that cannot be changed.

3   Assess how much time you have available to complete the tasks, apart from the routine work which you must get done. Also assess what resources, such as your own staff, are available to get the work done.

4   Draw up a provisional list of priorities by reference to the criteria of significance, importance and urgency listed at Stage 2 above.

5   Assess the possibility of fitting this prioritised schedule of work into the time available. If it proves difficult, put self-imposed priorities on a back-burner and concentrate on the significant tasks. Negotiate for completion or delivery times

where you believe they are possible, and when successful, move those tasks down the priority list.

6   Finalise the list of priorities and schedule the work you have to do (or you have to get others to do) accordingly.

Set out step-by-step like this, prioritisation looks a formidable task. But experienced managers go through all these stages almost unconsciously, although systematically, whenever they are confronted with a large workload or conflicting priorities. What many of them do is simply write out a 'Things to do' list at the beginning of the week, or quickly run through in their minds all the considerations described in the above six-stage sequence and make notes on a piece of paper.

EXERCISE 2.2

You are the personnel manager of a manufacturing plant based in the Midlands which is part of an American-owned engineering company. You report directly to the plant manager but you are functionally responsible to the group personnel director. On your return from two weeks' holiday on 5 July you find the following email messages:

1   From the plant manager
    We're running into services problems getting contract A5612 out on time. There is a serious shortage of skilled assemblers on that project. Contact me as soon as you return. (2 July)

    The union has put in a pay claim for a 'substantial increase'. They want to hold a preliminary meeting with us on 9 July. We shall need to discuss our response. (30 June)

    You didn't let me have your proposals on the new pay structure before you went on holiday, although I understand they are just about complete. We really need to get on with this. Please contact me on your return. (23 June)

2   From the group personnel manager
    The director of Comp and Ben from the States is joining our group personnel conference on 7 July. He would like to hear your ideas about a new pay structure in your plant; so would everyone else. I should like you to make a presentation – 30 minutes or so. (28 June)

3   From the production manager
    I had to suspend John Smith of the Assembly Shop on Wednesday, 30 June for fighting. I didn't want to take immediate action pending an enquiry in which I think you should take part – there are complications. But the shop steward has complained to me that nothing has happened yet. We need to get on with the enquiry as soon as you return. (2 July)

    I am worried about the shortage of skilled assemblers – it's holding up work. Can we discuss when you return? (1 July)

4   From the sales manager
    Karen Brown, one of my best reps, has just told me that she's been offered a
    much better job (a 20 per cent increase in salary). I really need to keep her – she
    looks after one of our key clients. Can we discuss this urgently when you are
    back? (30 June)

5   From Bill Robinson
    You interviewed me for the position of progress co-ordinator on 18 June but I
    have heard nothing since then. I should like to know the outcome of the inter-
    view. (1 July)

6   From your secretary
    Ruby Sharpe came into my office in tears today, saying that she has been
    harassed by her manager. I think you should see her as soon as possible after
    your return. (23 June)
       Group is pestering me for our personnel return which they said should have
    been with them on 24 June. Can you give it to me to send to them on Monday?
    (2 July)

You have left Monday and Tuesday free before you attend the two-day group personnel conference which is to be held in Central London on Wednesday and Thursday,
7 and 8 July (a three-line whip commands your presence).

What approach will you adopt in sorting out your priorities?

Organising

Organising involves dividing the overall management task into a variety of processes and
activities, and then establishing the means of ensuring that they are carried out effectively.
As a manager you have to decide who does what in your team. This may not involve a grand
re-design very frequently, if at all, but it may be necessary to make frequent adjustments in
response to changes in activities, demands and people.

Organising means defining who does what (teams and individuals) and establishing
reporting relationships between them. It is also concerned with deciding how activities
should be co-ordinated and controlled and the means of communication that will be used.

Your aim will be to clarify roles, accountabilities (responsibilities for results), relationships
and expectations so far as this is possible in fluid, even turbulent, conditions. You will also
have to ensure that people are given the scope and opportunity to use their skill to good
effect and to develop their competencies.

Organisation design is considered more fully in Chapter 8.

The process of allocating work

Managers have to define their own objectives as well as those of the members of their
teams. They have then to manage their own workload. But if, in the familiar phrase, managing is getting things done through people, they must also be concerned with allocating

and delegating work to other people in the light of agreed objectives and targets. They would not be managers if they could do it all themselves. They have to get contributions from other people if they are to achieve their overall task.

Allocating work means assigning it to a person or a group of people in order to achieve a purpose and/or result. Managers are usually responsible for a related group of activities. They cannot do them all on their own. They must allocate them – dividing the overall task into a number of subsidiary tasks, defining what they are, what has to be achieved, and how it is to be achieved.

The process of allocating work is carried out in stages:

1   Define the overall task – what the unit, section or team is there to do.
2   Analyse the activities required to achieve the task/result.
3   Decide how best to allocate the activities – to individuals or amongst groups of individuals. This is the process of organisation design as described in Chapter 8.
4   Define the tasks which teams or individuals have to carry out. Each task should ideally consist of three elements: planning, executing and controlling. If this can be achieved, the work is likely to be more satisfying and motivating to the team or individuals, and you will get better results. Your aim should be to empower the individual or the team as far as you can. Empowerment gives people singly and in groups more scope or 'power' to exercise control over and take responsibility for their work. It provides greater space for individuals to use their abilities or teams to deploy their collective skills to take decisions close to the point of impact – for example, handling a customer query or complaint. (Allocating work to teams is discussed in more detail in Chapter 7, and individual job design is covered in Chapter 8.)
5   Define and explain the purpose of the tasks to the people who will carry them out. It is important for them to understand how what they do contributes to the achievement of the overall purpose of their department or team and to the achievement of the purposes of other related activities. (This is particularly important when horizontal processes are cutting across organisational boundaries.)
6   Define expectations of the standards of performance required and any quantitative targets that must be achieved. As far as possible these expectations should be discussed and agreed with the people or team concerned – it is important that they have a sense of 'ownership' – 'This is what we have agreed to; we believe we are capable of doing it; we're going to do it.' Targets and standards should be defined so as to be related to (integrated with) organisational or functional objectives and the organisation's standards and core values.
7   Agree performance measures which indicate how well the individual or team performs in carrying out the task and achieving targets and standards. Performance measures can relate to such criteria as work, quality, output, timelines (delivery or completion on time, speed of reaction or turnaround) and income/costs. The aim should be to place people in a position in which by referring to each of the measures they can use information on performance to control their own work.
8   Agree any procedures to be used for measuring and reporting on progress and performance.
9   Define the skills and competences needed to achieve a satisfactory level of performance, and make arrangements as required for individuals to acquire or develop these skills.

10   Emphasise that people will be encouraged to think out for themselves the best way to carry out the work wherever there is any choice. Indicate also that you will encourage and welcome any suggestions on how work methods could be improved or how the allocation of work could be altered for the better.

EXERCISE 2.3

You are a manager in an insurance company where the present arrangement is that the work is divided into four sections: processing initial enquiries about insurance policies, amending existing policies, underwriting new policies, and dealing with bad claims. The company has decided to focus attention more on customer service and has asked you to form teams of people who will deal with all these activities jointly for groups of customers from different regions.

How do you set about allocating work to the newly formed teams?

Giving instructions

The process of allocating work is concerned with the permanent or at least longer-term distribution of duties and tasks to people. But on a day-to-day basis you will certainly need to get new or different things done by individual members of your team or by the team as a whole. What you then have to do is to define and agree

- what has to be done
- why it has to be done
- how it has to be done (if it is new or different)
- what resources are available to do it (people, money, materials, time)
- what results are expected
- when it has to be done
- how you and everyone else involved will know that it has been done (performance indicators).

The more you can involve people in reaching agreement with you under each of these headings the better. It is particularly important to get their views about how they will do the work. Every time you give an instruction, a learning opportunity is created. People will learn much better if they are encouraged to think through for themselves the best way to do something. This is called 'self-managed learning' and it is the best form of learning. Of course, you may have to provide some guidance and help, and you may have to arrange for special training.

But if people are encouraged to do their own thing, they will learn faster and be more capable of getting on with it themselves. Your aim should be to minimise the amount of close supervision you have to exercise. This frees you for more important planning, development and monitoring activities, and for liaising and networking with your colleagues.

The process of delegating work

Delegation is defined by the *Oxford English Dictionary* as 'the commitment of authority or power' to someone. Delegation involves giving people the authority to do something rather than doing it yourself.

You delegate work when you want someone else to do something because you do not have the time to do it yourself, or because you do not want to do it yourself (for good reasons – because you have more important things to do, not because you want to get rid of a tedious task!), or because there is someone who can carry out the task better than you can, or because delegation is one of the best ways of developing and motivating people – extending their skills and increasing their sense of responsibility and confidence in themselves.

EXERCISE 2.4

You have an experienced assistant buyer in your team who is efficient in the basic task of placing and processing orders with suppliers. However, as part of a quality management programme it has been decided that buyers should be more involved in specifying and monitoring quality standards.

How do you approach instructing your assistant buyer in these new duties?

To summarise, you delegate when

- you have more work than you can effectively carry out yourself
- you cannot allocate yourself sufficient time for your priority tasks
- you believe the task can be done adequately by the individual (or even better if he or she has expertise you do not have)
- you want to develop the skills and competencies of the individual
- you want to empower the individual, giving him or her more scope and authority to do things without reference back to you.

Delegation can be distinguished from work allocation. Delegation involves relinquishing part of your own authority – something that you are accountable for – to someone else. When work is delegated to people, they receive authority to do things which they previously did not have. But you cannot delegate responsibility, for ultimately you are accountable for the actions of the people to whom you have delegated work.

Work allocation is the process of defining what people are expected to do to carry out their role on a continuing basis. From time to time they will be allocated specific tasks – given instructions – but these will not be activities that you would normally be expected to carry out yourself. Yet the distinction between giving instructions and delegating is a fine one.

When you delegate you have to decide:

- what to delegate – You delegate tasks that you do not need to do yourself or tasks which will develop the skills of people or enhance their sense of responsibility for what they are doing. You may also delegate work to those with particular expertise. You will generally know what needs to be done and how it should be done, but others may have in-depth knowledge which you cannot be expected to possess. The ability to make the best use of specialists through delegation is one of the hallmarks of an effective manager.

- who does the work – Ideally, the person you select should have the knowledge, skills, motivation, confidence and time to get the work done to your complete satisfaction. But you may have to choose someone who does not meet the ideal specification. In which case, identify someone with the basic attributes and the willingness to learn to do the work with your help and guidance. This is how people develop, and the development of people should be your conscious aim whenever you delegate. You will also be looking for people you can trust to get on with it – you do not want to be constantly breathing down their necks. You can find out who can be trusted by progressively trying people out, first on relatively small and unimportant tasks and then by giving them increasingly more scope. With inexperienced or untested people, start by relinquishing relatively little of your authority and limiting their freedom to act independently. Progressively thereafter, give them more scope, until finally they have almost complete freedom to do the work.

- how to give out the work – Basically, your approach to delegating work should follow the pattern of giving instructions described earlier in this chapter. A distinction can be made between 'hard' and 'soft' delegation. Hard delegation takes place when you tell someone what to do, how to do it, and when you want the results. Soft delegation takes place when you agree generally what has to be achieved and leave the individual to get on with it. You still need to agree limits of authority, define any decisions which should be referred to you, and indicate when and how you will review progress. Whether a soft or a hard approach is adopted, you should always delegate by the results you expect.

- how you can guide and develop – Delegation not only helps you to get your own work done, it also helps to develop skills and confidence and increase the degree to which you can trust people to take on additional tasks with more freedom to act. Guidance, helping people to learn and coaching are all parts of the process of delegating. You may also have to provide specific guidance to relatively inexperienced people at the start of a task. And without interfering unduly, you should be prepared to provide guidance as necessary. Your role is not to let your people sink or swim. You have to keep them afloat. Remember, however, that there is a delicate balance to be maintained between undue interference and helpful guidance. This distinction may be difficult. But delegation, although important, is never an easy option – you have to work at it.

- how to monitor performance – At first you may have to monitor performance fairly carefully if someone is new to the task. But the sooner you can relax and watch progress informally, the better. You have to try to restrain yourself from undue interference in the way the work is being done. You do not want people to make mistakes, but you can help them to learn from them if they do occur. And you have to accept that some mistakes are likely – this is where trust is important. There should be an understanding that people should come to you in good time before things get out of hand. There should be no recriminations – rather congratulations that you have been informed. A joint problem-solving approach can then be adopted in which agreement is reached on the cause of the problem, what can be done about it now, and what can be done to prevent its recurrence in the future. That is what is meant by allowing people to learn from their mistakes.

1   The capacity to trust someone to do something well is an important require-
    ment for effective delegation.
    a) How do you build up your trust in other people?
    b) How can you ensure that people learn to trust you?

2   The phrase 'delegate by the results you expect' was used earlier: how can you
    do this in practice?

3   The phenomenon of 'riverbanking' has been described as what happens when
    a manager delegates something that is very difficult to do without proper guid-
    ance or help. As the individual is going down in the river for the third time, the
    boss is observed in a remote and safe position on the riverbank saying 'It's easy,
    really. All you need to do is to try a bit harder.'

    What should you do to avoid riverbanking?

Leading

Leading, according to Stoner, Freeman and Gilbert (1995) is

> **'the process of directing and influencing the task-related activity of group members or an entire organisation'.**

Managers are there to set the direction, to ensure that their function, department or team is moving purposefully towards a defined goal. But this should not be regarded as a process of simply commanding people to do what they are told. Good managers are not in the business of requiring compliance. They should seek willing co-operation rather than grudging submission. They need to involve people in deciding what needs to be done and how it should be done. Managers should see themselves as facilitators rather than commanders.

But it is still necessary to provide a sense of direction, to get people to understand where the organisation and their team are heading, and the part they are expected to play in getting there. Directing is therefore about furthering understanding and agreement on where the team and its members are expected to go. It is a key aspect of leadership. As Kotter (1971) wrote:

> **'The direction-setting aspect of leadership does not produce plans: it creates visions and strategies. These describe a business, technology or corporate culture in terms of what it should become over the long term and articulate a feasible way of achieving the goal.'**

The driver model of leadership

Leading can be said to be at the centre of managerial activity, because it directly relates to co-ordinating people and work as well as dealing with a range of interpersonal relationships with people in the organisation. A recent study which gave rise to what is known as the 'driver model of leadership' (Maitland, *People Management*, 2003, Vol. 9, No.11) was conducted over a three-year period and included information provided by 40 major global companies. The research revealed that a key driver of business profitability was the level of commitment shown by a firm's employees – and that key factors behind this were (Maitland, 2003):

- the leadership skills of managers
- the opportunities given to staff for personal development
- the extent to which employees are empowered to discharge their responsibilities effectively.

This model reinforces much of the traditional model of leadership in that it talks of directing and informing, but goes further in a discussion of values, respecting and role models.

The researchers compared UK companies with US equivalent businesses and found that leaders in UK organisations were rated less favourably by their employees. They suggest therefore that a UK employee's level of commitment to his or her organisations will be lower. As a consequence they assert that an organisation's profitability suffers. The leadership behaviours of the top-performing global organisation that achieved above-average financial results in its sector, the study maintains, are a factor in the organisation's ability to outperform its competitors.

The six qualities that the researchers suggest are essential skills for successful leadership are:

- imparting direction – Successful leaders have clear goals and objectives for their companies. They provide an inspiring vision of what they want their companies to be now, and what they want to become.
- showing respect – Successful leaders respect their employees and include them in their thinking. They recognise the value of the diverse talents and outlooks which they bring to their joint enterprise.
- being informative – Successful leaders keep their employees in the picture regarding plans and progress. They communicate rapidly and effectively about important matters that affect them.
- having values – Successful leaders have values that they believe in, and that they live up to. They promote the ethics and standards that they wish their organisations to subscribe to, and their own decisions and behaviours are consistent with these structures.
- acting with energy – Successful leaders cut through corporate bureaucracy and red tape to establish clear action plans and priorities. They take prompt decisions to ensure that their company achieves and maintains a lead in the market.
- being role models – Successful leaders set an example that their followers are motivated to and aspire to emulate. Their management style encourages their employees to give of their best.

Co-ordinating

Co-ordination is the process of ensuring that the tasks carried out by people are integrated so that they mesh together to achieve a common purpose through unified effort. Activities cannot be carried out in isolation. They have to be linked together so that they are conducted in the required sequence or in conjunction with one another. Organisations have to distinguish, or differentiate, the various activities required to achieve their purpose, but they also have to integrate these activities so that the required flow of work is maintained between different areas of operation. It may be furthered by a business process re-engineering exercise which, obviously, is concerned with business processes – the combination or sequence of activities that takes one or more kinds of input and creates an output that is of value to the customer. In this way order fulfilment may be seen as a process that starts with one order as the input and results in the delivery of the ordered goods. The various activities at each stage in this process must be sequenced and co-ordinated to ensure that all happens according to plan.

Co-ordination is required because individual actions may have to be synchronised. Activities must follow each other in sequence. Others must be carried out simultaneously in order that all elements of the enterprise finish together. People may want to do their own thing. Initiative and a spirit of independence are desirable qualities – yet if people who display them do not contribute alongside the efforts of others to achieve the goal, they may or may not be wasting their own time but they will undoubtedly be hindering the achievement of the required end-result.

Co-ordination involves getting people to work together. Recall that Fayol (1949) highlighted co-ordinating as a separate activity – here we include it as part of the leadership role. In general it means integrating activities, exercising leadership, and team-building (see Chapter 7). It also means carrying out specific activities:

- planning – Co-ordination should take place before the event. This means deciding what needs to be done, and when. It also means sequencing activities through processes such as networks and deciding when they have to be carried out jointly and how the mutual support required is to be provided.
- organising – When dividing work between teams and people, avoid breaking apart those tasks which are linked together and which you cannot separate clearly from one another. You have to identify potential barriers between related activities and get rid of them by emphasising that the sequence of work is a continuous process and that all concerned have a responsibility not only for carrying out the work in their own area but also for ensuring that it flows smoothly into the next area. People must be encouraged to appreciate that they must link up with other people – co-ordinated teamwork should be emphasised as a core value, and the ability to work well in a team should be an important factor in assessing performance.
- communicating – You should not only communicate what you expect people to do but also convey the importance you attach to your staff's communicating with each other. The key to effective co-ordination is good communication.
- monitoring – The steps listed above should help to enhance co-ordination but they cannot guarantee that it will happen. Managers must monitor what is going on and take swift action if there is evidence of poor co-ordination.

EXERCISE 2.6

What do you think are likely to be the main barriers to achieving good co-ordination?

How would you overcome them?

Controlling

Controlling is about monitoring and measuring performance, comparing results with plans, and taking corrective action when required. But control is not simply a matter of putting things right. Control is relative. It is concerned with comparing the difference between planned and actual performance. It also has a positive side – getting more or better things done on the basis of information received. Good control is dependent on monitoring and evaluation processes (as noted later in this section).

Exercising control

To exercise good control you must:

- plan what you aim to achieve
- measure regularly what has been achieved
- compare actual achievements with the plan
- take action to correct deviations from the plan or to develop opportunities revealed by the information.

Control need not be oppressive. You should not make people feel that you are watching them all the time, waiting for them to make a mistake. In fact, you should do everything possible to get them to control themselves – to monitor their own performances and take action as required. Self-control is far better than top-down command and control.

Setting up a control system

In accordance with the points above, it is preferable to involve people in setting up their own control system. This is one of the ways in which empowerment can be achieved. Your main task will then be to guide them on two essential requirements:

- how to set appropriate and fair targets, standards and budgets
- how to decide what information is required for control purposes and ensure that it is made available in a readily assimilated form, in good time, and to the right people (ie those carrying out the work) so that they can take action – control information should be the property of the team, not just the team leader.

Monitoring

To exercise control, managers have to be continuously aware of what is going on in their departments or teams. They must know how well their unit is performing against its objectives and how well individual team members are performing. Monitoring is the process of measuring and observing what is happening as it happens so that action can be taken as required – swiftly, if need be. Managers should also monitor their own performance against plans, budgets, objectives and standards.

Effective monitoring requires managers initially to define or establish clearly the plan or programme they have to implement, the targets and standards of performance they have to achieve, and the budgets within which they have to operate. They should then identify the performance measures they can use for monitoring purposes. These can be classified under several headings:

- Finance – income, shareholder value, added value, rates of return, costs
- Output – units produced or processed, throughput, new accounts
- Impact – attainment of a standard (quality, level of service, etc), changes in behaviour (internal and external customers), completion of work/project, level of take-up of a service, innovation
- Reaction – judgement by others, colleagues, internal and external customers
- Time – speed of response or turnaround, achievements compared with timetables, amount of backlog, time to market, delivery times.

The next step is to identify the feedback information that will be available to measure performance. This may be control data generated by the process itself, management reports based on data collection, direct feedback of results from returns or observations, or personal feedback from individuals in the form of progress or activity reports.

EXERCISE 2.7

1. What problems is a manager likely to meet when setting up a control system?
2. How might they be overcome?
3. How can a manager encourage people to carry out their own procedures?
4. How can a manager retain overall control while simultaneously delegating authority to people to carry out and monitor their own performance?

Finally, monitoring means comparing feedback information with plans, targets or budgets, and evaluating results as a basis for action (as described below).

Evaluating

Evaluating follows monitoring. It involves analysing, gauging and appraising outcomes. A diagnosis is made of the causes of any problems and of the issues that must be addressed. The analysis and diagnosis provide the basis for planning – to make the best use of opportunities or to deal with weaknesses or threats. Evaluation may require an assessment of the pros and cons of alternative courses of action in order to come to a balanced decision on what must be done and the priorities that should be attached to the various tasks involved.

Challenges to the traditional school

Sune Carlsson (1951), a researcher into management, wrote that:

'If we ask a managing director when he is co-ordinating, or how much co-ordination he has been doing during the day, he would not know, and even the most highly skilled observer would not know either. The same holds true of the concepts of planning, command, organisation and control.'

And Rosemary Stewart (1967) pointed out that:

'They [management theorists] could talk about the manager's job because their description of his functions was so general as to be universally valid; but such a level of generalisation has a very limited usefulness in practice.'

Common sense as well as the evidence collected by the empirical researchers as in this chapter tell us that managers do not sit down and divide their day into neat segments labelled 'planning', 'organising', 'leading' and 'controlling'.

But the traditional concept of management should not be dismissed out of hand. Planning, organising, leading and controlling are what managers do at least some of the time, even if each takes place haphazardly, almost unconsciously, during a complex working day. And it is clear that when the originator of this school, Henri Fayol, writes: 'In every case the organisation has to carry out [the following] managerial duties,' he is making it clear that he is writing about management in general, not the behaviour of individual managers. In fact, the traditional theorists tried to describe what management is. They did not attempt to describe how individual managers behave. That was left to the empiricists who succeeded them.

THE MANAGER'S ROLE

This section of the chapter is concerned with the manager's role. The traditional model of management is that it is a logical and systematic process of planning, organising, leading and controlling. But the work that managers actually carry out is characterised by fragmentation, variety and brevity. They may indeed be engaged in planning, organising, leading and controlling activities from time to time. However, because of the pressures under which they work and the constant need to cope with new situations, their working life is much less orderly than the traditional management theories indicate.

A manager can be defined as 'someone who is responsible for the operation of a discrete organisational unit or function and who has been given authority over those working in that unit or function'.

The key words in this definition are *responsible* and *authority*. Responsibility involves people being accountable for what they do or cause others to do. Authority means having the right or power to get people to do things. It involves the exercise of personal influence arising from position or knowledge.

The definition also indicates that a manager is someone who leads a team of people. This is the usual meaning attached to the term 'manager' and is the one adopted in this book. But people can be called managers even if they have no staff – for example, an investment manager could be solely responsible for controlling investments without any help. And managers are, of course, also responsible for managing other resources: finance, facilities, information, time, and themselves.

People can be specialists or professionals as well as managers, and much of their time could be spent in using their professional expertise to make decisions and solve problems rather than in getting someone else to do that for them.

Managers are like everyone else in an organisation in that they carry out roles. A role is the part a person plays in fulfilling his or her responsibilities. A role is not the same as a job, as set out in a job description, which is a list of duties and, perhaps, a statement of the overall purpose of the job. The role someone plays relates to how the person carries out the job. It is the concept and performance of a role that distinguishes individuals in organisational positions through the way they confront the demands and situational pressures within the role.

The demands of a role can be classified in terms of explicitness, clarity and coherence. They can refer to expectations – what must be done, what should be done and what can be done. 'Role expectations' consist of what individuals perceive to be their positions and the demands attached to them. People interpret what they are expected to do in the light of their perceptions of the context in which they work. When confronted with new demands or pressures from outside the organisation or from people within the organisation, they may have to re-interpret their roles and be prepared to respond flexibly. Roles, especially managerial roles, can therefore be fluid, and managers have to adapt rapidly – they cannot remain within the rigid confines of a prescribed set of duties. 'Role performance' refers to managers' actual behaviour, either in response to perceived expectations or in pursuing individual aims and projects. Managers may have to work in conditions of role ambiguity, when they are not sure what they are expected to do, or role conflict, when what they feel they should do is not in accord with what others believe they should do.

In carrying out their roles people are engaged in activities and tasks. Activities comprise what managers do – their behaviour. Tasks are what managers are expected or seek to achieve. In defining managerial work a distinction has been made by Hales (1986) between managers' behaviours and actions and the desired outcomes of those behaviours. This can be described as an 'input-process-output' model in which inputs are the knowledge and skills managers bring to their role, process is their behaviour in using their knowledge and skills to make decisions and take action, and output is the result or outcome of the behaviour.

The process of management can crudely be defined as getting things done through people. But there is more to it than that. Management can be described as deciding what to do and then getting it done through people. But even that description is insufficient. Managers work with people (their colleagues, customers, outside suppliers and their teams) as well as through people. Managers are part of the action. They are not there simply to tell other people what to do. In one sense, the members of their teams are their internal customers to whom managers have the obligation to provide help and support, as well as to provide direction so as to ensure that the required end-results are achieved.

Managers are also concerned with other resources besides those working directly for them. Managers have to manage themselves and make the best use of their key resources – expertise, leadership qualities and, importantly, time. They may have to 'manage' or at least interact with other people on inter-functional teams as well as with colleagues who are their internal customers. Managers are also managed, and they may – more or less subtly – have to manage their bosses to ensure that the right direction, guidance and support are provided. Finally, managers have to manage other resources: money, equipment, plant and facilities. They may do this through other people, but they could, for example, be entirely responsible for financial management. To emphasise this multifaceted role, a better definition of management might be 'deciding what to do and getting it done through and with other people by making the best use of the available resources'.

So far, so good – but this definition contains a degree of precision which may not exist in practice. Management could be defined much more broadly, albeit tautologically, as what managers do. Silverman and Jones (1976) have suggested that managers actively define their own work and create its constituent activities – communication is not simply what managers take a long time doing but the medium through which managerial work is constituted. As Hales (1986) points out, 'The work of managers is the management of their work,' or as Gowler and Legge (1983) contend, 'The meaning of management is the management of meaning.'

It is against this somewhat nebulous background that findings of the empiricists should be considered. These are examined below.

Rosemary Stewart

Rosemary Stewart et al (1980) studied 160 senior and middle managers for four weeks each. Her main findings on how they spent their time were:

- The managers worked an average of 42 hours per week.
- Discussions took 60 per cent of their time: 43 per cent informal, 7 per cent committee, 6 per cent telephoning, and 4 per cent social activity.
- They spent 34 per cent of their time alone, 25 per cent with their immediate subordinates, 8 per cent with their superiors, 25 per cent with colleagues and 5 per cent with external contacts.
- Fragmentation in work was considerable. In the four-week period, managers averaged only nine periods of 30 minutes or more without interruption, and averaged 20 contacts a day, 12 of them fleeting ones (of less than five minutes' duration).

Henry Mintzberg

Henry Mintzberg (1973) observed five chief executives over a period of five weeks. He found that the proportion of time they spent on different activities was as shown in Table 2.2.

Table 2.2 *The allocation of managers' time*

	Percentage(s) Average	Range
Desk work	22	16–38
Telephone calls	6	4–9
Scheduled meetings	59	38–75
Unscheduled meetings	10	3–8
Tours	3	0–10
Proportion of activities lasting less than 9 min	49	40–56
Proportion of activities lasting more than 60 min	10	5–13

Source: H. Mintzberg, *The Nature of Managerial Work*, Harper & Row, 1973

The managers' days were characterised by a large number of brief informal two-person contacts (telephone calls and unscheduled meetings) and relatively few scheduled meetings which nevertheless took most of their time.

Subordinates consumed about half the managers' contact time and were involved in two-thirds of the contacts. The managers initiated less than one-third of their contacts and only 5 per cent were scheduled regularly.

The broad conclusions emerging from this study confirmed that 'management' is

- highly interactive
- very much concerned with communication
- about getting things done with or through other people
- not much about office work.

Mintzberg also contrasted findings such as these on the work of managers with those of the traditional school, stating that his own results 'paint an interesting picture, one as different from Fayol's view as a Cubist abstract is from a Renaissance painting'. Traditional management theory defends managers as being systematic planners in control of the working day. In reality, however, Mintzberg allows us to see managers as being continually involved in a variety of concentrated, quite intense, often brief, sometimes disconnected practices/encounters that make up their day. To be successful in these activities we need managers who can balance the systematically oriented nature of managerial work with the people-centred interpersonal-encounter-focused aspects of the work. The later work of Mintzberg (1990) enables us to acknowledge that being a 'good' manager in the traditional sense is not enough. In citing his ten roles of managerial work he is attempting to suggest that the skills base of managers should be widened in order for them to gain results and be successful in the future.

Mintzberg's study drew some interesting conclusions about managers' work methods and the roles that they play. Prior to this, the popular image of managers, as suggested above, was as reflective, systematic planners who spend most of their time in their offices reading reports and making decisions. However, three of Mintzberg's findings contrasted sharply with this image:

- pace of work – Mintzberg's managers worked constantly from the minute they arrived at the office until they left in the evening. Rather than take coffee breaks, they tended to drink coffee while attending meetings, and 'working' lunches were the norm. On average, the managers attended eight meetings and handled 36 pieces of mail per day, as well as dealing with other written and verbal communication. Any spare time tended to be very quickly taken by subordinates wanting a word with the manager
- brevity, variety, and fragmentation – The managers in Mintzberg's study were found to handle a great variety of issues during their working day, ranging from social events to important strategic issues. Mintzberg was surprised to find that many of the activities were brief; most took less than nine minutes, and only 10 per cent took over an hour. Telephone conversations and meetings were short, and most managers left meetings early. The managers' activities were constantly interrupted by phone calls or people calling in to speak to them. Because of this fragmentation and interruption, most managers had to do any important thinking – planning, reading, etc – outside normal work hours, either at the office when most other people had left or at home
- verbal contacts and networks – Mintzberg's managers preferred to use verbal communications such as telephone conversations and meetings to conduct their business, rather than written communication (letters, memos, etc). They depended heavily for this on networks of contacts, both within and outside the company. (A network is a set of co-operative relationships with individuals whose help is needed in order for a manager to function effectively.) Examples of contacts within these networks included subordinates, peers, senior managers, customers, suppliers and trade associations.

Managerial roles

Mintzberg (1973, 1990) used the data he had collected in his study to group management activities into roles, albeit deriving them all together as from managers vested with formal authority within a particular aspect or work unit in the organisation. This in turn led to status, which he then contended led to the identification of ten roles – and these he categorised in three types:

- interpersonal,
- informational, and
- decisional.

The *interpersonal* type of role primarily has to do with work relationships that are instigated because of the manager's formal authority. The function is therefore one of contact with others rather than of analysing data or decision-making.

The *informational* category depicts managers as having a significant set of contacts which form into networks. The networks enable the manager to distribute and disseminate large amounts of data.

In essence the *decisional* category suggests that management requires action, and the prerequisite to action is decision-making. Organisations are committed to certain actions by the decisions of their managers.

The ten roles within the above-listed categories are summarised in Table 2.3.

Table 2.3 *Mintzberg's ten managerial roles*

Role	Description
Interpersonal	
Figurehead	Performs symbolic duties of a legal or social nature
Leader	Builds relationships with subordinates, and communicates with, motivates and coaches them
Liaison	Maintains a network of contacts outside work unit, who provide help and information
Informational	
Monitor	Seeks internal and external information about issues that can affect the organisation
Disseminator	Transmits information internally that is obtained from either internal or external sources
Spokesperson	Transmits information about the organisation to outsiders
Decisional	
Entrepreneur	Acts as initiator, designer and encourager of change and innovation
Disturbance-handler	Takes corrective action when organisation faces important unexpected difficulties
Resource allocator	Distributes resources of all kinds, including time, funding, equipment and human resources
Negotiator	Represents the organisation in major negotiations affecting the manager's areas of responsibility

Adapted from H. Mintzberg, *The Nature of Managerial Work*, Harper & Row, 1973

We can use them to identify the key skills required by a manager in order to perform competently.

It is clear that in every one of the roles that Mintzberg describes, the manager is required to communicate in some form or other. It is in the course of this communication that a manager demonstrates his or her management competence (or otherwise!) to others, so it is essential to have well-developed written and verbal communication skills.

In none of the roles does the manager work in isolation – each role requires interaction with a variety of other people from the manager's network. The successful manager must therefore have well-developed interpersonal skills, and be able to work effectively in groups.

Within the Decisional category, the manager is required to collect and interpret information to make decisions and solve problems.

Managers of today are operating in a rapidly changing global environment, which means they must adapt accordingly. Innovative ability is becoming increasingly important. This requires the manager to be constantly acquiring new knowledge and learning new ways of producing the desired results.

Leonard Sayles

Leonard Sayles (1964) also examined the role of the manager. He interviewed 75 lower- and middle-level managers in a large American corporation, and in his subsequent analysis identified three aspects of managerial work.

Managers are *participants in external work flows* – an aspect that led Sayles to identify seven basic relationships with people outside their immediate managerial responsibility:

- trading relationships: making arrangements with other members of the organisation to get work done
- work-flow relationships: making contacts concerning the work preceding or following that supervised by the manager
- service relationships: making contacts relating to the giving or receiving of services or support by specialist groups – for example, market research or maintenance
- advisory relationships: arranging the provision of counsel and advice to line managers by experts – for example, in industrial relations
- auditing relationships: making contacts with those who evaluate or appraise organisational work – for example, personnel in management accounts or quality control
- stabilisation relationships: making contacts with those who are empowered to limit or control the manager's decision in accordance with organisational policy – for example, concerning production planning and control
- innovative relationships: making contacts with groups specially isolated to perform a research function.

Managers are *leaders* – which results in three basic types of leadership behaviour:

- leadership as direction: getting subordinates to respond to the requests of the manager
- leadership as response: responding to initiatives from subordinates who are seeking aid or support
- leadership as representation: representing subordinates in contact with other parts of the organisation.

Managers are *monitors* – managers follow the progress of work through the system, detect variations and initiate action as required.

Peter Lawrence

Peter Lawrence (1984) observed the work of 16 German and 25 British general and production managers. His analysis of the proportion of time spent on different activities was as shown in Table 2.4.

Table 2.4 *Lawrence's allocation of production management time*

	Percentages	
	German	British
Formal scheduled recurrent meetings	9.78	15.50
Convened special-purpose meetings	12.62	14.46
Ad hoc discussions	20.07	17.93
Time spent in works	16.87	17.35
Telephoning	10.56	7.23
Office work	11.56	11.16
Explanations to researcher	10.45	13.08
Miscellaneous	8.02	4.08

Source: P. Lawrence, *Management in Action*, Routledge and Kegan Paul, 1984

Note that in both Germany and Britain the highest proportion of time was spent in ad hoc discussions. This demonstrates the extent to which managerial work is unplanned and frequently involves brief responses to sudden events.

The research into how managers spend their time confirms that their activities are characterised by fragmentation, brevity and variety. Because of the open-ended nature of their work, managers feel compelled to perform a great variety of tasks at an unrelenting pace. As Mintzberg (1973) comments:

'The manager actually appears to prefer brevity and interruption to his [sic] work. He becomes conditioned by his workload; he develops an appreciation of the opportunity cost of his own time; and he lives continuously with an awareness of what else might or must be done at any time. Superficiality is an occupational hazard of a manager's job ... The manager gravitates to the more active elements of his work – the current, the specific, the well-defined, the non-routine activities.'

EXERCISE 2.8

From your observation of managers at work, how realistic do you think Mintzberg's analysis is? Can anything be done to change this situation?

Mintzberg also indicated that even senior managers spend little time on planning, are subject to constant interruption, hold short face-to-face meetings which flit from topic to topic, and respond to the initiatives of others far more than they initiate themselves.

Why does this happen?

Fragmentation, variety and brevity in managerial work occur for the following six reasons.

- Managers are largely concerned with dealing with people – their staff and their internal and external customers. But people's behaviour is often unpredictable; their demands and responses are conditioned by the constantly changing circumstances in which they exist, by the pressures to which they have to respond, and by their individual wants and needs. Conflicts arise and have to be dealt with on the spot.
- Managers are not always in a position to control the events that affect their work. Sudden demands are imposed upon them by other people within the organisation or from outside. Crises can occur which they are unable to predict.
- Managers are expected to be decisive and deal with situations as they crop up. Their best-laid plans are therefore often disrupted; their established priorities have to be abandoned.
- Managers are at the beck and call of their superiors who also have to respond instantly to new demands and crises.
- Managers often work in conditions of turbulence and ambiguity. They are not clear about what is expected of them when new situations arise. They therefore tend to be reactive rather than proactive, dealing with immediate problems rather than trying to anticipate them.
- For all the reasons given above, managers are subject to constant interruptions. They have little chance to settle down and think about their plans and priorities or to spend enough time in studying control information to assist in maintaining a 'steady state' as far as their own activities go.

The varying nature of the managerial work, as Hales (1986) points out, varies by duration, time-span, recurrence, unexpectedness and source. Little time is spent on any one activity and in particular on the conscious, systematic formulation of plans. Planning and decision-making tend to take place in the course of other activities. Managerial activities are driven by contradictions, cross-pressures and the need to cope with and reconcile conflict. A lot of time is spent by managers accounting for, and explaining what they do, in informal relationships and in 'participating'. The role of the manager is therefore a challenging and at times difficult one. It is also a rewarding and exciting role to play, particularly for those who like to achieve.

EXERCISE 2.9

Read the case study on Leeds Leathers below, and answer the questions at the end.

Case study: Leeds Leathers International

Leeds Leathers International is an international player in the specialist motorcycle clothing industry. Originally based in the UK it has now spread its influence to Europe, the United States and Japan. Operations worldwide are co-ordinated from the UK (Head Office in Leeds) – these include production, marketing, finance and sales strategies. However, there is scope for parts of the organisation in different parts of the world to have some say in their own country's marketing and sales strategies, particularly in Italy (Milan). In terms of production, the Leeds-based operation in the UK manufactures full-length biker suits, off-road (moto-cross) apparel and face-masks, and a range of on-road jackets and trousers, while a newly acquired factory in Milan manufactures top-of-the-range boots and gloves.

As yet there are no other manufacturing centres. However, the company has a sales and marketing presence in the United States (Tampa Bay, home of drag racing), Spain (Madrid), Germany (Cologne) and Japan (Tokyo), as well as in Italy (Milan) and the UK (Leeds). Each of these areas is managed by an area manager who acts as the main sales agent in that particular country and who is the link person with the retailers. Meetings of area managers are held in Leeds once every month.

Competition in the industry is fierce. Individual products are major purchases for customers who are themselves knowledgeable about the products. Companies attempt to differentiate themselves from rivals by creating brand image and loyalty. To do this a lot of time is spent on promoting the products at fashion shows and races around the world – for instance, at the Isle of Man TT Races and at the Tampa Bay circuit in the United States. Sponsorship deals are contested with rival companies to gain the right to have champion riders race in their products emblazoned with their logo.

Quality of design, manufacture and performance are paramount. Biker magazines regularly review and compare products from the manufacturers.

Leeds Leathers had humble origins. It was established in the early 1960s by Donald Smith, an ex-moto-cross rider. Smith knew the value of effective protection from wind, rain and the occasional tumble. However, he also knew that the so-called 'protective' clothing of the time was heavy and cumbersome – and far from what anyone might call a 'fashion item'. For a while the business catered for the UK market and was a good source of income for Smith and his family members, several of whom joined the company as it grew. But it was the arrival on the scene of Fiona Smith, Donald's eldest daughter, that turned the company into the international organisation it is today.

Inheriting the role of managing director upon the retirement of her father, Fiona was intent on transforming the company. She had been brought up with the smell of high-octane fuel and burning rubber, and was passionate about the business. Not content with the UK she had set her sights upon the lucrative German and US markets. When family members who held senior managerial positions retired, they were replaced by key people Fiona had personally 'head-hunted' from rival companies.

At the Leeds manufacturing operation the focus was on quality and innovation. One of the most highly respected departments was that of new product design, which was headed by Frances Collingwood, a fashion graduate, now in her third year at the company. All new products were designed and the prototypes tested here. Frances had originally thought of a more conventional career in fashion, but the appeal of something more challenging was always at the back of her mind, and when the opportunity to apply to become a design assistant had presented itself, she had taken it with alacrity. She soon developed a desire for innovation bordering on the obsessive – but to her it wasn't work. She earned the respect of her peers in the industry for her work on design style, which coupled quality of performance with flair of design aesthetics.

There is a close working relationship between her department and the sales and marketing departments globally. One-offs are also manufactured in Leeds for special show events, and for top riders individually tailored suits are prepared. Frances strives to integrate her work with that of production as well, taking it upon herself to promote the practice of training the production staff in the specific details of new products – for instance, the order in which to assemble garment components and other assembly techniques. She reasons to herself that this training will have a dual benefit: ensuring effectiveness of production and being of assistance to staff.

Production staff are recruited from the local area; they are semi-skilled. Many current workers are family members of the previous generation of employees during Donald Smith's time. Wages are good, and being piece-work-related, regularly exceed the pay of the salaried new product design department staff. Generally, staff appear content to do their work and to work within the friendly atmosphere of their colleagues. However, work can be tough at times. If a deadline on a particular order is required, workers are expected to work overtime, with no questions asked.

Some staff want to progress further. Two routes present themselves for such people: to transfer into new product design (which is not easy, because positions are few and competition intense), or to join the sales and marketing team(s) (which usually requires a lot of travelling and a dynamic, outgoing personality).

James Clarkson was the Operations Manager at Leeds. A tough, seasoned individual, his main focus was upon production output and efficiencies. Once per week he held what he called a 'Team Briefing' in which he told the staff where targets had been achieved that week and what the targets were for next week. This briefing normally lasted for 10 minutes.

There is an intense rivalry between the Leeds manufacturing process and the Milan factory. Milan carries on the Italian tradition of manufacturing superlative boots and gloves. It was a struggling fashion manufacturer of women's shoes and gloves when Fiona Smith first found it. Nevertheless, it remains proud of its history. Fiona invested heavily in it and transformed its operations to what they are today. Giovanni Abruzzio is the head of the Milan operation. His main focus still echoes that of the previous product – quality of finish is, for him, the most important aspect of the business, in line with the fine tradition handed down to him. This attitude sometimes causes tension between him and Fiona, particularly when an important order is put through for an important customer and it is delayed as Abruzzio focuses on product finish to the highest standards.

EXERCISE 2.9 QUESTIONS

What does the fact that Fiona waited until the retirement of family members before replacing them with key people from outside the organisation indicate to you?

What do you think about Frances' practice of training production staff in the manufacture of new products? Discuss any benefits or disadvantages as you see them.

Reflect upon the 'driver model of leadership' (earlier in this chapter) with regard to Fiona, Frances and James, and summarise relevant points from the previous questions and add further points from your analysis of the case study.

SUMMARY

Planning

- Planning involves deciding what to do, getting the resources required, and scheduling work.
- The main planning activities are: objective-setting, activity analysis, forecasting, scheduling, resourcing, procedure-planning, setting targets and standards, and deciding on monitoring procedures.
- Prioritisation means deciding on the relative importance of tasks so that the order in which they should be done can be determined.
- Listing things to do can effect prioritisation, classifying them in terms of their significance, importance and urgency, assessing how much time is available, and fitting the scheduled tasks into this timescale.

Organising

- Organising means analysing what has to be done and then deciding who does what, setting up the reporting relationships between people, and establishing methods of communication, co-ordination and control.
- Direction is concerned with getting understanding and agreement on where the team and its members are expected to go – ie their objectives and targets.
- Direction means agreeing objectives and targets, and allocating and delegating work.
- Delegation involves giving people the authority to do something rather than doing it yourself.
- Managers delegate when they do not have the time to do everything themselves.
- Delegation means that individuals can develop their skills and competencies.
- Delegation involves empowerment – giving people more scope and authority.
- When delegating, you must decide what to delegate and to whom. You have to select people who are capable of doing work immediately or with a reasonable amount of guidance.
- A distinction can be made between 'hard' delegation – giving people full instructions on what to do – and 'soft' delegation – indicating what people have to do and letting them get on with it.
- You should always delegate by the results you expect, and set up arrangements for monitoring and reporting on performance.

Leading

- Leading involves a range of inter-related behaviours that include exhibiting: direction, respect, informing skills, values, energy, and the ability to become a role model for others.
- Co-ordination involves the achievement of unity of effort so that individual actions are synchronised and sequenced properly.
- Co-ordinating requires planning and scheduling activities, organising work so that it can be co-ordinated, communicating and monitoring.
- Effective implementers know what they want done and provide the guidance and leadership necessary to ensure that it does get done.

Controlling

- Controlling is concerned with monitoring and measuring performance, comparing results with plans, and taking corrective action if and when required.
- To exercise good control it is necessary to plan, monitor, measure, evaluate, compare, and take action.

Managerial role

- A manager is someone who is responsible for the operation of a discrete organisational unit or function and who has been given authority over those working in that unit or function.
- Management is about deciding what to do and then getting it done through and with other people by making the best use of available resources.
- The traditional writers defined the nature of management in terms of basic universal elements – eg planning, organising, leading and controlling.
- This does not, however, describe how managers actually spend their time – which, as research has shown, is characterised by fragmentation, variety and brevity.
- Managers tend to be doers who react to events and think on their feet. They often exercise choice over what they do and how they do it. Much of the time of managers is spent in communicating. Planning tends to take place during the course of carrying out other activities.

REFERENCES

BROWN A. (1995) *Organisation Culture*. London, Pitman Publishing.

CARLSSON S. (1951) *Executive Behaviour: A study of the workload and the working methods of managing directors*. Strömberg.

FAYOL H. (1949) *General and Industrial Administration*. London, Pitman.

GALLAGHER K., ROSE E., MCCLELLAND B., REYNOLDS J. and TOMBS S. (1997) *People in Organisations: An active learning approach*. Oxford, Blackwell Business.

GOWLER D. and LEGGE K. (1983) 'The meaning of management and the management of meaning: a view from social anthropology', in EARLE M. J. (ed.) *Perspectives on Management: A multidisciplinary approach*. London, Oxford University Press.

GULLICK L. (1937) 'Notes on the theory of organisations', in GULLICK L. and URWICK L. (eds) *Papers on the Science of Administration*. New York, Columbia University Press.

HALES C. P. (1986) 'What managers do: a critical review of the evidence', *Journal of Management Studies*, Vol. 23, No. 1, January, p8.

HANDY C., (1985) *Understanding Organisations*. Harmondsworth, Penguin Books.

KOTTER J. (1971) 'Power dependency and effective management', *Harvard Business Review*, July–August.

LAWRENCE P. (1984) *Management in Action*. London, Routledge & Kegan Paul.

MAITLAND R. (2003) *People Management*, Vol. 9, No.11.

MINTZBERG H. (1973) *The Nature of Managerial Work*. New York, Harper & Row.

MINTZBERG H. (1990) 'The manager's job: folklore and fact', *Harvard Business Review*, March–April, pp163–76.

PETERS, T. J. and WATERMAN, R. H. Jr (1982) *In Search of Excellence*. New York, Harper & Row.

SAYLES L. (1964) *Managerial Behaviour*. New York, McGraw-Hill.

SCHIEN E. H. (1985) *Organisational Culture and Leadership*. San Francisco, Jossey-Bass.

SILVERMAN D. and JONES J. (1976) *Organisational Work*. London, Macmillan.

STONER J. A. F., FREEMAN R. E. and GILBERT D. R. (1995; 6th edition) *Management*. Englewood Cliffs, NJ, Prentice Hall.

STEWART R. (1967) *Managers and Their Jobs*. London, Macmillan.

STEWART R., SMITH P., BLAKE J. and WINGATE P. (1980) *The District Administrator in the National Health Service*. London, Pitman.

INTRODUCTION

Management development is a difficult yet necessary activity – difficult, because any development must address the needs of both individual and organisation and it must take into account the skills and attributes that the individual already possesses; necessary, to maintain a vibrant, well-motivated managerial workforce and, therefore, to sustain a competitive business environment.

The UK government's own report *Twenty-First-Century Century Skills: Realising our potential* (2003) highlights these issues by pointing out that:

> **'effective leadership and management are key to the development of competitive business and high-quality public services. Good leaders and managers recognise the importance of workforce skills development as a fundamental building-block of high performance.'**

A further point this report extols is that

> **'around 4.5 million people in the UK have significant management responsibilities but fewer than a quarter hold a management-related qualification'.**

Other reports continue to show deficiencies in the level of management skills (the Council for Excellence in Management and Leadership, 2002, as featured in the CBI's *A Results Overview of the Regional Survey of UK Economic Trends*, 2003) and state that they are likely to be evident in lower and middle management (Porter, 2003).

In response to this the Management Standards Centre and the CIPD, among others, are ensuring that they review and develop new standards that underpin management development, learning, and qualifications at various levels. These serve as benchmarks that relate to the skill and competency requirements for the levels and functions (eg HR) of management education and development.

The emphasis in this chapter is on the need for organisations and their managers to be aware of the pressing requirement for effective management development in the UK.

Learning objectives

In particular, by the end of this chapter the reader will be able to:

- articulate why management development is essential
- outline various approaches to learning and development (L&D)
- write SMART objectives
- compare and contrast the competence and competency debate with infrastructure and differentiator behaviours
- appreciate the importance of becoming a reflective practitioner
- critically evaluate methods of managerial development – eg action learning, coaching, mentoring, personal development plans (PDPs).

LEARNING AND DEVELOPMENT

What do we mean by 'learning'? Some key learning concepts

There are many definitions amongst psychologists and educators of what learning is and how we learn. One writer (Jarvis, 1990) has offered five meanings for the concept:

- any more or less permanent change in behaviour as a result of experience
- a relatively permanent change in behaviour which occurs as a result of practice
- the process whereby knowledge is created through the transformation of experience
- the processes of transforming experience into knowledge, skills and attitudes
- memorising information.

Interestingly, the last of these meanings – memorising information – is the one we tend to think of first, because as Kolb *et al* (1991) remind us:

> 'For most of us, the first associations we have with the word "learning" are teacher, classroom and textbook ...
>
> As students, our job is to observe, read and memorise what the teacher assigns, and then to repeat "what we have learned" in examinations ... The textbook symbolises the assumption that learning is primarily concerned with abstract ideas and concepts. The more remembered, the more you have learned. The relevance and application of these concepts to your own job will come later. Concepts come before experience.'

Of course we do need to remember facts and figures. However, as Kolb goes on to say:

> 'As a result of these assumptions, the concept of learning seldom seems relevant to us in our daily lives and work.'

He talks of learning from our experiences and he sees learning as a continuous process. It is also individualised and self-directed. In other words, you take charge of your learning, and what you learn is what you decide you need to learn for your own particular situation. His work has been very influential in adult education and training. The following quote from Kolb (1991) emphasises that what we really need to acquire is the ability to keep learning from our experiences.

> **'And yet ... in a world where the rate of change is increasing rapidly every year, in a time when few will end their careers in the same jobs or even the same occupations they started in, the ability to learn seems an important, if not the most important, skill.'**

Kolb (1984) proposed a cyclical model of learning – Kolb's experiential learning cycle. In this model the learner goes through a four-stage sequence:

- having an experience ('concrete experience')
- reflecting upon this experience ('reflecting')
- forming more abstract theories and generalisations ('theorising')
- planning for the next time the experience occurs and testing out new ideas ('planning', 'testing').

The learner may enter the cycle at any of the above stages. Effective learning occurs by going through all four stages. Further learning occurs by going through more cycles.

As mentioned previously, Kolb's model (1984) has been widely used in training and development. The work of Honey and Mumford considers the learning styles appropriate to each stage of the cycle ('activist', 'reflector', 'theorist', 'pragmatist'); they have put forward a well-established Learning Styles Inventory. This takes the form of a questionnaire (administered by approved users) which rates an individual against each of the learning styles and then explains what this means to the individual in terms of how he/she presently learns.

The ability to measure learning styles leads to further debate concerning whether or not it is appropriate to attempt to improve 'weak' learning styles. Certainly, the concept of learning styles is widely known and debated among educationalists and trainers. Delivering training to suit various learning styles is an obvious area; less obvious, perhaps, is the preferred style of the mentor/trainer compared with that of the learner, and the effect that this has upon their relationship and the effectiveness of learning.

Donald Schön

Donald Schön (1930–1997) has also contributed immensely to the field of reflective practice and learning systems. His books – in particular *Educating the Reflective Practitioner* (1987) – are seminal works. However, Schön thought that learning by reflection did not have to take place in a cycle (as suggested by Kolb) but could take place independently. Doing justice to Schön's work lies beyond the scope of this book. Nonetheless, it was he who with Chris Argyris developed the concept of 'double-loop' learning (the ability to have a major re-think – a so-called 'paradigm shift' on the system of learning itself) which is mentioned later in this chapter.

Also, he broke reflection down into two components:

- *reflection in action*, sometimes described as 'thinking on one's feet' – in other words, thinking about how the activity is proceeding at the time of doing
- *reflection on action* – thinking back over a particular experience or event some time afterwards.

Jennifer Moon

Jennifer Moon (1999a) in her book *Learning Journals* raises an interesting point when she says:

'Although it seems obvious that reflection is associated with learning, there is little research that relates the two in a more analytical way than the instructional approach of the experiential learning theorists (eg Kolb, 1984).'

Moon's work on reflection, and in particular *Learning Journals*, will probably appeal to the development practitioner who requires sound theoretical underpinning but also needs to adopt a pragmatic approach. For instance, in her book *Reflection in Learning and Professional Development* (1999b) Moon states that:

'the experiential learning cycle ... is generally used in the context of guiding learners ... it is actually used to structure teaching, learning, training or the guidance of learning.'

However, she goes on to state that this 'might not necessarily be representative of what goes on in the brain', and in her discussion of learning journals (1999a) she proposes that, rather than being antagonistic, the approaches of Kolb and Schön are complementary.

Reflection on practice

Boud, Keogh and Walker (1985) talk of reflection as 'turning experience into practice' – how for the most part this idea helps us evaluate our learning and development experiences, and how we can improve our work practice because of our measured reflections. They define reflection thus (Boud, Keogh and Walker, 1985):

'Reflection is an important human activity in which people recapture their experience, think about it, mull it over and evaluate it. It is this working with experience that is important to learning.'

They go on to say,

'The capacity to reflect ... may characterise those who learn effectively from reflection.'

This may be one of the differentiating factors that enables individuals to grow and progress in their work lives. In this context reflection is presented as a cognitive process, whereas others see it as an active process (Jarvis, 1992). As noted above, Schön (1987) expresses it as both 'reflection in action' and 'reflection on action', the former occurring during the event or experience, the latter occurring after the event (or perhaps when we pause to stop and think).

In discussing this concept of reflection the model produced by Boud, Keogh and Walker (1985) can be of service. They talk of 'preparation', 'engagement' and 'processing' (see Figure 3.1).

- Preparation – In this, learners prepare for the particular reflection by considering 'self': this is our own role in the process and what we can learn from 'the event'. We may then understand what skills and strategies we need to employ during the event.
- Engagement – In this, we can link to Schön's 'reflection in action' stage in that it is ongoing throughout the particular event or activity. At this stage we move from using a cognitive process like thinking about what is 'intended' through 'noticing' skills (eg apprehending what is happening) to an 'affective' action-oriented process. These Schön describes as 'intervening' and 'adapting', in that we actually perform a particular action and adapt to the situation or environment.

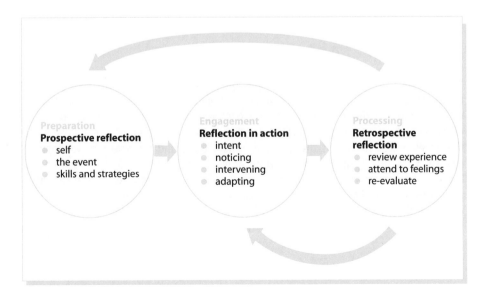

Figure 3.1 *Three-stage model of reflection*
Source: Boud, Keogh and Walker, *Reflection: Turning experience into learning*, Kogan Page, 1985

■ Processing – The engagement process itself throws up many questions. These have to be processed. To do this Schön suggests retrospective reflection – 'reflection on action'. In this, we review the experience and ask questions like 'What has been learned from this?' During this phase we 'attend to our feelings' about the experience. We recognise at this stage that not all experiences in the work environment are positive. We must therefore try to unpick the positive and the less positive and deduce what we have learned from both. This, then, will enable us to 're-evaluate' the engagement process and the process as a whole.

It is hoped that this discussion will clarify as well as emphasise the need for reflection in the development process, and again suggest its importance as a differentiating factor.

EXERCISE 3.1

Use the points below to write a reflection for your experience linked to your management practice:

■ Describe a recent significant problematic event in the workplace in which you were personally involved.
■ Summarise the main points of the experience.
■ Identify what you learned from this situation.
■ Consider how you will use this information in future situations – eg what behaviours you will change; what behaviours you will retain.
■ How will you follow up what you have learned from reflecting on this experience?

IMPROVING THE ORGANISATIONAL SYSTEM FOR DEVELOPMENT: DIFFERENTIATING

So far we have covered a range of concepts, ideas and theories that have been geared to the development of our managers. We have mentioned competence and competency and will elaborate on them soon, and go on later to discuss particular techniques – eg coaching. However, what distinguishes – ie differentiates – the superior management of the development process is the ability to reflect upon and improve the development process itself. This is an example of what Argyris and Schön (1978) term 'double-loop learning', which is itself part of the performance-enhancement process. This process questions *why* a particular problem or issue arose in the first place. It is through focused reflection that the learner/manager can have a greater understanding of the situation. He/she may then go on to challenge the original assumptions or actions that led to the problem.

What do we mean by 'management development'?

Adopting the approach of Mumford (1997), we suggest here that management development is seen as the whole process by which managers are enabled to 'learn and grow' in order to 'manage for results'. We all learn through formal, informal and integrated techniques – therefore we should not exclude any of these learning processes when considering how to develop managers.

The formal process

The formal process includes planned education/training and learning linked to individual and organisational needs, which are themselves concurrent with the organisation's strategic development requirements. The formal process itself takes place through a planned intervention either by the development manager, by the line manager or by the individuals themselves. Planned interventions may be desirable to achieve personal goals and aspirations, as well as those derived from an appraisal process. A range of interventions can be utilised here:

- internal courses
- external courses (eg master's qualifications)
- Action learning sets: work on projects
- coaching
- mentoring
- feedback on work performance
- modelling
- reading
- personal development plans (PDPs).

The informal process

An informal process of learning, arguably, is one by which we acquire tacit knowledge. It is within the 'normal course of events' in the workplace. Learning through acquiring tacit knowledge can occur unconsciously, without clear direction, and is difficult to classify as learning because of the inadequacy of the outcomes. Nonetheless, we do gain from the process. In fact, it is an important aspect of our development – for example, we learn about the organisation's culture ('the way we do things here') by informal processes, largely just by being there.

We might observe others and can find ourselves often emulating their behaviour or trying out a different procedure. This, however, can be conscious or unconscious behaviour depending on whether we have reflected on the 'event' and made a conscious decision to change and work in a different way.

The entrepreneurial process

Although Mumford (1997) in his writing suggests that an informal process can be planned, this position throws up a dichotomy in that he also suggests that informal learning can be unplanned and happens in general work practice. This state of affairs is only rationalised by the use of a halfway position that accepts both planned and unplanned methods of learning and merges them into one – a process that has formal and informal characteristics (Mumford and Gold, 2004). Stewart (1999) refers to 'opportunist learning' in this context: we shall take this further and suggest here the title 'entrepreneurial learning' to describe the process.

Table 3.1 *Three forms of learning*

Form	Learning
Formal	▪ deliberate ▪ a planned process
Informal	▪ takes place in the normal course of events
Entrepreneurial	▪ impromptu; may be accidental ▪ by monitoring the environment ▪ by trying things out for yourself ▪ by 'seizing the day' – opportunist

Adapted from A. Mumford, *Management Development Strategies*, IPD, 1997

Table 3.1 is adapted from Mumford (1997) and brings together three forms of learning in the workplace.

For instance, we might be observing the mannerisms, body language and behaviour, and the listening skills (involving verbal and non-verbal cues) of a senior manager who is busy networking. On a subsequent occasion we might find ourselves acting in a similar way to this manager. This would have been an unconscious decision. It is when we actually realise the value of reflection in our own practice that we *consciously* make a decision to change. In so doing we are beginning to capitalise on both the formal and informal learning and using a technique that merges or transforms them into deliberate actions. It is then that we are using the third process: the process we describe as *entrepreneurial learning.* The entrepreneurial process takes the issue of opportunity a step further by not only suggesting that development can take place through the managers' experiences at work but also by stating that the managers can themselves consciously seek out, plan and take advantage of developments presented to them. This may mean that they take on new projects, ask for specific developments, learn from the pathway of others, plan learning that will advance their career and/or take advantage of having a mentor or coach.

Cotton's (1995) concepts are also relevant here. She produces a model that links to our focal point that learning merges or is entrepreneurial, in her quadrant (see Figure 3.2) that describes constantly 'making and taking learning opportunities at work'. This process can use deliberate and planned scenarios of formal learning, yet can also use informal or tacit learning. It is accomplished mainly by being alert to events and for the most part opportunistic in our approach to personal development. Hence we suggest the individual can be entrepreneurial in his or her pursuit of development opportunities.

It is through merging our tacit learning into explicit learning that we can truly use the concept of differentiation. An example of this could be the way we approach personal development plans (PDPs) or continuing professional development (CPD). Let us take the case in which we become aware that improvement in, say our networking skills can be advantageous to career development and enhancement. From this we may choose to devise a PDP to achieve learning goals. We can do this through formal (planned) learning, and informal (a given situation in the workplace) learning, transforming the informal opportunities for networking into planned opportunities (possibly emulating the senior manager

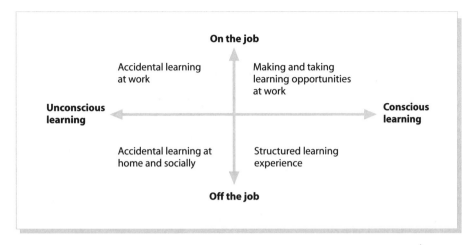

Figure 3.2 *'Making and taking learning opportunities at work'*
Source: J. Cotton, *The Theory of Learning*, Kogan Page, 1995

we mentioned earlier), and in so doing make a deliberate attempt to improve, using the opportunities available to us. Hence the suggestion that we can be entrepreneurial in developing our own learning plans, and that this learning process itself can be a differentiator between one person and another.

Later on in the chapter we will examine some of the learning methods discussed above.

The competence *v* competency debate

When assessing managerial effectiveness in terms of behaviour the concept of the competent manager as originally developed by Boyatzis (1982) has relevance.

Competence

Boyatzis defines competence as:

> **'A capacity that exists in a person that leads to behaviour that meets the job demands within the parameters of the organisational environment, and that in turn brings about desired results.'**

Thus for our purposes competences are the things people need to be able to understand and do to perform effectively. They provide the basis, for instance, for national vocational qualifications (NVQs) at levels 1, 2 and 3. The NVQs use the terms 'competent' and 'not yet competent' to describe whether a pass has been achieved or the individual is still working towards the qualification. Higher levels 4 and 5 also incorporate the use of behaviour – see below.

Competency

Boyatzis (1982) describes management competency as

> **'an underlying characteristic of a manager causally related to superior performance in a management position'.**

Competency thus relates to behaviours that produce effective performance. Such behaviours – competencies – are defined in the tailored competency frameworks and profiles many organisations are now using to provide guidance on selection, on training and development, and sometimes on increases in pay. A competency framework or profile provides guidance for managers on the sort of behaviour expected of them. Such frameworks can be used to provide criteria for assessing performance in its widest sense. Woodruffe (1990) maintains that competency is a

> **'dimension of overt manifest behaviour that allows the person to perform competently'.**

When do we stop being OK and start being superior?

Certainly in terms of management it is one thing to be an effective administrator and to give instructions for tasks (competence-/task-based), and quite another to be an inspirational leader (competency-/behaviour-based). In between lie grey areas.

Clearly, there are links between the two. For instance, we might be able to chair a meeting, but to do so to a superior standard involves the extra something that is our behaviour.

EXERCISE 3.2: DISCUSSION OF COMPETENCE AND COMPETENCY

1 How can we develop competence in a particular skill?
2 How can we develop competency (for instance, leadership)?
3 How are competencies useful to the organisation?

Unconscious and conscious competence

Figure 3.3 gives a perspective of a learning process that takes us through a journey from unconscious incompetence to unconscious competence, and is adapted from the work of Reay (1994).

Unconscious incompetence is the state in which you are unaware that you are incompetent in a particular task or in a range of skills: you have no idea of what you don't know. Reay used the example of a child in a car pretending to drive:

> **'They can't drive it – but they don't know they can't drive it.'**

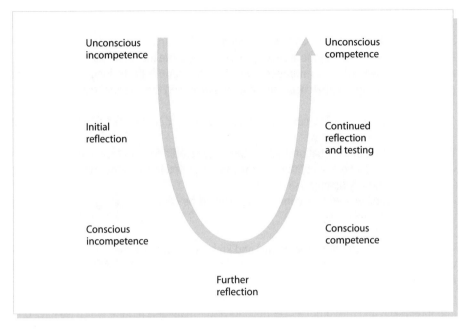

Figure 3.3 *Unconscious and conscious competence*
Adapted from D. Reay, *Understanding How People Learn*, Kogan Page, 1994

The event or reflection that should come next is the 'wake-up call' or realisation that one is inadequate in a particular knowledge, skill or behaviour. At the *conscious incompetence* stage the learner knows that there is more to know, and must decide what it is that he/she needs to learn in order to become competent. A personal training needs analysis can lead to the action stage. This, we suggest, is where the new learning experience takes place – again, a level of reflection may facilitate learning. The following stage is *conscious competence* – at which we are very aware that the new learning has to be tested and that further experience must be acquired. This can then initiate a 'taking stock' or reflection on results so far. We can then emerge 'consciously competent'. Finally, *unconscious competence* is the stage at which the learning is internalised and the process/task/skill/procedure becomes pretty well automatic or part of us. This is not to say that the learner does not still need support, advice and encouragement from his or her manager (coach/mentor) and personal time for reflection.

EXERCISE 3.3

To what extent do you think it possible for managers themselves to develop their own competencies as set out above?

How might they set about doing it?

What help might they need?

Core competence and competitor differentiation

In their bestselling book *Competing for the Future* (1994) Gary Hamel and C. K. Prahalad talk about 'core competences' as those set of competencies (note the use of both terms) – probably between five and 15 in number – which 'really contribute to long-term corporate prosperity'. Each core competence must meet the following three requirements:

- customer value – The customer must agree that it contributes significantly to the organisation's services
- competitor differentiation: that which is uniquely different to the competition's services – To be one of a number of organisations offering the same competence is not to be uniquely differentiated
- extendability – All core competences should be capable of being carried to future products and services.

An important point to note is that Hamel and Prahalad emphasise the integrative nature of these competences – that no one individual or unit is likely to hold all of them. The thrust of their work is strategic and is particularly concerned with the 'bigger picture' of how organisations compete in the marketplace. Clearly, however, there is a correlation between these integrated skills and the competences that individual managers require, which we have previously discussed.

Managers can help themselves

As described in the last chapter, managers work in conditions of turbulence, uncertainty and ambiguity. That is why one of the characteristics of effective managers is their resilience – they have to be able to cope with these inevitable pressures. But there are competencies and skills which can help them to manage in these circumstances. To a considerable extent it is up to managers to be aware of these requirements, the behaviours expected of them, and the skills they can use to help in carrying out their often demanding responsibilities. They must treat these as guidelines for personal development plans. Managers can learn from the example of their senior managers, by taking guidance from those individuals as well as from mentors, and through formal training courses – but self-managed learning is all-important.

The next section covers the role of the appraisal process in learning and development and then considers different learning/development methods in the workplace.

AN EVALUATION OF MANAGERIAL DEVELOPMENT INITIATIVES

This section of the chapter considers some of the development techniques that can be used to help managers learn. These processes are generally those that enable managers to benefit from experience. As Mumford and Gold (2004) suggest:

'All professional and managerial work are replete with opportunities for learning.'

The appraisal process

Some of the learning processes we highlight in this chapter can be initiated by the individual; others can be part of the training and development intervention initiated by the organisation. Appraisals, which evaluate an employee's performance or contribution on a work-related basis, are an essential part of the development process. Appraisals should give both employees and their line managers the opportunity to discuss performance and development issues. This can then lead to an agreement being reached between both parties as to what development activities are to be undertaken by the employee. Sadly, in far too many instances appraisal systems fall short of their goals, mainly because the aims (Reid, Barrington and Brown, 2004) are fragmented or unclear at times and because of a lack of commitment. However, on a more positive note, even in such cases an appraisal system allows for a dialogue between manager and employee and offers both an opportunity to give and receive feedback.

EXERCISE 3.4

Evaluate the appraisal system that operates in your workplace.

- How does it work?
- Is it a developmental system?
- Has it been a positive experience?
- How could it be improved?

Appraisals and learning objectives

Specifically, a sense of direction can be achieved by agreeing objectives and targets. An objective is something that is to be accomplished. For individuals or teams, objectives express what they are expected to achieve. A target is a quantified objective. But objectives can also be defined in qualitative terms as standards of performance. These set out the levels of performance required in a statement such as 'Performance in this area will be at the required standard when ... [something specified happens].'

A performance standard might therefore be expressed like this:

> **'Performance will be up to standard when callers are dealt with courteously at all times, whatever the circumstances.'**

Objectives should be agreed rather than 'set'. The latter word implies a top-down command – as in 'This is your objective because I say it is.' Agreement is important because commitment to achieving objectives is much more likely to exist when individuals and teams have taken part in formulating objectives they believe they can reasonably be expected to achieve. It is, however, a joint process. Managers must have their say. They have to meet the challenge set by the overall corporate objectives. It is up to them to present to their teams the challenge to which they are expected to respond, but also to listen to their views about what realistically can be done.

The agreement of objectives should be a top-down *and* bottom-up process. The top-down aspect is what management wants achieved; the bottom-up part is what individuals and teams believe they can achieve. The top-down views may ultimately prevail in general terms. For example, management may have no choice but to take steps to increase share-holder value because of pressure from institutional investors who have the power to demand better returns on their investment. However, the work objectives of teams and individuals may be modified to take account of their particular circumstances as long as, overall, they will be contributing sufficiently to the achievement of the goals of the business.

The process of agreeing objectives need not be unduly complicated. It should start from an agreed list of key result areas or main activities. It is then simply a matter of jointly examining each area and agreeing targets or standards of performance as appropriate.

Some organisations use the acronym SMART to define a good objective – an objective that is therefore

- **S**tretching/specific
- **M**easurable
- **A**greed/achievable
- **R**ealistic/relevant
- **T**ime-related.

The process requires that we write learning or development objectives which describe what the individual should be able to do on completion of the training and development programme. They should be SMART.

- stretching – The learner has yet to achieve the objective, but it is suggested that there must also be an element of challenge set within the objective. An objective too easily achieved is not challenging enough
- specific – Each objective should be as specific as possible (not vague) in its description of the performance/behaviour the individual should be able to demonstrate/achieve
- measurable – Objectives should be written in such a way that it is possible to get a clear 'yes' or 'no' answer if asked whether the learner has achieved any one objective or not
- agreed with the individual – The development of learning objectives should be a negotiated process with as much involvement of the learner as possible. An example (as we suggested earlier) of this is that many organisations operate performance appraisal systems in which the culmination of the appraisal is the writing of development objectives. In some cases the appraisee is primarily responsible for the 'first draft'
- achievable – Learning objectives should be challenging (by definition they should describe something more than the individual can achieve now) but they must be achievable. Obviously there is no point in objectives that are so far removed from what an individual is capable of that they become demoralising or demotivating before the learner begins

■ realistic and relevant, primarily to the individual's and organisation's needs – Achievement of the objectives must correspond to a significant improvement in the performance of the employee and in turn contribute to the achievement of organisational aims and objectives

■ time-related – Objectives should never be open-ended but should always stipulate a target date by which the individual should be able to perform the required behaviour.

EXERCISE 3.5

The following problems can arise in agreeing objectives:

■ It may be difficult to define specific and meaningful targets.
■ Where quantified targets cannot be set, it may be difficult to define qualitative standards.
■ Individuals may not be prepared to accept the targets or standards their managers think they should be set for their jobs.
■ Individuals may agree too readily to targets or objectives without thinking through how they are going to attain them, and as a result may fail.

How would you deal with these problems?

Targets

A target is a quantified and time-based objective. It defines measurable outputs and when they have to be achieved. The target may be to attain a specific level of output or to improve performance by a given amount. Targets can be expressed in financial terms, such as profits to be made, income to be generated, costs to be reduced or budgets to be worked within. Or they may be expressed in numerical terms, as a number of units to be processed, sales to be achieved, responses to be obtained or customers to be contacted over a period of time.

MANAGERIAL EFFECTIVENESS

Managerial effectiveness denotes the extent to which managers actually achieve, in terms of results, what they are supposed to achieve (Mumford, 1997). It is about performance, which refers both to what people do (their achievements and results) and to how people do it (their behaviour). To measure effectiveness it is necessary to understand and define both sides of the equation – that is, inputs (skills and behaviour) and outputs (results). The measurement of effectiveness and performance therefore compares expectations of achievements and behaviour with actual results and behaviour.

Action learning

Action learning (AL) was developed by Reg Revans (1983) as the 'best' way to educate and develop managers. He suggested that:

> **'There is no learning without action and no (sober and deliberate) action without learning.'**

He devised a method of planned learning that is relevant to management in general, and in particular to project management. It is, however, a method that requires collaboration and co-operation between managers in order to solve problems.

In Action learning a group of managers work on a common task/problem/project and by so doing learn from the process. It is thus designed to help managers think through the problems or the issues they encounter in their working life. This 'learning group' scenario may help managers share experience, gain new experiences and develop practical solutions to or a new point of view of their shared problems. This occurs while they continue with their usual management tasks. Learning while doing is thus essentially the key, and it is question-based (Reid, Barrington and Brown, 2004) and does not rely on established practice unless it fits the requirement of the task.

The process itself requires that the participants' rate of learning (**L**) is equal to or greater than the rate of change (**C**) they experience. In other words we learn at least enough prior to the changes we need to make. Revans suggests that organisations and the individuals in them cannot develop unless this relationship **L > C** is realised. Learning has two distinct elements: traditional instruction or programmed knowledge (**P**) and 'critical reflection' or 'questioning insight' (**Q**). This gives then gives the learning equation: $L = P + Q$.

Action learning sets

A Revans group acts as an Action learning set. It can include individuals from different departments in the organisation, different cultures, different backgrounds and so on, all on a voluntary basis.

The process allows individuals to work together in order to:

- work on problems
- work on problems that are of concern to set members and that they bring to the set for discussion
- ascertain set members' understanding of the problem, to clarify the points and enable them to become more manageable. This will help when the set discusses alternatives for action
- initiate action in the light of new ideas and decisions. This will change the situation. A review of the effects of the action is fed back to the set members for further reflection and analysis
- give support, although keep the process challenging. This will help set members to learn effectively
- be aware of the set dynamics and develop effective teamworking
- focus on effective learning.

An Action learning initiative would expect each set member to join voluntarily. Set members should have their own managerial project or issue to bring to the set for discussion with a view to initiating action. The set members may well become friends as part of the socialisation process, although that is not a requirement. Their main purpose is to exchange ideas, act and learn from the process, and help each other solve their managerial problem or issue. The Action learning set members frequently come back together for discussion so that the process of learning from the effect of taking action can continue.

Coaching

Coaching requires one person to have the talent to help someone else achieve. In the case of sports coaches, a coach is often attempting to get his or her charge to give a better performance than he or she is personally capable of achieving. Coaching is therefore a means of encouraging someone's (a successful person's) development and improving his or her performance and reaching his or her full potential.

The CIPD (2004) fact-sheet on Coaching defines a number of core characteristics of coaching:

- Coaching is a fairly short-term activity.
- It consists of one-to-one developmental discussions.
- It provides people with feedback on both their strengths and weaknesses.
- It is aimed at specific issues/areas that may nonetheless be wide-ranging.
- It is time-bounded.
- It focuses on improving performance and developing/enhancing individuals' skills.
- Coaching activities have both organisational and individual goals.
- It works on the belief that clients are self-aware and do not require a clinical intervention.
- It focuses on current and future performance/behaviour.
- It is a skilled activity.
- Personal issues may be discussed but the emphasis is on performance at work.

The CIPD (2004) defines coaching as:

> **'developing a person's skills and knowledge so that [his or her] job performance improves, hopefully leading to the achievement of organisational objectives. It targets high performance and improvement at work, although it may also have an impact on an individual's private life. It usually lasts for a short period and focuses on specific skills and goals.'**

Salisbury (1994) defines coaching as:

> **'the release of talent and skills, previously untapped by training, through a process of self-awareness initiated by the coach'.**

However, many companies fail to help their staff realise their potential and consistently throw talent away either through the minimal use of the skills/experience etc of staff or through seeing them 'leave and employ their talents elsewhere' (*ibid*).

The popularity of coaching as a development initiatives has risen markedly in the last few years. The CIPD (2004) suggests the following reasons:

- a rapidly evolving business environment – Targeted development interventions have become popular in helping individuals adjust to workplace changes
- the structural features of modern organisations – Organisational downsizing and flatter structures mean that newly promoted individuals often have to quickly fit into the higher performance requirements of their new roles. Coaching can assist individuals to achieve these changes
- the need for targeted, individualised, just-in-time development – The development needs of individuals can be diverse and in smaller organisations there are often too few individuals with specific development needs to warrant the design of a formal training programme. Coaching offers a flexible option which can be delivered 'just-in-time' to strengthen under-developed skills
- the financial costs of the poor performance of senior managers – There is a growing acceptance of the costs associated with poorly performing senior managers/executives. Coaching provides an opportunity to undertake pre-emptive and proactive interventions to improve their performance
- improved decision-making by senior employees – For senior-level executives it can be 'lonely at the top' because they have few people they can confide in, and with whom they can develop ideas and discuss decisions and concerns. A coach can be used as a 'safe and objective haven' to discuss issues and provide support
- individual responsibility for development – There is an increasing trend for individuals to take greater responsibility for their personal and professional development. Coaching can help individuals identify development needs, plan development activities and support personal problem-solving
- support for other learning and development activities – Coaching provides a valuable way of providing ongoing support for personal development plans, especially in assisting the transfer of learning in the workplace
- a popular development mechanism – People enjoy participating in coaching because they get direct one-to-one assistance and attention that fits in with their own timeframes and schedules. There is the potential to see quick results.

According to the CIPD Training and Development Survey (2004), coaching is being used for the development of staff at many levels: in that year 52 per cent of senior managers and 37 per cent of directors received coaching.

Produce a list of what you see as the attributes of a good manager.

The list you produce in response to Exercise 3.6 will almost certainly contain many positive attributes and behaviours – eg (expressed as competencies):

- values people
- shows respect
- is visible
- exhibits positive behaviour
- leads by example
- gives relevant feedback

and so on.

Some of these attributes are also those we would expect from a coach: someone who keeps us motivated, guides us to a higher level performance, engages our brains, taps into our skills and attributes, and enables us to feel a sense of achievement, even 'self actualisation' (Maslow, 1959). One role of the manager is thus evidently that of coach.

However, not all managers have those attributes. A planned process of transformation from managing to coaching staff will have many variables. The organisation's aims and culture can be a barrier against or a positive environment for developing coaching skills. It largely depends on the organisation's philosophy on the development strategies it chooses to adopt. A change in philosophical direction is not to be undertaken lightly. Managers will find the process of letting go of a leading/directing role in order to adopt a coaching role to be uncomfortable. They may feel a lack of control, although that is also part of the process of change. Caplan (2003) describes what she believes a coaching style of management to be about:

> **'A coaching style of management is not about "being the boss", giving directions and instructions and telling people what to do, how they should do it, should have done it, or jumping in with the answer. Rather, a leader's role today is to enable, encourage and facilitate so that staff have a stronger sense of control over their own work and their own time, and so that they identify their own options and solutions to problems. To achieve this the manager also needs to act as a role model of the desired behaviours. Nonetheless, there may be times when the manager will still need to be more directive with a member of staff.'**

Salisbury (1994) suggested a three-step plan for helping managers to coach:

- *Step 1:* Managers must learn about their own skills and attributes and whether their own perceptions of their interaction with people have congruence. In other words, do the manager's attributes match his/her actual ability to perform a coaching role? This stage of becoming more self-aware is difficult and some individuals will not go beyond this first phase. However, it is an important hurdle, because the would-be coach must understand his/her motives for wanting to develop.
- *Step 2:* In this phase managers are relinquishing control or responsibility for the performance of others. Instead, they provide relevant support, reach consensus on an aspect of personal and professional responsibility and provide relevant feedback to enable both parties to evaluate the likelihood of the task's being completed. This phase requires each person to be responsible for his or her own tasks and for the 'manager' to exhibit delegation skills.
- *Step 3:* The final stage requires the 'coach' to ask his/her colleague to repeat the task to fulfil a tighter deadline, or set his/her own time limitation. Giving an individual the autonomy to complete tasks at his/her own pace with some input and direction from the 'coach' can evoke a better performance than from staff who were previously told what to do. In this scenario individuals should know what to expect from each other and what contribution they should make. People invariably set higher goals for themselves than the traditional manager ever would – a position that is not always beneficial.

Clutterbuck and Megginson (1997) suggest that there are four coaching styles. These are termed: 'assessor', 'demonstrator', 'tutor' and 'stimulator'. The *assessor* role requires the coach to be an 'appraiser and teacher'. This is an important stage because some learners will lack the ability to judge their own performance and so will not be aware of what improvements are needed. The *demonstrator* role is necessary when learners need to see a task shown to them to increase their confidence. The *tutor* role is initiated as the learner grows in both skill and confidence. The tutor helps the learning experience by providing structure. The *stimulator* role is needed when the learner already has a high degree of skill and confidence. The coach's role here is to encourage learners to *reflect* on their performance and then go on to ascertain what can help them improve. The stimulator role is probably the one most favoured by management consultants.

Executive coaching

Whichever method is employed by the coach or the organisation to train managers to become coaches, there is no shortage, in the present climate, of consultants in this field offering their services. In particular, many offer executive coaching (EC). Unhappily, according to Carter (2001),

> **'there are no standards of practice or widely recognised certification of executive coaches in the UK and Europe'.**

This view is endorsed by the CIPD (*Coaching* fact-sheet, 2004), which suggests that 'there is a lack of established standards, professional bodies and qualifications frameworks'. Assessing the quality of service these consultants provide is therefore difficult. In her report,

Carter (2001) suggests that we 'should be concerned' because not only can 'coaching envy' occur in an organisation (ie everyone may want a coach), this phenomenon also represents a significant investment in both time and money. At the time of her report Carter stated that a charge of £2,000 per day was not uncommon for some consultants. We must assume, therefore, that this figure has risen in the last few years. The CIPD offers a guide to buying coaching services (Jarvis, 2004) to help the unwary HR manager charged with buying in coaching services.

We must nonetheless offer this cautionary note: executive coaching seems to be the current 'buzz word' – the new 'must have' for executives – and will consequently remain with us as such until the next consultancy craze hits Europe. But although executive coaching is part of 'popular-executive-culture', it does also have a place in developing staff. The CIPD (2004) Training and Development Survey reported that 90 per cent of respondents thought that when applied in an appropriate manner, coaching positively influenced the bottom line.

Executive coaching for the most part is a US import (Berglas, 2002). It has become fashionable to have a management coach in boardrooms in the UK to help these 'strategic thinkers' perform their roles. It is a phenomenon, the necessity for which has been brought about by recent changes in the workplace as outlined by Carter (2001):

> **'The downsizing and de-layering of the 1990s has produced a generation of isolated (and even lonely) senior managers. The larger gaps resulting between hierarchies mean that when people are promoted there are more skills to learn and less time to support one another. This has led to a new reliance on executive coaching as a way of imparting missing skills and improving existing ones.'**

Another situation, which Carter (2001) attributes to Business School courses of the past and company development programmes, is that the 'soft skills/people skills' have been ignored as part of the learner-development process. It is thus this that has caused the skills gap in some people at executive level – and executive coaching can therefore fill that gap.

Executive coaching is a one-to-one interactive process that is designed to enable the learner to learn at a rapid rate. It is focused on improving work-related performance and/or behaviours and is goal-oriented.

In her study of executive coaching in 30 UK organisations, Carter (2001) identified several steps in the learning process that were evident in many of the schemes she surveyed. These are:

- entry and contracting with the individual
- identifying the issue to be addressed
- reaching a shared analysis
- planning to address development needs arising
- action-taking, practice and reflection
- withdrawal from the relationship.

The next aspect of management development we discuss is mentoring.

Mentoring

Coaching and mentoring are often confused, although there are quite distinct differences. Coaching is current-job-oriented whereas mentoring is oriented towards both the current situation and the future, focusing on personal and career development. Mentoring enables the mentee to reflect on his/her own practice and thus his/her development. The mentor can then go on to suggest ways to develop his/her mentee in his/her current job or new appointment. The role of the mentor usually belongs to a more experienced member of staff, and is to offer advice and assistance to a less experienced member of staff. The mentor may also help to advance the career of the mentee, although that is not obligatory. Many observers believe that having a mentor is a significant factor for success; we would therefore suggest that it is part of our differentiator criteria for success.

Mentors can, in fact, play quite a varied role depending upon how the mentoring process is set up. It can range from emotional support for new starters to encouragement and advice for those progressing in their careers. The mentor should be in a good position to point out learning opportunities, help develop the mentee's self-confidence and stimulate and motivate. However, Clutterbuck (2001) makes the point that the mentor is not there to specifically guide the mentee's career development and progression, is not there to solve problems, and should not be in a role where he/she assesses the mentee.

Certainly, mentoring processes differ depending on whose guidance or theory we follow. Essentially, however, such theories break down into variations on the following themes: relationship-building, analysis and planning, and moving the process forward – ie 'getting on with it'.

- *relationship-building* – Cummings (2004) describes what she believes the relationship between mentor and mentee should be and what it should contain:

> **'Mentoring is a relationship. Through this developmental partnership, the mentee, with assistance from the mentor, sets goals for the key purpose of the development of the mentee. Enhancing skills, gaining new knowledge and implementing new behaviours are the intended targets of the mentoring programme.'**

  We should also take account of what both parties want to achieve, then go on to agree the way the process will work and produce a contract. The relationship must also be founded on agreement on what will be kept confidential.
- *analysis and planning* – Here the parties develop the mentee's learning plan which may in turn be linked to a personal development plan or a learning log. The mentor and mentee must analyse the mentee's needs: the tools of analysis must therefore be used – eg SWOT (strengths, weaknesses, opportunities and threats analysis), reflection on previous experiences, the appraisal process, line managers' feedback, etc. Both can then decide upon the personal competences/skills/qualifications the mentee might reasonably achieve.

■ *the moving forward phase* – This needs constant reflection and review of progress. The mentor offers structure here and is in a supporting role to keep the process on track, review what has been achieved, and acknowledge and celebrate those achievements.

This relationship should add value for both participants. The mentor may refresh his/her own knowledge by answering questions and being in discussion with the mentee. This can create renewed motivation on the part of the mentor. The mentee benefits both personally and professionally. The whole process may help both parties recognise their talents, and possibly their limitations, which can form the basis of future development.

The company also benefits. For instance, Gold (1999) in his study on teacher retention rates, pointed out some benefits of mentoring. After the first year of a mentoring programme, attrition rates were 5 per cent whereas before the programme started they had been at 18 per cent. In supporting female executives, Clutterbuck and Megginson (1999) found that mentoring had enabled the mentees to gain in confidence and enhance their self-image to the extent that they actively sought advancement and engaged in learning the organisational politics. Mentoring, unlike executive coaching, is usually an internal process, the intervention being undertaken by a more senior member of staff (the mentor). Organisations may choose to encourage this type of development intervention to build talent, support diversity initiatives, help career development, increase retention rates and build relationships.

This type of learning (mentoring) focuses very heavily on the learner, and along with coaching, fits in with the 'change agenda' (Sloman, 2003) proposition. This calls for a shift from traditional training to learning, and makes the case on sound business reasons:

> **'New business forces demand a different approach to the development of employees. Capable and committed people have become the critical source of competitive advantage. Emphasis must be shifted from training as a series of top-down interventions to a focus on individual learning.'**

Such a focus on individual learning makes coaching, mentoring and personal development plans part of that shift from training to learning by which employees take on more responsibility for their own development, albeit from an organisational agenda designed to ensure that appropriate learning takes place.

EXERCISE 3.7

Coaching and mentoring schemes are popular choices in contemporary organisations. However, even with top management commitment, some schemes fail to deliver the desired results.

Consider those factors in your own organisation (or an organisation with which you are familiar) which you think would be necessary to enable such schemes to succeed.

Personal development plans (PDPs)

Personal development plans (PDPs) are an essential tool in facilitating life-long and learner-centred learning – ie through mentoring, coaching, etc. They also form the backbone of delivering a continuous professional development (CPD) plan, much favoured by professional bodies including the CIPD. These plans encourage the members of such bodies to structure their learning, keep a record of the learning and provide evidence of CPD (CIPD, 2005). Candidates have to demonstrate CPD when applying for CIPD membership upgrades.

To be successful, these types of plans require a commitment to self-development on the part of the learner and a commitment of support on the part of the organisation. Gibb (2002) suggests that two axioms inform this issue:

> **'First is that any L&D [learning and development] is a good thing because it involves embracing the new, and changing capabilities and behaviours. Second is that the L&D that has the most potency to achieve change is that chosen and specified by the learners themselves.'**

The first point links to assessing employee development (Hamblett and Holden, 2000). The second identifies the learner as having a pivotal responsibility not only for his/her own learning but for managing the whole learning process.

The CIPD (2005; see http//www.cipd.co.uk) suggests that the key issues in developing a CPD plan are that:

- development should be continuous in the sense that the professional should always be actively seeking improved performance
- development should be owned and managed by the individual learner
- CPD is a personal matter, and the effective learner knows what he or she needs to learn – development should come from the individual's current learning state
- learning objectives should be clear and wherever possible should serve organisational or client needs as well as individual goals

- regular investment of time and learning should be seen as an essential part of professional life, not as an optional extra.

To support this effectively, the learner – along with his/her adviser (manager, mentor, coach, etc), after using relevant diagnostic processes – devises a learning plan. The plan itself may also link to a learning log (an ongoing continuous process of recording and reviewing learning events). This PDP method of experiential learning again emphasises the shift from training to learning (CIPD, 2004). Swart *et al* (2003) support this 'change agenda' (Sloman, 2003) from training to learning by taking the stance that in some cases training courses are of little value in that they do not endorse the need for sharing information. This reinforces some of the points made in this book regarding continuous improvement and those that promote differentiator behaviours – eg managing your own learning.

EXERCISE 3.8: REVIEW

In an attempt to give more prominence to management development in your organisation, senior management have asked you to prepare a critical review.

Specifically they require you to:
  a) evaluate what management development is taking place in the organisation
  b) benchmark these findings against a similar or competitor organisation
  c) analyse the results and recommend future developments.

SUMMARY

- Managers must recognise the requirement for effective management learning and development processes if they are serious about wanting to achieve excellent results.
- Successful management development helps to create a well-motivated managerial workforce and to maintain a competitive advantage. There therefore continues to be a need for management development related to management qualifications.
- Learning is the key factor in developing managers within their role. Many training and development programmes take into account both the learners' experience and their learning style(s) in the learning delivery.
- Some writers advocate reflection on experience as an important activity for managers, especially when linked to the learning process itself.
- Effective learning can be developed from informal, formal and entrepreneurial learning methods.
- To cope with the nature of their work managers have to be competent. However, to perform effectively we advocate that managers need to develop competency.
- One of the distinguishing – ie differentiating – characteristics of superior management is the ability to reflect upon and improve the development process itself.
- The appraisal process should use SMART learning objectives to develop the learning plan best suited to the needs of the individual manager.
- Action learning is a process that encourages 'set' members (managers) to exchange

ideas, interact and learn from the process of discussion, interaction and taking action as a continuous learning strategy.

■ Using the most effective learning method(s) of development is important. Thus a discerning overview of some of these processes (eg coaching, mentoring, etc) is worthwhile.

REFERENCES

ARGYRIS C. and SCHÖN D. A. (1978) *Organisational Learning: A theory in action perspective.* Reading, MA, Addison-Wesley.

BERGLAS S. (2002) 'The very real dangers of executive coaching', *Harvard Business Review*, Vol. 80, No.6, June, p92.

BOUD D., KEOGH K. and WALKER D. (eds)(1985) *Reflection: Turning experience into learning.* London, Kogan Page.

BOYATZIS R. (1982) *The Competent Manager.* New York, Wiley.

CAPLAN J. (2003) *Coaching for the Future: How smart companies use coaching and mentoring.* London, CIPD.

CARTER A. (2001) *Executive Coaching: Inspiring performance at work.* IES Report 379.

CIPD (2004) Fact-sheet: *Coaching.* November.

CIPD (2004) Training and Development Survey. http://www.cipd.co.uk/surveys

CIPD (2005) Continuous professional development. http//www.cipd.co.uk

CLUTTERBUCK D. (2001) *Everyone Needs a Mentor: Developing skills at work.* London, CIPD.

CLUTTERBUCK D. and MEGGINSON D. (1997) *Mentoring in Action.* London, Kogan Page.

CLUTTERBUCK D. and MEGGINSON D. (1999) *Mentoring Executives and Directors.* London, Butterworth-Heinemann.

COTTON J. (1995) *The Theory of Learning: An introduction.* London, Kogan Page.

COUNCIL FOR EXCELLENCE IN MANAGEMENT AND LEADERSHIP (2002) *Managers and Leaders: Raising our game.* A results overview of the Regional Survey of UK Economic Trends. London, CBI.

CUMMINGS J. (2004) Telephone interview. Jan 27, 2004. In Bob Crosby *Mentoring: Matching the mentor and mentee* at http://www-rohan.sdsu.edu/~crosby/index.htm

GIBB S. (2002) *Learning and Developing: Processes, practices and perspectives at work.* London, Palgrave.

GOLD Y. (1999) *Beginning Teacher Support.* http//www.ericfacility.net/databases/ERIC-Digest/ed436487.html

HAMBLETT J. and HOLDEN R. (2000) 'Employee-led development: another piece of left luggage?', *Personnel Review*, Vol. 29, No. 4.

HAMEL G. and PRAHALAD C. K. (1994) *Competing for the Future.* Boston, MA, Harvard Business School Press.

JARVIS P. (1990) *An International Dictionary of Adult and Continuing Education.* London, Routledge. As cited in M. TIGHT (1996) *Key Concepts in Adult Education and Training.* London, Routledge.

JARVIS P. (1992) 'Reflective practice in nursing', *Nurse Education Today*, 12: 174–81.

JARVIS J. (2004) *Coaching and Buying Coaching Services. A Guide.* London, CIPD.

KOLB D.A. (1984) *Experiential Learning as the Science of Learning and Development.* Englewood Cliffs, NJ, Prentice Hall.

KOLB D.A., RUBIN I.M. and OSLAND J. (1991) *Organisational Behaviour: An experiential approach.* Englewood Cliffs, NJ, Prentice Hall.

MASLOW A. H. (1959) *Motivation and Personality.* New York, Harper & Row.

MOON J. (1999a) *Learning Journals: A handbook for academics, students and professional development.* London, Kogan Page.

MOON J. (1999b) *Reflection in Learning and Professional Development.* London, Kogan Page.

MUMFORD A. (1997; 3rd edition) *Management Development Strategies.* London, IPD.

MUMFORD A. and GOLD J. (2004; 4th edition) *Management Development: Strategies for action.* London, CIPD.

PORTER M. (2003) *Competitiveness: Moving to the next stage.* ESRC/LSE/DTI.

REAY D. (1994) *Understanding How People Learn.* London, Kogan Page.

REID M. A., BARRINGTON H. and BROWN N. (2004; 7th edition) *Human Resource Development: Beyond training interventions.* London, CIPD.

REVANS R. W. (1983) *The ABC of Action Learning.* Bromley, Chartwell-Bratt.

SALISBURY F. S. (1994) *Developing Managers as Coaches.* London, McGraw-Hill.

SCHÖN D. A. (1987) *Educating the Reflective Practitioner.* London/San Francisco, Jossey-Bass.

SLOMAN M. (2003) *The Change Agenda.* London, CIPD. www.cipd.co.uk/changeagendas

STEWART J. (1999) *Employee Development and Practice.* London, Financial Times/Pitman Publishing.

SWART J., KINNIE N. and PURCELL J. (2003) *People and Performance in Knowledge Intensive Firms.* Research Report. London, CIPD. p71.

Twenty-First-Century Skills: Realising our potential – individuals, employers, nation (2003) White paper. The Stationery Office.

WHITTAKER J. and JOHNS T. (2004) 'Standards deliver', *People Management*, June, pp32–4.

WOODRUFFE C. (1990) *Assessment Centres: Identifying and developing competences.* London, IPM.

Communication: how we inter-relate

CHAPTER 4

INTRODUCTION

The Managing for Results model shows communication to be an integral concept that links all segments of the model. Its significance is such that without adequate or successful communication any hope of achieving results would be confounded. This would also hamper attempts by an organisation in differentiating for excellence.

This chapter will give a perspective of communication that can be used as a basis for discussion in both a personal and an organisational setting. It also leads us to the acknowledgment that good communication can be a major differentiator for success. It continues with an overview of communication techniques.

Learning outcomes

On completing this chapter the reader will be able to:

- explain various methods of communication
- critically evaluate some of the differences between intra- and inter-communication
- explain why managers need to be skilled in communication techniques – for example, to influence and persuade others.

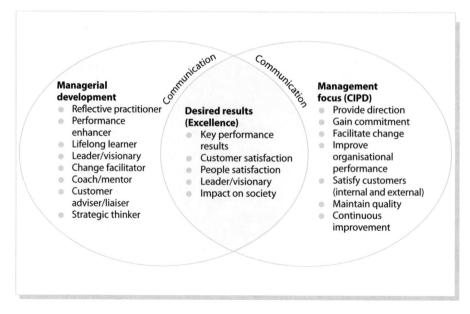

Figure 4.1 *Managing for Results: book schema–communication*

COMMUNICATION

A significant amount of our time in organisations is taken up by communicating with others as well as ourselves. Communicating with ourselves could be described as speaking with and listening to an 'inner voice', whereas communicating with others corresponds to the interaction between people in the organisation.

Types of communication that endorse these distinct ways of communication are:

- *intra-communication*, which takes place 'inside' the individual/body/group/network/organisation
- *inter-communication*, which takes place 'outside' – in other words, it is in the open domain.

It is important that managers develop a level of awareness of these concepts, because the need for effective communication in the workplace cannot be overstated. It is the means of

Table 4.1 *Intra- and inter-communication*

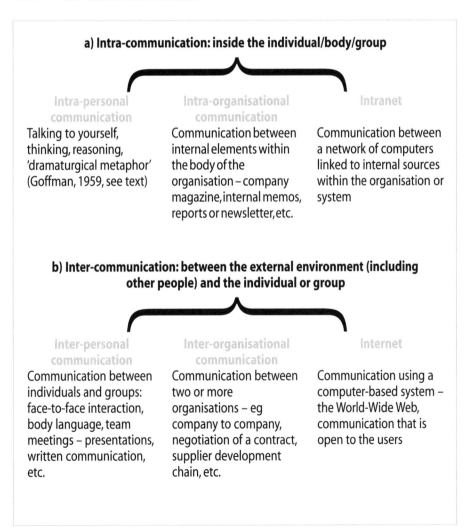

a) Intra-communication: inside the individual/body/group

Intra-personal communication	Intra-organisational communication	Intranet
Talking to yourself, thinking, reasoning, 'dramaturgical metaphor' (Goffman, 1959, see text)	Communication between internal elements within the body of the organisation – company magazine, internal memos, reports or newsletter, etc.	Communication between a network of computers linked to internal sources within the organisation or system

b) Inter-communication: between the external environment (including other people) and the individual or group

Inter-personal communication	Inter-organisational communication	Internet
Communication between individuals and groups: face-to-face interaction, body language, team meetings – presentations, written communication, etc.	Communication between two or more organisations – eg company to company, negotiation of a contract, supplier development chain, etc.	Communication using a computer-based system – the World-Wide Web, communication that is open to the users

developing and co-ordinating the activities of others and a means by which good working relationships can be fostered and motivation enhanced.

Table 4.1 categorises the concepts mentioned above as well as depicting how other forms of communication might fit into the overarching communication framework.

From the table it is evident that intra- and inter-communication have wider sub-sets that further define these concepts and increase our understanding of their significance. We note that:

Intra-communication **(a)** takes place 'inside' the individual/body/group/network/organisation and may be considered in the three ways below:

- *Intra-personal communication* takes place 'inside' the person; the process of intra-personal communication involves the transmission of data/information/feelings between the various senses or pathways.
- *Intra-organisational communication* classifies communication that is internal within the organisation: it describes the use of company magazines or newsletters which are used as the communication channel.
- *Intranet communication* is a form of communication channel using computer-based technology harnessed by the organisation to allow internal communication to take place – eg an internal email network.

The model of inter-communication **(b)** highlights that inter-communication takes place 'outside' – in other words, it is in the open domain and may be considered in the three ways below:

- *Inter-personal communication* involves the exchange of the message/information/dataacross communication channel/s from one person to another or one group to another.
- *Inter-organisational communication* describes communication between separate organisations – for example, a negotiation for a long-term business agreement such as a supplier and development chain or network.
- *Internet communication* uses a computer-based system that is open to the users – eg the World-Wide Web. Individuals and companies are able to buy, sell, advertise, investigate – in fact, conduct all manner of communication processes – in a way that might be person-to-person, person-to-company, or company-to-company.

However, communication involving organisations will be considered later in Chapter 5. For now we will discuss the importance of intrapersonal communication in more detail.

Intra-personal communication

Intra-personal communication includes the internal process of communication by which we converse with ourselves. This type of communication can be conscious or unconscious, using mainly (though not exclusively) non-verbal media. The process involves elements of the conscious mind (psyche) used to communicate thoughts between mental systems – this we could term the 'inner voice'. Our brain allows these 'thought' messages to be communicated as well as our 'feeling' messages to the stimulus response system, thus allowing interaction between areas of the brain.

To illuminate this consider the following:

a) You are sitting in your office, at the end of the day, having a cup of tea/coffee before starting your journey home. You are reviewing the events of the day – eg 'Should I have mentioned staff appraisals today? I need to complete them by the end of the month. I will talk to the staff about them tomorrow.' You are having a conversation with yourself. This reflection helps you clarify your thoughts, interpret events, make decisions for action, and so on.

b) The following internal sequence occurs: (thought) I will go home; (action) look out of the window; (thought) it looks as if it is going to rain; (decision) take my umbrella 'just in case …'; (thought) where did I put that umbrella?

In the case of both a) and b) you are engaged in intra-personal communication: you have made initial and final statements, asked yourself questions, reflected, debated them and made decisions. You are thus exhibiting the ability to communicate with yourself – possibly the basis for all good communication. Here one of the most relevant points of this intra-communication process is the thinking and 'encoding' stages, which are the precursors to intra-personal communication. Reasonably, a person cannot communicate a thought or a decision effectively unless he or she knows what to say and how to say it, and possesses an understanding of how the recipient will 'receive' and interpret the message (the perceived meaning or intended meaning).

Goffman (1959) interprets our actions as a 'dramaturgical metaphor' by which we act out in our minds what will happen in a particular interaction. In this type of inner discussion the individual plays the role of himself or herself as well as the other 'actors', and the whole scene unfolds as the individual prescribes. The actual outcome is determinant upon every aspect of the individual's interpretation of how the message will be per-ceived and its accuracy. In reality, then, that response is not always what actually transpires, because others will have their own interpretation of the message, which may or may not coincide with the originator's. The main point here is that that the originator has previously formed a clear vision of an interaction in his/her mind by a process of intrapersonal communication.

Fisher (1993) describes two fundamental factors which he maintains influence how we interpret and conduct communication and how this communication stimulates external action:

- internal stimuli derived from motives, attitudes personal schema (cognitive frame-works people use to select and organise the raw data available to them) and self-concept (what a person believes he or she is like)
- external stimuli selected from events, objects and people outside the individual, including the outcome of the individual's action.

From the discussion above, areas of consideration for management development would include: self-concept (knowing your self), self-confidence and self-perception. Gaining a level of understanding as well as the ability to evaluate these concepts is therefore essential for successful communication to take place. These concepts and their development are inte-gral to becoming a reflective practitioner, a fundamental aspect of management development in our Managing for Results model.

We must acknowledge that to engage in intra-communication is a fundamental requirement for a manager to become a reflective practitioner. It is part of our overall decision-making process. Intra-communication is a critical factor in our state of mind, our emotions, and whether we trust someone or not.

Emotional states are complex. A list of emotions could include anger, disgust, grief, fear, love, joy, contentment, and surprise. We are, however, taught from childhood to control emotion. Our learning process encourages logic in decision-making and in our dealings with others. Yet we might also argue that humans allow instinct and emotion (Berko *et al*, 1995) to control their decisional approach. As reflective practitioners, managers should therefore at least take responsibility for their feelings and their reactions to them. They should also acknowledge that decisions made purely on emotion should be avoided.

Trusting someone relies on our feelings, however, which are dependent upon interaction between the people concerned. We might well have discussed 'trust' in the following section (*Inter-personal communication*) but because of the intra-communicative practice involved in trusting we will continue our discussion here.

Trusting also involves those aspects of self-concept/perception. Indeed, in deciding to trust we are allowing a level of openness and disclosure. We decide who to trust and who to confide in – and who to distrust – the inclination to do so being a process learned through experience (Berko *et al*, 1995). Trust can be created through developing a rapport. The underlying factor here is risk. We put ourselves at risk through disclosure if this is supported and reciprocated (eg positive feelings are evidenced) by the other party and trust can begin to be incorporated into the relationship. Fundamentally, we look for consistency and congruence between the various messages we are receiving. This affects the level of confidence we have in predicting the other person's behaviour – which in turn links to whether we see the other person as dependable. Trusted individuals are often labelled as dependable. Feelings of trust are important in forming our attitudes and perceptions of another person and thus the communication process as a whole.

Inter-personal communication

Take another look at Table 4.1. Inter-personal communication consists of interactions between an individual/group and other individual(s)/group(s). Interaction can consist of face-to-face exchanges, team meetings, presentations, letters, emails, etc. In a face-to-face encounter (which is what takes place any time we talk to each other), when a person has decided on what to say and how to say it, the next stage is ensuring that the intended meaning (message) gets across. However, not every communication exchange is successful – things can and do go wrong. The message is not always accurately transmitted and/or received.

These concepts centre on one of the earliest and well-known models of communications, namely the Shannon and Weaver (1949) model. Shannon and Weaver devised a model that is somewhat linear and lacking in feedback loops, yet an appreciation of it remains adequate for our purpose. Byers' (1997) interpretation of the model is incorporated in Figure 4.2.

In the model the source transmits a message, which consists of signs, which are then relayed as a signal or encoded. Fisher (1993) suggests 'encoding' to be 'the process by which a sender converts ideas into the symbols that comprise a message'. These symbols could consist of gestures, words, or even pictures. In effect, the sender is predicting that the receiver will

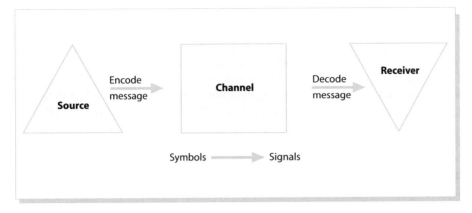

Figure 4.2 *The Shannon and Weaver model of communication, as represented by Byers, 1997*
Source: P. Y. Byers, *Organisational Communication*, Allyn & Bacon, 1997

understand and therefore interpret the message as the sender intended. The signs are sent via a channel and are 'decoded' by the receiver. The receiver interprets the message as the idea the receiver thinks the sender intended to convey (Fisher, 1993): the receiver has thus 'decoded' the message. The level of accuracy of the sender's message or the sender's prediction of its reception has an overwhelming influence on the quality of the message and how it will actually be received.

As we have already stated, communicating effectively with others is fundamental to the management role. Giving and receiving information is an everyday occurrence between staff in all organisations. Managers' communications encompass minor aspects of organisational life, like whose turn it is to make the coffee, as well as major events such as communicating impending redundancies or the current state of the organisation's finances. Outcomes of all such eventualities can rest with the manager's ability to communicate face-to-face (inter-personally) with others. Examples are shown below:

- Interviews are needed to select, appraise and discipline employees.
- Meetings (see Chapter 5) are used to develop ideas, give information, make decisions and resolve misunderstandings.
- In countless other situations getting the message across is essential: in other words, a manager must be able to persuade, sell, negotiate and present.

Although the list above is not comprehensive, it does signify the necessity for managers to have a high level of competence in communicating.

The effectiveness of any one-to-one communication is dependent on the relationship between the two people involved. The more trust and investment in the relationship, the more likely the two parties are to reveal their feelings. Developing the ability to share information in the form of confidences, opinions, values and beliefs is therefore important. This in itself involves the participants in a 'give-and-take' (trust) scenario, which becomes the basis for interpersonal transactions in the form of the sending and receiving of messages which are successfully encoded and decoded. Arguably, the more successful the interpersonal communication that takes place between participants, the greater the level of understanding and openness that should prevail.

A manager's ability to communicate on an inter-personal basis with others can therefore be significant, in that it has a marked effect in benefiting the organisation. Goffman (1959) maintains that we are continually seeking information from others that is not readily revealed. Instead, we constantly infer meaning from a range of cues – eg gestures. Simultaneously, Goffman suggests, we are attempting to deceive people who are trying to obtain the same information from us, mainly by creating an impression that is favourable; in this way communication can become, sadly, 'the performance that people present to others' (Goffman, 1959).

Be that as it may, what remains is the need for managers to develop good communication technique that is influential in persuading others that the message they and their organisation are transmitting has merit – and that thus is a differentiator, an indicator of competitive advantage.

EXERCISE 4.1

A colleague asks you to explain intra-personal communication and say why it is important to your personal development as a manager. How do you respond?

In your recent appraisal you and your manager agree that it would be beneficial for you to undertake a training course on influencing skills. However, she (your manager) requires you to present a case for taking up this course to the HRD (human resource development) manager. How do you respond?

Time spent by managers communicating

Managers spend a great deal of their time communicating. They exert influence, write reports, make presentations, manage meetings (scheduled and unscheduled), reply to or create email messages, etc – in fact, they use a wide range of forms of intra- and inter-communication to enable them to be effective in the completion of their tasks. Henry Mintzberg (1973) enabled us to gain further insight into the significance of communication when he considered the time managers spend in communicating. Even if we take into account the brief list of tasks suggested above, it is no surprise to learn that research indicates that managers spend up to 80 per cent of their time in communication of various types. In a detailed study (see Figures 4.3 and 4.4) of five chief executives, Mintzberg found that they spent 78 per cent of their time communicating orally, and that this accounted for 67 per cent of their activities.

It is reasonable to suggest, therefore, that if so much time is devoted to communicating, managers at all levels must exhibit skill and competence in the actual practice of communication. Consequently, the rest of this chapter considers the influencing and persuading skills that managers have to acquire in order to fulfil their tasks.

INFLUENCING TECHNIQUES

Managers exert influence – on their managers, on their colleagues and on their teams. They have to persuade people to do things, possibly against their will. It can be said that the manager's job is 60 per cent getting it right and 40 per cent putting it across.

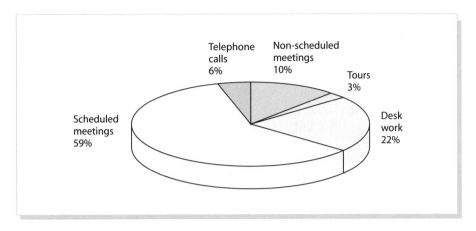

Figure 4.3 *Distribution of managers' hours (Mintzberg)*
Source: H. Mintzberg, *The Nature of Managerial Work*, Harper & Row, 1973

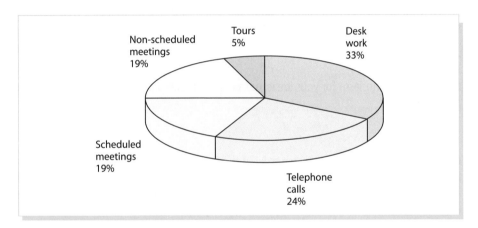

Figure 4.4 *Distribution of managers' activities (Mintzberg)*
Source: H. Mintzberg, *The Nature of Managerial Work*, Harper & Row, 1973

How are people influenced?

People are influenced by arguments or proposals which are logical and practical, which help them to get their work done better or improve results, and which provide them with a new perspective. They are more likely to be swayed by an argument if they see that the proposal benefits them, and are even more likely to agree if the suggestion accords and has congruence with their own views and/or feelings.

It follows that if you want to influence others (possibly against their will) *and gain their commitment*, you must not only present powerful, well-balanced and fully backed-up arguments. You must also take pains to understand each other person's point of view (or the collective view of a group of people) and take account of it in presenting your proposal or idea.

There are four basic influencing skills:

Asserting

This means making your views clear, expressing your views in direct ways. Assertive statements

- are brief and to the point
- indicate that you are not hiding behind someone, are speaking for yourself by using such clauses as 'I think that …', 'I believe that …', 'I feel that …' – your beliefs and views are important
- are not over-weighted with advice
- use questions to find out the views of others and test reactions to your views
- distinguish between fact and opinion
- are expressed positively but not dogmatically
- indicate that you are aware that other people may have different points of view.

Bridging

Draw out other people's points of view; indicate that you understand what they are getting at; give credit to their good ideas and suggestions; join your views with theirs: 'Well, we both seem to be saying the same things, so let's agree to proceed.'

Attracting

Convey your enthusiasm for your ideas; get people to feel that they are taking part in an exciting project.

Observing and listening

Observe people's reactions and listen to what they say. You should be able to spot the glassy look in someone's eyes when he or she is bored by what you are saying. You need to detect any feelings of hostility so that you can counter them. It is sometimes a good idea to come out into the open and say 'I don't seem to be getting my case across – what's the problem?'

EXERCISE 4.2

Think about a proposal that you want to make to someone who may resist it.

Plan how you would set about influencing that person using the suggestions in this chapter.

Persuasion

A key influencing skill is persuasion – using facts, logic and reason to present your own case, emphasising its strong points, anticipating objections to any apparent weaknesses, and appealing to reason.

The ten rules for persuading others are:

1 Define your objective.

2 Get the facts. Assemble as much data as possible. Even if you do not use it all, it may come in useful later as supporting material.

3 Organise your argument. Your aim should be to ensure that you devise a powerful argument which clearly addresses the problem and which is developed logically and inexorably from the facts. You should assemble the supporting data in a way that substantially supports your conclusion.

4 Anticipate objections. When marshalling your arguments and developing your proposition, anticipate any objections that may be raised. You can then either deal with them in your proposition – putting them up so as then to knock them down – or you can prepare yourself for dealing with them if they crop up in discussion. It is often useful to suggest different patterns of action, list the pros and cons for each, and come down firmly in favour of one. There is no harm in admitting that you have made this judgement 'on balance'. You accept that points can be made against your proposal, 'but the points for significantly outweigh those against – for the following reasons . . .'.

Remember that there are at least 12 ways of saying No, so prepare to deal with them:

■ It won't work.
■ It's good in theory but not in practice.
■ It will cost too much.
■ We've tried it before and it didn't work.
■ This is not addressing the real problem.
■ The benefits won't be realised until it is too late.
■ This is not the right time.
■ It will set a dangerous precedent.
■ We haven't got the resources to implement it.
■ Our shareholders, managing director, sponsors, trustees, shop stewards, workers, customers, clients, suppliers, sales outlets, sales representatives, agents (etc) won't like it.
■ We need to consult with . . . (etc) before we go any further.
■ We must spend more time considering the implications of this proposal.

5 Find out what the other person or people want. Never underestimate a person's natural resistance to change. But bear in mind that such resistance is proportional not to the total extent of the change but to the extent to which it affects that person. When asked to accept a proposition, the first questions people ask themselves are: 'How does this affect me?', 'What do I stand to lose?' and 'What do I stand to gain?' These questions must be answered before persuasion can start. The key to all persuasion is empathy – seeing your proposition from every other person's point of view. If you can really put yourself in their shoes, you will be able to foresee objections and present your ideas in the way most attractive to them. You must find out how they look at things and what they want. Listen to what they have to say. Don't talk too much. Ask questions. If they ask you a question, reply with another question. Find out what they are after, then present your case in a way that highlights its benefits to them, or at least reduces their objections or fears.

6 Look for the 'hidden agenda'. A meeting may be called for a particular purpose, but behind this there may be different and more significant things people want to

achieve. Some people, for example, may be more interested in improving their status or extending their authority than in achieving something that benefits the organisation.

7 Prepare a simple and attractive presentation. Your presentation should be as simple and straightforward as possible to emphasise the benefits. Don't bury the selling-points. Lead them in gently so there are no surprises. Anticipate objections.

8 Make your audience, and especially potential doubters, party to your idea. Get them to contribute, if at all possible. Find some common ground in order to start off with agreement. Don't antagonise them. Avoid defeating them in arguments. Help to preserve self-esteem. Always leave a way out for them.

9 Sell the benefits positively. Show conviction. You are not going to influence anyone if you don't believe in what you are proposing and communicate that belief. To persuade effectively, you must spell out the benefits of what you are proposing. What you are proposing may be of less interest to the individuals concerned than the effects of that proposal on them.

10 Clinch things and take immediate action. Choose the right moment to clinch the proposal. Make sure that you are not pushing too hard – but when you reach your objective, don't stay and risk losing it. Take prompt follow-up action. There is no point in going to all the trouble of getting agreement if you let things slide afterwards.

EXERCISE 4.3

Carry out the plan you devised for Exercise 4.2.

Review the outcome. What worked for you, and what did not?

What have you learned from this process?

EXERCISE 4.4

Consider a manager with whom you work. Drawing on the concepts outlined in this chapter construct a brief half-page account of your relationship. Analyse whether the relationship is effective in terms of task and personal criteria.

The intra- and inter-communication practices discussed in this chapter have helped demonstrate the need for managers to use their skill in influencing and persuading as tools of their work. These considerations are evident in an article that appeared in *People Management* (October, 2004), which reported on how the BBC has been communicating internally.

EXERCISE 4.5

Read the following article and answer the questions at the end.

A Season of Drama

by Claire Warren, **People Management***, 28 October 2004*

David Kelly, a government weapons scientist, committed suicide in July 2003 after he was revealed as the source for Radio 4's *Today* programme reporter Andrew Gilligan's story, which infamously claimed the government had 'sexed up' a dossier on Saddam Hussein's weapons capability.

Kelly's death prompted an inquiry, led by retired law lord Brian Hutton, which could have threatened the position of the prime minister. Instead, it was damning in its criticism of the BBC.

For Stephen Dando, head of HR at the corporation, the events that unfolded in the immediate aftermath of the Hutton Report catapulted him straight to the heart of one of the worst crises in the BBC's history.

The period between the departure of chairman Gavyn Davies and director-general Greg Dyke in January (2004) and the arrival of their replacements was, he says, 'a bit of a blur'.

'A profound and unplanned change of that sort clearly creates a lot of implications, most of which are to do with people and communication. Whether you like it or not, as the HR director you find yourself right at the heart of helping the organisation through that sort of crisis ... In my career it certainly goes down as one of the periods of massive learning and growth for me, personally. You develop your skills and your experience, but you also learn an awful lot about yourself and your own resilience.'

On the day the Hutton Report was published, Davies resigned and, following a meeting of the BBC governors, Dyke left the next day, prompting thousands of BBC staff to stage impromptu walkouts.

At the time the then acting chairman Lord Ryder apologised 'unreservedly' for errors made by the BBC. But in his recently published autobiography *Inside Story*, Dyke says:

> 'I didn t believe it was necessary for either of us [Davies and himself] to go.
>
> I didn't believe then, and I still don't believe today, that the BBC had done
>
> enough wrong to merit such a drastic response.'

Dyke goes on to say that Dando, director of BBC People, told the governors that 'getting rid of [him] would be a terrible blow to the staff and the BBC'.

Dando, however, does not comment on the rights or wrongs of the departures, although he does agree that this kind of shock has an inevitable short-term impact on morale. He says:

> 'My feeling is that if you can demonstrate to people that there is continuity
>
> about the things they care most deeply about, then you can look back and
>
> regard that impact on morale as being a dip rather than anything fun-
>
> damental.'

Within 24 hours of the resignations, Dando and acting director-general Mark Byford had organised an event to bring the BBC's top 400 people together to talk about what had happened.

'We just knew instinctively that it was vital to bring people together and to begin the process of making sense of what happened,' says Dando.

> 'We could then be in a better position to start to talk about the kind of
>
> leadership that we needed to bring to the rest of the organisation. There
>
> was a lot of emphasis on communicating very openly and giving people
>
> the time and the space to get through their own emotional reactions to
>
> what had occurred.'

Since those early days it seems there has been an endless stream of reviews and announcements designed to show that the BBC has learnt from its mistakes.

The organisation set up a disciplinary inquiry, led by Dando and Caroline Thompson, director of policy and legal, into the actions of the executives most directly involved in the Kelly affair.

According to national newspaper reports, before the results of the inquiry were known, many BBC journalists regarded it as a 'kangaroo court', some even saying it was like a 'medieval Star Chamber'. In May, the BBC announced that 'no dismissals were involved'. It would not comment further on individual decisions, but Dando says he believes other HR professionals will understand his determination to keep it as a strictly confidential internal management process.

He adds:

> 'Sadly, that meant I could not and would not comment on what, frankly, I
> thought was all the drivel that was being written on a daily basis by the so-
> called quality press. I am content to trust that most people who know me
> would be confident that anything of this sort would be rigorously, fairly
> and sensitively handled.'

A separate process to identify the editorial lessons from the Hutton inquiry was chaired by Ron Neil, a former BBC director of news and current affairs.

Plans to improve training and set up a multi-million-pound international college of journalism were included in the review, which was unveiled in June. Neil also recommended an enhanced role for programme editors and lawyers in the corporation's editorial process.

Neil's report came a day after Mark Thompson used his first day as the new director-general to outline a restructuring of the BBC's executive committee, replacing it with a smaller board and introducing two new boards for journalism and creativity. He also announced four reviews – which the unions expect to result in job losses – into commercial strategy, including BBC Worldwide, content supply, value for money and the transfer of departments out of London. All were expected to report before the end of the year.

Says Dando:

> 'We have to move very quickly with these reviews because of the whole
> context of the review of the Royal Charter [which expires in 2006] and the
> need for the BBC to be asking itself questions that, not unreasonably,
> others will ask of it … The world that we are part of is changing rapidly, and
> we need to continue to evolve and change. So the expectation is that
> there will be considerable change coming from these reviews – but
> exactly what that will look like has yet to be determined in detail.'

As part of the process, staff views are being taken into consideration and 'Shaping our future' sessions have been organised to enable employees to contribute their ideas.

Dando goes on:

'Mark Thompson has come back and made a very strong impact very quickly on the organisation. I think people see him as a very decisive, authoritative leader; he knows the organisation inside out, yet he had the benefit of two years away in a very different organisation. [Thompson left the BBC in early 2002 to become chief executive of Channel 4.] People can see that Mark is willing to ask some fundamental questions about the future shape and size of the BBC, but I think they can see that he is doing it in a way that is building on a lot of what we've put in place in the past few years.'

After Greg Dyke took the helm in January 2000, the BBC mounted a series of initiatives that resulted in huge changes in structure and morale. First came One BBC, which was fundamentally structural in nature but also included challenging the non-output divisions to significantly reduce costs. As a result, the HR department embarked on a three-year programme that has led to about £20 million being removed from its cost base.

When Dando joined the BBC in 2001 there was a lot of change being brought about under One BBC, but, he says, Dyke was beginning to feel that it wasn't really setting out to effect profound cultural change.

By February 2002, One BBC had evolved into the ongoing Making It Happen initiative, which aims to get the whole organisation to focus on developing much deeper audience insight.

Making It Happen kicked off with a new mission statement – to become the world's most creative organisation. This contrasts dramatically with another BBC mission statement dating back to John Birt's time as director-general – to be the best-managed organisation in the public sector.

Dando continues:

'The recent vision statement feels like the right one for the BBC because it is still incredibly ambitious, yet we are the BBC and we already have lots of examples of world-class creativity in so much of what we do ... The *challenge* is to continue that quest. It is about getting the whole organisation really focused on becoming more creative, more audience-focused.'

At the launch of Making It Happen, Dyke also produced the famous yellow cards with the statement 'Cut the crap'. Thousands of the cards, which encapsulated Dyke's desire to establish some straight talking at the BBC, were sent out to staff across the BBC and even translated into Chinese and Arabic.

The launch of a four-day induction programme for all employees who join for three months or more was also one of the first HR initiatives under Making It Happen.

Says Dando again:

> 'If you create a really powerful induction experience for people at the start
> of their career, it is a very powerful lever for changing the culture.'

More recently, leadership has also been moved right up the agenda, and a multi-million-pound leadership development programme has been launched. Over the course of the next five years the BBC, working in partnership with Ashridge Business School, is putting 7,000 staff through this course.

Other initiatives focused on areas such as the degree of flexibility staff can be offered and the spaces people work in. This has varied from installing a roof garden at the BBC's Belfast office to opening up an atrium at White City that had been closed on spurious health and safety grounds.

A new set of values has also been launched and recruitment practices have been steered away from placing too much emphasis on a narrow set of skills-based criteria.

'One of the very important things about the whole process of change is that there has been huge ownership from all of the executive committee,' says Dando.

> 'It is all too easy to define this kind of change programme as an HR
> initiative. I felt very strongly from Day 1 that we would only be successful
> if we had very strong line management ownership.'

The BBC has also worked hard to give everyone who wants to take part a serious voice in the process. As with the current reviews, events were organised to give employees an opportunity to express their views.

> 'In many ways what we did was democratise the process of change within
> the BBC. I think the degree and the reach and the scope of the consultation
> we've done has been very distinctive. It goes well beyond what most
> organisations are doing.'

A staff survey in 2003 revealed that around 60 per cent of employees were in favour of the Making It Happen culture change, and 20 per cent of that group were what the BBC would define as 'change champions'.

Declares Dando:

'We wouldn't have dreamed of results like that three years ago. This is quite an extraordinary snapshot of the degree to which people inside the BBC have really taken ownership of the change … It takes a huge amount of effort and work to shift the culture of an organisation in a sustainable way. I think we have achieved that, but we need to keep it going and accept that things move on as well. We are moving into a period of significant change, which is unsettling, but I think we are a lot better prepared for the change that we are going into as a result of the work we have done in the past few years.'

Organisations can do all sorts of things when the good times roll, but it is the tough times that prove just how strong an organisation really is.

As Dando says:

'At the end of the day, the BBC is a very resilient organisation. The impact of the Hutton inquiry was considerable at the time, but I think the BBC has demonstrated yet again that it can move on from its difficult moments very effectively.'

EXERCISE 4.5 QUESTIONS

1   From the discourse in the article, what are your perceptions of Stephen Dando (director of BBC People)?
2   How would you describe the relationship between Stephen Dando and Greg Dyke (former director-general)?
3   Do you believe that the BBC is getting its message across? Is it influencing and persuading?
4   Analyse the techniques used in communicating with the BBC staff. Were they adequate?
5   Would any of these techniques and interactions work in your organisation?

SUMMARY

■   An examination of the underlying aspects of communication was undertaken. These aspects centred on intra- and inter-communication, both of which are important in effective communication.
■   Influencing techniques involve asserting, bridging, attracting, observing and listening. Powerful, logical arguments must be developed and deployed which take account of each other person's point of view, which persuade him or her that the proposal is beneficial, and which answer any objections he or she may come up with.

REFERENCES

ARGYLE M. (1993; 2nd edition) *Bodily Communication*. London, Routledge.

BERKO R. M., WOLVIN A. D. and WOLVIN D. R. (1995) *Communicating*. Boston, MA, Houghton Mifflin.

BYERS P. Y. (1997) *Organisational Communication: Theory and practice*. Boston, MA, Allyn & Bacon.

FISHER D. (1993) *Communication in Organizations*. Minneapolis/St Paul, West.

GOFFMAN E. (1959) *The Presentation of Self in Everyday Life*. New York, Doubleday.

GOWER E. (1962) *The Complete Plain Words*. Harmondsworth, Penguin Books.

GREENBERG J. and BARRON R. A. (1993) *Behaviour in Organizations*. Boston, MA, Allyn & Bacon.

MINTZBERG H. (1973) *The Nature of Managerial Work*. New York, Harper & Row.

Communication: practical applications

INTRODUCTION

This chapter is designed to give some practical advice on a range of communication activities that managers engage in. It is therefore hoped that after reading this chapter, readers can enhance their skills in various communication areas including making presentations, report-writing and managing meetings.

Skills in interpersonal communication activities are regarded by many managers and theorists as essential qualities, and it is recognised that it is these skills that help organisations compete. Guirdham (1999) suggests:

> **'There is clear evidence that organisations value skilled interpersonal communication extremely highly.'**

Additionally, because the CIPD recognises that this is an important area of management development it has included these relevant skills as a required part of the Managing for Results specifications.

Learning objectives

On completing this chapter, the reader will understand and be able to explain:

- how to plan and prepare a presentation
- how to conduct a presentation
- how to write a report
- the nature of meetings, working parties and committees
- why and when meetings are necessary or unnecessary
- the criteria for a successful meeting
- how to be a member of a meeting.

MAKING PRESENTATIONS

Employers often refer to oral communication as a basic requirement that they seek in prospective employees. The skill of making presentations requires a considerable demonstration of oral communication as well as exercising us in a range of transferable skills. By alluding to elements that make up successful presentations, this section of the book aims to:

- increase self-confidence
- ensure good preparation
- support success, and
- help to ensure that the activity is both enjoyable and repeatable.

The three keys to effective speaking are:

- thorough planning and preparation
- good delivery
- overcoming nervousness.

Thorough planning and preparation

The amount of time you spend presenting is far less than the proportion of the time spent planning and preparing. It is therefore vital that you allow yourself ample time for planning and preparation. You will probably need at least ten times as much as the actual duration of your talk. The amount of time actually required will depend upon a range of factors, some of which are listed below:

- the level of importance the presentation represents
- the character and length of the presentation
- your level of understanding and in-depth knowledge of the subject matter
- the sophistication of the aids/visual aids you might require
- whether you need help from someone else.

Other considerations at the initial planning stage require a level of reflection involving a tried and tested analytical tool of who?, when?, where? and what?

- *Who* is the presentation for? Will you be alone, or will there be other speakers? How will your presentation fit in? And most importantly, who is the audience?
- *When* will the presentation take place? Do you know the date and time of the presentation? How long is your input?
- *Where* is the presentation to take place? Can the chosen venue accommodate your needs? Is there scope to arrange the room to your specific requirements? The layout of the room can denote formality or informality depending on the tone you wish to portray.
- *What* subject matter is to be presented, and what is its particular nature (eg scientific, informative, persuasive, etc)?

These considerations should help you clarify your ideas and help you begin to develop a coherent plan. Having established your broad criteria, it is appropriate to focus on some specific objectives for the presentation. Remember, objectives are statements which relate to what you want to achieve. Their function is:

- as a constant reminder of your aims
- to help manage the process and reduce/lessen complexity
- as a means of measuring your success – eg were all the objectives achieved?

The main stages of preparation are:

- Get informed
  - Collect and assemble all the facts and arguments you can get hold of.

- Decide what to say
  - Define the main messages you want to get across. Limit the number to three or four.

- Few people can absorb more than this number of new ideas at any one time. Select the facts, arguments and examples which support your message.

▪ Structure your talk: it should have the classic beginning, middle and end.
  - Start thinking about the middle first, for that should contain your main messages and the supporting facts, arguments and illustrations.
  - Arrange your points so that a cumulative impact and a logical flow of ideas are achieved.
  - Then turn to the opening of your talk. Your objectives should be to create attention, arouse interest and inspire confidence. Give your audience a trailer to what you are going to say. Underline the objective of your presentation – what they will get out of it.
  - Finally, think about how you are going to close your talk. First and last impressions are very important. End on a high note.

▪ Think carefully about length. Never talk for more than 40 minutes at a time: 20 or 30 minutes is better. Very few speakers can keep people's attention for long. An audience is usually very interested to begin with (unless you make a mess of your opening) but interest declines steadily until people realise that you are approaching the end. Then they perk up. Hence the importance of your conclusion.
  - To keep their attention throughout, give interim summaries which reinforce what you are saying, and above all, hammer home your key points at intervals throughout your talk.
  - Continuity is equally important. You should build your argument progressively until you come to a positive and convincing conclusion. Provide signposts, interim summaries and bridging sections which lead your audience naturally from one point to the next.

▪ Prepare your notes
  - In the first place write out your introductory and concluding remarks in full and set out in some detail the main text of your talk. It is not usually necessary to write everything down. You should then reduce your text to the key headings to which you will refer in your presentation. Your aim should be to avoid reading your speech if you possibly can, because that can completely remove any life and vitality from what you have to say. So as not to be pinned down behind a lectern, it is better to write your summarised points on lined index cards to which you can refer easily as you go along.

▪ Prepare and use visual aids
  - Because your audience will only absorb one-third of what you say, if that, reinforce your message with visual aids. Appeal to more than one sense at a time. PowerPoint slides, on disks or a 'memory stick'/USB Flash Drive, or alternatively overhead projector acetates, provide good back-up – but don't overdo them, and keep them simple. Too many visual aids can be distracting (keep them down to 15 or so in a half-hour presentation) and too many words, or an over-elaborate presentation, will divert, bore and confuse your audience. As a rule of thumb, try not to put more than five or six bullet-points on a slide. Each point should contain not more than six or seven words. Audiences dislike having to read a lot of small print on an over-busy slide. Use diagrams and charts wherever possible to break up the flow of words and illustrate points. If you

want the members of your audience to read something fairly elaborate, distribute the material as a handout and take them through it. So, to reiterate, the design of the visual aids should make it easy to understand the information provided and they should give clarity to the message. They should:

■ be visually effective/bold so that even the most distant member of the audience can see their purpose

■ be clean-looking and uncluttered so that details stand out

■ show key words rather than whole sentences (unless you are using a quote and require accuracy) and a minimum number of numbers and symbols.

– If you are producing handouts, ensure that they are of good quality. Avoid distraction by handing them out at the beginning or the end.

■ Rehearse

– Rehearsal is vital. It instils confidence, helps you to get your timing right, and enables you to polish your opening and closing remarks and co-ordinate your talk and visual aids. Rehearse the talk to yourself several times and note how long each section takes. Get used to expanding on your notes without waffling. Practise giving your talk out loud – standing up, if that is the way you are going to present it. Some people like to tape record themselves, but that can be off-putting. It is better to get someone to hear you and provide constructive criticism. It may be hard to take, but it could give you constructive feedback in a non-threatening environment.

■ Check arrangements in the room

– Ensure that your computerised PowerPoint projector, overhead or slide projector works and you know how to operate it. Check also on focus and visibility. Before you begin your talk, check that your notes and visual aids are in the right order and to hand.

Good delivery

To deliver a presentation effectively the following approaches are desirable.

■ Talk audibly and check that you can be heard at the back. Your task is to project your voice, not to shout at the audience. When you shout you raise the pitch of your voice and the tonal quality can then become quite harsh and the diction can suffer. Projecting your voice makes it audible without the harshness that is present when shouting. It's easier when there is a microphone, but even then you have to think about getting your words across.

■ Vary the pace (not too fast, not too slow) to add variety in the pitch and emphasis of your delivery. This does not, however, mean including long gaps between sentences, but varying the actual rate at which the words are spoken. Use pauses to make a point because using a pause at an appropriate point can add emphasis and increase attention. Be careful not to make the pause too long because the audience may deduce that you have forgotten your word. If using the pause in your presentation, maintain eye contact with the audience – this expresses the earnestness or sincerity of your intention.

■ Try to be conversational and as informal as the occasion requires (but not too casual).

- Give every indication that you truly believe in what you are saying: audiences respond well to enthusiasm.
- Avoid a stilted delivery. That is why you must not read your talk. If you are your natural self, people are more likely to be on your side. They will forgive the occasional pause to find the right word.
- Light relief is a good thing, but don't drag in irrelevant jokes or, indeed, make jokes at all if you are no good at telling them. You do not have to tell jokes.
- Use short words and sentences.
- If you can manage without elaborate notes (your slides or a few cards may be sufficient), come out from behind the desk or lectern and get close to your audience. It is generally advisable to stand up so that you can project what you say better, unless it is a smallish meeting around a table.
- Body language: audiences will always interpret behaviour. Body language and non-verbal cues must therefore be controlled as in face-to-face communication the majority of the message is determined by body language as well as the tone, clarity and pace of our voice. It is evident that in some instances non-verbal characteristics of communication can have more emphasis than the oral statements alone.
  - Keep your eyes on the audience, moving from person to person to demonstrate that you are addressing them all, and also to gauge their reactions to what you are saying.
  - Use hands for gesture and emphasis in moderation (but don't put them in your pockets). Make sure you avoid repetitive and irrelevant gestures.
  - Facial expression can also be used to add meaning or change the mood – from serious to lighthearted. We often express feelings by using the upper part of our face, especially our eyes. So as well as smiling with your lips, endeavour to smile with your eyes.
  - Don't fidget: fidgeting can be extremely off-putting, and switch off your audience very rapidly. Be aware of any habits you might have: playing with keys, adjusting spectacles, tapping a pen on the desk, etc. Learn to avoid these activities.
  - Stand naturally and upright: avoid slouching because it gives the impression that you are not interested in what you are saying; the audience will match your mood.
  - You can move around the platform a little to add variety – you don't want to look as if you are clutching the lectern for much-needed support. But avoid pacing up and down like a caged tiger.
  - Always be aware of your general appearance: first impressions count and have an impact. So plan your wardrobe carefully.

Overcoming nervousness

Some nervousness is a good thing. It makes you prepare, makes you think, and makes the adrenaline flow, thus raising performance. But excessive nervousness ruins your effectiveness and must be controlled.

The common reasons for excessive nervousness are: fear of failure, fear of looking foolish, fear of breakdown, a sense of inferiority, and dread of the isolation of the speaker. To overcome nervousness you should:

- practise – Take every opportunity you can get to speak in public. The more you do it, the more confident you will become. Solicit constructive criticism and act on it
- know your subject – Get the facts, examples and illustrations you need to put across

- know your audience – Who is going to be there? What are they expecting to hear? What will they want to get out of listening to you?
- know your objective – Make sure that you know what you want to achieve. Visualise, if you can, the thoughtful departure afterwards of each member of your audience having learned something new which he or she is going to put to practical use
- prepare – If you know that you have prepared carefully as suggested above, you will be much more confident on the day
- rehearse – This is an essential method of overcoming nervousness.

EXERCISE 5.1

Seize any chance you can get to make presentations. The more practice you get, the better.

Assuming you receive your chance, how well did it turn out, with reference to the points made above?

EXERCISE 5.2

For this exercise you need to have observed (or be in the process of observing) a presentation of some sort. This is an exercise in reading body language and non-verbal cues. Read the following sections, take two behaviours from each section, and describe and analyse what you believe is being communicated.

1	Description and analysis
■ frequently shrugging shoulders ■ weak and incomplete gestures ■ slouching ■ looking around somewhat aimlessly	
2	Description and analysis
■ stiff, upright ■ chin raised ■ chest out ■ staring intently at the audience ■ quick, forceful gestures	

3 <ul><li>uptight, yet relaxed</li><li>smiling</li><li>flowing gestures</li><li>gradually looking at all the people in the audience</li></ul>	Description and analysis
4 <ul><li>fidgety</li><li>pacing up and down</li><li>frowning</li><li>indecisive gestures</li><li>avoiding looking at the audience</li></ul>	Description and analysis

EXERCISE 5.3

Prepare an analytical presentation on a topic about which you have relevant knowledge. Evaluate your performance.

Prepare a persuasive presentation on an issue that is either controversial, an idea you believe in, or one where you are attempting to convince the audience about the value/worth of a particular product. Evaluate your performance.

REPORT-WRITING

Most of us in a managerial position are required to write reports within our working lives. Some will be based on research, some an account of a meeting or discussion, etc. This section of the chapter is constructed to provide general guidelines to make your report-writing more effective. Report-writing is part of the communication process, the report itself being a 'message' (see Chapter 4) exchanged between the writer and the reader. We must therefore consider the perspective of both the writer and the reader.

As the writer you might consider:

- Are you writing to precipitate action?
- Who will read the report?
- How many people will read the report?
- What is their level of knowledge and understanding of the subject?

Put yourself in the reader's position, then consider why someone should read the report. You should note that:

- A reader will only read the whole document if he or she is led to believe he or she will gain from the process. The gain is usually in the form of new insight, but any insight that might help the reader's future development is regarded as particularly valuable.

- A reader should be able to negotiate his or her way through the report without difficulty.

Criteria

A good report has specific characteristics:

- a logical structure
- the use of plain words to convey meaning
- messages presented lucidly, persuasively and, above all, succinctly.

Structure

A report should be structured in a way which ensures that the reader is taken through a sequence of sections that are clearly linked to one another and that proceed logically from the introduction to the conclusions and recommendations.

A report might be required to inform two sets of readers: one set might want to grasp the salient point of the report quickly (possibly a senior manager who only requires the essential information); another set may want to take a more critical and evaluative perspective, looking at the reasoning and conclusions before acting on its recommendations. To aid the first category of reader, the title, contents page, summary and conclusion should be separate.

A typical structure might incorporate the following sections:

- Title*
- Acknowledgements
- List of contents (index)
- Summary
- Introduction*
- Method
- Main body of the report (possibly under subheadings)*
- Conclusion*
- Recommendations
- Action plan
- References
- Appendices
       * indicates what is essential in any report; the remainder is as and if required.

Title page

In the first instance the title page has the function of providing a means by which the piece can be identified and subsequently retrieved. The title page may also include a subtitle, the name of the author of the report, the name/s of the recipient/s of the report, its date, and the organisation of origin, and the report's degree of confidentiality.

Remember, the title is in itself a marketing tool: it persuades the reader to open it. Unless the title is prescribed (and there is therefore no choice), it is often advisable to make a final decision on the wording of the title on the completion of the document.

Acknowledgements

In this section you take the opportunity to acknowledge/thank those who have given you substantial help. This might include a client, supervisor/manager or an academic mentor or tutor.

In an academic piece of work – eg a dissertation – many students wish to thank members of their own family. However, it is advisable to also thank the lecturer who helped/gave advice.

Cameron (2005) also cautions us to mention 'key members of a client organisation', because omitting to mention their contribution may have negative connotations for the future.

Contents list

A contents list/page may be unnecessary in short reports. In a longer document, however, it helps to reassure the reader that it is worthwhile continuing to read the report.

The contents page is made up of subtitles of all sections in the report. They help identify the contents of all the sections within it.

Summary

The summary is a précis of the whole report. It should not be just a recap or the conclusions and recommendations. Its function is to provide someone who has a demanding schedule (such as the CEO) with a quick review of the report.

It is advisable to write it after the main document is completed.

Introduction

This explains what the report is about, why the report has been written, its aims, its terms of reference, and why it should be read. If the report is divided into sections, readers should be given an indication of the logic of the structure as a signpost to direct them through the report.

Methods

This section advises the reader of the research philosophy and the research methods used to aid the investigation. It may include the following:

- pilot studies
- places and people visited
- measuring devices
- questionnaires
- interviews (semi-structured interviews).

Some of the material generated from the list above may have to be consigned to the Appendices. However, the main aspect of the particular research method under discussion should be included in this section. Any fundamental obstacles that affect the work should be stated.

Main body of the report

You must have ideas, data and results to relate to the readership of the report. Within this it is important to address the analysis, signposting and similar concepts.

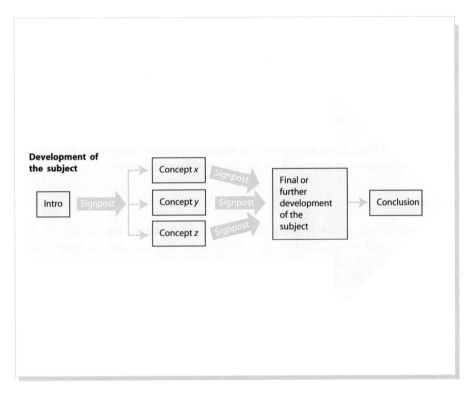

Figure 5.1 *Signposting and addressing similar concepts*

Analysis

This is a factual review of the situation or problem. It could describe the present arrangements, breaking them down into their elements – the main areas for attention. It could refer to data collected as part of the study – the key facts that have been assembled – although too much detail should not be included (such detail might perhaps be attached in an appendix). The analysis would identify the symptoms of any problems and should lead from discussing 'signposts' and similar concepts to the conclusion/diagnosis.

Signposting

Signposting is a method of guiding the reader. It is particularly useful in longer reports. It is simply a method of telling readers where they are in the text. It may also be used to tell readers where they are going (what will be discussed) in the next section. However, this technique should be used sparingly. (See Figure 5.1.)

Similar concepts

Similar concepts or even opposing concepts must be discussed if more than one definitive idea is to be explained and conceptualised before their significance and meaning in the report can be fully evaluated.

The diagnosis/conclusion

This is prepared by reference to the factual analysis. It sets out the issues to be addressed and establishes the causes of any problems. The diagnosis provides the basis for any conclusion and recommendation.

The conclusion is, however, a critical arena, because it becomes the forum in which the writer executes his/her judgement. He/she will deliver the reason for a particular course of action having already related the options available. This section may have to be persuasive because the reader may have to be convinced that the arguments put forward are valid, reasonable and, possibly, deliverable.

The writer should *not* introduce new material at this stage.

An indication of the benefits arising from the proposals should be made (such benefits may already have been linked to costs in the form of a cost/benefit analysis).

Recommendations

The recommendations specify the proposed action(s) based on the conclusions. They should flow logically and clearly from the main body, the diagnosis and conclusions. Where there is no obvious solution, options may be presented and evaluated, but a clear recommendation should emerge from this evaluation. An indication should be given of what the recommendation involves, and why and how it addresses the issue(s).

Action plan

The action plan sets out what must be done to implement the recommendations. It should identify:

- precisely what will have to be done
- who will be responsible
- the resources required (internal staff, external advice, materials and equipment)
- the estimated costs
- the timescale for implementation
- the programme of work.

Plain words

To convey meaning without ambiguity and avoid giving the reader unnecessary trouble, it is advisable, as suggested by Gower (1962), to:

- use no more words than are required to express the meaning: if too many are used, the meaning may be obscured and the reader will become tired. Do not use superfluous adjectives and adverbs, and do not use roundabout phrases where single words would serve
- use familiar words (in a business report) rather than academic ones if they express the meaning equally well, for the familiar are more likely to be understood
- use short words with a precise meaning rather than those that are vague, for they obviously serve better to make the meaning clear. In particular, choose concrete words over abstract ones, for they are more likely to have a precise meaning. Too many long words may be off-putting
- avoid jargon. If its use is essential, explain what it means in plain language.

Presentation

The way in which the report is presented and written affects its impact and value. The reader should be able to follow the argument easily and not get bogged down in too much detail.

Paragraphs should be short, and each one should be restricted to a single topic. Cotterell (2003) suggests that each paragraph should have arguments (ideas, theories, opinions and a line of reasoning), main information (types of evidence that support your line of reasoning) and supporting detail (lesser details, facts, names, statistics, dates). It is also helpful to use bullet points in order to list and highlight a series of observations or comments.

In long reports it may be a good idea to number paragraphs for ease of reference. Some people prefer the system which numbers main sections 1, 2, etc, subsections 1.1, 1.2, etc, and sub-subsections 1.1.1, 1.1.2, etc. However, this can be clumsy and distracting. A simpler system, which also simplifies cross-referencing, is to number each paragraph – not the headings – 1, 2, 3, etc; sub-paragraphs or tabulations can be indicated as bullet points.

Use headings to guide people on what they are about to read and to help them find their way about the report. Adopt a visibly distinctive hierarchy to separate main headings from lesser headings. Main headings might, for example, be in **BOLD CAPITALS** or **Bold Upper and Lower Case**, and subheadings might be in smaller ***Bold italics*** or even just *text italics*.

Truss (2003), in her book *Eats, Shoots and Leaves*, encourages the writer to use good punctuation at all times – yet another ingredient that if not executed correctly can be off-putting to the reader.

The report will make most impact if it is brief and to the point. Ask someone to proofread your work. Read and re-read the draft to cut out any superfluous material or flabby writing.

EXERCISE 5.4

Look at any report, preferably one from your organisation or one you have written yourself.

1   How does it measure up to the criteria given above?
2   Consider how it could be improved.

MANAGING MEETINGS

Meetings are an inevitable and often necessary part of a manager's job. A lot of time can be spent in them, and that time can easily be wasted. Cynics say that committees are made up of the unfit, appointed by the incompetent, to do the unnecessary – or that a camel is a horse designed by a committee. These comments may be gross exaggerations, but many a manager at the end of a long day entirely filled with meetings feels that it has all been a waste of time and that the day could have been spent much more productively on 'real' work. There is a lot that needs to be done and that can be done to improve the effectiveness of meetings.

The nature of meetings, working-parties and committees

Meetings are gatherings of people convened to discuss a particular issue and reach a collective decision. Meetings may be ad hoc to deal with a particular issue, or they may be held on a regular basis.

Working-parties are groups of people who are brought together to get something done – to deal with a problem, to discuss and plan an innovation, or to prepare for and oversee a project. They may also be called project teams or taskforces.

Committees are formally constituted bodies of people who meet regularly to discuss policy and planning issues, review performance and agree on actions in accordance with terms of reference.

Table 5.1 shows a variety of meetings ranging from the informal/ad hoc type of meeting to the formal type of meeting.

The rest of this chapter is concerned mainly with meetings and committees, although the suggested approaches apply equally well to project teams and working-parties.

Why and when meetings should be held

A meeting is a gathering of people with relevant expertise, experience and interests who contribute through discussion to the analysis of a situation and to a decision or recommendation on a course of action. The key point about meetings is that they exist for a purpose and their participant members should all be capable of contributing to the achievement of that purpose.

Why have meetings?

There are four assumptions usually made about why meetings are necessary.

1   They bring together people with different experience, roles and points of view. By taking account of all the considerations brought forward by this range of people (exchanging ideas) a solution will be produced that will be superior to one developed by any single person or number of people working independently. This is the principle of synergy – the whole is greater than the sum of the parts.
2   They ensure that the major interests in an issue or a problem are represented so that appropriate account can be taken of those interests when reaching a decision.
3   They provide a means for communicating views and information to interested parties.
4   They save time by assembling relevant people in one place at one time.

When to have meetings

The first two of the reasons given above may provide a sufficient justification for convening a meeting. But the use of a meeting as a vehicle for communication may not always be justified. There are other, more efficient, ways of communicating. And meetings can easily waste, rather than save, time.

Table 5.1 *Range of meetings*

Informal meetings	Meetings that have elements of the formal and the informal	Formal meetings
■ Managerial meetings (un-minuted) ■ Brainstorming (mind mapping) groups ■ Inter-departmental meetings – eg staff conference discussion ■ Intra-departmental meetings – eg team meeting (ad hoc) ■ Informal meeting: even an encounter in the corridor ■ Project team meetings (informal liaison between members) *Lists are not exhaustive*	■ Board of directors ■ Executive committee meetings ■ Advisory body – committee meetings ■ Inter-departmental meetings (cross-functional team – eg marketing, HR, finance, etc) ■ Team scheduled meetings (two-way process) ■ Voluntary sector group meetings ■ Working-party meetings (sub-group working on the task) ■ Project team meetings	■ Local government committee meetings ■ Council meetings ■ Public inquiries ■ Annual General Meetings ■ Shareholder meetings ■ Management v trade union meetings (perhaps a dispute) ■ Tribunals – judicial ■ Working-party meetings – eg sub-group formally reporting back to the main body ■ Departmental briefings (formal official progress meetings)
This type of meeting has an informal procedure which may mean that at times it has a group leader rather than a chair. Notes will be taken possibly on an informal basis; no formal rules may exist. The balance between formal and informal within these types of meeting may depend on the particular organisation culture and/or the attitude of the chair or group leader.	These meetings have elements of both informal and formal types of meeting. They have a chair and, for the most part, a set of officials. However, the proceedings have the potential for being conducted on a congenial basis, although these meetings have formal agendas and minutes taken by a secretary.	This type of meeting is the most formal – even at times, judicial – in nature. Such meetings have formal structures of agenda/motions/minutes etc, and follow a set of prescribed rules set down in the charter or statute of the organisation. They have a specific constitution over which certain officials preside. A list of attendees is drawn up of those required to attend. Accurate records are kept.

It is too easy for people to believe that a meeting is the only way to sort something out. They say 'Let's get together and talk about it,' without considering whether two or three brief conversations with interested people might suffice, and without deciding on the specific purpose of the meeting.

More meetings fail because the purpose has not been defined clearly enough than for any other reason. The end-result expected from a meeting – a decision, proposal or recommendation – should be spelled out so that people at the meeting know why they are there and understand what they are collectively expected to deliver.

Criteria for effective meetings

An effective meeting is one that in as short a time as possible achieves consensus by listening to and assessing different viewpoints and then proposes a specific, relevant and practical course of action.

What can go wrong at meetings

But meetings do not always work as well as this. Things that can go wrong include:

- wasting time – too many people talk (waffle) too much
- failing to come up with a solution – meetings can be slow, exasperating and frustrating, and they can legitimise procrastination and indecisiveness (meetings are sometimes called by people as a means of putting off the taxing process of having to make an independent decision)
- being dominated by a few people with strong personalities
- making lowest-common-denominator decisions – ie decisions which represent an easy way out favoured by the majority of people attending the meeting
- encouraging political decisions reached where vested interests prevail by means of lobbying and pressure
- diluting responsibility.

Conducting an effective meeting

Putting these failures into reverse, an effective meeting is one in which:

- people talk to the point (or are kept talking that way)
- decisions are made swiftly but after proper debate
- everyone with something to say contributes
- consensus is achieved without going for the easiest or most generally acceptable solution
- discussions are open – there are no hidden agendas, the meeting is responsible for the decision, and that decision will not already have been taken behind closed doors (ie the meeting is not acting as a rubber stamp)
- no individual's authority is usurped – it will be for someone designated by the meeting to take action afterwards
- managers are not allowed to shift their individual responsibility to the assembly – if they are there to make decisions, then they should make them (this does not, of course, preclude them from talking to other people and networking)
- overall duration is restricted to no longer than two hours (one hour is better) – this

may sound arbitrary, but long meetings tend to encourage discursiveness and people lose interest because they are preoccupied with their 'real' work: 'What am I doing here?', they say to themselves

- issues are addressed which are within the members' comprehension – if asked to agree to something big or complex, members will in any case want to leave it to the experts (so why raise it at the meeting?).

Setting up meetings

There are six things to do when setting up a meeting.

1   Ask yourself: 'Is this meeting really necessary?' What can be achieved by dragging all these busy people into a room to talk away possibly for hours about something which possibly does not really concern them and on which they possibly have little or nothing to contribute? One reason for irrelevant and waffly discussions is that people at meetings often feel compelled to say something, however inappropriate, to justify their presence there at all.

2   If the answer to the first question is 'Yes' (the meeting *is* really necessary), the second question is 'Why?' The purpose of the meeting must be defined: 'This is the issue. This is why it needs to be addressed. This is what the meeting has to achieve in the shape of a decision or recommendation.' It does not, of course, mean spelling out what the decision or recommendation should be, but it does mean indicating what it should be about. The chair of the meeting must be in a position to say something like: 'We are here to consider the following issue. We have to make up our minds what to do about it so that a firm recommendation can be made to management.'

3   Decide who is going to chair the meeting. The qualities you are looking for are: understanding of the issues (without necessarily knowing the answers) and demonstrated skills as a chair (these skills are described in the next section of the chapter) with the likelihood of retaining the respect and trust of the members of the meeting.

4   Decide who should attend the meeting. You should consider people who have a strong interest in the main issue and who can make a contribution. You do not want too many – six to eight is probably the most you need – but actually, the fewer the better. A meeting of two or three people may well achieve more than a meeting of 10 or 12. But you must ensure that the really interested parties are represented or the outcome of the meeting may be regarded as a 'stitch-up'. The people you invite should be told what the meeting is about and why they have been asked to attend.

5   Draw up terms of reference (this is what the meeting is for) and an agenda (this is what we are going to talk about). Supporting papers can be attached to the agenda but they should be brief. People have better things to do than wade through reams of paper.

6   Finally, fix the time and place, inform people accordingly, and give them the agenda and supporting papers.

Preparing for a meeting

Chairing

If you are chairing a meeting, you should familiarise yourself with the issues in advance and ensure that you have absorbed the relevant information. You should try to avoid leaping to conclusions before the meeting – conclusions should come out of it; they should not be pre-judged. Think about who is going to be present and what they may contribute so that you can draw them out if they do not come forward with their views. Finally, study the agenda and very broadly allocate a duration for each item so that you can complete the meeting in good time. You cannot be precise about timings but it is useful to have some guidelines.

Acting as secretary

If you are acting as secretary to the meeting, ensure that everyone knows when and where it is to take place and who will be present. Get the agenda and supporting papers out in good time. Nothing irritates committee members more than being confronted with a heap of papers only 24 hours before the meeting. Ensure that the meeting room is adequate – enough space, quiet, reasonably comfortable chairs, good ventilation, visual aid equipment as required, refreshments as necessary. Take along spare agendas and supporting papers – someone always leaves theirs behind.

Chairing a meeting

To chair a meeting effectively, you should:

- Start by defining the purpose of the meeting, also setting a timescale which you intend to keep.
- Go through each item on the agenda in turn, ensuring that consensus is achieved as far as possible, and that a firm conclusion on each is reached and recorded.
- Initiate the discussion on each item by setting the scene and inviting contributions.
- Allow no one person or clique to dominate the discussion.
- Generally, invite contributions from members of the meeting.
- Bring people back to order if they drift from the point.
- Where the discussion is going on too long or dragging, remind people that they are there to get something agreed, not just to talk – 'Let's make progress.'
- Encourage the expression of different points of view.
- Avoid crushing, and allow no one else to crush, a contribution even if it is not particularly relevant – 'That's an interesting point: are there any other views?'
- Allow a level of disagreement between members of the meeting but step in smartly if the discussion becomes too contentious.
- Chip in with questions or brief comments from time to time to clarify a point or help to make progress, but avoid dominating the discussion yourself.
- At appropriate moments, summarise the discussion and express views on where the meeting has got to, especially if the meeting is straying from the point or getting bogged down.
- If an interim or final conclusion appears to have been reached, outline your perception of what has been agreed. Next, check that the meeting concurs with this summary, amending it as necessary. And finally, ensure that the decision is recorded and agreed exactly as made.
- At the end of the meeting summarise what has been achieved, setting out action points for the record and indicating who is responsible for taking action, and when.
- If a further meeting is required, agree the purpose of the meeting, when and where it is to take place, and what has to be done by those present before it happens.

EXERCISE 5.5

Think about any meeting you have attended. How would you rate the chair (excellent, good, OK, not so good, poor) against the criteria listed above?

You are chairing a meeting.

- Two members get into an argument which appears to be degenerating into a slanging match. What do you say to them?
- You cannot get consensus on a decision. What do you do?
- You disagree strongly with the conclusions that are emerging from the discussion. What do you do?

Being an effective member of a meeting

To be an effective member of a meeting, you should:

- Prepare thoroughly – have all the facts at your fingertips, with any supporting data you need.
- Make your points clearly, succinctly and positively – try to resist the temptation to talk too much.
- Remain silent if you have nothing to say – 'keep your powder dry' until you can make a worthwhile contribution.
- Listen, observe and save your arguments until you can make a really telling point; don't plunge in too quickly or effusively – there may be other compelling arguments.
- Avoid making such statements as 'I think we must do this' if you are not sure of your ground; instead, pose a question to the chair or other members of the meeting in such a form as 'Do you think there is a case for doing *this*?'
- Be prepared to argue your case firmly, but don't persist in fighting for a lost cause – don't retire in a sulk because you cannot get your own way: accept defeat gracefully.
- Remember that if you are defeated in committee there may still be a chance for you to fight another day in a different setting.

EXERCISE 5.6

Think about the last meeting you attended. How did you measure up to the criteria set out above?

EXERCISE 5.7

Consider the case study below and answer the questions that follow.

Case study: Midton Bakery

Meeting

Scenario and key players:

- Time: 5.30 p.m. Saturday (the end of a busy day)
- Date: 5 July 2003
- Location: Midton Bakery, situated in a small picturesque village in the Durham Dales
- Setting: the kitchen.

Present:

BOB – owner and manager (he owns the bakery along with his wife Joan, who does the baking; they live on the premises)

MIRA – senior permanent member of staff (she usually works through the week rather than at weekends) who has worked at the bakery for a long time and deputises as manager on various occasions

CLARICE – senior part-time (weekends) member of staff (she has worked at the bakery for over ten years, which is longer than the present owners have been in the business. The job has helped fund her through school, 'A'-levels and university, and it is now helping to pay off her student loan)

BARRY – Mira's son, working at the bakery for the second time (he has just finished his 'A'-levels this year and is planning to go to university in September).

Scenario:

The kitchen. Having just finished cleaning the restaurant, bakery counter and kitchen areas, the bakery staff are taking a few minutes at the end of the day to hold a meeting and have a cool drink before going home.

MIRA:	I'm exhausted. I don't remember it being this busy between 4 and 5 p.m. – we actually had to lock the door.
CLARICE:	It's the bikers and walkers from the towns who always come at the end of the day, although we don't usually get a mini-bus load of girls!
BOB:	Oh! Is that the reason you spent so much time outside, Barry?
BARRY:	They had been on a Duke of Edinburgh's Award Outward-Bound trip and were just on their way home. They couldn't decide what to have. I was making suggestions [waving the menu in his hand]. Although I know I did get behind in clearing the dishes away …

MIRA:	It is only his second shift. I think he is doing quite well.
CLARICE:	'Making suggestions' aside, I agree. I'm glad he is here. It's murder when those bistro tables are outside and there's only three of us to look after everything.
BOB:	Well, you cope, don't you?
CLARICE:	Only just, Bob. I am rushed off my feet most of the time, and sometimes customers wait a long time to be served. For example, if you are cooking and Mandy [who sometimes works weekends] is stacking the dishwasher, that leaves the counter, the restaurant and the bistro area for me to cover – and I only have one pair of hands.
MIRA:	It seems to me, Bob, that you could do with more staff at weekends, particularly over the summer.
BOB:	We have always managed with three staff on a weekend.
CLARICE:	Yes, but that was before you started putting tables outside.
BOB:	I'll have to think about it.

Pause.
A somewhat uncomfortable silence comes over the company.

Bob looks uncomfortable as he sits on a chair at the end of the table and folds his arms in a rather defensive manner. Clarice on the other hand gives an exaggerated shrug. She is thinking 'Why do I bother?', and 'Do I really need this job?' Mira, realising a) that weekend work is very intensive, and b) that Clarice's patience is wearing thin, decides to change the subject and bring up more mundane practical matters, intending to return to the relevant issues later in the discussion.

MIRA:	Bob, is there something wrong with the grill? I thought it was slow today, and with all those girls wanting bacon butties I'm surprised we managed to serve them all. And another thing – why *did* they all want bacon butties, Barry?!
BOB:	Oh, *I* told Barry to encourage people to have them. I had quite lot of bacon in the fridge – and besides, butties are good for profit.
CLARICE:	Not if people leave without ordering, they aren't.
BOB:	What do you mean?
CLARICE:	Two of the 'walkers' left. I think they were sick of waiting. I was serving at the counter at the time.
BOB:	Why didn't you call me or Mira?
CLARICE:	I did. Mira was cooking bacon. You were cooking and serving. Barry was taking orders outside.
BOB:	Everyone was busy, then?
BARRY: MIRA: ⎫ CLARICE: ⎭	Yes.
BOB:	I'll get the engineer to come out and look at the grill. That might help.
MIRA:	That won't solve all our problems, and issues really need to be resolved.

Pause.
Again Bob looks rather reflective, realising that he has to do something about staffing – he cannot afford to lose staff. He hits on an idea (though not a solution)!

BOB:	Joan and I think we have been doing quite well this year, and today's profits will be good. I've decided to give all of you £10 extra today.
CLARICE:	That's great, Bob! ... Is there anything else?
BOB:	You do all work extremely hard, and it is appreciated. I promise I'll talk to Joan about some extra staff at weekends. Could you work most weekends, Barry?
BARRY:	Yes, that would be great! I need the money.
BOB:	Good. I think this discussion has been quite valuable. [A broad, satisfied, smile comes across his face.]

EXERCISE 5.7 QUESTIONS

1   What type of meeting was taking place at the Bakery? Give reasons for your analysis.

2   With reference to the Bakery scenario, but also in respect of the four assumptions made in the section *Why have meetings?* (above):
   - describe whether synergy was reached
   - would you say that the meeting provided an adequate forum for members to pass on information and represent their views to interested parties?
   - were all relevant individuals present at the meeting? If they were, explain; if they weren't, who else should have been there, and why?

3   Using the nine-point bullet-list provided in the section *Conducting an effective meeting*, evaluate all nine points in relation to the meeting at the Bakery to analyse its effectiveness.

SUMMARY

- Presentations are most likely to be effective if they are prepared and rehearsed thoroughly, are well-structured, are well-delivered and make use of visual aids.
- Reports are most likely to be effective if they have a clear and logical structure, use plain words to convey meaning and present the material in ways which enable people to grasp the point and follow the argument easily.
- Meetings are gatherings of people who discuss and come to conclusions on particular issues. Working-parties are set up to tackle a problem or a project. Committees are groups of people who meet regularly to discuss policies and plans and come to decisions on actions.
- Meetings are held because they bring together different experiences and points of view to discuss and resolve an issue.
- An effective meeting reaches a firm conclusion based on the contributions of its members.
- Meetings must be carefully planned.
- Chairing a meeting is a demanding role which requires considerable inter-personal skills in controlling and progressing discussions to reach a firm conclusion.
- Effectiveness at a meeting depends on preparation, clarity of expression, and taking part in discussions in a measured and careful way.

REFERENCES

ARGYLE M. (1993; 2nd edition) *Bodily Communication*. London, Routledge.

CAMERON S. (2005; 5th edition) *The MBA Handbook: Skills for mastering management.* London, Prentice Hall.

COTTERELL S. (2003; 2nd edition) *The Study Skills Handbook*. London, Palgrave.

GOWER E. (1962) *The Complete Plain Words.* Harmondsworth, Penguin Books.

GUIRDHAM M. (1999) *Communicating Across Cultures*. Basingstoke, Palgrave.

TRUSS L. (2003) *Eats, Shoots and Leaves: The zero-tolerance approach to punctuation.* London, Profile Books.

INTRODUCTION

This chapter investigates and makes suggestions on the important subject of 'working with your manager'. Working with your manager involves responding to expectations, requirements and objectives, delivering completed and acceptable work, and dealing with your manager's demands. It is one of the most influential aspects of a person's work environment. The work environment, and the organisational culture it sustains, plays a significant part in our work lives. It can dictate whether work is an enjoyable part of our lives or, conversely, something that feels oppressive.

The 'Microsoft experience' is considered in this chapter – in particular, its record in recent years of being prominent in 'Best Company to Work For' awards. This example demonstrates that the level of commitment from the organisation's hierarchy and its employees rests with how the psychological contract is managed, and if that is done well, it is a differentiating feature of a 'great company'.

Learning outcomes

After reading to the end of this chapter, the reader will therefore:

- be able to evaluate and critically discuss the processes involved in the psychological contract
- understand the need to respond to expectations and requirements (agreeing and achieving objectives)
- be aware of the importance of delivering timely, completed and acceptable work
- appreciate the value of 'managing' one's own manager
- appreciate the need for the workforce to have a 'voice'.

RESPONDING TO EXPECTATIONS

In accordance with the concept of the 'psychological contract', managers have expectations about how their staff should behave and perform, and staff have expectations about how their managers should treat them. But these mutual expectations may not only be unwritten, they may be no more than assumptions. On the other hand, where there is a more formal approach to performance management, objectives and standards of performance will have been agreed. This section of the chapter considers responses to the unwritten (psychological) contract. The next section covers managing the agreement of expectations – setting and agreeing objectives.

The psychological contract

Managing expectations is vital if we believe the management focus of *gaining commitment* is important. Essentially, theories that relate to the psychological contract are themselves associated with gaining the commitment of staff, thus creating conditions in which organisational performance can be maintained.

From the point of view of most managers, the psychological contract (between them and you – ie their staff) implies that you should display specific behaviours and characteristics:

- competence
- effort
- commitment
- willingness
- compliance
- loyalty.

Expectations of competence, effort and commitment are not unreasonable. You should receive guidance, support and coaching from your manager, but in the last analysis it is up to you to develop your competencies or capabilities and deliver results accordingly. This is the principle of self-directed learning. People learn most effectively if they take responsibility for identifying and meeting their own learning needs, thus upholding their commitment to enhancing their own performance. You can ask for guidance and help, and your organisation may have a personal development planning process which structures your learning endeavours and programmes. What you have to do for yourself, however, is to review and *reflect* upon how well you are doing your work, to identify what you need to learn in order to do your work better, and to take steps to acquire the knowledge and skills you need with whatever help you can get from your manager, your colleagues and the organisation.

Guest and Conway (2001) suggest a definition of the psychological contract that we can readily accept. They describe it as constituting:

> **'the perceptions of both parties to the employment relationship – organisational and individual – of the reciprocal promises and obligations implied in that relationship'.**

The emphasis here is on perception – whether we believe someone's 'word' or promises, and whether obligations have been met. This in turn leads to the perception that the manager is being fair in his or her dealings, which will determine whether you decide to trust him or her. Your decision may have a significant impact on the work relationship that follows and on what you might think is reasonable for your manager to expect from you.

It is reasonable for your manager to expect you to direct the required amount of effort to getting the work done. People may be criticised for being incompetent, but they will be damned once it is believed that they are lazy.

Commitment is also a reasonable expectation. Commitment requires that you demonstrate your identification with the goals of the organisation and of your area of operation, that you actively support the values of the organisation, that you show a desire to remain part of the organisation (you are not constantly and obviously looking for another job), and that you demonstrate by your actions and behaviour that you are prepared to put yourself out on behalf of the organisation, your boss and the colleagues in your team. If someone says of you that you are fully committed, then that is praise indeed.

Willingness could be regarded as evidence of commitment but is rather more problematic. It is not reasonable for your manager to expect blind obedience, but it makes managers happy if, when they ask someone to do something extra or special, the response is 'Yes, I'll do my best' (unless the task is clearly impossible). What managers do not want to hear is endless grumbles following quite proper and reasonable requests to do something. A sullen and grudging acquiescence is almost as bad.

Where the expectations are of compliance or blind loyalty, they become even more problematic. To demand compliance is in effect to say, 'You will do what I tell you to do – or else.' It is a process of bending someone else's will: 'Give me no buts.' There will, of course, be occasions when managers can reasonably say 'Look – this is important. I'd like you to drop everything and get on with this.' They may be under equally strong or even greater pressure from above. But these should be rare occasions, not a habitual approach which requires instant obedience. Martinet managers like this still exist, even in these more easygoing and democratic days.

As for loyalty, it is reasonable to expect people to be loyal to their managers, in the sense of providing support and not indulging in snide criticisms or comments to other people. But blind and unswerving loyalty upwards cannot be demanded. It should never be the case that 'I shall be loyal to my manager through thick and thin, right or wrong.' Managers who behave impossibly and make impossible demands, managers who refuse to recognise good work, do not deserve loyalty. And loyalty is a two-way process. If managers are not loyal to their staff (supporting and developing them, trying to provide security), why indeed should their staff be loyal to them?

This issue extends to organisations as well as managers. Organisations expect commitment and loyalty from their staff – but do they display any commitment and loyalty in return? Some do; others don't. Loyalty should be two-way. Loyalty towards its staff on the part of the organisation may be implied when there are adequate rewards for length of service, further implying that the organisation promotes from within, so denoting its commitment to its staff. But does the prevailing belief in the organisation suggest on the contrary that loyalty of service does not matter? For example, if an employee of long service is in some difficulty (bereavement, illness, etc), does the organisation help (good HR policies) or does it turn its back? Further, are managers in the organisation aware that it is demoralising for employees if someone is brought in from outside when existing staff are trained and capable of taking up the position? Another more strategic consideration of loyalty may arise when organisations make people redundant at the first sign of a business problem, in order to downsize or (an even worse euphemism) to 'rightsize'. All these examples of organisational loyalty and commitment fall far short of the characteristics of commitment and loyalty that organisations demand from their employees.

Guest and Conway (2001) explain the importance of the 'deal', expressed in terms of a reciprocal process that involves both employer and employee delivering on the psychological contract. The good employer would be delivering a high-quality work environment in which an employee could expect:

- progressive human resource practices
- a climate of positive organisational support

- flexible employment practices
- employee partnerships.

If these elements are in place, Guest and Conway (2001) suggest that both employee and employer can deliver on the 'deal' that thus encompasses fairness, trust, commitment, well-being and performance, preserving the two-way process essential to upholding the psychological contract.

RESPONDING TO REQUIREMENTS – OBJECTIVES AND STANDARDS

Managers should manage performance. They have to respond to the targets and objectives set at the top of the organisation, which management want to 'cascade' down to ensure that at every level the contribution expected of people towards the achievement of the overall purpose of the business is understood and agreed. This is the process of integrating objectives, and each manager will want to ensure that this happens within his or her own area.

Cascading objectives is a top-down process, but there should be a bottom-up element which provides for people to make proposals on what they believe they can achieve and to comment on what their bosses say they are expected to achieve. Clearly, there is room for disagreement here, but it is one of the key skills of a manager to achieve consensus on what he or she believes or is told is necessary, and what the staff believe they can deliver. Managers will want to get people to accept objectives that extend them because of the thrust for continuous performance improvement and their staff to be 'performance enhancers'. Some people will resist unreasonably; others may have valid points to make about what it is possible for them to achieve. When they are indeed valid, it is up to the manager to agree to modifications.

Hamel (2000) expresses a view that senior executives realise more than ever that they cannot command commitment from the generation now entering employment. Moreover, he suggests that they are 'more authority-adverse than any in history'. He also maintains that organisations that manage in an authoritarian, control-oriented manner are 'bound to fail'. Some, more enlightened, organisations now value intellectual capital and also encourage their staff to become shareholders in the company. Hamel actually makes sweeping statements on the matter in describing what he argues is the age of revolution in business and management that we now find ourselves in. He states (Hamel, 2000) that we do not require

'diligent soldiers, throwing themselves at the enemy en masse, but guerrilla fighters, highly motivated and mostly autonomous'.

His advice to organisations also extends to suggesting that senior managers should not seek 'courtiers' bending to their egos and prejudices. Rather, they should encourage pioneering, inventive, imaginative people prepared to fight for their ideas.

What should managers reasonably expect from their staff?

To work well with your manager, you may have to accept that this kind of thing will happen from time to time. What you should not do is to raise unreasonable or frivolous objections. Your manager may be equipped with benchmark information, which shows that the expected targets or standards are being achieved by people within the business, or in other organisations. You would have to make out a good case to counter this sort of data.

If there is a formal process for agreeing objectives and standards – as there should be – then your part in it should have been defined by those setting up the process. Where it has not been defined, you can always ask politely if it can be done.

Typically, before a meeting to agree objectives you will be asked if you know what your key result areas are. (A *key result area* is any critical part of the job which strongly influences the achievement of its overall purpose. Key result areas should have been formally defined in a job description. If they are not in your job description, make sure that they become part of it forthwith.) Having listed these areas, the next thing to consider is what targets (output, service delivery, response time, etc) can be set in quantified terms, and what standards of performance you should be expected to achieve in any area in which quantified targets cannot be set. A standard of performance is a statement of the expected behaviour and the conditions that will exist when a task has been well done. If you have carried out this exercise before, you can look at the targets and standards agreed last year and assess how you have got on with them. This will give you a lead towards what new targets or standards may be set. In some cases no changes need be made. This process of self-assessment is used as the basis for performance review in some company schemes.

As well as setting new or revised targets, this pre-meeting analysis on your part can include some thought on how you are going to achieve the targets and what help you will need from your manager – guidance, support, coaching, or the provision of extra resources. This gives you an opportunity to express your expectations of what you want your manager to do for you and can lead to overall satisfaction (people satisfaction is one of the desired results for excellence) of both manager and staff member.

Performance reviews should be a two-way process which provide for the definition and agreement of mutual expectations. In many organisations there is no such provision for this exchange of views although it is a potentially productive process. Good managers will recognise that they can learn from their staff just as their staff can learn from them. In one sense managers' teams are composed of their internal customers who have the right to expect proper leadership, guidance and support.

Responding to objectives

Managers take part in agreeing objectives with their own managers as well as with the people who report to them. In objective-agreement sessions they have to find answers to such questions as:

- What are the key result areas of my job?
- What objectives can I set for each of these key result areas? Each objective will define what I have to achieve in terms of targets or standards of performance.
- Are these objectives SMART? That is, are they stretching/specific, measurable, likely to be agreed/achievable, realistic and time-related?
- How do these objectives support the achievement of the objectives of the organisation? The aim should be to align individual and organisational objectives.
- What are the critical success factors that will affect the achievement of the objectives? *Critical success factors* are the parts of a job which make a particularly

significant contribution to the achievement of its overall purpose and for which objectives can be set. Defining them indicates the areas to which most attention should be given and what elements of work should be measured, monitored and evaluated.

- What resources do I need? Resources might include people, money, equipment, materials, time, and support from your manager.
- What are the budgets and timescales I have to work to? This information indicates what controls have to be maintained over expenditure, and provides the basis for planning and project management.
- How will I and my manager know how well I have done? This requires identifying performance measures.
- How am I going to monitor my work against targets and standards by reference to the performance measures?
- On what basis will I and my manager evaluate my performance?

DELIVERING COMPLETED AND ACCEPTABLE WORK

If you are asked to do something, you should come up with solutions, not problems. You should present a completed proposal with whatever supporting arguments or evidence you need. Managers want answers, not questions. They want a well-argued proposal based on a thorough analysis of the problem, a diagnosis of the issues to be addressed, and recommendations which logically flow from the analysis and diagnosis and for which a carefully thought-out methodology is specified.

Consider your own job or another one with which you are familiar and use the above bullet-point checklist as a guide to defining objectives. Then write a report about overcoming a problem – any specific problem – that you and your manager are aware of in your work. Analyse the situation, explain your diagnosis and derive recommendations that could demonstrably deal with the problem. Then come to a conclusion which sets out the actions required to implement the proposal (an action plan) together with an estimate of the costs involved and the benefits that will accrue to the organisation.

When you have finished your report and studied your recommendations and conclusions, ask yourself the question, 'If I were my manager, would I stake my reputation on this piece of work and put my name to it?' If the answer is No, tear up your report and do it again. It's incomplete.

Meeting deadlines

The ability to meet deadlines is one of the most important qualities managers must possess when they have to take on a project or carry out a special task. If they are responsible for a project, they are most likely to complete work on time if they:

- prepare a project plan and programme that is based on an analysis of the work to be carried out in such a way that it can be sequenced and divided into its constituent elements or tasks
- estimate the time to complete each element or task
- add up the element times to produce a total time (on a complex project network-planning techniques can be used)
- prioritise the tasks

- allocate responsibilities for carrying out each segment of work according to the priorities
- define the deadlines everyone involved has to meet for each part of the project for which they are responsible
- set up information systems which monitor work-in-progress against the programme and the deadlines
- call for regular progress reports
- conduct 'milestone' meetings at critical stages through the project to assess progress and, if necessary, re-schedule the work
- throughout the project exert all their powers of leadership to motivate their team and maintain their commitment
- keep their manager informed of progress and, realistically, their ability to meet the deadline
- are prepared to apply extra resources (including their own time) if there is slippage in the programme.

If in this situation things go horribly wrong and managers come to believe that whatever they do, the deadline will not be met, they should inform their bosses – it is better to warn them of the problem so that corrective action can be initiated at that level in good time than to attempt to hide the unpalatable truth.

EXERCISE 6.1: THE MICROSOFT CASE STUDY

The Microsoft case study is concerned with the concepts of working for and with others. The study describes why Microsoft was voted 'best company' in the *Sunday Times* Best Companies to Work For survey, 2003. It talks of culture, being self-critical and recognising expectations, from the point of both the employer and employee. Read the case study and address the questions that follow.

Case study: Microsoft UK

Microsoft UK has had considerable success in Best Company to Work For employee surveys. This is validated by the company's record in the *Sunday Times* Best Company to Work For competition, being number one in 2003, in the top 20 in 2004, and still in the top 100 in 2005.

In 2003 93 per cent of Microsoft staff said that Microsoft was the best company to work for, and that they felt pride in the company. Indeed, 89 per cent of employees stated that they 'loved' working for Microsoft and went so far as to say that they believed the organisation made a positive difference to the world in general.

Certainly the Microsoft philosophy is to continue to recruit the best employees who will potentially fit in at Microsoft and to meet their aspirations. Given the maturity, in employment terms, of the Information Technology recruitment market, attracting new and committed staff is a challenge for all companies in this sector. Microsoft faced this scenario along with its competitors and yet still managed to keep its people well motivated and engaged even when rewards were being reduced.

In managing this dichotomy, Microsoft maintained its positive internal interface with its staff in spite of cutting the workers' share options. The reason for this success is probably in part due to its internal HR policies that have led to Microsoft's winning accolades for its work-life balance policy. For instance, flexible working is commonplace. Employees have broadband Internet access and laptops enabling them to work at home. A crèche and a subsidised gym, free private health care and clinics for 'life partners' all add to the appeal of working for Microsoft (Persaud, 2003). Certainly, Microsoft believes it is giving its workforce a choice by empowering them to balance their home and work lives.

This success is endorsed still further by Microsoft UK's thirteenth place in the *Sunday Times* 2004 Best Company survey, which featured the statement that 88 per cent of staff were proud to work for Microsoft and added that because of 'gold star' bonuses and profit-related pay (McCall, 2004) workers can earn an extra 86 per cent of their salary (84 per cent of staff earn more than £35,000 annually).

The *Sunday Times* article goes on to state that 'Four out of five staff find their work stimulating, feel trusted by managers and get support when they need to learn new skills.' Although, again in the article above, some workers found the increasing work-loads a problem, they did however appreciate the range of benefits and rewards the company offered. These included:

> '– private health care (with family cover) and life insurance
>
> – holiday entitlement from 25 days to 32 days with long service
>
> – the company pays 5 per cent of salary to the pension scheme,
>
> – the company gives 15 per cent discount on shares, [consequently] 90 per
>
> cent of staff have a stake in the organisation.'

It is perhaps no surprise to learn that staff turnover is low (1 per cent) and that the 'company is still pressing the right buttons' in respect to the values it and the staff seem to share.

A much deeper issue can also explain Microsoft's success – that of culture. People who join the organisation have to fit in to the prevailing way in which things are done and how people interact with each other. For example, those who adopt the 'technology-loving' culture will be readily accepted; those who do not, face isolation and eventually leave of their own volition.

Microsoft puts great emphasis on recruiting and retaining its staff and has a company scheme to inform employees of Microsoft's vision. This shows the workforce where it is heading and what all of this means to the employees, so enabling them to be more engaged in the long-term strategy of the organisation.

Steve Harvey (Microsoft UK director) stated that Microsoft was a self-critical organisation. He went on to say (Persaud, 2003) that:

> 'You cannot issue a stupid policy because it will get thrown back at you. In

the first two minutes of it being launched via email or on the web, you get

feedback pretty quickly about whether it's sensible or not.'

The fact that feedback can be critical shows a level of openness and trust between staff – trust that, for the most part, appears to be earned.

Further commentary: Microsoft Ireland/Europe

Anna Pringle, human resources director of Microsoft Ireland, speaking from its European Operations Centre in Dublin (in January 2004), endorses some of the sentiments expressed previously by stating that 'Microsoft is a great company and is very successful. It is also a great place to work,' and she asserts, 'Microsoft has maintained its success by treating its people well.'

Part of this success strategy links to the company's values. Anna suggests that:

'One of the key values is having respect for one another.'

Anna says, 'The internal telephone directory is organised on a first-name basis,' and that 'from time to time people do receive email from Bill G [Bill Gates]'.

She emphasises that:

'The reason Microsoft is a great place to work is a combination of factors –

a great company, great work environment, and above all, great jobs that

allow individuals to learn and have an impact.'

It is worth remembering that Microsoft has a presence in many countries in Europe and its employees seem to endorse Anna's point of view, which is borne out by several surveys. One such notable investigation was one sponsored by the European Commission (Moskowitz and Levering, 2004), in which Microsoft took first place in Germany, Ireland, France and Belgium for 2003. Microsoft Germany and Belgium repeated their top place in 2004, and Ireland also featured in the top ten.

What is clear from this debate is that the Microsoft operation in Dublin is strongly supportive of a staff development environment in which people are encouraged to learn and develop. Indeed, Microsoft uses career development as a way of both attracting and retaining its staff. However, this must link to the Microsoft business environment of 'Constantly challenging [staff] to improve their performance' (Moskowitz and Levering, 2004) and offering rewards to encourage high performance.

Anna helps us to conceptualise the business environment thus:

> 'The point is that the culture of the company, the approach to employee development, and the links to business goals and the focus on employees are consistent across very different national cultures.'

There seems therefore to be a concurrent emphasis across Microsoft Europe on meeting agreed objectives, deadlines and performance criteria from a cultural perspective that encourages loyalty and personal competence linked to development. This in turn upholds the psychological contract.

EXERCISE 6.1 QUESTIONS

Consider the various headings below (which correspond to section headings earlier in the chapter) and list instances in the Microsoft case study that help to support the concepts of working with your manager and the expectations developed because of the psychological contract.

Responding to expectations	Responding to requirements
What is required of employees?	How does the organisation respond to the requirements of its employees?

Responding to objectives	Delivering efficiency
How does the organisation enable its employees to fulfil their objectives?	Why is the pursuit of high performance and efficiency so critical to the organisation's survival?

Meeting deadlines
How critical is it to the organisation for workers to meet their deadlines?

EXERCISE 6.2

Give your own rationale for Microsoft's success.

You may also wish to compare and contrast these factors and those highlighted above with your own organisation.

EXERCISE 6.3

What do you think are the most likely problems people face when they have to meet deadlines?

How would you overcome them?

HOW TO DEAL WITH DIFFICULT MANAGERS

Managers can make entirely unreasonable demands. They can refuse to give any feedback – positive or otherwise; they can ignore your requests; and they can act as bullies. There are no easy answers to these problems. Managers who behave in any of these ways do not deserve to be managers. It is to be hoped that they will be found out – but in the real world this sort of behaviour can still be accompanied by good results, and this may be all that higher management is looking for.

One thing is certain. No one should have to take bullying or harassment. If this is happening to you, a complaint must be made to the personnel department or to higher management. You can ask for a transfer – but that, of course, does not solve the real problem. The prevalence of bullying in organisations has at last been recognised in recent years, and personnel specialists and their managers are much more likely nowadays to take action, at least to investigate the complaint. This itself may have unpleasant consequences for you – it is in the nature of bullies to take it out on people who are not in a position to fight back – but it is better to face these consequences than to put up with the bullying.

The other ways in which managers behave badly may not be quite as stressful. And the dividing line between a reasonable and an unreasonable demand is not always precise. But you have every right to question an entirely improper demand – although you will have to be certain that you can provide supporting evidence for your belief that it is unreasonable. Again, bosses who persist in making such demands are ineffective managers. If they are not spotted from above, you have the right to make it known that a problem exists, if only by giving it as a reason for a transfer request. (If other people feel the same and can join in your protest, so much the better.)

EXERCISE 6.4

1 Your manager doesn't bully you because he/she knows you will fight back. But you observe him/her bullying other people who are not as well placed as you are. What do you do about it?
2 Your manager keeps on demanding the impossible. You know that he/she is being unreasonable because no one else in similar positions is expected to do what he/she expects. What do you do about it?

MANAGING YOUR MANAGER

Managers need managing as much as anyone else. Managers exist to get results. They are not there simply to please their own managers. But they are more likely to get things done and progress in the organisation if they can:

- get agreement from their managers on what they are expected to do
- deal with their managers effectively when problems arise
- impress their managers generally with their efficiency, effectiveness and willingness to put themselves out to get a result.

Getting agreement

Getting agreement from managers involves:

- finding out what they expect – their likes and dislikes, their quirks and prejudices, how they like things presented to them, how they like things to be done
- establishing the best ways, times and places to tackle them with a proposal, request or problem
- avoiding open confrontation. If you can't get your own way at first, return later at a more propitious moment. If you get into an argument, leave an escape route – a way open for them to consent to without having to climb down
- not trying to achieve too much at once. It is often better to tackle one or two things at a time. Managers have many other preoccupations and their boredom thresholds are often low. Avoid overwhelming them with detail. They will always prefer a clear-

cut proposition supported by arguments which are compelling but limited in number and complexity.

Dealing with problems

If things are going wrong, managers should adopt the following approach with their superiors:

- Keep them informed. Never let them be taken by surprise. Prepare them in advance for any bad news.
- Explain what has happened and why (no excuses), and what you propose to do about it.
- Emphasise that you would like their views on what you propose, as well as their agreement – everyone likes to be consulted.

Impressing your manager

Your manager needs to trust you, to rely upon you, and to believe in your capacity to come up with good ideas and to make things happen. He or she doesn't want to wet-nurse you or to spend time correcting your mistakes or covering up for them.

To succeed in impressing your manager without really trying (it is fatal to push too much), you should:

- Always be frank and open. Admit mistakes. Never lie or even be economical with the truth. If there is the faintest suspicion that you are not perfectly straightforward, your boss will never trust you again.
- Aim to help your manager to be right. This does not mean being subservient or time-serving. Recognise, however, that you exist to give support – in the right direction.
- Respond fast to requests on a can-do/will-do basis.
- Not trouble him or her unnecessarily with your problems.
- Provide protection where required. Loyalty is an old-fashioned virtue, but you owe it to your manager. If you cannot be loyal, you should get out from under as quickly as you can.

Guy Browning (2003a and b) in part expresses some of the sentiments already expressed in dealing with difficult managers and managing your manager (this links to the desired result factor of people satisfaction) in the two articles below. They are to a great extent somewhat tongue-in-cheek, although they do have quite serious implications.

EXERCISE 6.5

Read through the articles which follow – *How to get noticed* and *How to manage office politics* – and discuss them with colleagues (those you trust), or alternatively, use a SWOT (strengths – weaknesses – opportunities – threats) analysis to consider the merits of the suggestions in the articles. This might help you establish in your own mind whether they are feasible options for you. You can decide (taking account of your personality) whether you would be likely to put some of them into practice or not!

Whichever method you use, the exercise should help give to you an insight into the politics in your particular place of work as well as helping to establish whether getting noticed is one of your goals. Being armed with this data may also help you manage your manager.

'How to get noticed'

by Guy Browning, *People Management*, 9 October 2003

They say that promotion in a large company is case of who you know rather than what you know. In fact, it's more often the case of who knows you and what they know about you. Here's how to keep a high profile at work.

Have good ideas and keep the credit

Good ideas are in short supply in life, and nowhere more so than in the workplace. Having good ideas will get noticed fast, especially if they are good for business. Not every idea you have will be a good one, but if you're thinking about things constantly, the good ones will come. When you've had a good idea, make sure your name stays attached to it.

Volunteer for projects

Many people view their jobs as work avoidance schemes. There's always work to be done, so making yourself available for it will mark you out as someone with ambition.

Ideally, volunteer to work on your own good ideas to make them happen. At the same time avoid becoming a delegation monkey where people will quite happily work you to death to make their life easier.

Visit other departments

Homo sapiens are possibly the least adventurous of all mammals. They work in the same place, live in the same place, go on holiday in the same place, and every day take the same route from the car park to the desk.

Make a point of visiting every corner of your company. This has two advantages: you see what's going on everywhere and everyone sees you.

Talk to senior management

Senior managers often say it's a lonely life at the top. That no one talks to them is because subconsciously we feel they must know more than we do. They don't. They know different things – and they certainly don't know as much about your job as you do.

When you get the chance, have a chat with them. They'll feel better informed about the company and will already know you when you're interviewed for promotion.

Organise social events

Don't try this if you're shy and retiring and have never organised your own party.

However, if you are a naturally outgoing person, organising a company social event gives you the ideal opportunity to talk to everyone in the organisation because no one, especially top management, wants to be seen as a party-pooper.

Ask people what they want

Prince Charles knows more about this country than any other living person, principally because the question he asks everyone is 'What do you do?' If you make a habit of asking this at work, you will have a better understanding of what's going on and also where your next opportunity lies.

Learn to love finance and IT

They may not be your natural lunch partners but there is no part of the organisation untouched by IT or finance.

Having a good profile with these departments means they will help spread the word about you throughout the organisation.

Try to cultivate a genuine interest in finance and IT so it's a good word that they are spreading.

Say good morning

Communication with other people is the bedrock of networking and career progression. You can't communicate telepathically with most people, so at some stage you will have to open your mouth and take the plunge. Saying good morning is the best possible way of starting, and no one is ever going to mind you being friendly (except in London and the south-east).

'How to manage office politics'

by Guy Browning, *People Management*, 6 February 2003

In the office, as in every human arena, politics often raises its ugly little head. Politics is the pursuit of power. The more interested you are in power, the more political you are likely to be. People who place more value on other things often find office politics difficult to deal with.

Don't play

Normally it takes two sides to play politics. If someone is being political and underhand with you, the right response is to treat them with the utmost fairness and openness. And, equally importantly, you need to treat all other sides just as fairly and openly. When it's clear there is no 'side' to you, the politicians will stop trying to get you on their side.

Radar

The main weapon in the fight against office politics is good communication. The more everyone shares the same information, the more difficult it is to play politics with information, the more difficult it is for people to use spin. Make sure you know that everyone important thinks that they know what you think.

Gossip

There are two types of gossip in the office. The first is malicious briefing against people and is widely used by office politicians. The second is the good old natter with your mates about what's happening generally. The more you do of the second, the more protected you are against the first. A good grapevine can alert you to political moves afoot before they happen.

Avoid corners

Office politics tries to back people into corners. When you find yourself being pressed into making a decision where you feel you haven't been consulted, you don't know enough or you haven't had the time to think about it, always hesitate. Just say 'Let me get back to you.'

Get it in writing

Whenever you feel that someone's playing politics with you, keep a record of what's happening, especially any relevant emails. If there's one thing the politicians can't stand, it's being held accountable. Having a paper trail of what they've been doing can help you do exactly that.

Manage upwards

Every office politician has a boss. Every office politician probably wants their boss's job. That makes their boss your natural ally when dealing with office politicians. However, only making contact when the chips are down won't work. The boss should be someone you already talk to before you really need to talk to him or her.

Think ahead

Politicians are schemers. They have a vision and they plot to achieve it. Yet everyone knows who the politicians are. Their ambitions are usually quite plain and their motivations simple. By thinking ahead and planning your own course, you put politicians on the back foot. And no politician is at their best when forced to react.

Be good at your job

People play politics because they think it's a way of getting ahead without working hard. People who clearly have talent and work hard don't need to be so political. If you make it abundantly clear that you're by far the best person for the job, then you'll probably get it despite the politicians.

Win-win

Office politics is based on 'I win, you lose'. When you approach everything on a win-win basis, you might not get what you want but you'll always be a potential winner. But the office politician will always have a scheming and equally political opposition.

(Note that the second article here – *How to manage office politics* – is particularly relevant to Chapter 11's discussion of power and politics.)

EXERCISE 6.6

Discuss the following questions:

1. Why should you have to manage your manager?
2. Is managing managers just about pleasing them, or is there more to it than that? If so, what is it?

CONCLUSIONS

How people feel about their work, their workplace and their managers can affect the overall performance of the individual (performance enhancement), the organisation (organisational performance) and the overall key performance result of the business as a whole. The processes discussed in this chapter can be seen as strong differentiators between good companies and great companies. Leary-Joyce (2004) believes 'success lies in congruence'. She maintains that

> **'the added factor of greatness lies in the intention behind the principles themselves.'**

This may allude to the fact that key performance results and people satisfaction in the workplace are brought about by exceptional organisations' acting on principles others only talk about (see the Microsoft case study).

SUMMARY

- It is necessary to clarify mutual expectations – what managers expect from their staff; what staff expect from their managers. It is reasonable for managers to expect competence, effort and commitment. It is unreasonable for them to expect compliance or loyalty unless the latter is two-way.
- The manager and the individual should agree expectations in the form of targets and standards. The individual should be encouraged to think through what can be achieved, and the manager should listen to these suggestions and take account of them, although ultimately it may be necessary to accept that overriding corporate objectives will have to prevail.

- Managers have the right to expect finished work from their staff.
- Managers can be unreasonable, even bullies. Bullying behaviour should never be tolerated, and a reasoned response to an unreasonable demand should be made.
- The work environment and the way in which staff are treated will have an effect on whether they feel they are working for a 'best company'.
- It is necessary for staff to give consideration to how they can best manage their managers by being aware of expectations and making every effort to meet them.
- Be aware of your own expectations and aspirations; manage yourself accordingly.
- Take account of office politics – we all have to deal with this phenomenon in one form or another.
- Last but not least, it is reasonable that a two-way level of commitment should prevail: the psychological contract. This will help to differentiate the good companies from the great companies.

REFERENCES

BROWNING G. (2003a) 'How to manage office politics', *People Management*, 6 February.

BROWNING G. (2003b) 'How to get noticed', *People Management*, 9 October

GUEST D. E. and CONWAY N. (2001) *Employer Perception and the Psychological Contract.* London, CIPD.

HAMEL G. (2000) *Leading the Revolution.* Boston, MA, Harvard Business School Press.

LEARY-JOYCE J. (2004) *Becoming an Employer of Choice: Make your organisation a place where people want to do great work.* London, CIPD.

MCCALL A. (ed.) (2004) '100 best companies to work for, 2004', *Sunday Times*, 8 March.

MOSKOWITZ M. and LEVERING R. (2004) 'Ten great companies to work for', *Fortune* (Europe), 26 January, Vol. 149 Issue 1, p36.

PERSAUD J. (2003) 'Keep the faithful', *People Management*, July.

INTRODUCTION

Organisations allocate people to work-groups as part of their infrastructure (see next chapter) so as to enable staff to function successfully in an effective work unit and at the same time maximise their individual potential for growth and development. Such groups may well involve people working together in a co-ordinated manner on common tasks that would be unachievable by individual effort alone. We talk of 'teams' and 'teamwork' in such instances. Increasingly, teams can also be formed on a temporary or permanent basis with members from across various groupings within the organisation. Many variables account for team success or failure. What is clear, however, is that teams must be supported by top management, they require training and development, and individuals must be recruited with the requisite skills and attributes.

This chapter further considers the difference between groups and teams, and considers how groups and teams develop and function. We reflect on how to create effective teams, and in so doing discuss the Belbin assessment methodology to represent how effective teams can be created. The chapter also suggests an alternative to the Belbin process – that of Margerison and McCann. It concludes with a review of working in virtual teams – a growing phenomenon in many international organisations.

Learning objectives

On completing this chapter, a reader will understand and be able to explain:

- the essential nature of group behaviour
- how groups develop
- how teams function
- how to build effective teams, and the importance of team roles
- how to work effectively as a member of a team
- how to lead and build teams
- the value of virtual teams.

GROUP BEHAVIOUR

Organisations essentially consist of groups of people who work together. They may be formal groups or teams set up to achieve a defined purpose, or they may be informal groups set up to include people who have some affinity with one another. It could be said that formal groups satisfy the needs of the organisation whereas informal groups satisfy the needs of their members. These needs may not necessarily coincide. Management generally likes to take what is called a 'unitarist' view of organisations, which is the belief that everyone works together and has the same interests at heart. In practice, however, organisations are 'pluralist' in nature – there are different interest-groups whose needs and expectations are not necessarily in accord with those of the organisation's management.

The ways in which people work together are affected by the nature of the task, the technology they use, and the culture of the organisation – its values and norms: 'the way we do things around here'.

Groups must carry out two major functions:

- tasks – initiation, information-seeking, decision-making, taking action, responding to demands or requests
- maintenance – encouraging, clarifying, summarising, standard-setting, working amicably and co-operatively together.

In the course of carrying out their tasks, groups can develop feelings and beliefs about how they work and should work together. This 'ideology' affects the attitudes and actions of group members and the degree of satisfaction they get out of being part of their group. If the group ideology is strong, its members identify closely with it. This may be a good thing, but it can go too far. There is the phenomenon known as 'group-think' (Orwell, 1949 and Janis, 1982) which can lead to irrational decisions and the inhibition of flexibility and independent judgement. Undue group pressures exerted by members on one another can do great harm to the organisation's work practice and culture.

How groups develop

Groups show signs of maturation. To support this theory some authors suggest that groups develop in five stages (Tuckman and Jenson, 1977):

1 *Forming* – when there is anxiety, dependence on the leader, and testing to find out the nature of the situation and the task, and what behaviour is acceptable. At this stage group members are becoming acquainted with each other – they use this period to establish ground rules both in the task-related area and the interpersonal-relationship arena. Individuals may now appear uncertain how to act and interact. They are deciding whether they want to affiliate with the group. However, once a person has decided to commit to becoming a group member, the forming stage is complete.

2 *Storming* – when there is conflict, emotional resistance to the demands of the task, resistance to control, and even hostility towards the leader. This aggression may also be focused on other group members. However, after initial conflict and difficulties within the group have been resolved and the group leadership established, the storming stage is complete.

3 *Norming* – when group cohesion is developed, norms emerge, mutual support and co-operation increase, and the group acquires a sense of identity. Good working and personal relationships may develop as well as sentiments that the group has a common purpose and shared responsibility. The norming stage is considered complete when the group decides to hold to a set of values and agrees the way they will function.

4 *Performing* – when interpersonal problems are resolved, roles are flexible and functional, there are constructive attempts to complete tasks, and energy is available for objective work. The group has reached a stage of maturity and is able to 'get the job done' and perform well in the process of meeting its goals.

5 *Adjourning* – when groups, having met their objectives, may disband. This can be fairly abrupt, or the the group may gradually diminish over a period of time. A

project or task group, for example, may have an agreed point at which its task has been completed and there is no need for it to continue.

EXERCISE 7.1

In groups, discuss ways in which groups can work positively or negatively towards management goals.

EXERCISE 7.2

Think of any team to which you belong or of which you are familiar. Analyse at which one of these five stages it is functioning, and put forward evidence – in terms of how the team performs – to back up your analysis.

The process of group development does not, however, always follow such a predictable path. There are many variables – for example, the period of time a group might spend at each stage: clear boundaries may not exist between the stages because of pressures placed on the group – eg a deadline (Gersick, 1988). Nevertheless, the five stages enable us to see a general pattern of group behaviour that results in certain stages of group formation.

HOW TEAMS FUNCTION

Although a group may often be referred to as a 'team', there are several distinct differences between groups and teams. Groups can be social, meeting through a common interest – eg wine-tasting or as a book club, etc. A team, on the other hand, may still comprise people with a common interest although it is more likely to be made up of people with complementary skills. The difference lies in the fact that team members have to work together to achieve their goals. Teams have an energy, power or even opportunity to complete a task or project that would not have been possible had the team members not been in place. Although each member of the team may have distinct or unique skills, it is working together as a team that ensures a successful outcome.

In a group, members may amalgamate and use the overall resources available to them although individual performance is still key to the group's success. However, individuals would be accountable only for their own performance, not the group's as a whole. In a work group, employee rewards would be given on an individual basis. A team, on the other hand, has to focus on individual and mutual accountability, and would share the responsibility for results as well as the rewards.

Groups and teams can also differ in an organisational context, particularly in their relationship with management. Groups tend to respond to management-led demands whereas mature work teams may be set challenges by management. Management in this context establishes aims, goals or a mission and asks the team to respond. The team would have flexibility and have a degree of self-management and autonomy. It nonetheless remains part of the organisational structure, and as such would respond to demands from management.

Katzenbach and Smith (1993) give their definition of a team:

'A team is a small number of people with complementary skills who are committed to a common purpose, performance goals and approach for which they hold themselves mutually accountable.'

The characteristics of effective teams

The characteristics of teams, as described by Katzenbach and Smith (1993), are:

- Teams are the basic units of performance for most organisations. They meld together the skills, experiences and insights of several people.
- Teamwork applies to the whole organisation as well as specific teams. It represents 'a set of values that encourage behaviours such as listening and responding co-operatively to points of view expressed by others, giving others the benefit of the doubt, providing support for those who need it, and recognising the interests and achievements of others'.
- Teams are created and energised by significant performance challenges.
- Teams outperform individuals acting alone or in large organisational groupings, especially when performance requires multiple skills, judgements and experiences.
- Teams are flexible and responsive to changing events and demands. They can adjust their approach to new information and challenges with greater speed, accuracy and effectiveness than can individuals caught in the web of larger organisational conventions.
- High-performance teams invest considerable time and effort exploring, shaping and agreeing on a purpose that belongs to them, both collectively and individually. They are characterised by a deep sense of commitment to their growth and success.

Dysfunctional teams

The specification set out above is somewhat idealistic. Teams do not always work like that. They can fail to function effectively in the following ways:

- The atmosphere can be strained and over-formal.
- Either there is too much discussion which gets nowhere, or discussion is inhibited by dominant members of the team.
- Team members do not really understand what they are there to do or the objectives or standards they are expected to achieve.
- People don't listen to one another.
- Disagreements are frequent and often relate to personalities and differences of opinion rather than to a reasoned discussion of alternative points of view.

- Decisions are not made jointly by team members.
- There is evidence of open personal attacks or hidden personal animosities.
- People do not feel free to express their opinions.
- Individual team members opt out or are allowed to opt out, leaving the others to do the work.
- There is little flexibility in the way in which team members operate – people tend to use a limited range of skills or specific tasks; there is little evidence of multi-skilling.
- The team leader dominates the team; more attention is given to who takes control than to who is getting the work done.
- The team determines its own standards and norms, which may not be in accord with the standards and norms of the organisation.

Types of teams

There are many different types of teams in organisations. The main categories are:

- organisational teams: any fairly loose groupings in an organisation – for example, the top management team
- work teams: teams formed of people who are dependent on one another to deliver the specified results for which the team has been formed
- project teams: teams set up to plan and control a project which may carry on for months or even years
- ad hoc teams: teams set up as taskforces or working-parties to deal with specific issues.

DEVELOPING WORK TEAMS

Importantly, if organisations are serious about developing work teams, then how a team is actually formed and developed must be given due consideration. The list below outlines typical organisation-related issues, person-related (team member) issues and developmental (personal and/or team) issues that are related to team development.

Organisation-related issues

Organisational fit

Most businesses tend to be configured on a hierarchical structure often depicted as a pyramid (see Chapter 8). This may suit teams that need to meet deadlines in producing a particular product. However, more ideas-based or creativity-based teams would perhaps work most effectively in a matrix structure. Some organisations may even use a combination of the two.

Management style

The organisation's philosophy, culture and style start at the top. Management's belief in teamworking must therefore be genuine and pervade all levels of the organisation. Teams work best when they are motivated and work in a supportive environment.

Aims

Organisations aiming to build effective teams must establish a focused view of what they want their teams to do, and why. There is no point in attempting to build effective teams if they are not utilised to perform focused tasks. A highly trained work team can quickly degenerate into a group if its skills are not being used effectively.

Person-related (team member) issues

Selecting team members

Selecting and recruiting staff as team members is of great importance. It is worth noting that even organisations with sophisticated HR systems can make mistakes and recruit people who will never fit into the team.

Whether you are recruiting from outside or making a selection from existing staff to be team members, the skills and attitudes required must be clearly thought through.

Motivation

A person's motivation is dependent upon many variables. However, many people seek congruence between their aims, the needs of the team and the aspirations of the organisation. A key aspect to team-building is participation in decision-making so that each member of the team believes his or her contribution is valuable. How people feel about the team and the organisation will therefore dictate the amount of effort they are prepared to expend.

Developmental (personal and/or team) issues

Personal development issues

People need to continually develop to enable them to attain their aspirations. Linked to this may be the aspirations and development of their work team. Excellent performances from the team may be the path to personal advancement.

Training

Learning is the main key to team development – from the point of view both of the team in learning to be a team, and of each team member bringing his or her own knowledge and experiences to help the team achieve its goals. However, a truly effective team has its development needs continually under review so that continued improvement takes place. There are always new skills and new knowledge to be learned under this philosophy.

Employee-related rewards

Although people carry out work purely for its intrinsic value, other rewards are extrinsic. Of these, pay is arguably the most important aspect of any reward-related initiative. In order to support effective teams, any reward package must be well thought through and fairly distributed to all team members, thus endorsing the team work ethic.

Career planning

Career planning and progression are factors that individual team members and the organisation as a whole must consider. Within the progression agenda people will need to 'grow' within the team. This may involve structured personal development and the opportunity to take a leading role in certain initiatives.

EFFECTIVE TEAMS: TEAM ROLES

Various writers have suggested that a vital factor for successful teams is the mix of team roles. The concept of 'roles' is one with which we are already familiar. We only have to reflect on the roles we perform in a working day. For example, a parent may 'act out' some of the following home roles: chauffeur, cook, child-minder, teacher, etc. In just the same way Belbin (1981, 1993) and Margerison and McCann (1986 and 2000) have analysed the roles we undertake in the workplace. Both Belbin and Margerison and McCann use their models in consulting situations. For our purposes we will discuss Belbin's work in detail; Margerison and McCann's framework will also be highlighted.

EXERCISE 7.3

This exercise invites you to consider how effective you are as a team member.

How would you rate yourself on a scale of 1 (poor) to 5 (excellent) as a team member under each of the following headings?

Score

1–5

An effective team worker

- understands the part or parts he or she is expected to play as a member of the team
- is multi-skilled – capable of carrying out a number of team-member roles
- is prepared to work flexibly
- takes a full part in team meetings and contributes useful ideas – is not afraid to express a point of view
- is tolerant and supportive of colleagues and respects other people's points of view
- works co-operatively with other members of the team.

Total score

Breakdown of results
25–30 excellent – alternatively, are you seeing things as they really are?
20–25 very good: you are an effective and committed member of the team who keeps abreast of all team issues.

10–20 an acceptable score but there is room for improvement: seek further development.

0–10 poor: you are not working in an effective team – perhaps it is a group.

Analysis
Develop your own explanation for your score.

Reflect on the result with reference to the list in the section *Developing work teams* above. This will help you determine whether your high, medium or low score is organisation-, person- or/and development-related.

Belbin

In this section we consider the benefits – in terms of roles – of developing and choosing the right team. However, in order to be effective a balance should be struck between 'the task', 'the team' and 'the individual' (see Figure 7.1, which was adapted from Adair, 1986, by Barrie Watson as part of his extensive work within Belbin Associates). Our discussion will refer back to this model.

The 'task' is related to the action-driven process of using both the individual and the team to complete a task. The 'team' process is linked to the socialisation that takes place. The 'individual' has to be able to 'fit in', to contribute to achieving the 'task' and be part of a successful team. 'Fitting in' may relate to the way the individual thinks or his/her overall attitudes and characteristics that contribute to the role he/she plays in the team itself.

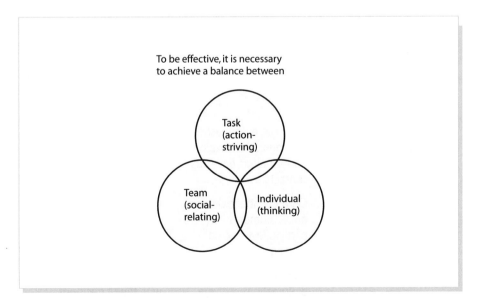

Figure 7.1   *The inter-relationship between task, team and individual (the Belbin team roles)*
Source: Belbin material, used by kind permission of Belbin Associates

Belbin (1993) thus describes team roles as

> **'our tendency to behave, contribute and interrelate with others in a particular way'.**

The type of team roles that we already have help to define our actions and sometimes the roles we adopt within any given team. Task- or action-related team roles (see Table 7.1) include those of 'shaper', 'implementer' and 'completer-finisher'. Social-related roles (see Table 7.2) include those of 'resource investigator', 'co-ordinator' and 'teamworker'. Roles that are considered more individualistic or those that are classed as thinking-related team roles (see Table 7.3) are 'plant', 'monitor-evaluator' and 'specialist'.

Table 7.1   *Task- or action-related team roles*

Team role	Strengths	Weaknesses
Shaper	Challenging, dynamic, goal-oriented, has drive and courage	Prone to provocation, often offends people's feelings
Implementer	Disciplined, organised, efficient, turns ideas into actions	Somewhat inflexible, slow to respond to new possibilities
Completer-finisher	Accurate, conscientious, meticulously prevents error	Inclined to worry unduly, reluctant to delegate

Source: Belbin material, used by kind permission of Belbin Associates

Table 7.2   *Team- or social-related team roles*

Team role	Strengths	Weaknesses
Resource investigator	Extrovert, enthusiastic, communicative, explores opportunities, develops contacts	Over-optimistic, loses interest once initial enthusiasm has passed
Co-ordinator	Calm, confident, clarifies goals, promotes participative decision-making	Can be seen as manipulative, offloads personal work
Teamworker	Co-operative, caring, diplomatic, sensitive, a good listener, averts friction	Indecisive when faced with tough decisions

Source: Belbin material, used by kind permission of Belbin Associates

Table 7.3 *Individual- or thinking-related team roles*

Team role	Strengths	Weaknesses
Plant	Creative, imaginative, unorthodox, solves difficult problems	Ignores incidentals, too pre-occupied to communicate effectively
Monitor-evaluator	Logical, analytical, discerning, judges accurately	Lacks drive and ability to inspire others
Specialist	Single-minded, motivated by the pursuit of knowledge	Contributes on a narrow front, dwells on technicalities

Source: Belbin material, used by kind permission of Belbin Associates

Identifying a person's team roles therefore helps to:

- improve self-awareness and personal effectiveness
- foster mutual trust and understanding between work colleagues
- facilitate team selection and team-building
- match people to jobs more effectively.

Self-awareness has an important place in reflecting how we manage and conduct ourselves within the team. Many organisations use assessment centres or human resource development professionals to compile questionnaires or psychometric tests to help us become more self-aware. These assessments, however, often rely on our own self-reporting, the outcomes of which are almost certainly less than objective and usually positive. This is not surprising because we are in fact agreeing with ourselves. When defining our own prominent team roles, Belbin suggests our perception may be unrealistic and open to faking, because we may be unaware of attributes that others may regard as significant.

He also contends that reliability may suffer as the data produced from only one source (self-perception/self-reporting) will not be as robust as that produced from a combination of self- and observer-reporting. A combination of data collection helps to normalise the results and in so doing makes them potentially more reliable. Hence, to produce a Belbin team roles profile the combination method is preferred. We must acknowledge that the 'Belbin Assessment' measures behaviour, not specifically personality (as in some psychometric tests); however, our personality, along with our mental abilities, experiences, values and motivations, and role-learning all constitute what Belbin (1993) calls 'behaviour'.

Underlying factors in team role behaviour

When discussing his team role model, Belbin (1993) states:

> **'that individuals eventually arrive at a stable pattern of association with their fellows based on a personality propensity, modified by the thought process, modified still further by personal values, governed by perceived constraints, influenced by experience and added to by sophisticated learning'.**

Expanding upon this we may consider the following six factors:

- Psycho-physiological factors – especially extroversion/introversion and high anxiety/low anxiety – underlie behaviour.
- Nevertheless, high-level thought can override personality to generate exceptional behaviour. (A naturally shy person taking on a 'resource investigator' role would be a case in point.)
- Cherished values can provide a particular set of behaviours. These are probably developed from our background and the particular traits we might value in our selves and others – eg loyalty, trust, etc (behaviours that we could attribute to the 'teamworker' and 'company worker' roles).
- Behaviour can depend on factors in the immediate environment. This may be determined by our reaction to the particular work environment – eg deadlines, change, etc. (For example, someone with a prominent 'completer-finisher' role will ensure that the team meets its deadlines. However, the need for achievement by someone with a prominent 'shaper' role will, at times, ensure that he/she drives the team to finish the task, even though it is not his/her usual inclination to do so.)
- Personal experience and cultural factors may serve to conventionalise (individual) behaviour, or behaviour is often adapted to take account of experience and conventions. (An example of this might be when a man expects to take the role of 'co-ordinator' when in a group of women even though there is a woman in the team with a high propensity for the 'co-ordinator' team role.)
- Learning to play a needed role improves personal versatility. This helps individuals to maximise their potential and value to the team and the department.

The challenge of using team role analysis

The challenge for the individual, the team and the organisation is often to use the information gathered on the staff members' team role profiles effectively.

The individual might question what to do with this new knowledge. The answer has surely got to include the level of reflection on the results (eg 'This is how others see me') and a personal development and effectiveness strategy that would require the individual to decide how to make the most of them. Roles would probably separate into:

- least preferred
- manageable
- preferred.

Table 7.4 *Making the most of one's team role*

Least preferred	Manageable	Preferred
Try to avoid using for prolonged periods	Be prepared to adopt these roles if necessary	Develop and perfect the role
Delegate and make use of complementary roles of others		Plan career to maximum use of these natural strengths
		Build a balanced team

Source: Belbin material, used by kind permission of Belbin Associates

Belbin suggests using the information constructively as in Table 7.4

As stated previously (in our pursuit of an effective team), the purpose of the team and the type of organisation in which it operates must all be considered as well as the individual team member. Table 7.4 suggests that a person's team roles can be a fundamental arbiter when planning a career or matching the person to the job role. This may, indeed, allow individuals to maximise their strengths, adopt the perfect role or at least manage the job requirements. An awareness of one's team role can also enable both individuals and their managers to acknowledge the role that is least preferred by team member and act accordingly. Consequently, managers may choose to recruit the person that fits the demands of the job and make the Belbin profile part of the recruitment process. The Belbin team roles profile can therefore be used when matching people to jobs.

The usual recruitment process would include a consideration of the eligibility and entry criteria. However, when using the Belbin process, suitability and performance criteria also have prominence (see Table 7.5).

The first three steps in the recruitment process identify the eligibility and suitability criteria, and are:

1 The manager defines the job or project.
2 The manager completes a Job requirement assessment.
3 The manager and others who know the job complete a Job observation assessment.

Table 7.5 *Eligibility and suitability criteria*

Eligibility/entry criteria	Suitability/performance criteria
1 Qualifications	Aptitude
2 Relevant experience	Versatility
3 References	Assessments
4 Acceptability at interview	Individual 'fit' with the requirements of the job

Source: Belbin material, used by kind permission of Belbin Associates

Table 7.6 *Considerations when matching people to jobs*

Eligibility/entry criteria	v	Suitability/performance criteria
Skills		Behavioural tendencies
Qualifications		Temperament
Experience		Aptitude

Source: Belbin material, used by kind permission of Belbin Associates

The next two steps are what the Belbin process can help facilitate:

4   Produce a Job suitability report.
5   Assess the match between the job and the candidate.

Belbin uses the chart shown as Table 7.6 to emphasise that although entry criteria (eg the qualifications etc to secure the interview) are important, they are not in themselves guarantees that the person would be successful in the job. The data in Table 7.6 therefore allows for the distinguishing features encompassed within the performance criteria to be, potentially, of greater prominence, particularly when used as an overall measure of suitability for a job.

The Belbin team roles assessment in this way helps to define the candidate who is suitable with an assessment developed through both self- and observer-reporting. Belbin also makes a case for backing the suitable candidate in preference to the eligible by pointing out that a candidate who might not normally be considered eligible may have his or her eligibility improved by a well-executed training and development plan (if the effort is deemed justified).

The Belbin assessment produces a person's 'team role profile'. This of course can be used to compile the 'perfect' work team, with most if not all of the Belbin team roles represented and everyone in the team having a complementary part to play. The purpose and terms of reference of the team must therefore be considered before actual team-building occurs.

Belbin (1993) suggests:

'To build a well-balanced team demands that there is a reasonable supply of candidates, adequate in number and diversity of talents and team roles.'

Margerison and McCann

Margerison and McCann (like Belbin) are partners in a commercial consultancy business, obviously linking into their respective theories. Both consider the process of team-work and 'teaming'. Both also have produced books and journal articles to evaluate and promote their theories and to enable the reader/manager to critically evaluate if either process would be appropriate to use in the organisations in which they work.

Margerison and McCann's work can be used as a tool to analyse and develop teams. It centres on their 'Team Management Wheel'. In line with the Belbin process their overall 'team

Table 7.7 *Team management profiles*

Team management profile	Description
Reporter-adviser	Reporter-advisers' forte is producing and accumulating data and being able to synthesise the information so that it is understandable to others. They prefer to give what they see as accurate advice to decision-makers even if it means delaying action. Reporter-advisers are necessary as support members of the team.
Creator-innovator	These individuals offer ideas which may disrupt the 'traditional' way things are done. They are independent thinkers who enjoy developing their own ideas.
Explorer-promoter	Their value to the team is in their ability to explore potential outside the organisation and bring back contracts, resources and data, which support the team's initiatives. They are less interested in finite detail and prefer to see the broad picture and motivate their colleagues to see the value of the way forward.
Assessor-developer	They offer an analytical style/stance on life and work, which is best suited to development and testing new prototypes, and assessing how to make them work. They often respond well to a challenge and are good at organising aspects of work life.
Thruster-organiser	Action-oriented individuals who are essential for getting results. They tend to push forward action from discussion, ideas or experiments. They are not known for their patience and at times can be quite hasty.
Concluder-producer	They like to work to a standard set of procedures and prefer a regular pace to work life. They need to take pride in their activities and are not keen to make changes. Rather, they prefer to use their existing skills to their full potential. They are content to reproduce tried and tested results.
Controller-inspector	They ensure that facts and figures are correct, and are good at meticulous detailed work. They have the ability to devote long periods of time to in-depth work and to ensure that it is carried out efficiently and effectively.
Upholder-maintainer	They have the ability to ensure that the team maintains balance between its physical and social sides. These individuals often become the conscience of the team. They also have definite views on how the team should be run. They can be prone to obstinacy but have a strong belief in the ability of the team, and this can be a source of strength and support to the team.
Link	There is one role that every team member must pay attention to – that of linking. Linking is at the hub of the 'wheel' and is the distinct role of all team members because they are expected to help link, through communication, their own personal roles with the personal roles of other team members.

Source: C. J. Margerison and D. McCann, *Team Management: Practical applications*, Mercury, 2000

management system' considers how departmental/organisational performance can be enhanced through the development of teams that work effectively. They identified nine key areas that they suggest not only form a basis for feedback and discussion, but also help the team continuously improve. The system encourages organisations to assess their team-work practices and team members to improve their 'inter-group links and co-ordination' (Margerison and McCann, 1995). Organisations could go on to extend the use of the 'team management system' to evaluate personal strengths and weaknesses, and develop an action plan for improvement.

Margerison and McCann's Team Index is a sixty-item questionnaire that extracts data about an individual's work preferences and, they claim, it has been widely tested internationally (Margerison and McCann, 2000). The questionnaire data is then reconfigured into personal roles that are depicted on the Team Management Wheel. Each segment of the wheel reflects types of work-model. These link to a person's profile which purports to show how certain individuals fit into preferred roles within the team.

Margerison (2001) linked the nine factors in the wheel to team competences, suggesting that there has been an over-emphasis in the past on individual competences. His argument is that organisations devote much of their time and resources to the competences required across the organisation, which they use to help develop individual training plans. He maintains that the acquisition of 'team competences' is often not regarded as an important issue and thus receives little attention – whereas it is actually the team functions, competences and effectiveness on which organisations rely for their overall performance and success. Margerison (2001) therefore suggests that the development of individual competence should be seen in context. That context may be linked to teamwork, and the competences and attributes needed to develop team members to enable the team as a whole to perform effectively and meet their overall objectives.

The nine factors that make up the Team Management Wheel and that are linked to the attributes and competences the team requires are as shown in Table 7.8.

Table 7.8 *The nine factors of the Team Management Wheel*

Factors	Competences and attributes
Advising	Gathering and reporting information
Innovating	Creating and experimenting with new ideas
Promoting	Exploring and presenting opportunities
Developing	Assessing and testing new approaches
Organising	Arranging how things will work
Producing	Making and delivering outputs
Inspecting	Controlling and auditing the working system
Maintaining	Upholding and safeguarding standards and processes
Linking	Co-ordinating and linking with others

Source: C. J. Margerison, *Team Performance Management* (*Journal*), 2001

Team members' relationships with the nine factors in the wheel and the associated competences are, as stated earlier, diagnosed by the use of a questionnaire. The main aspects of the Team Wheel are twofold. Firstly the wheel relates to team tasks and functions; secondly it relates to personal issues and the individual's work performances. It is suggested (Margerison, 2001) that these two areas must complement each other and that adequate links must be constructed between them. Maintaining links is perceived as a key competence for all participants in the team process.

In the final analysis the process can aid organisations when considering team attributes and work preferences. It can aid in the development of these attributes and team competences as well as in how they integrate with work preferences (Campbell, 1998). The Team Management Wheel offers an alternative to the Belbin team roles analysis for managers when compiling and assessing teams in their organisations.

Having considered the composition of the team we now turn our attention to the specific role of the team leader.

HOW TO BE AN EFFECTIVE TEAM LEADER

Competency requirements

Competencies can be developed specifically for team leaders, as in the following example, which uses a differentiating competency approach (a differentiating competency distinguishes between high- and low-performers).

Definition

- guides, encourages and motivates teams to achieve the required result.

Positive indicators

- achieves high levels of performance from team
- defines objectives and plans clearly
- continually monitors performance and provides good feedback
- maintains effective relations with the team
- develops a sense of common purpose in the team
- builds team morale.

Negative indicators

- achieves poor team performance
- sets unclear objectives
- pays insufficient attention to team needs
- does not provide good feedback.

Achieving good teamwork

To achieve good teamwork, team leaders should:

- Establish urgency and direction.

- As far as possible select members who have the required technical and team-working skills.
- Pay particular attention to first meetings and actions.
- Agree team objectives and standards with the team.
- Assess people's performance not only on the results they achieve but on their capacity to work well in a team.
- Encourage team members to plan their own work, monitor control information and take action without reference to their team leader except in special circumstances (ie create a self-managed team).
- Stimulate team members to come up with joint suggestions on how the performance of the team could be improved or working methods changed for the better (ie treat the team as an 'improvement group').
- Hold special 'off-the-job' meetings regularly to discuss work-related issues, review progress and explore new ideas.

EXERCISE 7.4

Review the above list of actions. Which do you think are the most important, and why?

You have just been appointed a team leader. What are the first things you do?

EXERCISE 7.5

Think of any team leader you know (including yourself, if appropriate). Evaluate how well he/she performs on a scale of 1 (poor) to 5 (excellent) in each of the above-listed actions.

Team-building

Team-building activities can include helping people to learn about the interpersonal skills they need as team-workers and exercising team leadership skills as described above. The process of team-building as a method of influencing attitudes and behaviour is illustrated below.

If you are a team leader, you may be faced with a situation in which various forms of dysfunctional behaviour are being displayed. Training which covers the areas set out in Figure 7.2 can improve matters, but leadership by example is even more important. Team meetings can be held to explore what helps and hinders effective working, and to come to joint conclusions about what the team itself can do about it.

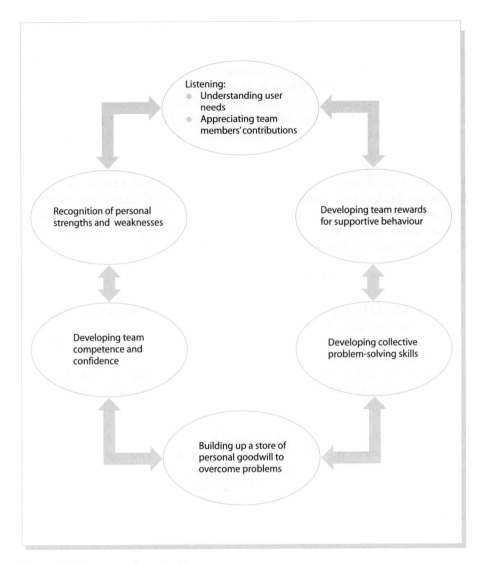

Figure 7.2 *The process of team-building*

If, however, there are individual team members who are not contributing well, they may possibly lack the required skills or not be well motivated. They might therefore have to be dealt with specifically through a performance review process. This will include agreeing the standards of performance and competencies required by team members, carrying out joint reviews of the behaviour of the individual with reference to actual examples, agreeing and implementing a personal development plan, giving positive feedback to recognise achievement and build on strengths, and providing encouragement, support, coaching and training as required.

Disruptive team members can be tackled in the same way, although their colleagues may exert some influence on them. If behaviour does not improve, consideration would have to be given as to whether such individuals should be allowed to remain members of the team.

VIRTUAL TEAMS

We owe many new and innovative procedures to the advance of the globalisation of business afforded to us by the Internet. The e-economy, e-learning, e-business, etc, all owe their existence to the transformation of business brought about by the 'dot.com revolution'. This new technology has enabled us to look again at many of our conventional practices, such as working in teams, and develop innovative ways of capturing the essence of 'the team' even though people are not necessarily in the same building or even the same country. Thus the concept of the 'virtual team' is born.

Johnson *et al* (2001) suggested that the team members of a 'virtual team' meet very infrequently and that face-to-face work practice occurs only seldom. Certain writers in this field have noted that 'virtual teams' consist of people who work in separate geographical locations, across space and time boundaries (Lipnach and Stamp, 1997) and who rely on modern technology to maintain the essence of their co-operation.

Benefits ascribed to working in virtual teams include:

- the capacity for employees to work for one or several organisations in one location or another country (Arnison and Miller, 2002)
- the workforce does not have to be relocated in order to take part in a particular project or innovation
- team members do not need to travel to see their counterparts in other countries – the organisation therefore does not need to continually purchase airfares or hotel accommodation to sustain their international business (Yukl, 2002).

One of the main differences between conventional and virtual teams is communication. The system of communication – that is, the technology adopted to manage the information system – must enable virtual team members to learn, share developments and connect on an inter-personal basis (Townsend *et al*, 1998). This process also requires the individual team members to acquire the necessary skills that will enable them to collaborate effectively in this virtual environment.

Skill requirements of the virtual team can be broken down into two interdependent areas – infrastructure and differentiators, as shown in Table 7.9.

Table 7.9 *Virtual team skills*

Infrastructure skills	Differentiator skills

Technologies
  - computer literacy
  - Internet/intranet
  - email
  - video-conferencing
  - mobile phone
 	
Geographical location
  - separated nationally
  - separated internationally
	Communication
	  - language written and verbal
	  - building and maintaining inter-personal relationships
	
	Team-building
	Motivation
	Maintaining the levels of creativity
	Cultural awareness
	  - national, international and cross-cultural

Arnison and Miller (2002) help illuminate the need for technology by describing it as

'the fundamental driving force behind the existence of pure virtual teams, and critical to their existence'.

Although we have previously mentioned the issue of geographical location and suggested that virtual teams are located over a wide global area, Hayward (2001) also elaborates on the issue of location by suggesting that people can work as a virtual team not because of the imperative of distance, but rather because of their use of the technology. This, he maintains, enables enhanced communication and more effective work practices.

The skills/development aspects of being a member of a virtual team therefore have certain distinct characteristics, especially in the development of good communication. As we have shown in Table 7.9, written and verbal communication skills are important. However, note the omission of non-verbal communication. People will not, in the virtual team, have eye contact or an across-the-desk exchange with a team member. Yet when a virtual team member is in communication with another, a response is warranted (as in face-to-face communication). This attention to detail/good communication in itself can help to build successful interpersonal relationships. We do acknowledge, however, that virtual team members can communicate through using technology which generates visual images (web cams, video-conferencing, etc), although this type of imagery can be distorted and does not replace the intimacy of one person in proximity to another.

It is also significant that when working in virtual teams there may be people from many nationalities, and that acknowledging and understanding cultural differences are therefore part of the attitude of professionalism that team members should include in their work ethic. It may be advisable, then, for a virtual project team to (physically) meet on at least one occasion for team-building purposes. This process may help sustain and even develop levels of motivation, consistency and creativity within the virtual team.

Whichever methods organisations adopt to build their virtual teams, one factor seems to be consistent: many large global organisations are adopting the concept of using virtual teams. To that end they need to meet the challenges such ways of working bring. Meanwhile, organisations that do *not* work over widely dispersed geographical areas are also increasingly harnessing the technologies and skills to enhance their communication, knowledge management and work practices to enable the traditional team to work more effectively and efficiently (Arnison and Miller, 2002).

EXERCISE 7.6: TEAM-BUILDING – THE VIRTUAL TEAM

This exercise may be carried out on an individual basis, but because the chapter is considering groups and teams, it makes a useful group exercise and has been devised with this in mind.

You are to work in a group of three to five people. Your group will be asked to fulfil the tasks below. These tasks are challenging, and you and your colleagues will need to spend several hours in preparation.

You have been asked as Management Consultants to devise a team development programme (two days) for a proposed or existing virtual team with the aim of fostering team development. The exact nature of the work of the team members (perhaps from the same company or perhaps people working together on a specific project) is something on which your group may decide for themselves. Your programme will outline the nature of various events and relevant scheduling.

You are required, as a group, to present your team development programme to members of the organisation's management for approval.

As part of the exercise you should keep a Team Learning Log. This may take any of various forms but will need updating as your plans are developed. As a minimum, your Learning Log should cover the following areas, although not necessarily under these headings:

> Brainstorming on initial ideas for the team development programme
> Allocation of work tasks amongst group members
> Group interaction

Team members' thoughts before and after the group presentation of the programme, especially in relation to things learned during this exercise that can be put to good use in future.

Your presentation should aim to present the team development programme to the management team over a duration of some 15 to 20 minutes. The management team should then give you feedback on the likelihood of adopting your proposals. The focus will purely be on demonstrating the team development programme.

SUMMARY

- Organisations are composed of formal and informal groups.
- The ways in which groups function are affected by the nature of their task and the organisation's culture. Groups essentially have two functions: task and maintenance.
- Groups go through stages of development: forming, storming, norming, performing and then adjourning.

- Teams are the basic units of performance and can outperform individuals.
- Teams can be dysfunctional – groups may encounter conflict, disagreements and lack of consensus, and create for themselves norms in conflict with those of the organisation; individuals may be subject to oppression and allow themselves too little flexibility.
- The main types of teams are organisation teams, work teams, project teams and ad hoc teams.
- Team members play a number of different roles. The Belbin assessment may help to create 'perfect teams'; it can also aid in the recruitment process.
- Team members' preferred ways of working can affect the overall success of the team. The Margerison and McCann team profiles seek to show how important it is for team roles to link together.
- Effective team-workers are multi-skilled and prepared to work flexibly; they play a full part in the team and work co-operatively with colleagues.
- To achieve good teamwork, team leaders must establish urgency and direction, select the right people, agree team objectives, assess the performance of individuals as team-workers, encourage the development of self-managed teams, and hold regular meetings.
- Team-building activities can include various methods of influencing attitudes and behaviours, including performance reviews and training.
- The use of virtual teams has become popular with large global organisations that have staff dispersed over wide geographical areas. Increasingly, other organisations are utilising the skills and technologies of the virtual team to introduce more efficient work practices.

REFERENCES

ADAIR J. (1986) *Effective Teambuilding*. Aldershot, Gower.

ARNISON L. and MILLER P. (2002) 'Virtual teams: a virtue for the conventional team', *Journal of the Workplace*, Vol. 14, No. 4, pp166–73.

BEE R. and BEE F. (1977) *Project Management: The people challenge*. London, CIPD.

BELBIN R. M. (1981) *Management Teams: Why they succeed or fail*. London, Butterworth-Heinemann.

BELBIN R. M. (1993) *Team Roles at Work*. London, Butterworth-Heinemann.

CAMPBELL R. A. (1998) 'Team leadership review', *Journal of Management Development*, Vol. 22 No. 10, pp919–21.

HAYWARD B. (2001) 'Wake up after the dot-com fry', *BRW* (online), available at: www.brw.com.au/stories/20011004/11763.asp

GERSICK C. L. G. (1988) 'Time and transition in work teams: towards a new model of group development', *Academy of Mangement Journal*, Vol. 31, pp9–41.

JANIS I. L. (1982; 2nd edition) *Groupthink: Psychological Studies of policy decisions and fiascos*. Boston, MA, Houghton Mifflin.

JOHNSON P., HEIMANN V. and O'NEIL K. (2001) 'The Wonderland of virtual teams', *Journal of Workplace Learning*, Vol. 13, No. 1.

KATZENBACH J. and SMITH D. (1993) *The Magic of Teams Learning*. Boston, MA, Harvard Business School Press.

LIPNACH J. and STAMPS J. (1997) *Virtual Teams: Reaching across space, time and organisations with technology*. Ontario, Wiley, p7.

MARGERISON C. J. (2001) 'Team management, team competence', *Team Performance Management: An International Journal*, Vol. 7, Nos 7/8, pp117–22.

MARGERISON C. J. (2002) *Team Leadership: A guide to success with Team Management Systems*. London, Thompsom Learning.

MARGERISON C. and McCANN R. (1986) 'The Margerison–McCann team management resource theory and application', *International Journal of Manpower*, Vol. 7, No. 2, pp1–32.

MARGERISON C. J. and McCANN D. (1995) 'Quality in team work', *Journal for Quality and Participation*, Vol. 18, Issue 22.

MARGERISON C. J. and McCANN D. (2000) *Team Management: Practical Applications*. London, Mercury.

ORWELL G. (1949) *Nineteen Eighty-Four*. London, Secker & Warburg.

TOWNSEND A., DEMARIE S. and HENDERSON A. (1998) 'Virtual teams: technology and the workplace of the future', *Academy of Management Executive*, Vol.12, No. 3.

TUCKMAN B. (1965) 'Developmental sequences in small groups', *Psychological Bulletin*, No. 63.

TUCKMAN B. E. and JENSON M. A. (1977) 'Stages of small group development revisited', *Group and organisational studies*, Vol. 2, pp 419–27.

YUKL G. (2002; 5th edition) *Leadership in Organisations*. Englewood Cliffs, NJ, Prentice Hall.

INTRODUCTION

That the term 'organisational structure' can inspire, is rarely a thought that crosses the minds of most people. Certainly, it embodies many of the 'infrastructure' aspects we mentioned in the introductory chapter. The tendency might be to regard it as a sort of 'given', a necessary evil which, once established, can be forgotten about. The need for structure is obvious: its importance less so. And yet, if we regard it as being the framework through which the organisation exists and operates and grows, then it clearly is not static but dynamic, and we would do well to pay it adequate respect. Indeed, the links between structure and organisational strategy (see, for instance, the work of Chandler et al, 1999) demonstrate its strategic importance – although analysis at this level lies outside the scope of this book. However, we regularly observe organisations which are 'de-layering', 'centralising' or 'decentralising', 'divisionalising', etc, and are aware that such restructuring can mean dramatic changes for both those who work for the organisations concerned and their customers. In this chapter we are going to consider some of the structural variables and perhaps give structure back its rightful place.

Learning outcomes

On completing this chapter, the reader will understand and be able to explain:

- the meaning of the terms 'organisation', 'organisation structure', 'organisation design' and 'organisation development'
- how organisations function, including the need for specialisation and autonomy
- the different types of organisation structure – formal, informal, unitary, divisionalised, centralised, decentralised, matrix, process
- the concepts of the flexible firm, the core-periphery organisation and the 'ad hocracy'
- the considerations affecting organisation and job/role design
- how to construct an organisation chart and write a job description or role definition
- approaches to organisation development.

DEFINITION OF TERMS

Organisation

Organisations get results by designing, developing and maintaining a system of co-ordinated activities in which individuals and groups of people work co-operatively under leadership towards commonly understood and accepted goals.

Organisational structure

When most people think of organisational structure, the areas that spring to mind are organisational charts, the allocation of work to individuals and groups, and the reporting

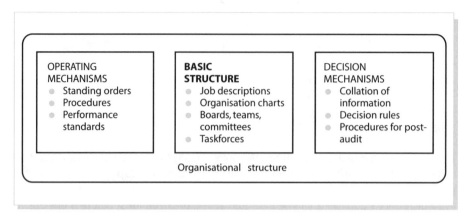

Figure 8.1 *The three aspects of organisational structure*
Adapted from J. Child, *Organisation*, Paul Chapman, 1988

mechanisms of the organisation. This view is true but is not complete. What we are describing here is only one element of structure – what Child (1988) would call the 'basic structure' (see Figure 8.1). Organisational structure is the entire framework of this 'basic structure' *together with* what he calls 'operating mechanisms' and 'decision mechanisms' as shown in Figure 8.1.

Basic structure

We will look in further depth at job descriptions and organisation charts later in this chapter. For now we can note that the basic structure covers the following:

- how the activities required are grouped together into units, functions and departments
- who is responsible for what
- who reports to whom
- the lines of authority emanating from the top of the organisation.

Organisation charts are used to illustrate the structure, but they can never represent the reality of how organisations operate – the cross-functional interactions and the different ways in which people work together. Job descriptions are used to define what is done – but again, they cannot convey the full flavour of the work carried out. If they do attempt to describe it in detail, they defeat their own purpose through over-elaboration and by attempting to capture what is commonly an evolving role rather than a static set of duties.

Boards and teams also form part of this basic structure. Boards might be a board of directors or a board of examiners; teams may include work groups and functional teams (eg engineering team, admin team, personnel team); committees may consider (eg) health and safety; taskforces are groups established for the duration of a particular project – for instance, the installation of a new management information system.

Operating mechanisms

These relate to how tasks are carried out in terms of both what is to be done and how it is to be done, and to what standard. Procedures give rules, guidelines and typical sequences of activities (for instance, in a hospital's Accidents and Emergency department there will be an established protocol for prioritising patients' injuries) which may be applied to each different situation. Standing orders are more precise, laying down what must happen in a given situation. Performance standards indicate what level of action is acceptable: this may be in the form of a 'charter' (eg the Patient's Charter in the NHS, the Student's Charter in a university) or may refer to industrial/ work sector codes of practice.

There are clearly links between basic structure and operating mechanisms. For instance, an engineer may be in a team and this will be shown on an organisation chart and his job description will reflect this. When designing, the engineer must comply with engineering codes of practice, again linked to the job description.

Decision mechanisms

How do we make decisions? Do we rely upon the information already in the heads of our senior managers? Do we carry out research to gather (collate) information? And how do we make decisions in the organisation? This could be on the basis of some financial consideration or it might be linked to other considerations. Are we democratic, autocratic, or somewhere in between when it comes to the final decision? And what do we do after we have carried out checks (ie post-audit) – how do we inform people of results, and what do we do if something needs corrective action?

Again, these mechanisms are linked to basic structure and operating mechanisms. A change in any one of these areas is likely to have a knock-on effect into the other.

Putting basic structure, operating mechanisms and decision mechanisms together gives us a comprehensive, holistic framework for the organisation. An organisation needs this basic 'infrastructure' in order merely to be in a position to operate effectively. It does not, as we stated in the introductory chapter, guarantee success, but without it, success cannot be achieved.

Organisation design

The design of the structure is contingent upon the type of organisation, the activities carried out, the organisational culture (as described in Chapter 10) and the views or whims of those in charge. In traditional theory, organisation design is not affected by the characteristics of the members of the organisation. In practice – and increasingly so in these days of 'the flexible firm' – organisation structures are adjusted or flexed in response to the type of people who are available or can be obtained to carry out the work.

Organisational development

Organisational development activities aim to improve the effectiveness of the organisation as a place where work gets done. They constitute the dynamic aspect of organising – breathing life into the structure.

HOW ORGANISATIONS FUNCTION

Organisations can be regarded as systems which exist in ever-changing and turbulent environments. As systems, they transform inputs (human, financial and physical resources) into outputs (goods and services).

An organisation has been described by Trist *et al* (1963) as a 'socio-technical' system in which social processes (interactions between people) are inter-related with the technologies and operational methods used in the organisation.

In describing what goes on in organisations, the term 'process' is frequently used today. 'Process' refers to *how* things get done, not *what* gets done. It embraces such aspects of organisational behaviour as leading, motivating, networking, working in teams, and planning and co-ordinating activities. Structures and systems are ways of helping to make 'process' work. There are a number of different views about how organisations function, as examined below. But there is consensus on the fact that all organisations are concerned with specialisation and autonomy.

Traditional views on how organisations function

The classic or scientific management school as represented by Fayol (1949), Taylor (1911) and Urwick (1947) believed in order, control and formality. It was thought that organisations should minimise the opportunity for uncontrollable, and therefore unfortunate, informal relations, leaving room only for the formal ones. The term 'bureaucracy' was coined by Max Weber (1864–1920) to describe the type of organisation in which impersonality and rationality are developed to the highest degree (see posthumous work of Weber, 1946). The ideal bureaucracy, according to Weber, has characteristic features:

- close job definitions concerning duties and boundaries
- vertical authority patterns
- decisions based on expert judgement
- disciplined compliance with the directives of superiors
- maximum use of rules
- the impersonal administration of staff.

The traditional approach to organisation emphasised formality – informality was not allowed. The approach was largely based on the military model such that a distinction was made between the line and the staff who both had rigidly defined functions – the line did the fighting and the staff planned and provided support. The line-and-staff organisation became the model formal structure – the line exercises delegated authority to perform the functions of the enterprise and the staff organisation offered advice and provided the services required by the line organisation.

Recent views on how organisations function

The rebellion against the rigidities of the classic school was led by the contingency school, the best-known of whom were Burns and Stalker (1961), Woodward (1965) and Lawrence and Lorsch (1969). Their overriding theme is that organisations are a function of the circumstances in which they exist. They oppose those who impose rigid principles of organisation irrespective of the technology or environmental conditions.

Pascale (1990) believes that the new organisational paradigm should be regarded as having changed

- from the image of organisations as machines, with the emphasis on concrete strategy, structure and systems, to the idea of organisations as organisms, with the emphasis on the 'soft' dimensions of style and shared values
- from a hierarchical model, with step-by-step problem-solving, to a network model with parallel nodes of intelligence which surround problems until they are eliminated
- from the status-driven view that managers think, and workers do as they are told, to a view of managers as 'facilitators', with workers empowered to initiate improvements and change
- from an emphasis on 'vertical tasks' within functional units to an emphasis on 'horizontal' tasks and collaboration across units
- from a focus on 'content' and the prescribed use of specific tools and techniques to a focus on 'process' and a holistic synthesis of techniques
- from the military model to a commitment model.

Specialisation

Organising is about getting teams and individuals to work collectively together to achieve a common purpose. But this involves a number of specialised activities which have to be catered for. For example, marketing is a general activity but within it there are specialisms such as market research. Production management requires specialists in computer-controlled manufacturing systems. Personnel management may need a specialist in employee reward (pay and benefits or compensation and benefits) systems.

These specialisms have to be identified and the expertise required obtained and developed to enable the practitioners to contribute in their particular field to achieving the collective effort. This raises an organisational problem: how can specialists, who may well be individualists, be made to fit into a team? How can the specialist contribution be consolidated into the overall effort?

The answer to both these questions is to ensure that from the very start the purpose of the specialist activity is identified as being part of the whole. The role it is expected to play has to be specified precisely. The contribution that the specialist is expected to make to the team should be clarified, and the need to integrate specialist with generalist activities must be addressed. Specialists can often make their best contribution if it is established that they are members of multi-disciplinary or multi-functional teams in which the part they play is defined.

Autonomy

According to the *Oxford English Dictionary*, 'autonomy' means the right of self-government and personal freedom. In organisations it means being given devolved authority and freedom to act without reference to another person, although such authority and freedom are constrained to some degree by the organisation's policies and core values and by external legislation and the expectations of stakeholders.

Enabling people to act autonomously within reasonable limits is desirable because:

- it means that decisions can be taken at the point of action by people who are 'close to the customer' or aware of the particular circumstances in which a decision has to be made
- it speeds up action and response time
- it empowers people, giving them greater job satisfaction – they are in control of their own actions and their work becomes meaningful because they can influence how it is done as well as what is done
- it focuses the attention of people on their responsibilities – it is more difficult for them to say that a complication is someone else's problem or that 'it's not in my job description'
- it is a means of developing initiative, a sense of responsibility and increased expertise.

But there are limits to autonomy. People have to conform to corporate policies and uphold core values. And, importantly, they have to work as members of teams, which may mean sacrificing a certain measure of individual autonomy for the good of the team.

Teams can be given a degree of autonomy as well as individuals. Self-managing teams (autonomous work groups) can be set up which may be largely self-regulating and work without close supervision. Such teams can be given the authority to plan, monitor and control their own work as long as they meet the targets and standards they have agreed.

Finally, autonomy can be given to strategic business units in a decentralised organisation. This autonomy may be governed by the requirement to deliver results, although how they deliver results is up to them.

FORMAL AND INFORMAL ORGANISATIONS

The formal organisation may be defined as a structure and described by means of an organisation chart. But that is not how it works. Some time ago, Chester Barnard (1938) emphasised the importance of the informal organisation – the network of informal roles and relationships which, for better or worse, strongly influences the way formal structures operate. He wrote:

> **'Formal organisations come out of and are necessary to informal organisations: but when formal organisations come into operation, they create and require informal organisations.'**

Barnard's views were influenced by the so-called 'Hawthorne experiment', a large-scale investigation of productivity and industrial relations which took place at Western Electric's Hawthorne plant in the late 1920s and early 1930s. This highlighted the importance of informal groups and how they affected the way work was carried out.

More recently, Child (1988) has pointed out that it is misleading to talk about a clear distinction between formal and informal organisation. Formality and informality can be built into the structure. And Burns and Stalker (1961) have criticised the view that formal and informal organisation are mutually opposed social systems as described in 'the Manichean world of the Hawthorne studies'. It is perhaps better to make a distinction between the rigidly defined 'line-and-staff' organisation, loved by the scientific management school, and the more flexible organisation of today, where it is recognised that process and interactions between people make them work, and that the lines on an organisation chart do not describe what really goes on. As Child has said, informality can be built into the structure if it is recognised that the structure need not be rigid. The 'process' organisation described later in this chapter illustrates how organisation design can cope with both the formal and the informal elements in one structure.

TYPES OF ORGANISATION STRUCTURE

Unitary (functional) structure

A unitary structure is one that is found in self-contained organisations (those without divisions or subsidiaries) or in the separate units of divisionalised or decentralised organisations. In a unitary structure the heads of each function (you will also see this sort of structure referred to as a 'functional' structure) or department report directly to the top, as illustrated in Figure 8.2.

A unitary structure is the most basic type of organisation. It has the obvious advantage of clearly defining relationships – everyone knows where they are and a distinction is made between the line (production and sales) and staff (finance and personnel). The disadvantage of such a structure is that the departments might operate as separate 'organisational chimneys' – pursuing their ends without considering corporate needs and erecting boundaries between each other. Much depends on the capacity of the chief executive as a leader and team-builder to hold the organisation together.

Centralised structure

A centralised structure is one in which divisions, subsidiaries and geographically separated activities are subject to close control from the centre, which dictates what products they make or services they provide and how they should operate, and severely limits the extent to which independent decisions can be made locally. A centralised structure is illustrated in Figure 8.3.

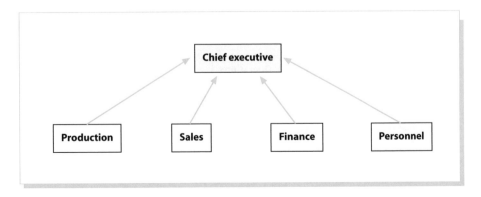

Figure 8.2 *A unitary (functional) organisational structure*

The advantages and disadvantages of centralisation

The advantages of centralisation are that:

- control can be exercised over divisional activities to ensure that they are complying with group policy
- well-tried and tested products and services can be offered in standard packages to customers supported by country- or worldwide marketing and advertising campaigns, thus establishing a global brand image
- standard procedures and systems can be used without the need to develop new ones at local level – group resources can readily be made available to each division
- highly qualified and expert staff are available at headquarters to spell out to divisions how they can perform effectively.

The disadvantages of centralisation are that:

- it constrains the ability of local management to determine what is best for their part of the business in the light of their understanding of their product, market or local circumstances
- it implies, incorrectly, that there is one best way to manage business affairs
- it restricts local enterprise and initiative to respond rapidly to new challenges and opportunities – the heavy hand of the centre is imposed on those in the business front line
- it creates double and unnecessary tiers of functional specialists and, often, an over-staffed and expensive headquarters.

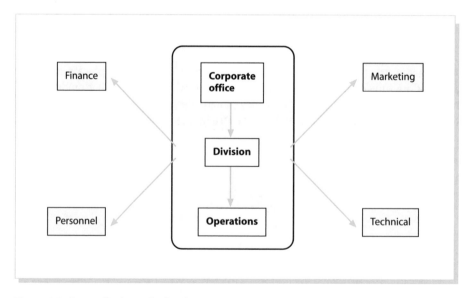

Figure 8.3 *A centralised organisational structure*

Decentralised organisations

Some organisations, especially conglomerates, decentralise their manufacturing or service delivery activities to subsidiaries or strategic business units (SBUs). Only a few specialists remain at headquarters to deal with financial, taxation and legal matters. Personnel issues concerning senior management (recruitment, transfer, development and remuneration) may sometimes – but not always – be catered for at the centre.

The essence of decentralisation is that authority is delegated almost completely to the chief executives of the strategic business units to operate in their particular markets, so long as they meet profit and performance targets.

The research carried out by Goold and Campbell (1986) established that there are three ways in which the centre can relate to its businesses:

- strategic planning – the centre develops strategy with the business units and sets broad, strategic performance targets
- financial control – the centre exercises control through financial budgeting processes and by measuring performance in relation to profit targets; planning influence is low
- strategic control – the centre leaves the units to develop their strategic plans but exercises tight control against strategic targets.

A decentralised organisation is illustrated in Figure 8.4.

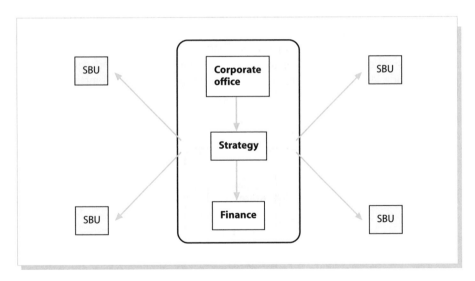

Figure 8.4 *A decentralised organisational structure*

The advantages and disadvantages of decentralisation

The advantages of decentralisation are that:

- authority is given to the management of strategic business units to develop their products and markets
- the strategic business units can operate closely with their customers and respond quickly to product/market opportunities
- the cost of the central operation is minimised.

The disadvantages of decentralisation are that:

- business unit managements do not receive much support, if any, from the centre
- the scope for strategic business units to work together to exploit joint markets is severely limited – the tendency will in fact be for them to compete against each other
- the best use may not be made of the organisation's human and financial resources across the strategic business units – for example, career development for executives may be limited to their unit although both they and the organisation would benefit from planned career moves to other parts of the organisation.

Divisionalised organisations

The process of divisionalising organisations, as first described by Sloan (1963) on the basis of his experience in running General Motors, involves structuring the organisation into separate divisions. Each division is concerned with discrete manufacturing, sales, distribution or service functions, or with serving a particular market. At group headquarters, functional departments are created in such areas as finance, planning, engineering, personnel and legal to provide services to the divisions. Importantly, they may exercise functional control

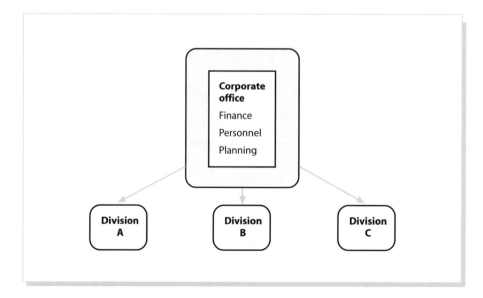

Figure 8.5 *A divisionalised organisational structure*

over the activities of divisions in their area. Thus personnel may lay down that a standard job evaluation system has to be applied in each division, and finance may stipulate how budgets are to be prepared and submitted to headquarters. The amount of control exercised depends on the extent to which the organisation has decided to decentralise authority to divisions. Divisionalised organisations may appear to operate the same sort of structure as decentralised organisations but they treat each operational unit as a strategic business unit. The form a divisionalised organisation may take is illustrated in Figure 8.5.

The advantages and disadvantages of divisionalised organisations

The advantages of a divisionalised organisation are that:

- areas of responsibility can be clearly defined
- each division can be set up to carry out a discrete or closely linked set of activities
- functional services and control can be provided and exercised from the top so that a uniform approach to managing activities can be adopted.

The disadvantages are that:

- individual divisions, as the word implies, can go their own way without reference to what is happening in the other divisions of the organisation
- concerted efforts to develop and exploit particular markets may be prejudiced
- the functional control exercised from the centre may inhibit the development of systems and processes which are appropriate to the markets the divisions serve and the environment in which they operate.

Matrix organisations

Matrix organisations carry out projects in such fields as contracting, research and development, and consultancy. Staff from various disciplines – for example, electrical and mechanical engineering in a contracting firm, or finance and IT in a consultancy firm – are assigned to projects. When a project is set up, a project leader is appointed and draws staff from the appropriate disciplines. Project-leading may be a full-time occupation or leaders may be senior specialists from the key project disciplines. While working on the project, team members are responsible to the team leader for the project work they do, but the functional head of the discipline has a general responsibility for ensuring that proper standards are maintained by discipline members. The members continue to be functionally responsible to the head of the discipline, and when a project ends they return to the discipline until they are assigned to a new project. The head of the discipline is responsible for the recruitment and career development of specialist staff and for making decisions about their promotion and pay. While on a project, individuals are thus placed in the matrix intersection, being responsible on a day-to-day basis to the project leader but continuing to be functionally responsible to the head of their discipline.

A matrix organisation is illustrated in Figure 8.6. This particular example shows part of the matrix structure for a civil engineering project. Here you can see, for instance, how the Design engineers report to the Design director for issues such as: work allocation, training and development, and appraisals. They are accordingly part of the Design team which thus has a wealth of design expertise. However, engineers also report to Project managers on the specific projects upon which they are working. Here, the focus is very much upon

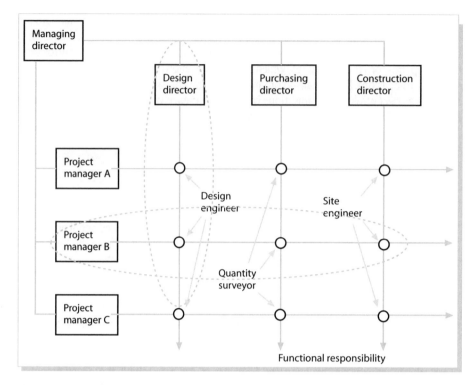

Figure 8.6 *A matrix organisation*

completion of the task, with particular emphasis upon co-operation and collaboration with other project team members.

The advantages and disadvantages of matrix organisations

The advantages of matrix organisations are that they:

- enable organisations in the business of conducting projects quickly to assemble teams consisting of people with the most appropriate expertise and experience
- help to achieve excellent speed of response and flexibility in the case of new demands
- recognise that project management is a special skill and that a pool of experienced leaders must be maintained
- recognise the need to develop and nurture expertise in the key disciplines which the business uses in its projects
- provide team members with a variety of experience, broadening their skills base in conjunction with members of other disciplines and developing project management skills.

The disadvantages of matrix organisations are that they:

- tend to be fragmented – it is difficult to develop and maintain commitment to the organisation
- can unsettle individuals, who will be constantly working for new bosses on different projects – there may be little continuity

■ require individuals to be responsible to two bosses simultaneously – their project leader and the head of their discipline – which may create ambivalence

■ necessitate careful planning to ensure that resources from the different disciplines are available when required without people spending too much time idle and waiting for work

■ may limit or appear to limit career progression for individuals because of those individuals' constant movement between projects and because of the consequent difficulty of developing coherent career plans.

The process-based organisation

A process-based organisation is one in which the focus is on horizontal processes that cut across organisational boundaries. Traditional organisation structures consisted of a range of functions operating semi-independently and each with its own, usually extended, management hierarchy. Functions acted as vertical 'chimneys', with boundaries between what they did and what happened next door. Continuity of work between functions and the co-ordination of activities was prejudiced. Attention was focused on vertical relationships and authority-based management – the 'command and control' structure. Horizontal processes that cut across organisational boundaries received relatively little attention. It was, for example, not recognised that meeting the needs of customers by systems of order processing could only be carried out satisfactorily if the flow of work from sales through manufacturing to distribution was treated as a continuous process and not as three distinct parcels of activity. Another horizontal process which drew attention to the need to reconsider how organisations should be structured was total quality initiatives. These are not top-down systems. They cut across the boundaries separating organisational units to ensure that quality is built into the organisation's products and services. Business process re-engineering exercises have also demonstrated the need for businesses to integrate functionally-separated tasks into unified horizontal work processes.

The result, as indicated by Ghoshal and Bartlett (1995), has been that

> **'managers are beginning to deal with their organisations in different ways. Rather than seeing them as a hierarchy of static roles, they think of them as a portfolio of dynamic processes. They see core organisational processes that overlay and often dominate the vertical, authority-based processes of the hierarchical structure.'**

In a process-based organisation there are still designated functions for, say, manufacturing, sales and distribution. But the emphasis is on how these areas work together on multi-functional projects to deal with new demands such as product/market development, or, as in Bass Taverns, commissioning new pubs. Teams jointly consider ways of responding to customer requirements. Quality and continuous improvement are regarded as a common responsibility shared between managers and staff from each function. The overriding objective is to maintain a smooth flow of work between functions and to achieve synergy by pooling resources from different functions on taskforces or project teams. An example of process-based organisation structure is shown below in Figure 8.7. Here we observe that the organisation has decided to treat Health and Safety issues as a process which impacts upon

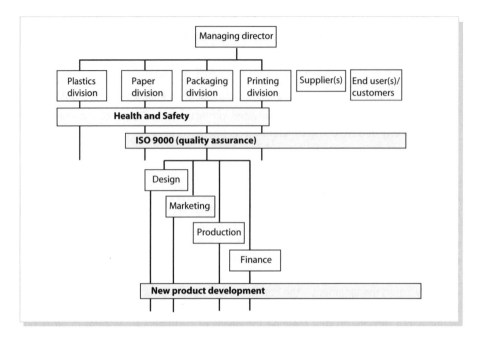

Figure 8.7 *Cross-divisional process and cross-functional process structure*
Source: Dimanescu, as cited in Maylor, *Project Management*, 1999

all of its divisions; it is considering the operation of the Quality Assurance process ISO 9000 in three of its four divisions – note here how the suppliers and customers are also part of the 'team'. While these cross-divisional processes may also be cross-functional, the diagram also depicts a specific example of a cross-functional team operating within the Packaging division in which the functions of Design, Marketing, Production and Finance are all present and, because the process is New product development, the decision has been made to also include suppliers and customers (in some form) within the team.

The advantages and disadvantages of process-based organisations

The advantages of process-based organisations are that they:

- provide for the smooth flow of work between and across functions to meet customer demands and enhance the thrust for quality and cost- effectiveness
- reduce the insularity which can plague functional 'chimneys' in a traditional organisation
- enable resources to be pooled on multi-functional project teams more easily to develop new products, markets or processes.

The disadvantages of process-based organisations are that they can:

- diffuse attention away from the core activities of particular functions
- lead to excessive attention to work flows rather than to what is actually produced, sold and delivered
- confuse people within and outside the organisation as to who is responsible for what
- diffuse responsibility.

THE FLEXIBLE FIRM

The concept of the flexible firm is often used to indicate an organisation which is able to respond quickly and flexibly to new demands generated by the market overall or by individual customers. Job-based flexibility means that people can be moved between different tasks and may be expected to use a wider range of skills. Rather than work at jobs, they carry out *roles* – behaving in appropriate ways depending on the situation. Organisation-based flexibility exists in core-periphery, 'shamrock' and 'ad hoc-racy' organisations.

Core-periphery organisation

A core-periphery organisation is one that retains a core of permanently employed key workers who carry out the fundamental tasks that the organisation exists to do. The 'periphery' consists of part-time, casual and contract workers who are employed when they are needed, or who carry out tasks that are not basic to the organisation. This is a form of team organisation, and a move towards a core-periphery structure often means downsizing, although those retained are offered a measure of security.

'Shamrock' organisation

The 'shamrock' organisation is Handy's (1989) term for a core-periphery structure. As he puts it:

> **'The core will be composed of well-qualified people, professionals, technicians or managers. They get most of their identity and purpose from their work. They are the organisation and are likely to be both committed to it and dependent on it.'**

In contrast, what Handy calls the 'contractual fringe' will be made up of both individuals and organisations. The individuals will be self-employed professionals or technicians, many of them past employees of the central organisation who ran out of roles in the core or who preferred the freedom of self-employment.

The core and the contractual fringe compose two leaves of the shamrock; the third leaf consists of the flexible labour force who carry out part-time or temporary work.

The 'ad hoc-racy'

The 'ad hoc-racy' is a term coined by Mintzberg (1981) for organisations where, as he expresses it,

> **'power is decentralised selectively to constellations of workers that are free to co-ordinate within and between themselves by mutual adjustments'.**

As the term implies, such organisations evolve and respond as required to the circumstances in which they exist. There is no fixed or permanent structure – it is constantly being adjusted to meet new conditions. Software houses, especially in their earlier stages, often take the form of ad hoc-racies.

Where these structures can be found

The structures described above can be found in any organisation. The choice of structure depends on the circumstances of the business, its purpose, the views of top management and its functions in accordance with the principle that 'form follows function'. One organisation could operate entirely on a decentralised basis with the maximum amount of autonomy devolved to strategic business units. Another could centralise some activities and decentralise others. A process-based approach may operate in one part of an organisation while elsewhere a more traditional 'line-and-staff' structure may be adopted. There is no one right way of organising. Organisation design is contingent on the situation.

EXERCISE 8.1

Charles Handy (1989) writes: 'It is the organisation's job to deliver; it is not its job to be everyone's alternative community, providing for all for life.'

To what extent do you agree or disagree with this statement, and why?

What type of structures might you find in the following organisations?

- a conglomerate owning a number of different but unrelated businesses
- a high-tech company in the defence industry with a strong research and development function and a computer-manufacturing system operated by technicians
- a company responsible for marketing a foreign car through a chain of distributors
- a national housing association delivering 'care' to people with learning difficulties in sheltered accommodation
- a brewing company managing a number of tied outlets
- an insurance company with a strong customer-focus
- a local authority
- a large comprehensive school
- a manufacturing company which produces a range of inter-related products that are marketed on the basis of quality and in which the key requirements are speed of response to customer requirements and effective after-sales service.

Consider your own organisation or one familiar to you. How would you describe it in terms of its type of structure?

ORGANISATION DESIGN

The process of organising may involve the grand design or re-design of the total structure, but most often it is concerned with the organisation of particular functions and activities and the basis upon which the relationships between them are managed. Organisations are not static things. Changes are constantly taking place in the business itself, in the environment in which the business operates, and in the people who work in the business. There is no such thing as an ideal organisation. The most that can be done is to optimise the processes in order to achieve the best 'fit' between the structure and the functions carried out in an ever-changing environment. This is one good reason why a flexible or decentralised approach is often desirable. It should also be borne in mind that although it may be possible to visualise an ideal structure, the organisation functions may have to be adjusted to fit the particular strengths and attributes of the people available – for changing and turbulent environments a flexible approach is desirable.

The approach to organisation design

Organisation design or re-design should be conducted in specific stages:

1. An analysis of the existing arrangements – their strengths and weaknesses in relation to the opportunities and threats facing the organisation.
2. A diagnosis of what needs to be done to improve the way in which the organisation functions.
3. A plan to implement any revisions to the structure emerging from the diagnosis, possibly in phases.
4. Implementation of the plan, bearing in mind that this may involve a major change management exercise as described in Chapter 16.
5. Evaluation of the impact of the reorganisation, and making adjustments as necessary.

Points to be covered

The things to do when designing or re-designing an organisation are:

- Identify the internal and external environmental factors which may influence the design.
- Clarify the overall purpose of the organisation.
- Define the key activities required to achieve that purpose.
- Group these activities logically together as units, teams, processes, taking into account interdependencies and the flow of work across the boundaries between possible groups.
- Define the role and function of each team, unit or process, paying particular attention to its relationship with other units so that the maximum amount of integration can be achieved.
- Decide on a management/team leader structure required to direct, co-ordinate and control activities in units or processes, and define who will be accountable for delivering results in each area.
- Define reporting relationships between managers/team leaders and the members of their teams.
- Design jobs and define roles to make the best use of the skills and capacities of those who will carry them out.
- Clarify with teams and individuals the results they are expected to achieve in terms of targets and standards of performance.
- Plan and implement organisational development activities to ensure that the various processes in the organisation operate in ways which contribute to organisational effectiveness.

Organisation guidelines

The original management theorists produced sets of principles of organisation they claimed were universally applicable. The best-known of these are 'unity of command' (no one should have more than one boss) and 'span of control' (no manager should control more than five or six subordinates whose jobs were different). Neither of these principles is wrong (having two bosses can create confusion, and too many people with different roles reporting to a manager can cause problems), but they are certainly not universally applicable. People can successfully report to both a line manager for their day-to-day activities and a functional manager for maintaining required standards and implementing company policies in their area. In today's de-layered organisations managers have to be responsible for much wider spans of control, which they achieve by delegation and empowerment and which is made easier by the ready availability of control information through computers.

There are, however, certain guidelines which are worth remembering, even if they should not be applied rigidly:

- differentiation and integration – Although it is necessary to differentiate between the different activities carried out, it is equally necessary to ensure that these activities are integrated and that the horizontal processes that cut across organisational processes are recognised and catered for
- teamwork – Jobs and roles should be described in ways which facilitate teamwork. Areas where co-operation between functions and individuals are important should be emphasised. Networking should be encouraged
- decentralisation – Authority to make decisions should be delegated as close to the scene of action as possible
- de-layering – Superficial layers of management or supervision should be removed to promote flexibility and responsiveness, give people more responsibility, facilitate better communication, and cut costs
- role clarification – People should be clear about their roles as individuals and members of teams.

EXERCISE 8.2

What are the things you would look for if you were asked to comment on the effectiveness of an organisation structure?

Mintzberg (1981) has commented that 'De-layering is the process of people who don't know how the organisation works getting rid of those who do.' What does he mean? Is there any validity in this opinion?

JOB DESIGN

Job design, or role definition, is the process of defining what activities are carried out by a job- or role-holder. Each activity consists of three elements: planning (deciding what to do, if there is any choice), executing (implementing the plan), and controlling (monitoring performance and progress and taking corrective action as necessary). A fully integrated role contains all these elements for each of the tasks involved.

Job design should define a job in such a way as to maximise the intrinsic motivation it provides (intrinsic motivation is the inspiration and encouragement provided by the work itself). These motivating characteristics are important:

- autonomy, discretion, self-control and responsibility
- variety
- the use of personal abilities
- feedback
- belief that the work is significant.

Overall, job design should consider the extent to which individuals can be 'empowered' by being given greater scope and responsibility for their work.

HOW TO DRAW UP AN ORGANISATION CHART

Organisation charts provide a generalised illustration of the allocation of work between functions and of formal reporting relationships. But they cannot convey the reality of how a business works. All they can do is indicate in very broad terms how activities are grouped together, who is responsible for what, and who reports to whom. They may indicate direct lines of control but they cannot illustrate the cross-functional lines of communication or the fact that although individuals may be supposed ostensibly to report to a manager, they may in practice spend much of their time working for or with other people in, for example, cross-functional project teams.

Notwithstanding these caveats, organisation charts are useful ways of summing up a structure and clarifying basic responsibilities and reporting relationships. To construct one you have to:

- Define who is responsible for groups of activities or a single set of related activities. These positions are placed in the boxes on the chart.
- Establish reporting relationships – the teams or individual positions which managers at the various levels direct, co-ordinate and control. These lines connect the various position boxes on the chart.
- Define any functional relationships between, for example, a plant personnel manager and the group personnel director. These are sometimes shown by a dotted line.
- Cross-reference positions to outline job descriptions or role definitions which set out in more detail what job-holders do.

EXERCISE 8.3

What are the limitations of a conventional organisation chart?

What purposes can it serve?

Draw up an organisation chart for your company or function, without reference to any existing chart.

HOW TO WRITE A JOB DESCRIPTION

Job descriptions (also known as 'accountability profiles' or 'role definitions') provide more detailed information on how organisations function. They also serve other important purposes: defining accountabilities for performance management, indicating the areas in which targets should be set, and providing the basis for competence analysis and employee development and job evaluation.

The aim should be to keep the job description short and simple – ideally on the classic one side of one sheet of paper. The days of elaborate descriptions that prescribe and describe every duty in great detail are gone.

The description should consist of three parts:

1   job purpose – a one-sentence definition of the overall purpose of the job – what it exists to do
2   reporting relationships – who the job-holder reports to and who reports to the job-holder
3   key result areas (also called 'principal accountabilities', 'main activities' or 'key tasks') – a description of the essence of the job in terms of the main areas in which the job-holder has to achieve results. There are normally no more than seven or eight key result areas in any job, however senior or complex it is. Each key result area or accountability should be described in one clause beginning with an active verb – 'plans', 'prepares', 'provides', 'despatches', etc. The object of the verb (what is done) is set out as briefly as possible: 'despatches planned output to the warehouse' (how it is done does not have to be described). Finally, the purpose of the activity is stated in terms of outputs or standards: 'despatches the warehouse planned output so that all items are removed by carrier within 24 hours of their being packed'.

AN EXAMPLE OF A JOB DESCRIPTION

Human resources manager

Job purpose
to provide advice and cost-effective HR services which enable the company to achieve its goals and meet its responsibilities to the people it employs

Reporting relationships
- reports to: plant manager
- reporting to role-holder: personnel officer, training officer, personal assistant

Key result areas
1   Advises on personnel strategies, policies and practices which support the achievement of the company's business objectives while fulfilling its obligations to employees.
2   Provides a recruitment and selection service to meet the company's needs.
3   Provides advice on all employment and health and safety matters, including issues arising in connection with employment legislation, to ensure that the company meets its legal and social obligations and avoids legal actions.

4 Develops and helps to maintain performance-management processes which are owned by line managers and employees, and makes a significant contribution to employee motivation, performance and development.

5 Plans and implements employee development programmes to meet identified needs, and satisfies the company's requirements for an effective and multi-skilled workforce.

6 Advises on reward management systems and the operation of the company's pay structure and performance pay schemes which obtain, retain and motivate employees.

7 Advises on employee relations issues and co-ordinates the company's involvement and communication processes in order to develop and maintain a co-operative and peaceful climate of employee relations in the company.

8 Develops and maintains an effective computerised personnel information system.

Job descriptions may be extended to become role definitions by listing the key competencies job holders have to possess in terms of their role.

ORGANISATIONAL DEVELOPMENT

Organisational development is concerned with the planning and implementation of programmes designed to improve the effectiveness with which an organisation functions and responds to change. The aim is to adopt a coherent approach which enhances the ways in which people carry out their work, especially in the ways in which they interact with others. The starting-point of an organisational development programme is an understanding of what constitutes organisational effectiveness. The next stages are analysis and diagnosis, followed by the design and implementation of organisational development programmes.

Organisational effectiveness

An effective organisation is one that achieves its purpose by meeting the needs and expectations of its stakeholders. The characteristics of an effective organisation include the following, as defined by Beckhard (1969):

- The organisation and its teams and individual contributors manage their work against goals and plans for the achievement of these goals.
- Form follows function – the activity, task or project determines how people are organised.
- Decisions are made by and near the source of information.
- Communication laterally and vertically is relatively undistorted. People are generally open and share relevant facts.
- There is a minimum amount of inappropriate win/lose activity between individuals and groups.
- There may be some clash of ideas about tasks and projects but relatively little over interpersonal difficulties because they have been worked through.

Analysis and diagnosis

The analysis of organisations from a developmental point of view can follow broadly the headings set out by Beckhard as listed above, with one additional point. The main questions to ask are:

- To what extent is the organisation goal-oriented, with clearly defined objectives that strongly influence plans and activities at all levels?
- Does the organisation structure properly reflect the nature of the work and the activities carried out? Are there any ambiguities? Has sufficient account been taken of the need for flexibility and the flow of processes across organisational boundaries?
- To what extent is decision-making devolved in the organisation close to the scene of action? How much authority have units and individuals got? Is it sufficient, too much, or too little? To what extent have teams and individuals been empowered to take responsibility?
- How effectively do communication flows work in the organisation – laterally as well as diagonally? To what extent are people open with one another, and to what extent do they share relevant information?
- How much unnecessary conflict is there in the organisation? Do people indulge in inappropriate win/lose activities? To what extent do politics and power-plays influence the way the organisation operates?
- How much interpersonal conflict is there? To what extent is there evidence that people work through differences of opinion?
- How effectively do team members work with one another? How well do teams co-operate with one another?

This analysis can be conducted by the processes of 'action research', which takes the form of collecting data from people about process issues such as those listed above. This can be carried on into a diagnostic phase by feeding reactions back to people to identify the likely causes of problems so that possible actions can be tested.

The diagnosis arising from the analysis can lead to various types of organisational development activities or programmes (sometimes called 'OD interventions') as summarised below.

Organisational development activities

Typical organisational development activities include:

- introducing new structures or processes
- working with teams on team development
- working on inter-group relationships, either in defining roles or resolving inter-group conflict
- change management programmes
- various learning activities to help people improve their personal or inter-personal skills.

EXERCISE 8.4

Jack Welch, chief executive officer of the General Electrical Company, has stated that he wants to achieve a 'boundaryless organisation'. What does he mean by this phrase, and why might it be important in a massive and successful manufacturing company?

A direct marketing organisation has two departments carrying out research into consumer preferences and choices. Internally, the operations research department analyses information about buying habits and trends from the database. Externally, the market research department conducts special projects to identify who customers are, what they prefer to buy, and what type of service they want. There is conflict between the needs of the two departments. Each of them claims that the other is encroaching on its territory and each believes that it should be entirely responsible for all internal and external research. They are both highly competent in their field and are delivering excellent information. How would you deal with this situation?

EXERCISE 8.5

The concepts and models of organisational structure have been outlined in this chapter. These provide the tools for us to analyse structure in a relatively systematic way, although of course there may well be arguments for different structural arrangements for a given situation. (So don't be surprised if you find that your structure is different from someone else's!)

Objectives for learners:
- to use the models and concepts of organisational structure covered in the chapter
- to create a feasible structure for a project in a case study situation
- to investigate possible tensions in the project structure they have identified

Read the case study below and answer the questions at the end.

Case study: education project

New product development (NPD)

You are the External Activities Manager for Sheerwater Business School, part of Grandpool University, reporting directly to the Head of School. The Business School offers a range of degrees and other qualifications. Whereas the majority of Business School income is generated from individual full- and part-time students who attend the Business School on conventional qualification routes, your job involves you in new 'product' development for companies and government bodies. In other words, you help create and sell various training and educational packages unique to particular companies or industries.

You rely upon the involvement of academic tutors drawn from across the subject disciplines at the University. These academic tutors are normally specialists in their own teams (eg Law, Human Resource Management, Operations Management) who work in the University teaching students on degree programmes; any work they do for you is thus additional to their normal workload, although they are paid a fee by the University for the additional work. This fee would cover development costs – ie cover time which they, as academic staff, spent in developing the training package; it would also be usual for the same staff to teach the training package and get a fee whenever they did this (this is regarded as the main incentive). However, team leaders still need to agree that their specialist tutors can work for you: team leaders tend to regard the Business School and the teaching of degrees as of prime importance and anything else, such as work for you, as secondary. Team leaders report to the Head of School.

You have recently been approached by the training director of a local hospital to establish a new training programme for some of their senior staff (senior nursing managers and specialist managers in charge of areas such as eye surgery, cancer care, the X-ray department, etc). The aim of this training programme is to deliver a mix of human resource management, law, operations management and computer skills. These are managerial and IT skills which have not traditionally been provided by the hospital's own trainers (training has been based upon providing specific skills in nursing, eye surgery, etc).

At the moment only these broad titles (eg 'Human Resource Management module') have been suggested, and there are no guidelines yet on possible training material content – but you do know that there will be four modules (Human Resource Management, Operations Management, Law, Computer Skills). In other words, you have an 'open page' as to what to include in the programme. However, you have been asked to somehow involve the hospital's own trainers in the development process to put your Business School's managerial and IT skills into a health context. Students will be assessed throughout the programme; this is something else you need to think about.

You have six months to get the programme up and running, but other than the initial contact with the hospital nothing has yet been done. Once you have established the programme and checked that it is running properly, the project – in terms of 'new product development' – is complete. The subsequent day-to-day running of the programme from then on is not your concern, although a requirement of the previous development process is that an operational structure is devised by you to facilitate this day-to-day running. The first thing you intend to do is create a development team for the new programme.

EXERCISE 8.5 QUESTIONS

Address the following tasks, stating clearly any assumptions that you make.

1 Who would you include in your (new product) development team? Why?
2 Draw up the subsequent *organisational structure* for the 'new product development' team, *as far as Business School staff are concerned*. Which of the structures covered in the chapter is the most similar to your structure?
3 How do you envisage the hospital trainers contributing to the development of the modules/programme? Show the hospital trainers on your previous structure in task 2 (you may have to be creative here!).
4 How do you envisage your development team operating in terms of procedures and decision-making?

SUMMARY

- Organisation structures define and clarify how required activities are grouped together, who is responsible to whom for what, and the lines of authority.
- Organisations function according to the situations in which they exist, with an increasing emphasis on flexibility and process.
- Organisations necessarily contain specialists, but they have to fit into teams.
- Autonomy is a desirable feature in organisations, but there are limits to the extent to which it can be granted to units, teams or individuals.
- The formal organisation is the structure defined in an organisation chart, but this creates and requires informal organisation – the network of relationships that make organisations work.
- Organisations may be:
  - unitary, with basic and very clearly defined boundaries
  - divisionalised, with discrete units or functions responsible for a range of associated activities
  - centralised or decentralised, with authority concentrated at the centre or devolved to a greater or lesser degree to strategic business units (SBUs)
  - matrix, with projects staffed by people drawn from different disciplines who are responsible to the project leader for their work on the project and also to the head of their discipline for employment, deployment and career development
  - process-based, with the focus on horizontal processes which cut across organisational boundaries
  - flexible, operating with a permanent core of key employees and a periphery of contract and temporary workers, or functioning as an 'ad hoc-racy' responding to particular demands as required.
- Organisation design will produce structures that are contingent on the circumstances and the environment of the organisation. The design process is concerned with identifying and grouping activities, defining who is responsible for what to whom, and establishing reporting relationships and lines of control.
- Job design is the process of deciding what activities should be carried out by a jobholder. It pays attention to the planning, executing and controlling aspects of the work, and how the job can be defined in a way which maximises intrinsic motivation.
- Organisation development is concerned with the analysis and diagnosis of the factors that determine organisational effectiveness, and the planning and delivery of programmes to increase that effectiveness.

REFERENCES

BARNARD C. (1938) *The Functions of an Executive*. Boston, MA, Harvard University Press.

BECKHARD R. (1969) *Organisation Development: Strategy and models*. Reading, MA, Addison-Wesley.

BURNS T. and STALKER G. (1961) *The Management of Innovation*. London, Tavistock.

CHANDLER A.D., HAGSTROM P. and SLOVELL O. (eds) 1999, *The Dynamic Firm: The role of technology, strategy, organizations and regions*. Oxford, Oxford University Press.

CHILD J. (1988) *Organisation: A guide to problems and practice*. London, Paul Chapman.

DIMANESCU D. (1995) *The Seamless Enterprise: Making cross-functional management work*. New York, Wiley.

FAYOL H. (1949) *Administration Industrielle et Générale*. Translated by C. Storrs as *General and Industrial Management*. London, Pitman.

GHOSHAL S. and BARTLETT C. A. (1995) 'Changing the role of top management: beyond structure to process', *Harvard Business Review*, January–February, pp86–96.

GOOLD M. and CAMPBELL A. (1986) *Strategies and Styles: The role of the centre in managing diversified corporations*. Oxford, Blackwell.

HANDY C. (1989) *The Age of Unreason*. London, Business Books.

LAWRENCE P. R. and LORSCH J. W. (1969) *Developing Organisations*. Reading, MA, Addison Wesley.

MAYLOR H. (1999) *Project Management*. London, Financial Times/ Pitman Publishing.

MINTZBERG H. (1981) 'Organisation design: fashion or fit', *Harvard Business Review*, January–February, pp103–16.

PASCALE R. (1990) *Managing on the Edge*. London, Viking.

SLOAN A. O. (1963) *My Years With General Motors*. New York, Doubleday.

TAYLOR F. W. (1911) *Principles of Scientific Management*. New York, Harper & Row.

TRIST E. L., HIGGIN G. W., MURRAY H. and POLLACK A. B. (1963) *Organisational Choice*. London, Tavistock.

URWICK F. L. (1947) *Dynamic Administration*. London, Pitman.

WEBER M. (1946) as cited in H. H. GERTH and C. W. MILLS (eds) *From Max Weber*. Oxford, Oxford University Press.

WOODWARD J. (1965) *Industrial Organisation*. Oxford, Oxford University Press.

Organisational communication | CHAPTER 9

INTRODUCTION

Organisational communications correspond to the various methods organisations use to inform employees about matters management believes to be important. Good organisational communications can be a valuable means of increasing commitment. Expect some degree of overlap between this chapter and Chapter 4, *Communication: how we inter-relate*. However, the emphasis in this chapter is on how communication is used in a workplace or organisational setting.

In this chapter we will be looking at the non-personal sections of the table we introduced in Chapter 4.

Table 9.1 *Intra- and inter-communication*

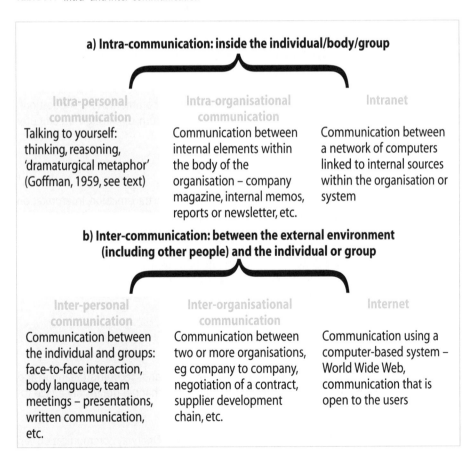

Learning outcomes

On completing this chapter, the reader will:

- recognise the need for communication
- be familiar with the nature of organisational communication
- recognise barriers to communication
- be aware of the various channels available.

THE NEED FOR ORGANISATIONAL COMMUNICATION

Organisations want to obtain the commitment of their employees. Managements would like people to identify with the goals and values of the organisation, to want to belong to it, and to work hard on its behalf. To develop a well-committed workforce it is necessary to create and maintain an effective system of two-way communications: from management to employees and back from employees to management. Management needs to explain its values and expectations. Employees need to have the chance to raise issues and questions directly with their managers without necessarily having to go through formal consultative channels.

The organisation in particular has to recognise that it functions by means of the collective action of people, yet each individual is capable of taking independent action which may not be in line with policy or organisational needs, or may not be reported properly to other people who ought to know about it. Good communication is required to achieve co-ordinated results.

Communication consists of the transmission of instructions, comments and suggestions, and the exchange of information in writing, by word of mouth or through a computer system.

The nature of organisational communication

Organisational communication is concerned with the creation, transmission, interpretation and use of information. The communication can be on a person-to-person basis, as when information is exchanged between people, a manager asks someone to do something, colleagues exchange information, or someone informs his or her manager that something has been done. Or it can be on a departmental/corporate basis, as when general instructions or pieces of information are passed down the line, and reactions, reports and comments float, more or less effectively, up again.

BARRIERS AND INFLUENCING FACTORS IN ORGANISATIONAL COMMUNICATION

Early models of communication talked in terms of 'encoding' and 'decoding' (Shannon and Weaver, 1949) messages which are sent via a communication 'channel' (for instance, face-to-face, telephone, written).

A television broadcast or a lecture may be said to be 'one-way'. One-way communication can be effective at conveying a lot of information efficiently and in an ordered format. However, its biggest problem is that the receiver does not have the facility to ask questions or ask for

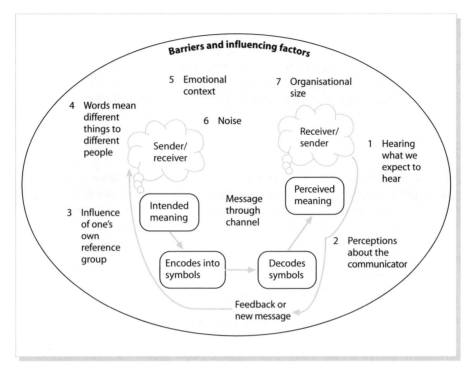

Figure 9.1 *Organisational communication: a model showing barriers to and influencing factors of communication*

points of clarification, nor to convey the acceptability or otherwise of the message. 'Two-way' or 'interaction' models overcome this problem by providing the facility for feedback from the 'receiver' to the 'sender'. Such models are somewhat mechanistic but they do allow for an appreciation of some of the variables. In reality, of course, we often act as both sender and receiver simultaneously, rather than sequentially (transaction models: Byers, 1997). For instance, even when you are delivering a presentation to an audience you are tuning in to their reaction to what you are saying, whether in their questions or their body language. For our purposes the model shown as Figure 9.1 depicts a feedback model of communication set in the context of the organisation and its typical barriers to communication. Each of these barriers is then discussed.

Barriers to communication

So many barriers exist to good communication that the constant cry in all organisations to the effect that communication is terrible is hardly to be wondered at – it is amazing that any undistorted messages ever get through. Some of the main barriers (shown in Figure 9.1 numbered 1 to 7) are summarised below.

1 Hearing what we expect to hear

What we hear or understand when someone speaks to us is largely based on our own experience and background. Instead of hearing what people tell us, we tend to hear what our minds tell us they have said. We all have preconceived ideas of what people mean – when we hear something new, we tend to relate it to something similar we have experienced in the past. When we receive a communication that is consistent with our own beliefs, we accept it as valid, seek additional information and remember accurately what we heard. But we tend to ignore or reject communications that conflict with our own beliefs. If they are not rejected, some way is found of twisting and shaping their meaning to fit our preconceptions. Communication often fails when it runs counter to other information that the recipient already possesses, whether that information is true or false.

2 Perceptions about the communicator

Recipients not only evaluate what they hear in terms of their own background, they also take the sender into account. Experience or prejudice may ascribe non-existent motives to the communicator. Some people see every collective action as a plot to get something done in an underhand way – the 'conspiracy theory' of organisational (or political) behaviour. Others look behind the message to read into it all sorts of motives different from those apparent on the surface.

3 Influence of one's own reference group

The group with which we identify – the reference group – influences our attitudes and feelings. 'Management' and 'the union' as well as our work group, family, ethnic set, political party and religious affiliation (if any) all constitute reference groups and colour our reactions to information. What each group hears depends on its own interests. Shared experiences and common frames of reference have more influence than messages containing information which conflicts with what employees already believe, from managers with whom they feel they have nothing in common.

An early example of a reference group in the work situation was the group of workers in the Bank Wiring Room experiments (1931–32) during the Hawthorne studies carried out by Elton Mayo, Fritz Roethlisberger and William Dickson. This group consisted of 14 men in total: three trios of workmen connecting wires in electrical assemblies, each overseen by a supervisor, plus two inspectors (for the entire group). Personalities within the group exerted a very powerful influence on the group's 'norms', in this case daily output (see management and organisational behaviour textbooks or read the original account given by Roethlisberger and Dickson, published 1939 and 1966) – to the extent that the men ignored incentives to work harder.

4 Words mean different things to different people

Words may have symbolic meanings for some people, with the result that they convey a quite different impression from the one intended. Profits, to management, for example, are a prerequisite for survival and growth: to employees, they may represent ill-gotten gains from keeping down pay or overpricing. Do not assume that something that has a certain meaning to you will convey the same meaning to someone else.

5 Emotional context

Our emotions colour our ability to convey or to receive the true message. When we are insecure or worried, what we hear and see seems more threatening than when we are secure and at peace with the world. When we are angry or depressed, we tend to reject out of hand what might otherwise seem like reasonable requests or good ideas. During arguments, many things can be said that are not understood or are badly distorted.

The work of Daniel Goleman (1996) looks in depth at how

'emotions play a far greater role in thought, decision-making and individual success than is commonly acknowledged'.

He considers the emotional part of the brain, the amygdala, and the thinking part of the brain, the neocortex, and shows how an overactive amygdala can cause problems as we become ruled by our emotions (recall Chapter 4 when we said that we should not make decisions based purely upon emotion). He explains that the brain is highly 'plastic' in young children and that a genetic predisposition to be (for instance) shy can often be overcome by appropriate exposure to situations where the child is encouraged to communicate with others. He states that the brain continues developing even until the mid- to late teens. The question we might ask ourselves is 'How does this help us, as post-teenage adults?' The answer he gives us is that that although old fears will still be triggered by certain stimuli (eg sight, sound, smell), we can learn to respond differently by using the neocortex, the thinking part of the brain (as in cognitive behavioural therapy), to overlay these emotions. The emotional response is less intense and our conscious thoughts and actions are more appropriate to the situation. The conclusion seems to be that it is never too late to improve our emotional response to events.

6 Noise

'Noise', in the sense of outside factors that interfere with the reception of the message, is an obvious barrier. It may be literal noise which prevents words from being heard, or figurative noise in the shape of distracting or confused information which distorts the message. The awkward forms in which messages are communicated – unclear syntax, unwieldy sentences full of long words – all help to produce noise.

7 Organisational size

The sheer size and complexity of modern organisations is one of the main barriers to communication. In the traditional hierarchical organisation messages have to penetrate layer upon layer of management or move between different functions, units, or locations. They thus become distorted or never arrive. Reliance is placed more on the written than the spoken word to get the message through, and this seriously restricts the effectiveness of the communication. Reducing this problem is, of course, one of the good reasons for de-layering an organisation, although cost considerations generally come first.

OVERCOMING BARRIERS TO COMMUNICATION

The overall implication of this formidable collection of barriers is that no one should assume that every message sent will be received in the form intended. But communications can be improved as suggested below, even if perfect understanding between people is impossible.

Adjusting to the world of the receiver

When you communicate, the tendency is to adjust to yourself. You have the need to say something and to say it in a particular way. But to get the message across, you have to adjust to your recipients. This means thinking ahead and trying to work out how they will grasp the message – understanding their needs and potential reactions. It also means using feedback and reinforcement techniques, as discussed later.

Using feedback

Feedback is the process of obtaining information on what has been happening in order to take action where necessary. In communications, feedback means ensuring that communicators get a message back from the recipient which tells them how much has been understood. This is why face-to-face communication is so much more effective than the written word, as long as the communication is truly two-way – in other words, when the recipients are given adequate opportunity to respond and react.

Using reinforcement

A message may have to be presented in a number of different ways to get it across. Good speakers know that if they can get more than three important ideas across in a 30-minute talk, they are lucky, and that they must repeat each idea at least three times in different ways to ensure that the message has been received and understood. In giving complicated directions it is wise to repeat them, perhaps in different ways, to guarantee successful transmission.

Using direct, simple language

This seems so obvious as to be hardly worth stating – but many people seem unable to express themselves clearly and without the use of jargon or an excessive number of adjectives, adverbs and sub-clauses.

Reinforcing words with actions

Communications are effective only if they are credible. If management says a thing, then it must mean it and do something about it. Next time it is more likely to be believed. The motto should be 'Suit the action to the words.'

Using different channels of communication

Some communications have to be in writing to get the message across promptly and without any danger of variations in the way it is delivered. But wherever possible, written communications should be supplemented by the spoken word. Conversely, an oral briefing should be reinforced by a written confirmation.

Reducing problems of size

Communication problems arising from organisational size can be reduced structurally by cutting down the number of levels of management, reducing spans of control, creating self-managed teams, generally ensuring that activities are grouped on the basis of ease of

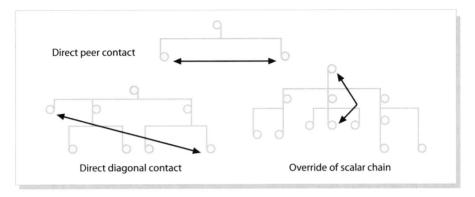

Figure 9.2 *Communicating outside the hierarchy (Mintzberg)*

intercommunication, and decentralising authority into smaller, self-contained (although accountable) units.

Sometimes people within the organisation deal with communication difficulties linked to organisational structure by communicating outside of the hierarchical reporting mechansisms (Mintzberg, 1979). See, for example, Figure 9.2.

COMMUNICATIONS STRATEGY

To achieve good results, communication should be seen as a strategic matter to be planned, developed and controlled on the basis of a full understanding of the requirements, problems and needs of everyone in the organisation.

The starting-point for the formulation of a communications strategy should be an analysis of the different types of communication with which it should be concerned. Communication studies embrace all human activities in an organisation, and the analysis must narrow the field down to well-defined areas in which action can be taken. The strategy should be based on analyses of:

- what management wants to say – Management usually aims to achieve three things: first, to get employees to understand and accept what management proposes to do in areas that affect them; second, to obtain the commitment of employees to the objectives, plans and values of the organisation; and third, to help employees to appreciate more clearly the contribution they can make to organisational success and how it will benefit them
- what employees want to hear – Employees want to hear about and to comment upon the matters that affect their interests. These will include changes in working methods and conditions, changes in the arrangements for overtime and shift-working, company plans which may affect pay or security, and changes in the terms and conditions of their employment.

The strategy will be concerned with the use of involvement processes, including team briefing and formal written communication systems, as examined in the next two sections.

Involvement

Employee-involvement processes such as consultative committees and team briefings provide important channels for two-way communication. Involvement can vary according to the level at which it takes place, the degree to which decision-making is shared, and the mechanisms of a greater or lesser degree of formality that are used.

Levels

Involvement can take place at the job level between team leaders and their teams. Processes at this level include the communication of information about work and the inter-change of ideas about how the work should be done; these processes are essentially informal.

At management level, involvement can entail sharing information and decision-making on issues that affect the way in which work is planned and carried out, and working arrange-ments and conditions.

At the policy-making level, where the direction in which the business is going is determined, total involvement would imply sharing the power to make key decisions. This is not much practised in the UK.

'Winning hearts and minds' is often referred to when considering a particular situation that is about to be subjected to change by senior management. Here, communication strategy must be coherent with the change strategy and indeed becomes an integral part of the change strategy. We will return to this area in Chapter 16 under *Future directions: managing change*.

Mechanisms for involvement

At the job level, involvement is usually informal. Teams are called together on an ad hoc basis to consider a particular problem or to digest and comment on new information. More formality can be injected by the use of a team briefing, as described below.

At the next higher level, more formality may be appropriate in larger organisations. There is scope for the use of consultative committees or departmental councils provided with defined terms of reference on the matters they can discuss.

At the enterprise level, company or works councils can be set up.

Team briefings

The concept of a team briefing (previously called a briefing group), as originally developed by the Industrial Society, is a device to overcome the restricted nature of joint consultative committees by involving everyone in an organisation, level by level, in face-to-face meetings to present, receive and discuss information. Team briefings aim to overcome the gaps and inadequacies of casual briefings by injecting some order into the system.

Team briefings operate by setting up groups at each level in the organisation. The subjects covered are:

- policies – explanations of new or changed policies
- plans – as they affect the organisation as a whole and as they affect the immediate group
- progress – how the organisation and the group is getting on
- people – new appointments, points about personnel matters (policies, pay, security, etc).

Team briefings work to a brief prepared by the board on key issues which is then cascaded down the organisation. The briefing meetings should, however, allow for discussion of the brief, and should also ensure that any reactions or comments are in turn fed back to the top. This provides for two-way communication.

FORMAL WRITTEN COMMUNICATION SYSTEMS

Formal communication systems use the written word as relayed in magazines, newsletters and bulletins and on notice-boards. The aim should be to make judicious use of a number of channels to make sure that the message gets across. These channels should be supplemented by direct spoken communications which can be structured in the form of team briefings (as described above).

Magazines

Glossy magazines or house journals are part of the organisation's intra-communication system, are an obvious way to keep employees informed about the company and are often used for public-relations purposes. They can extol and explain the achievements of the company and may thus help to increase identification and even loyalty. If employees are encouraged to contribute (although this may be difficult), the magazine may take on a more human face. The biggest danger in publishing this sort of magazine is that it becomes a public-relations exercise that is seen by employees as having little relevance to their everyday affairs.

Newsletters

Newsletters aim to appear more frequently and to angle their contents more towards the immediate concerns of employees than the glossier form of house magazine. To be effective they should include articles specifically aimed at explaining what management is planning to do and how this affects everyone. They can also include more chatty human-interest material about the doings of employees to capture the attention of readers. Correspondence columns can provide an avenue for the expression of employees' views and replies from management, but no attempt should be made to censor letters (except those that are purely abusive) or to pull any punches in reply. Anonymous letters should be published if the writer gives his or her name to the editor.

Bulletins

Bulletins can be used to give employees immediate information that cannot wait for the next issue of a newsletter. Or they can be a substitute for a formal publication if the company does not feel that the greater expense is justified. Bulletins are useful only if they are distributed quickly and are seen by all interested employees. They can simply be posted on notice-boards or, more effectively, given to individual employees and used as a starting-point for a briefing session if they contain information of sufficient interest to merit a face-to-face discussion.

Videos

Specially made videos can be a cost-effective method of getting personal messages across (eg from the chief executive) or relaying information about how the company is doing. They can, however, be regarded by employees as too slick to have any real personal impact.

Email (intranet and Internet)

Email has the advantage of being fast and giving efficient coverage to many readers. Documents may be attached which can give more detail. It is very good for dialogue between members. However, it lacks the impact of face-to-face meetings required for high-profile messages and discussion. Sacking people by email hits the headlines but for all the wrong reasons! It is also very easy to misuse in the heat of the moment and send a message which one later regrets. The recent display of government emails associated with the Hutton Inquiry (published 2004) investigating the circumstances surrounding the death of Dr David Kelly and the roles of the BBC and the government in the lead-up to the war in Iraq, has laid bare intimate thoughts very publicly and shown a 'treasure trove of documents that would not normally have seen the light of day for 30 years or more' (Douglas, 2003). As Hanney (2004) points out:

> **'Emails are seen as informal and immediate, rather like the phone. They're not seen as legal documents – but they are.'**

Also, the expectation is for a fast response, in tune with the ease of transmission. Email overload can also occur and important messages can be lost amongst a surfeit of unopened mail. Having said all of this, emails are now considered an indispensable part of office life.

Websites

Websites are now an essential method of disseminating information for any organisation, and a recent survey conducted in 2003 by Booz Allen Hamilton for the government's International Benchmarking Study used to assess the adoptions and application of information communication technologies found that '90 per cent of UK businesses access the Internet' (Chase, 2004). Through the use of passwords information can be available at various levels, from the employee to the general public. As Chase (2004) says:

> **'A website is, in effect, an organisation's shop window, setting out its wares – products and services – and at the same time communicating quite clearly somewhat less obvious messages about corporate values, market positioning, commitment to quality ...'**

Websites offer a highly versatile (depending upon the skill of the webmaster) source of information which can be linked to other sites and email addresses. Through the use of bulletin boards and chatrooms they can also offer interactive communication. However, a cautionary note is worth making here if we consider briefly the use of e-learning. Since the demise of the government's e-university – abandoned in 2004 (*BBC News*, 2004) due to a severe shortfall in the realisation of projected student numbers – the conclusion has been reached that many learners will not access courses if the only means of information is via the Web. The phrase now used to describe a more suitable approach (in general) is that of 'blended learning' in which the Web is only one of a number of channels used.

White (2004) talks of the many uses of the intranet and concludes that certain underlying requirements must be fulfilled. Employees need to be able to find the information they want; they need to trust it to be correct; and they need to know that it is current.

EXERCISE 9.1

Read the following case study and answer the questions that follow.

Case study: company takeover!

Enviricycle Ltd is a large company which specialises in the handling and recycling of industrial waste, from paper and plastics to used oils. Now in its tenth year of operations, the company has grown rapidly from its origins of supplying waste paper to a local mill to its present position – as one of the UK's leading players in the recycling industry. The company has grown through a policy of the aggressive acquisition of rival businesses and has a major presence in many of the North of England regions (Head Office is located in Newcastle) and is now seeking to expand into the 'M4 corridor' in the South of England and beyond.

Jamie Swift has been the Managing Director of Enviricycle from its earliest days; he is regarded as bold and with a keen eye for a good deal. By nature an apparently easygoing character with considerable charm, he is nevertheless somewhat autocratic at times – he did not get where he is today by being afraid to make tough decisions. Nothing if not adaptable, he senses that if his 'empire' is to continue to expand, he will need to keep all of its units focused and loyal to Enviricycle. At one time able to walk about his factories on a regular basis and chat to individuals whom he knew by name, he recognises that expansion has brought its own communication problems with it.

Six months ago, for instance, he bought out Partridge & Sons Ltd, a family-run business in Bristol. It was a medium-sized operation with two recycling plants in the Bristol area (Bristol North and Bristol South, each with 10 to 12 site operatives, between five and seven collection vehicles and its own office staff). However, the new acquisition is not performing as well as expected and Jamie has decided to pay a visit to the larger of the two sites – his first since the deal was done.

The first thing Jamie notices on his arrival is that the sign at the plant entrance still has the name 'Partridge & Sons Ltd', and so do the collection vehicles. 'Old Man Partridge' took the chance to retire after the takeover but his two sons, Julian and Barry, are site managers under the new regime. It is Barry whom Jamie is to meet today.

Jamie arrives promptly at the agreed time of 11 am, having driven down early from Newcastle with Steve Smith, Director of Finance. He is met by Wendy, Barry's secretary, who explains that Barry has had to rush off earlier in the morning to sort out a problem with an important customer but is 'due back any time now'. She makes him and Steve coffees.

Twenty minutes later, and still no Barry. Jamie asks to see Albert, the site foreman, and after a brief introduction by Wendy, the two go for a walk about the production plant, Jamie donning an old pair of overalls and boots which he keeps in his car. Unannounced, they tour the plant, with Albert explaining the operations and Jamie listening intently. He warms to Albert, who strikes him as a solid, trustworthy character. Albert explains that he has his own son and a niece (Wendy) who work for Partridges, a fairly common situation in the company. Albert apologises for the messy state of the production floor, hinting that since the takeover standards have slipped slightly because of the disruption. Jamie listens to Albert's views and ideas on running the plant but senses that Barry likes to do things his way without interference from his staff. Steve Smith in the meantime has been looking at the accounts with the site accountant (one of the old 'head office staff').

At 11.45 Barry arrives back at the site. He apologises for the 'brief but unavoidable delay' but hopes that Albert has given Jamie a useful site tour. Jamie, not best pleased, puts on a thin smile but says nothing. Barry then suggests that as it is about time for lunch that they carry on their conversation at a very good local restaurant which he has booked in advance.

'OK,' Jamie replies, '– but I'd like Albert to come along as well. He seems to know what goes on at the coalface!'

'Oh, I think he's pretty busy at the moment – and besides, he's hardly dressed for the occasion,' is Barry's immediate response.

Jamie is having none of it, and with the same thin smile as before says quietly but firmly, 'Barry, I want him to come along.'

And that is the last word on the matter. Lunch lasts for two hours, during which time they are joined by Nigel and Simon, who deal with transport and sales at Partridges. It is mid-afternoon by the time they all arrive back on site. Wendy makes them all more coffees. Barry explains how tough the market has been recently after prices for some of his products have been cut, but how he thinks they have 'turned the corner' – a claim of which Jamie is highly sceptical.

On the return journey to Newcastle in the car, Jamie and Steve discuss the situation. Steve points out that the wage rates are much higher than in the rest of Enviricycle and will have to be brought in line. He also queries the amount of business being generated by the sales staff and the cost of having a site accountant at each of the sites. Jamie agrees, and comments upon the the production staff who seem to be running operations in spite of the brothers' presence (or, as he suspects, the lack of it).

EXERCISE 9.1 QUESTIONS

What do you see as possible barriers to communication between:

- Jamie and Barry?
- Barry and Albert?
- Enviricycle Ltd's Head Office and the staff of the Bristol North and Bristol South sites?

How do you think Jamie could encourage better communication between Head Office and the Bristol sites?

SUMMARY

- Organisational communication corresponds to the various methods organisations use to inform employees of matters management believes to be important, together with the processes for obtaining the views of employees on matters that affect them. Communications are concerned with the creation, transmission and use of information.
- Barriers to communication include such personal effects as hearing only what we expect to hear, perceptions about the communicator, the influence of colleagues (the reference group), the fact that words mean different things to different people, the emotional context of the communication, and 'noise' (interference), as well as the size or complexity of the organisation.
- Overcoming barriers means adapting to the world of the recipient – using feedback, using reinforcement, using direct, simple language, reinforcing words with actions, using different channels of communication, and taking structural steps to reduce problems that arise from organisational size or complexity.
- To achieve good results, communication should be seen as a strategic matter to be planned, developed and controlled on the basis of a full understanding of the requirements, problems and needs of everyone in the organisation.
- Employee involvement processes such as consultative committees and team briefings provide important channels for two-way communication. Involvement can vary according to the level at which it takes place, the degree to which decision-making is shared, and the extent to which mechanisms of a greater or lesser degree of formality are used.
- Formal intra-organisational communication systems using the written word are represented by magazines, newsletters, bulletins and notice-boards, email and websites. The aim should be to make judicious use of a number of channels to make sure that the message gets across. Email in particular should be handled with care because it can be used as legal documentation.

REFERENCES

BBC NEWS, UK edition (2004) 'E-university's recruiting "abysmal"', [online] available from: http://news.bbc.co.uk/go/pr/fr/-/hi/education/3995295.stm

BYERS P. Y. (1997) *Organizational Communication: Theory and Behaviour*. Boston, MA, Allyn & Bacon.

CHASE E. (2004) 'Project managing website development', *British Journal of Administrative Management*, October–November, pp22–3.

DOUGLAS T. (2003) 'And lo, the Lord Hutton said: "Let there be light"', *Marketing Week* (UK), Vol. 26, Issue 27, p17.

GOLEMAN D. (1996) *Emotional Intelligence: Why it can matter more than IQ*. London, Bloomsbury.

HANNEY B. (2004) *Accountancy*, Vol. 133, Issue 1330, p45.

HUTTON J. B. E. (2004) *Report of the Inquiry into the Circumstances Surrounding the Death of Dr David Kelly C.M.G.* Address to the Honourable House of Commons dated 28 January 2004: available from http://www.the-hutton-inquiry.org.uk/content/report/huttonreport.pdf

MINTZBERG H. (1979) *The Structuring of Organizations*. London, Prentice Hall.

ROETHLISBERGER F. J. and DICKSON W. J. (1966) *Management and the Worker*. Cambridge, MA, Harvard University Press.

SHANNON C. and WEAVER W. (1949) *The Mathematical Theory of Communication*. Urbana, IL, University of Illinois Press.

WHITE M. (2004) 'Behind the firewall: does your intranet have a win-win strategy?', *EContent*, March, p41.

The living organisation: culture

CHAPTER 10

INTRODUCTION

The concept of organisational culture as described in this chapter is extremely important to managers because it explains much of what happens in organisations and provides guidance on what can be done to improve organisational effectiveness. The outsider who joins an organisation soon becomes acutely aware of 'how things are done around here' even when he/she has previously been employed in the same capacity by another organisation. Change industrial sector, and cultural differences in attitudes, behaviours and values can become even more diverse. Add to this the overarching concept of national culture and differences can, occasionally, become confusing and extreme. Attempting to understand culture is desirable because it aids managers' understanding. However, senior management may also wish to change, or at least influence, culture in the work situation. In particular, culture plays a key role in the management of change (see Chapter 16). Strategies to achieve this end are examined, even though their limitations are acknowledged. The process through which people become aware of and assimilate culture (known as 'socialisation') is another area that is covered in this chapter.

Learning outcomes

On completing this chapter, the reader will be familiar with:

- the concepts of organisational culture and organisational climate
- the significance to organisations of the concept of culture and how a culture develops
- the components of a culture
- approaches to the analysis and description of organisational culture and climate
- methods of supporting or of changing culture
- the impact of national cultural characteristics.

DEFINITION OF TERMS

Organisational culture

Organisational or corporate culture is the pattern of values, norms, beliefs, attitudes and assumptions which may or may not have been articulated but which shape the ways people behave and things get done. Values refer to what is believed to be important about how people and the organisation should behave. Norms are the unwritten rules of behaviour.

This definition emphasises that organisational culture is concerned with abstractions such as values and norms which pervade the whole or part of an organisation. They may not be defined, discussed or even consciously noticed. Nevertheless, culture can have a significant influence on people's behaviour.

Organisational climate

Organisational climate refers to how people perceive (see and feel about) the culture existing in their organisation.

Management style

Management style describes the way in which individual managers set about achieving results through people. It is how managers behave as team leaders and how they exercise authority. Managers can be autocratic or democratic, tough or soft, demanding or easy-going, directive or *laissez-faire*, distant or accessible, destructive or supportive, task-oriented or people-oriented, rigid or flexible, considerate or unfeeling, friendly or cold, keyed-up or relaxed. How they behave depends partly on themselves (their natural inclinations), partly on the example given to them by their managers, partly on the way in which they have been trained, and partly on organisational values and norms – accepted and typical ways of managerial behaviour.

THE SIGNIFICANCE OF CULTURE

The significance of culture is that it is rooted in deeply held beliefs. It reflects what has functioned well in the past, embodying responses which have been accepted because they have met with success.

Culture can work for an organisation by creating an environment that is conducive to performance improvement and the management of change. It can work against an organisation by erecting barriers that prevent the attainment of corporate strategies. These barriers include resistance to change and lack of commitment.

The impact of culture can be to

- convey a sense of identity and unity of purpose to members of the organisation
- facilitate the generating of commitment and 'mutuality'
- shape behaviour by providing guidance on what is expected.

Some organisations might already have a strong culture that they wish to retain; others might have cultures that are still embryonic. In both cases there will be a need to at least *maintain* if not *develop* these cultures. Some writers would argue that culture is extremely difficult to alter. Gareth Morgan in *Images of Organization* (1986) states:

'Managers can influence the evolution of culture by being aware of the symbolic consequences of their actions and by attempting to foster desired values, but they can never control culture in the sense that many management writers advocate.'

It is wise, therefore, to approach the influence which management can exert over culture in a realistic and careful fashion.

LEVELS OF CULTURE

One of the most influential writers on organisational culture has been Edgar Schein. If we now consider his definition (consistent with our previous definition), as given below, we see that he pays great attention to what he calls 'basic assumptions' and that culture is (Schein, 1985):

> **'a pattern of basic assumptions – invented, discovered, or developed by a given group as it learns to cope with its problems of external adaptation and internal integration – that has worked well enough to be considered valid and, therefore, to be taught to new members as the correct way to perceive, think, and feel in relation to those problems'.**

Schein views these 'basic assumptions' as the deepest level of culture. If we consider his model of culture we can see that culture has different levels, from the observable (which he calls 'artefacts') through to 'values' at a deeper level, to the taken-for-granted 'basic assumptions' – see Figure 10.1.

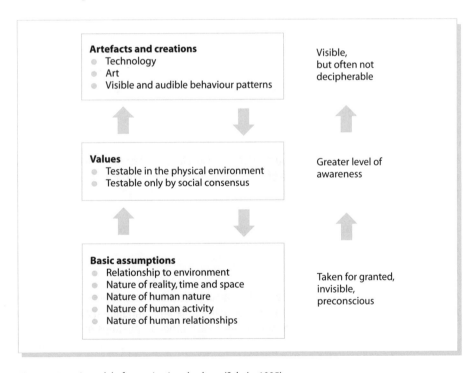

Figure 10.1 *A model of organisational culture (Schein, 1985)*

The next section expands on each of these elements.

COMPONENTS OF ORGANISATIONAL CULTURE

Values

Values reflect 'moral and ethical codes, and determine what people think ought to be done' (Brown, 1995). The 'value set' of an organisation may only be recognised at top level, or it may be shared throughout the business, in which case the business may be described as 'value-driven'. Beliefs 'concern what people think is and is not true' (Brown, 1995).

The stronger the values and beliefs, the more they influence behaviour. This does not depend upon their having been articulated. Implicit values which are deeply embedded in the culture of an organisation and are reinforced by the behaviour of management can be highly influential, whereas espoused values which are idealistic and are not reflected in managerial behaviour may have little or no effect.

Some of the areas in which values can most typically be expressed, implicitly or explicitly, are:

- performance
- competence
- competitiveness
- innovation
- quality
- customer service
- teamwork
- care and consideration for people
- ethical codes.

Values are translated into reality through norms and artefacts, as described below. They may also be expressed through the media of language (organisational jargon), rituals, stories and myths.

Artefacts and norms (Note: Schein talks of artefacts and creations – see fig 10.1)

Artefacts

Artefacts are the visible and tangible aspects of an organisation that people hear, see or feel. Artefacts can include: the working environment; the tone and language used in letters or memoranda; the manner in which people address each other at meetings or over the telephone; the welcome (or lack of welcome) given to visitors; and the way in which telephonists deal with outside calls.

Artefacts also include the manner in which people dress, company logos and mission statements. Some organisations also make obvious statements via the architecture of their offices and buildings. Stories that carry messages of the organisation's values are sometimes heard during coffee breaks or may be integrated into the historical overview of the company which new starters receive at their induction.

Norms

Norms are the unwritten rules of behaviour, the 'rules of the game' which provide informal guidelines on how to behave. Norms tell people what they are supposed to be doing, saying, believing, even wearing. They are never expressed in writing – if they were, they would be policies or procedures (themselves artefacts). They are passed on by word of mouth or by example and can be enforced by the reactions of people if they are violated. They can exert very powerful pressure on behaviour because of these reactions – we control others by the way we react to them.

Norms correspond to such aspects of behaviour as:

- how managers treat the members of their teams (management style) and how the team members relate to their managers
- the prevailing work ethic – eg 'work hard, play hard', 'come in early, stay late', 'if you cannot finish your work during business hours, you are obviously inefficient', 'look busy at all times', 'look relaxed at all times'
- status – how much importance is attached to it; the existence or lack of obvious status symbols
- how people dress (shirt and tie, for instance)
- ambition – in some organisations naked ambition is expected and approved of; elsewhere a more subtle approach is the norm
- performance – exacting performance standards are general; the highest praise that can be given in some organisations is to be referred to as 'very professional'
- power – recognised as a way of life; executed by political means, dependent on expertise and ability rather than position; concentrated at the top; shared at different levels in different parts of the organisation
- politics – rife throughout the organisation and treated as normal behaviour; not accepted as overt behaviour
- loyalty – expected, a cradle-to-grave approach to careers; discounted, the emphasis is on results and contribution in the short term
- anger – may be openly expressed; may be hidden, but expressed through other, possibly political, means
- approachability – managers are mostly expected to be approachable and visible; otherwise, everything happens behind closed doors
- formality – a cool, formal approach is the norm; forenames may or may not be used at all levels; there are unwritten but clearly understood rules about dress.

Basic assumptions

These are taken-for-granted truths – they are so deep as to be accepted without question. Because of this they are the least visible aspect of culture (and yet the essence of it, at least to those who have worked in the organisation for a number of years). To question such basic assumptions is to question the very fabric of the organisation. Take, for instance the nature of 'work'. Managers might have an inherent 'Theory X' style in which they treat employees as basically lazy individuals who have to be checked at every stage of the job and who only respond to a 'carrot and stick' approach of motivation.

Another basic assumption is the nature of time: closely linked to the prevailing national cultural characteristics of the team members is the sense of urgency and the meaning of language that indicates when something should occur. In some countries, for example, the word 'now' may mean 'immediately', or it may mean 'the next task which I will get around to doing'. It may be acceptable to be 30 minutes late for a meeting in one country but considered insulting in another.

(Geert Hofstede, in his well-known study of IBM managers (1980), discussed national cultural characteristics in terms of four variables: *masculinity/femininity* – a 'macho', directive managerial approach versus a nurturing, caring approach; *power distance* – the extent to which managers were allowed to interact with staff on an equal basis; *risk avoidance* – the level of risk that managers would accept; and *individualism/collectivism* – the extent to which the emphasis was on the individual or the group. We shall return to this later in the chapter.)

Then there is the 'nature of nature'. For instance, do we believe that, with our modern technology, we can permanently overcome the natural barriers that nature presents us with – perhaps by reclaiming a section of desert as fertile land? Or do we believe that, ultimately, we humans have little control over nature other than tinkering around the edges? Do we believe in living in harmony with the land and attempting to preserve it, or do we assume that it is a resource to use as we wish?

EXERCISE 10.1

Use Schein's framework of Artefacts, Values and Basic assumptions (see Figure 10.1 and text) to analyse your own organisation or one with which you are familiar.

HOW ORGANISATIONAL CULTURE DEVELOPS

The values and norms that are the basis of culture are formed in four ways. First, they are formed by the leaders in the organisation, especially those who have shaped them in the past. People identify with visionary leaders – how they behave and what they expect. They note what such leaders pay attention to and treat them as role models. Second, culture is formed around critical incidents – important events from which lessons are learned about desirable or undesirable behaviour. Third, culture develops from the need to maintain effective working relationships among organisation members, and this establishes values and expectations. Finally, culture is influenced by the organisation's environment. To a greater or lesser degree, the external environment may be dynamic, even turbulent, or it may be unchanging. Culture is learned over a period of time. Where a culture has developed over long periods of time and has become firmly embedded, it may be difficult to change quickly, if at all, unless a traumatic event occurs.

One model that has been used to show some of the above issues is that proposed by Richard Pascale (1985) which talks about 'socialisation' – a process that Schein (1968) defines as:

'the process by which a new member learns the value system, the norms, and the required behaviour patterns of the society, organisation, or group which he is entering'.

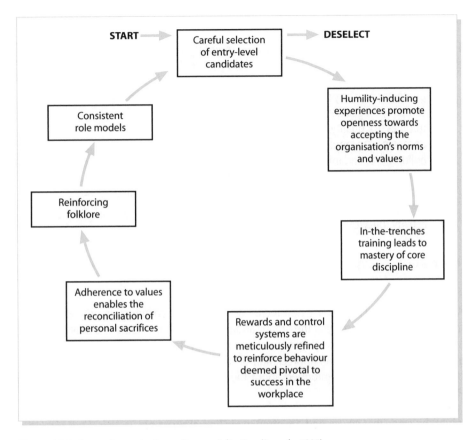

Figure 10.2 *Steps of organisation culture socialisation (Pascale, 1985)*

(Mintzberg uses the term 'indoctrination' to describe the process by which the organisation formally socialises its members for its own benefit.)

Richard Pascale's 'Steps of organisation culture socialisation' is shown in Figure 10.2.

The following section takes each of the elements of Pascale's framework and gives examples.

Selection of candidates

One of the ways to further or change the culture in an organisation is to select new recruits and promote existing staff who share similar values and basic beliefs to the idealised culture, as seen through the eyes of senior management. To some extent, an informal process of finding individuals who 'fit into' the organisation has traditionally been used, sometimes at the unconscious level, by many companies. In some cases this has focused on somewhat elitist requirements (eg membership of a certain school or college – the so-called 'old boy' network – or golf club) or, in others, a common social lifestyle to the cultural norm (such as heavy drinking at business lunches) or personal background. However, times move on. It is now fairly common for an organisation to consciously consider a list of competences from candidates which is consistent with its mission and goals. These competences include technical skills and qualifications but, perhaps more significantly, also desired behaviours and attitudes: thus, the requirement for 'team players', 'proactive attitude' and 'adaptability'.

Interviews and the selection process

The prospective candidate will observe the surrounding settings and gain an impression of the organisation through symbols such as (Gallagher *et al*, 1997):

- photographs (the product, aerial view of large site, 'team' and 'chairman')
- company magazines
- trophies (for quality/charity)
- decor (spartan/opulent)
- building size and importance
- building layout (open-plan/closed offices)
- quantity of personal computers and other high-tech equipment
- dress (formal/informal)
- activity (busy/quiet).

'Humility-inducing experiences'

Induction training

As part of the formal induction a new recruit will often go on an induction programme. This might include a brief history of the organisation, its founding members and their successes and failures, leading up through various critical incidents to where the company is today. It also gives the new recruit an appreciation of the sorts of expected and acceptable work behaviour. Recruits will be informed about the conditions of service and rules and regulations.

It is at this stage that newcomers are often made (more) aware of:

- stories – based on critical incidents, essentially truthful
- myths – exaggerated or distorted accounts of critical incidents; unproven beliefs (the 'Titanic' was supposed to be unsinkable)
- sagas – tales of epic struggles
- heroes – organisational figures who inspire
- written artefacts: slogans, logos, manuals.

Typical slogans include:

- *Just do it* – Nike (sports equipment specialist)
- *Trust is earned* – Berghaus (outdoor equipment specialist)

Typical logos include:

- Nike's well-known 'tick'
- Berghaus' blue- and red-banded inclined oblong.

In-the-trenches training

In-the-trenches training can be particularly effective at showing new recruits the ways in which to act and think (sometimes different from management ideas, in which case we might use the term 'sub-culture' to describe what is happening).

Table 10.1 *The effects of compliance versus non-compliance with cultural values*

Compliance with cultural values may lead to ...	Non-compliance may lead to ...
<ul><li>praise</li><li>a salary increase</li><li>promotion</li><li>keeping your job (!)</li><li>prestigious office, car, and other status symbols</li><li>being given interesting and challenging work</li></ul>	<ul><li>disciplinary action</li><li>a salary freeze</li><li>demotion, a sideways move</li><li>dismissal</li><li>loss of status symbols</li><li>being given too little, too much, or demeaning work</li></ul>

Adapted from Gallagher, Rose, McClelland, Reynolds and Tombs, *People in Organisations*, Blackwell, 1997

Again, some of the training might be 'humility-inducing' – sweeping the shopfloor, for instance. Such companies probably believe that it is important for their staff to appreciate even the menial tasks and to gain an appreciation of workplace feelings.

Rewards and control systems

A very critical way in which shared norms and values are communicated within the organisation is reward and control, as indicated in Table 10.1.

Reinforcing folklore and providing consistent role models

In time, those individuals who decide to accept the cultural norms of the organisation and who are prepared to make personal sacrifices by which they place the company ahead of their own interests, may well become role models for future recruits. They will become part of the stories and myths of the organisation – and they will have input as to who is selected as new recruits.

EXERCISE 10.2

Use the Pascale model of socialisation (see Figure 10.2 and text) to analyse how people learn the culture in your organisation or in one with which you are familiar.

THE DIVERSITY OF CULTURE

The development process described above may result in a culture which characterises the whole organisation. But there may be different cultures within organisations. For example, the culture of an outward-looking marketing department may be substantially different from that of an internally focused manufacturing function. There may be some common organisational values or norms, but in some respects cultures will differ between areas working in different environments.

Classifying organisational culture

There have been many attempts to develop culture typologies which can be used to analyse cultures as a basis for taking action to support or change them. Two of the best-known ones are Harrison's and Handy's.

Harrison (1972) categorised what he called 'organisation ideologies'. These are:

- *power-oriented* – competitive, responsive to personality rather than expertise
- *people-oriented* – consensual, rejecting management control
- *task-oriented* – with a focus on competency, dynamic
- *role-oriented* – with a focus on legality, legitimacy and bureaucracy.

Handy (1981) based his typology on Harrison's classification, although Handy prefers the word 'culture' to 'ideology' because 'culture' conveys more of the feeling of a pervasive way of life or set of norms. His four types of culture are:

- *the power culture* – one with a central power source which exercises control. There are few rules or procedures and the atmosphere is competitive, power-oriented and political
- *the role culture* – in which work is controlled by procedures and rules and the role, or job description, is more important than the person who fills it. Power is associated with positions, not people
- *the task culture* – in which the aim is to bring together the right people and let them get on with it. Influence is based more on expert power than on position or personal power. The culture is adaptable and teamwork is important
- *the person culture* – in which the individual is the central point. The organisation exists only to serve and assist the individuals in it.

In addition to referring to the typologies above, it is common practice to summarise the overriding characteristics of an organisation's culture in such terms as:

- *value-driven* – when the value set is put into practice as a way of life (operationalised)
- *customer-focused* – when the emphasis is on providing value for customers and customer-care programmes (see Chapter 15)
- *service-oriented* – when the focus is on service delivery and improving levels of service to customers or clients
- *high-performance* – when the focus is on achieving and sustaining high levels of performance in terms of profitability, output, productivity, innovation and quality: this might be expressed in the form of continuous improvement policies and processes (see Chapter 14)
- *high-involvement* – when management puts into practice involvement programmes which genuinely provide for employees to take part in decision-making processes on matters that affect them.

Assessing organisational culture

A number of instruments exist for assessing organisational culture. Assessment is not easy, because culture is concerned with both subjective beliefs and unconscious assumptions (which might be difficult to measure) and with observed phenomena such as behavioural norms and artefacts. One of the better-known instruments was developed by Harrison (1972). His questionnaire deals with the four orientations referred to earlier (power, role, task, self) and is completed by ranking statements according to what the respondent deems closest to the organisation's actual position. For example:

- A good boss is strong, decisive and firm but fair.
- A good subordinate is compliant, hard-working and loyal.
- People who do well in the organisation are shrewd and competitive, with a strong need for power.
- The basis of task assignment is the personal needs and judgements of those in authority.
- Decisions are made by people with the most knowledge and expertise about each problem.

Measuring organisational climate

Organisational climate measures attempt to assess organisations in terms of those dimensions that are thought to capture or describe perceptions of the organisation, its general operation and its culture. One of the best-known instruments was devised by Litwin and Stringer (1968) and takes account of the following specific dimensions:

- *structure* – feelings about constraints and freedom to act and the degree of formality or informality in the working atmosphere
- *responsibility* – the feeling of being trusted to carry out important work
- *risk* – the sense of riskiness and challenge in the job and in the organisation; the relative emphasis on taking calculated risks or playing it safe
- *warmth* – the existence of friendly and informal social groups
- *support* – the perceived helpfulness (or lack of it) of managers and co-workers; the emphasis (or lack of it) on mutual support
- *standards* – the perceived importance of implicit and explicit goals and performance standards; the emphasis on doing a good job; the challenge represented in personal and team goals
- *conflict* – the feeling that managers and other workers want to hear different opinions; the emphasis on getting problems out into the open rather than smoothing them over or ignoring them
- *identity* – the feeling that you belong to a company, that you are a valuable member of a working team.

APPROPRIATE CULTURES

It can be argued that a 'good' culture exerts a positive influence on organisational behaviour. It could help to create a 'high-performance' culture, one that will consistently produce a high level of business performance. As described by Furnham and Gunter (1993):

> **'a good culture is consistent in its components and shared amongst organisational members, and it makes the organisation unique, thus differentiating it from other organisations'.**

Nonetheless, a high-performance culture corresponds to little more than any culture that produces a high level of business performance. The attributes of cultures vary tremendously by context. The qualities of a high-performance culture for an established retail chain, a growing service business and a consumer products company that is losing market share may be very different. Further, in addition to context differences, all cultures evolve over time. Cultures which are 'good' in one set of circumstances or period of time may be dysfunctional in different circumstances or at different times.

Because the culture is developed and manifests itself in different ways in different organisations, it is not possible to say that one culture is better than another, only that it is dissimilar in certain ways. There is no such thing as an ideal culture, only an appropriate culture. This means that there can be no universal prescription for managing culture – although there are certain approaches that can be helpful, as described in the next section.

SUPPORTING AND CHANGING CULTURES

It may not be possible to define an ideal structure or to prescribe how it can be developed, but it is certain that embedded cultures exert considerable influence on organisational behaviour and therefore performance. If there is an appropriate and effective culture, it would be desirable to take steps to support or reinforce it. If the culture is inappropriate, attempts should be made to determine what must be changed and to develop and implement plans for change.

Culture analysis

In either case, the first step is to analyse the existing culture. This can be done through questionnaires, surveys and discussions in focus groups or workshops. It is often helpful to involve people of an organisation in analysing the outcome of surveys, getting them to produce a diagnosis of the cultural issues facing the organisation and to participate in the development and implementation of plans and programmes to deal with pertinent issues.

Culture support and reinforcement

Culture support and reinforcement programmes aim to preserve and underpin what is good and functional about the currrent culture by:

- reaffirming existing values through discussions and communications
- ensuring that values are put into practice (operationalising them)
- using the core values defined for the organisation (the value set) as headings for reviewing individual and team performance – emphasising that people are expected to uphold the values
- ensuring that induction procedures cover core values and explain how people are expected to achieve them

- reinforcing induction training with further training courses set up as part of a continuous development programme.

Culture change

In normal circumstances, cultural change programmes tend to focus on one or two particular areas which it is felt must be given priority. Such programmes rarely, if ever, try to cover every aspect of organisational culture. The areas might, for example, be performance, commitment, quality, customer service or teamwork. In each case the underpinning values have to be defined. It would probably be necessary to prioritise by deciding which areas need the most urgent attention. There is a limit to how much can be done at once. The effectiveness of culture change programmes largely depends on the quality of change management processes, as described in Chapter 16.

Levers for change

Having identified what must be done, and the priorities, the next step is to consider what levers for change exist and how they can be used. The levers might or might not include:

- performance – performance-related or competence-related pay schemes; performance-management processes; gainsharing; leadership training, skills development
- commitment – communication, participation and involvement programmes; developing a climate of co-operation and trust; clarifying the psychological contract
- quality – total quality programmes
- customer service – customer-care programmes
- teamwork – team-building; team performance management; team rewards
- values – gaining understanding, acceptance and commitment through involvement in defining values, performance-management processes and employee-development interventions.

THE IMPACT OF NATIONAL CULTURAL VARIATIONS

Geert Hofstede

We cannot ignore the fact that our values, beliefs and basic assumptions are heavily influenced by the society in which we live, and these will play a part in the organisation's culture. One of the key writers in this area is Geert Hofstede, whose early work in the 1980s considered a large number of managers working for IBM in different countries. Hofstede was able to distinguish the following dimensions along which people of different countries varied and could be measured:

- *power distance* – the psychological distance allowed between manager and staff members as a mutual expectation, measured from 'high' to 'low'
- *masculinity/femininity* – the extent to which actions are dominant and aggressive versus caring and sharing
- *risk* or *uncertainty avoidance* – linked to the amount of risk people are prepared to accept
- *individualism versus collectivism* – the extent to which people behave as individuals or groups.

EXERCISE 10.3

Use Hofstede's four dimenions to analyse typical differences between two national cultures of your own choice.

Fons Trompenaars

Fons Trompenaars (1999) talks of the need for managers who interact with different (national) cultures to be what he calls 'trans-culturally competent'. At the heart of this is the requirement of the manager to *reconcile* the differences between the cultures. Those who can reconcile, he argues, get better performance. He uses the following seven dimensions in comparing cultural differences:

1   Universalism versus particularism (Do you value rules applicable to all, or do you value relationships and loyalty?)
2   Individualism versus communitarianism (Me or the group?)
3   Specific versus diffuse (Are you superficially or deeply involved in relationships?)
4   Neutrality versus affectivity (Do you conceal or show your emotions?)
5   Inner-directed versus outer-directed (Do you feel that you control your environment or that your environment controls you?)
6   Achieved status versus ascribed status (Is your status derived from what you do or who you are?)
7   Sequential time versus synchronic time (Do you do things one after the other or several things at once?)

Sometimes differences can appear irreconcilable, especially if particular parties have very polarised views. Such an example of this would be mirrored by the statement 'If you're not for us, you're against us!'

Trompenaars would argue that we must take account of each other's cultural values, while not abandoning our own, so that we arrive at a situation that ideally satisfies both – although he is keen to point out that this should not be a compromise.

As an example, take the case of the National Health Service and the employment of doctors and nurses from India, the Philippines and South Africa. There is clearly a need for NHS managers to reconcile differences in the cultures of their overseas and British staff. Individual overseas workers themselves also need to reconcile these differences if they are going to be effective in the work situation. For instance, the British are in general fairly reserved about showing their feelings whereas someone from overseas might be quite demonstrative.

EXERCISE 10.4

Read through the following case study, noting that there are quite a few sections of background information of various kinds before the actual case commences.

Once you have read through all the data, answer the questions at the end.

Case study: socialisation

This case study raises some interesting and controversial points on the socialisation process. There is much here which concerns organisational culture, but there are also reminders of the social and political contexts in which site engineer Tom Smith has now come to work. With many organisations currently working internationally in countries that have value systems different from our own, it is important for us to be aware of national cultural differences. This may not always be an easy task, not least if it involves squaring ethical with business considerations: organisations and individuals must make their own decisions in this respect.

This particular case has been chosen because it is situated in a context which the majority of readers probably have some background information on, and because it allows for wide variation in cultural factors. It is also still fairly fresh in the minds of many people as a topical subject for debate. However, please note that there is no endorsement here, intentionally or otherwise, of the former apartheid political regime in South Africa.

The case to be studied is set in South Africa in the early 1980s when the apartheid system of racial segregation was still in force. *Apartheid* or 'apartness' was a political doctrine established in 1948 and carried further when South Africa became a republic (free of British influence) in 1961. It essentially enabled the white minority to govern the country while employing black workers from ostensibly black-controlled areas known collectively as the 'homelands' within South Africa (although other countries did not accept the 'homelands' concept). Behind the scenes during the late 1980s there was an ongoing secret dialogue between certain key members of the South African government (who had realised the unsustainability of their contemporary practices) and the outlawed ANC party (*South Africa Yearbook*, 1996) which was eventually to lead to the release from imprisonment of Nelson Mandela in 1990 and the establishment of the present democratic system of government. This transition was remarkably smooth, bearing in mind the latent hostilities on all sides.

There are various ethnic groups involved in this case study: black people from the Xhosa, Sotho, Tswana, Zulu and other tribes; Afrikaans-speaking white South Africans who held sway in government and the police force; English-speaking white South Africans who tended to be located in the coastal towns of Cape Town and Durban, and who by tradition held more liberal views; and expatriates from various countries, most notably the UK. Figure 10.3 shows the languages spoken in South Africa at about the time of the case study, thus indicating both the diversity of cultures and the relative sizes of the various factions, black and white.

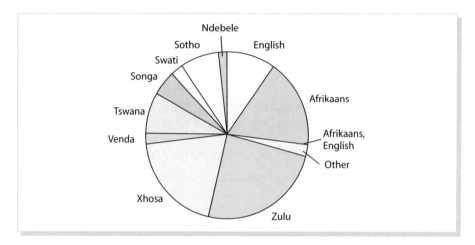

Figure 10.3 *Languages spoken in South Africa in the early 1980s*
Source: population census 1991

Since 1820 and the first great influx of British settlers in South Africa there had been tensions between the British and the Afrikaners (whom the British termed 'Boers' – simply the
Afrikaans word for 'farmers'). The Afrikaners were determined to free themselves from British
rule. This resulted initially in the Great Trek of 1836–38, when the Boers ventured into the
unknown interior and away from the British coastline in search of their own land, and later
in the (Anglo-)Boer War 1899–1902. There was also inevitable conflict between the
Afrikaners and the black tribes of the interior during the Great Trek. And there was a cen-
turies-old history of inter-tribal conflict between the various black tribes themselves. There
were also the Zulu Wars 1876–81 between the British and the Zulu peoples. Conflicts after
this time were largely political but no less influential. Add to this heady mix the discovery of
diamonds and gold during the same period, and you have a highly volatile context.

The case

The year was 1982; the place a steel town called Vanderbijlpark, some 100 kilometres south
of Johannesburg in the Republic of South Africa. Tom Smith had been recruited from Britain
the previous year as a site engineer to work for Scott & Anderson, a major construction
company. He reported to the site agent, Ron Murray, a veteran construction boss. He worked
alongside two foremen, one an old fiery Scot called Sam Munroe (who sported an
impressive chest scar from his recent heart by-pass operation) and the other an amiable
Yorkshireman, George Bell. In fact, Munroe was a drinking buddy of Murray's, and the two
had worked on the same projects for a number of years and now even shared the same
office. Both Munroe and Bell had a team of 15 or so workers whose job it was to fix steel or
pour concrete; every one of these workers had been hired from the Xhosa, Tswana or Sotho
peoples, the local black tribes.

But Tom Smith was not with any of them just now. He looked out from his vantage point
high on a partly constructed platform through the tangle of smoke and steam clouds rising
slowly from the cooling towers and pipework of the steelworks, and felt surges of rage
surface once more. Munroe was well and truly out of line this time! It was just as well,
though, to have walked away from the situation in order to give his anger time to subside
rather than lashing out physically at the man – in his state that might have been fatal.

Figure 10.4 *Organisation structure on site*

Perhaps, thought Tom, he was in the wrong job. Or maybe the wrong place. He didn't really know. He thought over everything that had happened in the last year.

It hadn't been an easy job to get. There had been the job interviews, of course, but there was the added complication that he'd had to apply for immigration status and a residency permit, and a further interview with the immigration people. At the job interview it seemed that what was being sought was not just a paper qualification; they seemed impressed that he had driven a Caterpillar bulldozer.

Attracted both by the job and the tourist brochures depicting superb scenery, the wildness of the mountains and the seemingly perpetual sunshine, Tom – a keen climber in his spare time – had been quite naïve when he first arrived. There was no doubting that South Africa was the most important African state in the Southern hemisphere and it appeared to offer a Westernised style of living. Little was the average citizen to know that within 10 years the entire political situation would be radically changed as Nelson Mandela was swept into power. But for now, the old apartheid regime of control by the white government remained in place, although occasionally the system appeared to be challenged and there was the feeling that one day, maybe sooner maybe later, something would happen.

He hated having to get up early for the 7 am starts and the occasional late finishes, but that was the price to pay in this job. It was no good leaving a concrete pour half finished! He liked to take pride in his work and would push himself and his foremen to hit targets. If only the steel and concrete gangs would show the same enthusiasm! For them there was always tomorrow. This was a hard lesson to learn. They were paid poorly although they lived in hostels provided by the company. Once a month they all went back to their 'homelands' with their monthly pay. This too was frustrating for Tom, because it meant that the workforce was down in numbers the following week awaiting their return. Sometimes he picked up on the simmering tensions of the political situation: the violence occurring in both homeland and township as evidenced by the demeanour of the workforce: the unspoken question of when apartheid would end, and of its manner.

He thought of Ron Murray, the site agent who was his boss. Ron had been in his position 10 years ago and was now successful. In many ways Tom admired him and knew he could ask him for advice. Ron was strict, a company man through and through, and tough, but someone he still felt he could trust. He could still remember the feelings of embarrassment, tinged with a hint of suddenly realised status, when Ron had introduced him for the first time to the workers as 'Boss Tom'. He acquired a 'chain boy' to carry his theodolite and measuring tapes.

He knew that if he completed projects on time and to budget he would get his own company vehicle. Later, he might move on to a more prestigious project. In the meantime he had to be careful. There was the well-known story of the engineer who had measured a set of positioning bolts incorrectly which had delayed the installation of a steel tower – he had been sacked. Other engineers he knew had rebelled against the strictness of the company system by taking liberties. One used to come to work on a Saturday and make private international calls on the office telephone. One had driven off in a company pick-up and simply dumped it at the airport and flown off home to the UK.

Engineers from overseas had to sink or swim in their new environment. They were expected to pick up the peculiarities of the job as they went about their business. Not all survived. It was a fact of life that few commented upon. Of course, they had all been given the 'big guy/little guy' pep-talk on arrival by the general manager, Piet Kopje, a huge bear of a man, an Afrikaans-speaking South African – a man whose name was mentioned in hushed tones if he was in the vicinity. They'd all had the grand site tour with Kopje and the not-so-coded warnings to obey the rules on apartheid, which included no liaisons with black women (a prosecutable offence) or else they'd be on the next flight home!

Living in their own (much better) hostels the engineers met socially, although on site they worked as individuals. This was in marked contrast to the workers who seemed to do (or not do, as Tom saw it) everything together and who shared a keen sense of humour – for instance, having nicknames for all of the site staff.

So why was Tom standing on top of that steel platform, slowly fuming? Well, he'd made a mistake in the positioning of a set of concrete bases. That wasn't the real problem, though. The real problem was that his foreman Munroe had sworn at him in front of the concrete team and thus caused him to 'lose face'.

EXERCISE 10.4 QUESTIONS

Using Pascale's model of socialisation (see Figure 10.2), analyse how Tom Smith has learned about and the extent to which he has adopted the organisational culture of his new company, Scott & Anderson, over the last year.

The case study gives some clues on national cultural characteristics (albeit as viewed from Tom's viewpoint only). Use Geert Hofstede's four dimensions and Fons Trompenaars' seven dimensions to further analyse the key players in the case.

Do you think that it is inevitable that someone in Tom Smith's position will be influenced in their values?

EXERCISE 10.5: FURTHER WORK

Do you think that it is only after the event that we can properly reflect (as a 'reflective practitioner') upon our experiences and arrive at some form of realistic evaluation?

Nelson Mandela has rightly been hailed as a remarkable man whose calls for restraint following his election as President enabled the relatively calm and successful transition of political ideologies to take place during the early 1990s. To what extent do you think this was due to his ability to reconcile the differences in cultural values, in particular between the Afrikaner and various black South African peoples?

SUMMARY

- Organisational culture consists of the beliefs, values, attitudes, ways of behaving and assumptions which pervade an organisation and strongly influence how the organisation functions.
- The concept is important because it can make a significant impact on the effectiveness of the organisation and because anything that is done to introduce change must take it into account.
- Culture support and reinforcement programmes aim to preserve and underpin what is good and functional about the current culture by reaffirming and operationalising values.
- Culture change programmes aim to develop more appropriate cultures by the application of 'levers for change' performance-management and performance pay systems and total quality and customer-care processes.
- National cultural characteristics can overlay the cultural values of the organisation and must be taken into account. Managers who are 'trans-culturally competent' can 'reconcile' apparent differences in cultural approach, and this ability is consistent with improved performance.

REFERENCES

BROWN A. (1995) *Organisational Culture*. London, Pitman.

FURNHAM A. and GUNTER B. (1993) *Corporate Assessment*. London, Routledge & Kegan Paul.

GALLAGHER K., ROSE E., MCCLELLAND B., REYNOLDS J. and TOMBS S. (1997) *People in Organisations: An active learning approach*. Oxford, Blackwell Business.

HANDY C. (1981) *Understanding Organisations*. Harmondsworth, Penguin.

HARRISON R. (1972) 'Understanding your organization's character', *Harvard Business Review*, 5, pp119–28.

HOFSTEDE G. (1980) *Culture's Consequences: International differences in work-related values*. London, Sage.

LITWIN G. H. and STRINGER R. A. (1968) *Motivation and Organisational Climate*. Boston, MA, Harvard University Press.

MINTZBERG H. (1973) *The Nature of Managerial Work*. New York, Harper & Row.

MINTZBERG H. (1979) *The Structuring of Organizations*. London, Prentice Hall.

MORGAN G. (1986) *Images of Organization*. London, Sage, p139.

PASCALE R. (1985) 'The paradox of corporate culture: reconciling ourselves to socialization', copyright by the Regents of the University of California. Reprinted from the *California Management Review*, Vol. 27, No. 2, Winter, p38, as cited in F. Luthans (1989; 5th edition), *Organizational Behaviour*. McGraw-Hill.

SCHEIN E. (1985) *Organizational Culture and Leadership: A dynamic view*. San Francisco, Jossey-Bass.

SCHEIN E.H. (1968) 'Organizational Socialization and the Profession of Management', *Industrial Management Review*, Winter, pp1–16.

South Africa Yearbook 1996 (1996; 3rd edition) Pretoria, South African Communication Service.

TROMPENAARS F. (1999) 'Cultured performers', *People Management*, Vol. 5, No. 8, pp30–7.

Power and politics

CHAPTER 11

INTRODUCTION

Formal organisation structures as described in Chapter 8 may define the framework for getting things done, but the ways in which people behave in their roles – the processes of exercising power and authority, acting politically, and, inevitably, conflicting with others – affect how things get done.

This chapter serves to introduce the reader to the concepts of power and politics. Conflict, which has close ties with these factors, is then discussed, followed by strategies for handling conflict. The reader should note that power and politics occupy a central position in the management of change, and that further critical discussion of these issues is featured in the final chapter, *Future directions: Managing change*.

Learning outcomes

On completing this chapter, a reader will understand how these various processes operate and how they affect organisational behaviour, and in particular will be able to:

- outline the definitions of authority, power, politics and conflict
- critically discuss key elements of power and politics
- analyse conflict situations and use the Thomas model of conflict resolution.

AUTHORITY

Authority is defined by the *Oxford English Dictionary* as the 'power or right to enforce obedience'. This rather fierce definition could be modified to read: 'Authority is the process of exerting influence on others in order to get things done.' This is sometimes referred to as the 'authority to command'.

Such influence can be achieved by the exercise of power or by more subtle means. According to the classical school of management theorists, such as Fayol (1949), organisations achieve order and regularity by the use of authority implemented through a defined hierarchy or chain of command. This 'command and control' approach to the use of authority is regarded with distaste by most recent writers on organisation. Handy (1989) advocates the development of a 'culture of consent' in which the emphasis is on the virtues of decentralisation, empowerment and self-managed teams.

But organisations do contain 'regularly occurring features which help to shape their members' behaviour' (Child, 1988), and one of these features is the use of authority. Ultimately, organisations exist to get things done, and this will involve exercising authority, although that may take place in the form of management by agreement rather than management by control.

Authority can be structured – vested in the role of manager – or it may be based on expertise or personal charisma. There is also moral authority exercised on the basis of the 'rightness' of the action because it is ethical, fair or equitable. It is possible to distinguish, as Cooper (1965) does, between authority exercised by people with expertise who are respected as such and authority based simply on position. Cooper coined the phrase 'authentic authority' which corresponds to a form of control that is not exercised by dominating others. It differs from power in the sense that people will respond willingly to authentic authority based on expertise (a culture of consent), whereas power requires compliance even if they disagree.

Leaders exercise authority, but only in Handy's (1989) sense:

> **'A leader shapes and shares a vision which gives point to the work of others . . . The vision remains a dream without the work of others. A leader with no followers is a voice in the wilderness.'**

Handy describes what he calls 'a post-heroic leader' as one who

> **'asks how every problem can be solved in a way that develops other people's capacity to handle it'.**

The term 'authority' also refers to the right to make decisions or take action (authority to act), and this right may be authorised by a more senior manager (authority to authorise).

POWER

Jay (1967) commented that:

> **'Power lies in the acceptance of your authority by others – their knowledge that if they try to resist you, they will fail and you will succeed.'**

Power is the capacity to impress the dominance of one's goals or values on others. Four different types of power have been identified by French and Raven (1959):

- *reward power* – derived from the belief of individuals that compliance brings rewards; the ability to distribute rewards contributes considerably to an executive's power
- *coercive power* – stemming from a conviction that non-compliance will bring punishment
- *expert power* – exercised by people who are popular or admired and with whom the less powerful can identify
- *legitimised power* – power conferred by position in an organisation.

Cyert and March (1963) developed a behavioural view of the firm as a coalition of individuals who are, in turn, members of sub-coalitions, each with different goals. There will, however, be a dominant coalition which will use power to impose its goals in the organisation.

Foucault, who wrote and spoke extensively about the concept of power, described it as ubiquitous and comprehensive (Foucault, 1981):

> **'Power is a machine in which everyone is caught, those who exercise it just as much as those over whom it is exercised.'**

He regarded the disciplinary drive as being particularly widely spread in bourgeois society (one of its great inventions), as exemplified by the control of the daily activities of workers. But Foucault did not always think of power as negative (although his views on this subject varied):

> **'We must cease once and for all to describe the effects of power in negative terms: it "excludes", it "represses", it "censors", it "abstracts", it "masks", it "conceals". In fact, power produces; it produces reality; it produces domains of object and rituals of truth. The individual and the knowledge that may be gained of him [sic] belong to this production.'**

Foucault also pointed out the intimate connection between knowledge and power:

> **'To know something is to create a new power relationship.'**

Exercising power responsibly

The responsible use of power occurs when managers do their best not to coerce people into taking action against their will. If something has to be done because it has been ordered by higher authority or because there is a crisis, such managers at least explain why the action is necessary, and request and listen to suggestions about the method of proceeding. When these conditions do not exist, power is exercised responsibly wherever a 'culture of consent' is nurtured. This is when a manager gets people involved in discussing courses of action and work methods. It also means that the manager takes steps to 'empower' people. Empowering is the process of giving people more scope (or 'power') to exercise control over, and take responsibility for, their work. The manager thus devolves authority, delegating more, and allowing individuals and teams more scope to plan, to act independently, and to monitor their own performance.

POLITICS

Power and politics are inextricably mixed, and in any organisation there will inevitably be people who want to achieve satisfaction by acquiring power, legitimately or illegitimately. They may do this by 'playing politics'. Political behaviour in organisations involves finding out who has the decision-making power and how decisions are made so that influence – which is often hidden – can be exerted without going through normal channels. Political behaviour in organisations has been described by Kakabadse (1983) as

'a process, that of influencing individuals and groups of people to your own point of view, where you cannot rely on authority'.

To be 'politic', according to the *Oxford English Dictionary*, you should be sagacious, prudent, judicious, expedient, scheming or crafty. So by this definition political behaviour in an organisation might be either desirable or undesirable. But it is the 'expedient', 'scheming' and 'crafty' aspects of political behaviour that makes it suspect even when it is widespread.

A political approach on the part of a manager means that he or she is aware of where power is based in the organisation, who are members of the dominant coalition, who holds the power, and who makes the key decisions. Organisational politicians know that such decisions are often made behind closed doors or by a coterie of people who are in the know and are in positions of power and influence. They know whom they should influence – and the best way to do so.

The essence of political behaviour is that it is not open behaviour. It is discreet. Organisational politicians exert hidden influence to get their way. They are 'politically sensitive' – they are aware of what is going on behind the scenes, who is a rising star, whose reputation is fading, and the less obvious factors that are likely to affect decisions. They use that knowledge to make things happen their way by exerting influence in the right quarter. Organisational politicians do not 'go through channels': they intrigue, they form factions, they go behind people's backs, they lobby (although sounding out opinion is often desirable before plunging into a proposal).

Put like this, political behaviour sounds unethical. But some organisations are webs of political intrigue – and in others, progress cannot be made unless the political climate within the organisation is understood and people act in the light of that understanding. It may be quite justifiable to sound out opinion and to line up support (to do a bit of lobbying) if you are about to launch what may be a contentious proposal at a meeting. Political systems exist and managers may find themselves having to operate within those systems.

But political behaviour can be subversive, divisive and counterproductive. It can create a climate of intrigue in which decisions are no longer visible and where people with more political nous do better than the straightforward organisational citizens who are simply and openly doing a good job. However, in the real world in which managers live, it is at least necessary to appreciate that decision-making in organisations is not always as transparent as it might be. Political sensitivity in this case means knowing 'how things are done around here', knowing how decisions are made, knowing who makes the running – and bearing all this in mind when faced with situations in which proposals have to be made or actions taken.

Organisations consist of individuals who, while they are ostensibly there to achieve a common purpose, are at the same time driven by their own needs to achieve their own goals. Effective management is the process of harmonising individual endeavour and ambition to the common good. Some individuals genuinely believe that using political means to achieve their goals will benefit the organisation as well as themselves. Yet others unashamedly pursue their own ends.

It can be argued that a political approach to management is inevitable and even desirable in an organisation in which the clarity of goals is not absolute, where the decision-making process is not clear-cut and where the authority to make decisions is not evenly or appropriately distributed. There can be few organisations in which one or more of these conditions do not apply. In this sense, it could be argued that a political approach can be legitimate as long as the ends are justifiable from the viewpoint of the organisation. But organisational politicians can subvert the proper ways in which decisions should be made, where the emphasis is on transparency and public accountability.

EXERCISE 11.1

Can you think of any circumstances in which political behaviour would be appropriate in an organisation?

What can go wrong if politics are rife in an organisation?

What is meant by 'political sensitivity'? Is it a quality that is worth developing? If so, how can it be developed?

CONFLICT

Conflict takes place in organisations because organisations function by means of adjustments and compromises among competitive elements in their structure and membership. People's views often conflict. If they hold them strongly, the result can be two kinds of conflict: horizontal between functions, departments, groups and individuals, and vertical between different levels in the hierarchy.

Conflict also arises when there is change, because change may be seen as a threat to be challenged or resisted. Or conflict can arise when there is frustration – this may produce an aggressive reaction: fight rather than flight. Conflict should not always be deplored. It is an inevitable result of progress and change. It would be strange if everyone's views in an organisation coincided. Conflict can and should be used constructively to bring issues out into the open and, through discussion, to arrive at a better solution or course of action.

Conflict between individuals raises fewer problems than conflict between groups. Individuals can act independently and resolve their differences. Members of groups may have to accept the norms, goals and values of their group. An individual's loyalty will usually be to his or her own group if it is in conflict with others.

Resolving conflict

As Mary Parker Follett (1924) wrote, there is the possibility that conflict can be creative if an integrative approach is used to settle it. This means clarifying priorities, policies and roles, using agreed procedures to deal with grievances and disputes, bringing differences of interpretation out into the open, and achieving consensus through a solution which recognises the interests of both parties – a win/win process. Resolving conflict by the sheer exercise of power (win/lose) will tend to lead to further conflict. Resolving conflict by compromise may lead to both parties being dissatisfied (lose/lose).

Most writers would argue that the best method of handling conflict is to adopt a problem-solving (collaboration) approach by:

- getting agreement on what the problem is
- jointly analysing the causes of the conflict
- identifying alternative means of dealing with the issue
- jointly evaluating the merits of each alternative from the perspectives of both parties
- working through the alternatives to find the one closest to meeting the needs of everyone concerned
- agreeing on how the preferred solution can be implemented to the satisfaction of both parties.

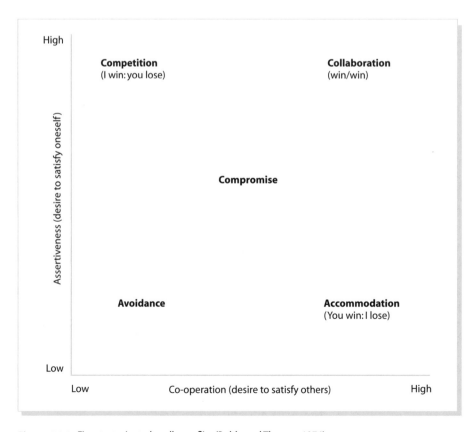

Figure 11.1 *Five strategies to handle conflict (Ruble and Thomas, 1976)*

However, we should note that there are other strategies for handling conflict, and Ruble and Thomas (1976) outline five strategies, as shown in Figure 11.1.

Verma (1996) takes a pragmatic view of using competition, avoidance, compromise and accommodation and collaboration which has elements of a contingency approach. He advocates using competition:

- when you think you're right
- in an emergency
- when you are more powerful.

He suggests that avoidance may be used to:

- gain more time
- give the problem time to solve itself
- maintain neutrality.

Accommodation may be used, he says:

- to 'maintain the peace'
- to build up favours
- when the outcome is not important to you.

Compromise, he declares, can be used for a temporary fix or as part of a negotiation strategy when you cannot win. Finally, collaboration is suggested for gaining long-term commitment from the other side and achieving synergy. This approach is probably more realistic than expecting collaboration as an outcome for all situations. It illustrates, for instance, the fact that repeated demands of a child to a parent will often (rightly or wrongly!) lead to capitulation (ie accommodation) on the part of the parent. Also, we might sometimes use more than one strategy – perhaps using avoidance as a stalling strategy before using one of the other strategies. And of course there is sometimes a tendency to try collaboration or compromise first before resorting to competition!

EXERCISE 11.2

Read the case study below and answer the questions at the end.

Case study: Helene

Zoë McGreal is the recently appointed marketing director for Godiva Beauty Products Ltd. Degree-educated (Marketing and French at Strathclyde University) and fresh from her previous post as assistant marketing manager to a baby-care manufacturer, she is still only 29. In the past Godiva has concentrated its product range on moisturising lotions and creams under the Dermiplex label designed to 'rejuvenate sagging and tired skin', as the sales blurb says. The company has enjoyed a degree of success with these but has recently been the subject of scrutiny from animal rights activists after a local newspaper revealed that the Dermiplex range had been initially tested on animals.

Zoë strongly believes that the future for Godiva Beauty Products lies in products that are made from natural ingredients, not tested on animals. She has thought of a name for the new product range – Helene (after Helen of Troy, famed for her beauty) – which will feature a soap, facial scrub, shampoo and aromatherapy oils.

Of course she is aware that this is no longer an unthought-of 'niche' market (Body Shop, in particular, is already well known) and is aware that she will have a tough fight on her hands to convince her own company to agree to her plans. However, she is adamant that this is the direction for the company to take. Already she is tired of those in the company's management who are afraid to 'move with the times' and feels passionately that the time to get into the 'natural market' is 'now or never'. In fact, she feels so strongly that she is prepared to resign if the board turns her down. (She has another job lined up as a fall-back.)

Deep down she feels that her role as marketing manager means that she *must* be the catalyst for new products, and she tries to communicate an appropriate self-image by always appearing buzzing with energy and wearing 'sharp' business suits.

Zoë has gained approval from Mr Giles Dermot, the managing director, to give a presentation of her ideas at the next monthly boardroom meeting. It had been Dermot's idea to recruit a university-trained 'ideas' person to replace the previous director who was leaving to join a rival company. Dermot is an entrepreneur who likes jetting off to arrange deals with buyers and suppliers. He was not 'business school educated' but rose to his present position by sheer drive and ambition. Initially, he had been quick to praise McGreal in her every effort, but Dermot's attention has been waning the more he wades through her detailed reports. She found that approval to present her latest ideas was not easy to obtain, for Mr Dermot is a busy man. Zoë made an appointment to speak to him but, as usual, Mr Dermot was behind schedule and was busily putting various papers into his briefcase prior to leaving for the airport when Zoë was beckoned in by the secretary. Zoë tried to quickly explain the whole business of 'Helene'. Mr Dermot, busy now searching for something or other in his desk, scarcely looked up, only acknowledging Zoë's idea with the occasional grunt. Zoë felt frustrated, thinking that Mr Dermot was not listening, but she persisted anyway. Wanting to complete his packing, Mr Dermot muttered 'Yes, McGreal. Put it on the agenda – see Norma on the way out. See you at the meeting.'

Zoë had indeed seen Norma (Mr Dermot's PA, now in her late forties) whom she got on well with. Zoë felt she could always ask for advice from Norma – someone who could give impartial advice about the workings of the organisation and to whom she could talk openly without feeling that any of her weaknesses might be revealed to others.

Zoë persuaded Norma to include a paper headed 'Natural products: the way forward?' to accompany her presentation, which was listed as item number 2 on the meeting agenda. This paper firstly showed how profits appeared to have stagnated at a moderate level, and secondly introduced the field of natural beauty products for future product portfolio consideration. All board members had now received this information, and with the monthly meeting only a week away, Zoë was already receiving nods of approval … and threats of some opposition.

Alan Fresh, the product testing and improvements manager, is tired of the standard work his department is carrying out and is enthusiastic about technical research into a new type of product. Zoë feels a natural rapport with Alan – he has been with the company for three years, is likewise a graduate of Strathclyde University, although four years her senior, and has a positive, outgoing attitude which she likes. Zoë agrees with Alan that there must be close links between marketing and product testing and the whole idea needs careful planning. They have already had quite a long discussion over Zoë's new ideas and have agreed to meet for breakfast at the local Post House Hotel on the day of the main board meeting so as to – in Zoë's words – 'discuss last-minute tactics'.

The finance director, Donald McTavish, likes the idea of an environmentally friendly product but has said privately that he would favour a two-phase introduction of the product to, firstly, manufacturing plant 'A', to be followed in due course by plant 'B' once the new product has demonstrated its ability to sell.

The production director, Alec Smallfield, the longest-serving of the present directors (15 years), on the other hand, is opposed to the idea to the point of being visibly hostile (at first sniggering at her ideas in the presence of others), and has pointed out to Zoë over the telephone that neither his staff nor his two manufacturing units were set up to manufacture the proposed range. Indeed, in a recent telephone conversation on the subject, Alec's voice seemed to become louder the more she talked, and at one point she thought she heard him bang the desk, as he is known to do sometimes. This particular conversation ended abruptly either because they were cut off or, as Zoë suspects, because Alec banged the phone down in a rage. Questioned later, Alec blamed the telephone system. Alec is a 'production man' to the core, and prides himself on having achieved great efficiencies with Dermiplex over the years. He dismisses the idea of what he calls a 'well tried and tested product being ousted by some politically correct fad!' Lately, Zoë has had the feeling that Alec is trying to avoid her since he always seems to be leaving as she enters the coffee lounge whereas previously he seemed to virtually live there.

Zoë believes that although difficulties do exist in manufacturing Helene, they are not insurmountable. However, she is aware that if Helene was adopted and placed in one of the manufacturing units, some sort of expansion of the site would be necessary because her intentions are to manufacture on a large scale. This could be carried out within a timescale of about four months if planning permission is granted quickly. Her initial enquiries have revealed that local residents feel that the present manufacturing plants detract from the neighbourhood and affect their house prices; the old plants do look somewhat dated and 'industrial' but Zoë hopes that new-style units will persuade residents that expansion will be to their advantage.

If her strategy receives company backing, Zoë will have to sell the idea to major stores and pharmacies because the company does not have its own retail sales outlets. However, final approval will only come from the customer!

It will be important to launch the Helene range at the most auspicious time. Zoë has decided that an ideal launch date would be immediately after a nationally publicised day of action by the animal rights activists AHF2! ('Animals have feelings too!') It will therefore be essential to have the first of the product range available and in the stores by this date, and to have all of the publicity sorted out well in advance.

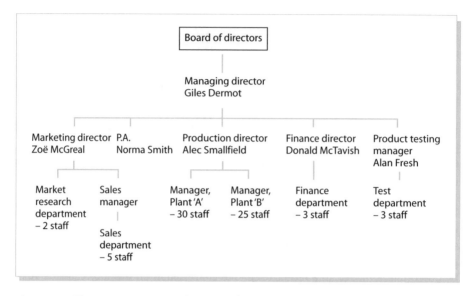

Figure 11.2 *The current organisational structure of Godiva Beauty Products Ltd*

EXERCISE 11.2 QUESTIONS

Analyse the case study and build a case for the power which each of the named characters possesses. Note: because power is relationship-oriented you will have to compare characters against each other.

Consider the case for applying each one of Thomas's conflict strategies of competition, avoidance, compromise, accommodation and collaboration (Figure 11.1), as seen from Zoë 's point of view in her relationship with Alec Smallfield.

SUMMARY

- Authority is the process of exerting influence on others in order to get things done.
- Authority can be exercised by means of a 'command and control' approach. But writers such as Charles Handy advocate the development of a 'culture of consent' in which the emphasis is on the virtues of decentralisation, empowerment and self-managed teams.
- Authority can be structured – vested in the role of manager – or it may be based on expertise or personal charisma. There is also moral authority exercised on the basis of the 'rightness' of the action because it is ethical, fair or equitable.
- In Cooper's phrase, 'authentic authority' is not exercised through dominating others. It differs from 'power' in the sense that people will respond willingly to authentic authority based on expertise (a culture of consent), whereas power demands compliance even if disagreed with.
- Power is the capacity to impress the dominance of one's goals or values on others. The four different types of power have been identified by French and Raven as reward power, coercive power, expert power, and legitimised power.
- Politics is described by Kakabadse as 'a process, that of influencing individuals and groups of people to your own point of view, where you cannot rely on authority'.

- A political approach means that managers (and others) are aware of where power is based in the organisation: who are members of the dominant coalition, who holds the power, who makes the key decisions.
- The essence of political behaviour is that it is not open behaviour. It is discreet. Organisational politicians exert hidden influence to get their way.
- Conflict is inevitable. It takes place in organisations because they function by means of adjustments and compromises among competitive elements in their structure and membership.
- The best method of handling conflict is to adopt a problem-solving approach which involves getting agreement on what the problem is, jointly analysing the causes of the conflict, identifying and evaluating alternative means of dealing with the issue to find the one that is closest to meeting the needs of everyone concerned, and agreeing on how the preferred solution can be implemented to the satisfaction of both parties.

REFERENCES

CHILD J. (1988) *Organisation: A guide to problems and practice.* London, Paul Chapman.

COOPER D. (1965) 'The anti-hospital: an experiment In psychiatry', *New Society*, March, pp4–6.

CYERT R. M. and MARCH J. G. (1963) *A Behavioural View of the Firm.* Englewood Cliffs, NJ, Prentice Hall.

FAYOL H. (1949) *General and Industrial Administration.* London, Pitman.

FOLLETT M. P. (1924) *Creative Experience.* London, Pitman.

FOUCAULT M. (1981) *Power/knowledge: Selected interviews and other writings.* Brighton, The Harvester Press.

FRENCH J. R. and RAVEN B. (1959) 'The basis of social power', in CARTWRIGHT D. (ed.)(1959) *Studies in Social Power.* Ann Arbor, MI, Institute for Social Research.

HANDY C. (1989) *The Age of Unreason.* London, Business Books.

JAY A. (1967) *Management and Machiavelli.* London, Hodder & Stoughton.

KAKABADSE A. (1983) *The Politics of Management.* Aldershot, Gower.

RUBLE T. and THOMAS K. (1976) 'Two-dimensional model of conflict behaviour', *Organisational Behaviour and Human Performance*, Vol. 16, p145.

VERMA K. (1996) *Human Resource Skills for the Project Manager* (*The Human Aspects of Project Management*, Vol. 2). Project Management Institute.

CHAPTER 12

INTRODUCTION

Mention the words 'health and safety' in some organisations and the response is one of indifference by employees and the paying of lip-service by managers. Too often it is a function carried out by people who are ignorant of their own responsibilities and who fail to appreciate its positive and negative impacts upon their working and personal lives. It is something that the prudent (rather than the ethical) organisation will assign to a Health and Safety Officer who is at best tolerated and at worst sidelined in the company. Health and safety in such organisations is synomonous with unnessary cost, time and effort.

Yet let us consider some of the facts. Despite improvements in the statistics issued by the Health and Safety Executive, some 226 people were killed at work in 2002–3, 28,000 people suffered major injuries, and 33 million days were lost to ill health. Upon further investigation we find that in 2002–3 there were 3,880 injuries to workers falling from a height, of which 49 were fatal (HSC, *Delivering Health and Safety in Great Britain*); 733 workers were struck by moving vehicles, 39 fatally; 1.1 million people suffered from work-related musculo-skeletal disorders (WRMSD) either caused or made worse by their work, with 240,000 new cases and a loss of 12.3 million working days; 'slips and trips' accounted for 37 per cent of major industry accidents and are the most common cause of injuries in UK workplaces (HSC 2002–3); and work-related stress is the second most common cause of occupational health (after WRMSD, to which there are links), leading to both physical and mental disorders.

The achievement of a healthy and safe place of work and the elimination to the maximum extent possible of hazards to health and safety are the responsibility of everyone employed in an organisation, including those working there under contract. But the onus is on management to achieve and, indeed, go beyond the high standard in health and safety matters required by the legislation – the Health and Safety at Work (etc) Act 1974, the Management of Health and Safety at Work Regulations (1992, updated 1999) and the various regulations laid down in the Codes of Practice.

The importance of healthy and safe policies and practices is, sadly, often under-estimated by those concerned with managing businesses and by individual managers within those businesses. But it cannot be emphasised too strongly that the prevention of accidents and elimination of health and safety hazards are a prime responsibility of management and managers in order to minimise suffering and loss.

This chapter offers an introductory awareness of some key health and safety issues; it gives an overview of some of the advice and legislation currently in force. It will not in itself give you sufficient information to carry out your own health and safety activities – however, the articles and websites should serve as good starting-off points for your own self-development and should enable you to contact qualified practitioners and organisations in the health and safety field.

Learning outcomes

At the end of this chapter the reader should have a basic understanding of:

- the importance of health and safety in the workplace
- the basic legislative requirements concerning health and safety at work
- the use of health and safety codes of practice
- the importance and content of health and safety policies
- methods of conducting risk assessments, safety audits and inspections
- methods of minimising health hazards (occupational health procedures) and pre-venting accidents
- how to investigate accidents
- methods of measuring health and safety performance
- how to promote healthy and safe working practices through communications and training, and the approach that can be used to advise a group of staff on the import-ance of health and safety in the workplace
- who is responsible for health and safety
- how to respond to contradictions between health and safety requirements and organisational constraints.

THE IMPORTANCE OF HEALTH AND SAFETY IN THE WORKPLACE

The achievement of the highest standards of health and safety in the workplace is important because:

- The elimination, or at least minimisation, of health and safety hazards and risks is the moral as well as the legal responsibility of employers – this is the overriding reason.
- Ill-health and injuries resulting from the system of work or from working conditions cause suffering and loss to individuals and their dependants.
- Accidents and absences through ill-health or injuries result in losses and damage to the organisation: this 'business' reason is much, much less significant than the 'human' reasons given above but remains a consideration, albeit a tangential one.

EXERCISE 12.1

What importance is attached to health and safety matters in your organisation, and for what reason? Is the level of importance satisfactory – and if not, why not?

The role of the Health and Safety Executive (HSE) and the Health and Safety Commission (HSC)

The HSC and the HSE were established in conjunction with the Health and Safety at Work (etc) Act 1974 (HASWA) and play a major role. The following definitions of the HSC and HSE are both taken from the Health and Safety Commission's document *Delivering Health and Safety in Great Britain* (2003):

'The HSC is a body of ten people, appointed by the Secretary of State for Works and Pensions for the administration of the HSWA. The HSC's primary function is to make arrangements to secure the health, safety and welfare of people at work and the general public. This work includes proposing new laws and standards, conducting research and providing information and advice....

The HSE is a body of three people which advises and assist the Commission in its functions. Together with local authorities, it also has day-to-day responsibility for enforcing health and safety law, investigating accidents, licensing and approving standards in particularly hazardous areas and commissioning research. The Executive has staff of around 4,050 – collectively known as the HSE – which includes inspectors, policy advisers, technologists and scientific and medical experts.'

Legislative requirements

The Health and Safety at Work (etc) Act 1974

This Act sets out the basic duties of an employer:

- to install a safe working system
- to provide safe premises, a safe working environment and safe equipment
- to employ trained and competent people
- to give proper instruction and supervision to ensure that healthy and safe systems and conditions of work are achieved.

The duties of employers apply not only to their full-time workers but also to part-timers, trainees, casual workers and subcontractors. They apply to anyone allowed to use the employers' equipment or visit their premises, and extend to anyone affected by what the employer does – for example, neighbours or members of the public and those who use the products of the organisation or the services it provides.

Employers who employ five or more people are required to set out written statements of their health and safety policy and the arrangements they have in force to further the intentions of the policy. They have to consult with their employees on measures for promoting health and safety, which implies discussing the contents of the policy with them before it is published. Annual reports of companies registered under the Companies Act are required to include presented information about accidents and occupational diseases suffered by the company's employees and about preventive measures taken by the companies.

The Act additionally lays down that it is the duty of employees to observe the legal health and safety provisions and to act with due care for themselves and others.

Regulations

A number of major regulations came into force during the 1990s. The six 1992 regulations – sometimes known as the 'six-pack' – were introduced to implement the European Framework Directive and its five associated directives in Great Britain.

The 'six-pack' regulations were:

- the Management of Health and Safety at Work Regulations 1992 (updated 1999) – These established a structured approach to the management of health and safety at work. They placed a specific legal duty on employers to carry out detailed risk assessments, as well as strengthening safety representatives' consultative rights
- the Health and Safety (Display Screen Equipment) Regulations 1992 (updated by minor amendments 2002 [SI 2002 No. 2174]) – These provide for eye tests and training for regular users of display screen equipment
- the Manual Handling Operations Regulations 1992 – These require employees to avoid hazardous manual handling operations wherever possible.
- the Personal Protective Equipment at Work Regulations 1992 – These set out comprehensive requirements on the provision of personal protective equipment.
- the Provision and Use of Work Equipment Regulations 1992 (updated 1998) – These cover the selection, suitability and maintenance of all equipment in the workplace
- the Workplace (Health, Safety and Welfare) Regulations 1992 – These set out minimum standards for cleanliness, ventilation, temperature, lighting and maintenance.

In addition, the Control of Substances Hazardous to Health (COSHH) Regulations (first introduced in 1988, now the Control of Substances Hazardous to Health 2002, amendments 2003 [SI 2003 No. 798]) make further provision for the health and safety of employees who work with dangerous substances.

Keeping up to date

As an aside we can note the regularity with which health and safety regulations are subject to change. It is essential to keep up to date in these matters. Tolley's *Yearbooks* (see *References*) provide an excellent means of keeping up to date with most recent changes. Another excellent method is to subscribe to Croner's, which offers regular updates thoughout the year as new changes are introduced.

Codes of Practice

Codes of Practice have been produced by the Health and Safety Executive (HSE) concerned with the implementation of the key regulations. They offer sound advice and information developed through the experience of the HSE field staff or gained from other professional bodies and organisations. They should be considered carefully when developing and introducing health and safety policies and procedures and when conducting risk assessments, safety audits and accident investigations.

HEALTH AND SAFETY POLICIES

Written health and safety policies are required to demonstrate that top management is concerned about the protection of the organisation's employees from hazards at work and to indicate how this protection will be provided. Such written policies are, therefore, first a declaration of intent, second a definition of the means by which that intent will be realised, and third a statement of the guidelines which should be followed by everyone concerned – which means all workers – in implementing the policy.

The policy statement should consist of three parts:

- the overall statement of policy
- a description of the facilities and the personnel provided by the organisation for health and safety
- details of arrangements for implementing the policy by means of those facilities and personnel.

The overall policy statement

The overall policy statement should be a declaration of the intention of the employer to safeguard the health and safety of employees. It should emphasise four fundamental points:

- that the safety of employees and the public is of paramount importance
- that safety takes precedence over expediency
- that every effort will be made to involve all managers, team leaders and employees in the development and implementation of health and safety procedures
- that health and safety legislation will be complied with in the spirit as well as the letter of the law.

EXERCISE 12.2

Obtain a copy of a relevant HSE Code of Practice. To what extent do the practices of your organisation in this area conform to the code?

Provisions by the organisation

This section of the policy statement should describe the health and safety arrangements of the company through which high standards are set and (hopefully) achieved by people at all levels in the organisation. It should underline the ultimate responsibility of top management for the health and safety performance of the organisation. It should then indicate how key management personnel may be held accountable for performance in their areas. The role of safety representatives and safety committees should be defined, and the duties of specialists such as the safety adviser and the medical officer should be summarised.

IMPLEMENTING A HEALTH AND SAFETY POLICY
Conducting risk assessments

Risk assessments are concerned with the identification of hazards and the analysis of the risks attached to them.

A hazard is anything that can cause harm (eg working on roofs, lifting heavy objects, potentially harmful chemicals, high-voltage electricity, etc). A risk is the chance, large or small, of harm being actually caused by the hazard. Risk assessments are concerned with looking for hazards and estimating the level of risk associated with them.

The HSE produces guidance on this. Its booklet *Health Risk Management: A practical guide for managers in small and medium-sized enterprises* gives a useful overview and sources of further information for those who fit into this category of organisation.

As suggested by Holt and Andrews (1993), risk can be calculated by multiplying a severity estimate by a probability estimate – that is,

$$risk = severity \times probability$$

The purpose of risk assessments is, of course, to initiate preventive action. They enable control measures to be devised on the basis of an understanding of the relative importance of risks. Risk assessments must by law be recorded if there are five or more employees.

There are two types of risk assessment. The first is *quantitative risk assessment*, which produces an objective probability estimate based upon risk information that is immediately applicable to the circumstances in which the risk occurs. The second is *qualitative risk assessment*, which is more subjective and is based on judgement backed by generalised data. Quantitative risk assessment is preferable if the specific data is available. Qualitative risk assessment may be acceptable if there is little or no specific data, as long as it is made systematically on the basis of an analysis of working conditions and hazards, and on an informed judgement of the likelihood of harm actually being caused.

Looking for hazards

The following, as suggested by the HSE and others, are typical activities in which accidents happen or in association with which there are high risks:

- receipt of raw materials – eg involving lifting, carrying
- stacking and storage – eg where there may be falling materials
- movement of people and materials – eg potential falls, collisions
- processing of raw materials – eg possible exposure to toxic substances
- maintenance of buildings – eg while carring out roof-work, gutter-cleaning
- maintenance of plant and machinery – eg when lifting tackle, installing equipment
- using electricity – eg in using hand tools, setting up extension leads
- operating machines – eg if operating without sufficient clearance, or at an unsafe speed; if not using safety devices
- not wearing protective equipment – eg hats, boots, clothing
- distributing finished jobs – eg when delivering vehicles
- dealing with emergencies – eg spillages, fires, explosions

■ using equipment or methods of working subject to intrinsic health hazards – eg display screens, possible repetitive strain injuries from badly designed workstations or working practices.

The HSE suggests that most accidents are caused by a few key activities. It advises that assessors should concentrate initially on those that could cause serious harm. Operations such as roof-work, machine-maintenance and transport movement cause far more deaths and injuries each year than many mainstream activities.

When carrying out a risk assessment it is also necessary to consider who else might be harmed – eg employees, visitors (including cleaners and contractors and the public when calling in to buy products or enlist services).

Hazards should be ranked according to their potential severity as a basis for reducing one side of the risk equation. A simple three-point scale can be used, such as 'low', 'moderate' and 'high'. A more complex severity-rating scale has been proposed by Holt and Andrews (1993):

■ *catastrophic* – imminent danger exists: hazard capable of causing death and illness on a wide scale
■ *critical* – hazard can result in serious illness, severe injury, damage to property and equipment
■ *marginal* – hazard can cause illness, injury, or equipment damage, but the results would probably not be serious
■ *negligible* – hazard should not result in serious injury or illness; the possibility of damage beyond requiring minor first aid is remote.

A 'risk matrix' that plots severity against probability (for an example see Tolley's, 2005) can be used to depict low risk, medium risk and high risk in the form of a diagram.

EXERCISE 12:3

Consider a typical office. If you were carrying out a risk assessment, what hazards would you look for?

Read the next section on *Assessing the risk* and then try to calculate how great are the risks of injury or threats to health arising from each of the hazards you specify above.

Assessing the risk

When the hazards have been identified it is necessary to assess how high the risks are. The HSE suggests that this involves answering three questions:

■ What would be the worst result?
■ How likely is that to happen?
■ How many people could be hurt if things go wrong?

A probability rating system can be used, such as the one recommended by Holt and Andrews (1993):

- *probable* – likely to occur immediately or shortly
- *reasonably probable* – probably will occur in time
- *remote* – may occur in time
- *extremely remote* – unlikely to occur.

Taking action

Risk assessment should lead to action. The type of action to be taken can be ranked in order of potential effectiveness in the form of a 'safety precedence sequence' as proposed by Holt and Andrews (1993):

1 hazard elimination – use of alternatives, design improvements, change of process
2 substitution – for example, replacement of one chemical substance with another that is less risky
3 use of barriers – displacing the hazard from the worker or displacing the worker from the hazard
4 use of procedures – limitation of exposure, dilution of exposure, safe systems of work (all these depend on human initiative)
5 use of warning systems – signs, instructions, labels (all these also depend on human initiative)
6 use of personal protective clothing – this depends on human response and is used as a side measure only when all other options have been exhausted.

Monitoring and evaluation

Risk assessment is not completed when action against the risk has been initiated. It is essential to monitor the hazard and evaluate the effectiveness of the action in eliminating it or at least reducing it to an acceptable level.

EXERCISE 12.4

Refer to the office for which you have carried out a risk assessment (Exercise 12.3). For each identified hazard – and taking into account the assessment of the risk of injury or illness – set out proposed actions with reference to the safety precedence sequence.

Health and safety audits

Risk assessments identify specific hazards and quantify the risks attached to them. Health and safety audits provide for a much more comprehensive review of all aspects of health and safety policies and procedures and practices programmes. As defined by Saunders (1992),

> **'A safety audit will examine the whole organisation in order to test whether it is meeting its safety aims and objectives. It will examine hierarchies, safety-planning processes, decision-making, delegation, policy-making and implementation.'**

Who carries out a health and safety audit?

Safety audits can be conducted by safety advisers and/or personnel specialists, but the more managers, employees and trade union representatives are involved the better. Audits are often carried out under the auspices of a health and safety committee whose members take an active part in conducting them.

Managers can also be held responsible for conducting audits within their departments. Even better, individual members of these departments can be trained to carry out audits in particular areas. The conduct of an audit is made considerably easier if checklists are prepared and a simple form used to record results.

Some organisations also use outside agencies (such as the British Safety Institute) to conduct independent audits.

What is covered by a health and safety audit?

A health and safety audit should cover:

Policies
- Do health and safety policies meet legal requirements?
- Are senior managers committed to health and safety?
- How committed are other managers, team leaders and supervisors to health and safety?
- Is there a health and safety committee? If not, why not?
- How effective is the committee in getting things done?

Procedures: how effectively do the procedures
- support the implementation of health and safety policies?
- communicate the need for good health and safety practices?
- provide for systematic risk assessments?
- ensure that accidents are investigated thoroughly?
- record data on health and safety which is used to evaluate performance and initiate action?
- ensure that health and safety considerations are given proper weight when designing systems of work or manufacturing and operational processes (including the design of equipment and workstations, the specification for the product or service, and the use of materials)?
- provide safety training, especially induction training and training when jobs or working methods are changed?

Safety practices
- To what extent do health and safety practices in all areas of the organisation

conform to the general requirements of the Health and Safety at Work (etc) Act and the specific requirements of the various regulations and codes of practice?

- What risk assessments have been carried out? What were the findings? What actions were taken?
- What is the health and safety performance of the organisation as shown by the performance indicators? Is the trend positive or negative? If negative, what is being done about it?
- How thoroughly are accidents investigated? What steps have been taken to prevent their recurrence?
- What is the evidence that managers and supervisors are really concerned about health and safety?

The audit should cover the questions above, but its purpose is to generate action. Those conducting the audit will have to assess priorities and costs and draw up action programmes for approval by the board.

Example

An example of an auditing system is provided by Sharp Manufacturing (*source*: IDS, 1997). This consists of four tiers:

1. A number of employees are nominated by their departmental managers to carry out safety sampling in their own section at least every two weeks. The safety samplers, who have received training by their managers in hazard-spotting, work from a checklist of key elements of safety in their own particular workplace. Sampling consists of 10–15 spot-checks, looking at such things as housekeeping, protective clothing and any risky elements of working to establish a picture of accident potential and the changes needed.
2. Monthly inspections are carried out by trade union safety representatives, who use the same checklist to ensure high safety standards.
3. Every three months, safety tours are made throughout the plant by the safety manager and the personnel manager together with representatives of the area being audited.
4. A formal audit of Sharp's safety systems is carried out every year by an outside agency. The British Safety Council undertakes a five-star health and safety management audit which examines 77 key elements in five areas of safety, ranging from safety organisations and housekeeping to machinery and personal safeguarding. (Sharp has on a number of occasions won a five-star award which requires a minimum of a 91 per cent rating by the British Safety Council.)

EXERCISE 12.5

What is the difference between a health and safety audit and a risk assessment?

How would you recommend that a health and safety audit should be carried out in your organisation?

What are the main aspects of health and safety that should be covered by an audit?

Safety inspections

Safety inspections are intended to examine a specific area of the organisation – an operational department or a manufacturing process – in order to locate and define any faults in the system, equipment, plant or machines, or any operational errors that might be the source of accidents. Safety inspections should be carried out on a regular and systematic basis by line managers and supervisors with the advice and help of health and safety advisers. The steps to be taken in carrying out safety inspections are:

- Allocate the responsibility for conducting the inspection to a specific individual.
- Define the points to be covered in the form of a checklist.
- Divide the department or plant into areas and list the points to which attention needs to be given in each area.
- Use the checklists as the basis for the inspection.
- Define the frequency with which inspections should be carried out – daily in critical areas.
- Carry out sample- or spot-checks on a random basis.
- Carry out special investigations as necessary to deal with special problems such as operating machinery without guards to increase throughput.
- Set up a reporting system (a form should be used for recording the results of inspections).
- Set up a system for monitoring safety inspections to ensure that they are being conducted properly and on schedule, and that corrective action has been taken where necessary.

Measuring health and safety performance

The saying that 'If you can't measure it, you can't manage it' is totally applicable to health and safety. It is essential to know what is happening; it is even more essential to measure trends as a means of identifying in good time where actions are necessary.

The most common measures are:

- the frequency rate:

$$\frac{\text{number of injuries} \times 100{,}000}{\text{number of hours worked}}$$

- the incidence rate:

$$\frac{\text{number of injuries} \times 1{,}000}{\text{average number employed during the period}}$$

- the severity rate: the days lost through accidents or occupation health problems per 1,000,000 hours worked.

Some organisations adopt a 'total loss control' approach which covers the cost of accidents to the business under such headings as 'Pay to people off work', 'Damage to plant or equipment' and 'Loss of production'. A cost severity rate can then be calculated, which is the total cost of accident per 1,000,000 hours worked.

ACCIDENT PREVENTION

The prevention of accidents is achieved by:

- identifying the previous and likely causes of accidents and the conditions under which they occur
- taking account of safety factors at the design stage – building safety into the system
- designing safety equipment and protective devices and providing protective clothing
- carrying out regular risk assessments, audits, inspections and checks, and taking action to eliminate risks
- investigating all accidents that result in damage to establish the cause and to initiate corrective action
- maintaining good records and statistics in order to identify problem areas and unsatisfactory trends
- conducting a continuous programme of education and training on safe working habits and methods of avoiding accidents
- leadership and motivation – encouraging methods of leadership and motivation which do not place excessive demands on people.

EXERCISE 12.6

What is the purpose of a safety inspection?

What items might be covered by an inspection?

Who should be responsible for conducting inspections?

What steps can an organisation take to prevent accidents?

What is meant when reference is made to the 'system of work' as a major cause of accidents?

Consider an accident at work (however minor) which you have experienced yourself or have first-hand knowledge of. How would you have investigated it? What were the causes? What recommendations would you make to prevent a recurrence?

COMMUNICATING THE NEED FOR BETTER HEALTH AND SAFETY PRACTICES

As Holt and Andrews (1993) observe, various forms of propaganda to sell the health and safety message have been used for many years, although

'They are now widely felt to be of little value in measurable terms in changing behaviour and influencing attitudes to health and safety issues.'

But they believe that it is still necessary to deliver the message that health and safety is important as long as this supplements rather than replaces other initiatives. They suggest (pp103–14) that specific steps can be taken to increase the effectiveness of safety messages:

- Avoid negatives. Successful safety propaganda should contain positive messages, not warnings of the unpleasant consequences of actions.
- Expose correctly. Address the message to the right people at the point of danger.
- Use attention-getting techniques carefully. Lurid images may only be remembered for what they are, not for the message they are trying to convey.
- Maximise comprehension. Messages should be simple and specific.
- Messages must be believable. They should address real issues and be perceived as being delivered by people (ie managers) who believe in what they say and are doing something about it.
- Messages must point the way to action. The most effective messages call for positive actions which can be achieved by the receivers and will offer them a tangible benefit.

Approaches to briefing staff on the importance of health and safety

Advice to a group of staff on the importance of health and safety in the workplace must be based on a thorough understanding of the organisation's health and safety policies and procedures and an appreciation of the particular factors affecting the health and safety of the group of people concerned. Identification of those particular factors can be based on information provided by risk assessments, safety audits and accident reports. But the advice must be positive – why health and safety is important and how accidents can be prevented. The advice should not be over-weighted by awful warnings.

The points to be made include:

- a review of the health and safety policies of the organisation, with explanations of the reasoning behind them and a positive statement of management's belief that health and safety is a major consideration because 1) it directly affects the well-being of all concerned, and 2) it can, and does, minimise suffering and loss
- a review of the procedures used by the organisation for the business as a whole and in the area concerned an assessment of the risks and audit safety situation
- an explanation of the roles of the members of the group in carrying out their work safely and giving full consideration to the safety of others
- a reiteration of the statement that one of the core values of the organisation is the maintenance of safe systems of work and the promotion of safe working practices.

Health and safety training in the work situation

Health and safety training is a key part of the preventive programme. It should start as part of the induction course. It should also take place following a transfer to a new job or a change in working methods. Safety training spells out the rules and provides information on potential hazards and how to avoid them. Further refresher training should be provided and special courses laid on to deal with new aspects of health and safety or areas in which safety problems have emerged.

An example of safety training

As reported by IDS (1997), Leyland Trucks provide Leyland employees with a minimum of 37½ hours' training every year, a sizeable chunk of it devoted to health and safety. In addition, operators receive extra health and safety training based on an analysis of needs.

Under the company's system of 'toolbox' training, 30 modules are available on safety. This allows weekly sessions to be run by the business unit manager as part of a 'quality hour' when the trucks are stopped. Around half the time is devoted to safety.

Immediate-response training is organised after any incident judged to need action. Managers receive refresher training, as do shop stewards who are safety representatives.

Organising health and safety: senior responsibilities

Health and safety concerns everyone in an establishment, although the main responsibility lies with management in general and individual managers in particular. The British Safety Council offers a one-day course entitled 'Health and Safety for Directors and Senior Managers' (online at www.britishsafetycouncil.co.uk) which provides them with

> **'a clear picture of their legal duties under the Health and Safety at Work Act, the Management of Health and Safety at Work Regulations and other associated regulations'.**

The specific roles of management are summarised below:

Management develops and implements health and safety policies and ensures that procedures for carrying out risk assessments, safety audits and inspections are implemented. Importantly, management has the duty of monitoring and evaluating health and safety performance and taking corrective action as necessary.

Managers can exert the greater influence on health and safety. They are in immediate control and it is up to them to keep a constant watch for unsafe conditions or practices and to take immediate action. They are also directly responsible for ensuring that employees are conscious of health and safety hazards and do not take risks. It is highly advisable for additional health and safety training to be given to managers at this operational level. Various courses and qualifications are available. The British Safety Council, the HSE, RoSPA, and Croner as listed at the end of this chapter are all good places to find out what is currently available.

Employees should be aware of what constitutes safe working practices as they affect them and their fellow-workers. Whereas management and managers have the duty to communicate and train, individuals also have the duty to take account of what they have heard and learned in the ways they carry out their work.

Health and safety advisers advise on policies and procedures and on healthy and safe methods of working. They conduct risk assessments and safety audits and investigations into accidents in conjunction with managers and health and safety representatives, they maintain statistics, and they report on trends and necessary actions.

Medical advisers have two functions: preventive and clinical. The preventive function is the more important, especially on occupational health matters. The clinical function is to deal with industrial accidents and diseases and to advise on the steps necessary to recover from injury or illness arising from work. Medical advisers in the workplace do not usurp the role of the family doctor in non-work-related illnesses.

Safety committees consisting of health and safety representatives advise on health and safety policies and procedures, help in conducting risk assessments and safety audits, and make suggestions on improving health and safety performance.

CONTRADICTIONS

Contradictions may arise between health and safety priorities and organisational constraints. The only response to such contradictions is to attach priority always to health and safety considerations. Operational necessity (real or assumed) is no excuse for cutting corners. Some work carried out in organisations may be inherently dangerous to a certain extent, but the dangers must be recognised and work should be allowed on these operations only when every possible precaution has been taken against accidents by developing a safe system of work and by other preventive measures, including training. It is also inevitable that some work may involve the use of dangerous substances, but such substances must be isolated from the worker or the worker isolated from them. Proper training and supervision is particularly necessary in these circumstances.

CHANGING ATTITUDES TO HEALTH AND SAFETY

The role of the HSE: enforcer v adviser

If the information so far in this chapter seems a little daunting to you, reading from the comparative comfort of your armchair, then you are not alone. So much to remember and to comply with, it may seem difficult to know where to start. No wonder, then, that many employers – especially in small businesses – feel that health and safety compliance is something that can be confusing and expensive to operate, and is really only appropriate for large companies. Moreover, they are fearful of the knock on the door of the HSE inspector; their stance is reactive rather than proactive.

The HSE has recognised the nature of this poor attitude and is now striving to help businesses to appreciate that health and safety is something that everyone has to get to grips with, that it is not the sole preserve of the large organisation, and that people should feel as though they can approach the HSE and local authorities for help and advice. In its document *A Strategy of Workplace Health and Safety in Great Britain to 2010 and Beyond* the HSC states:

> **'Appropriate health and safety management is an integral part of effective business management and as such is an *enabler* [authors' emphasis] and not a hindrance.'**

With regard to the fear factor mentioned earlier, the strategy goes on to say:

> **'We want to develop channels of support and advice that can be accessed without fear of enforcement action while allowing the regulators to continue to be tough on those who wilfully disregard the law.'**

Focus on health as well as safety

The construction industry has the second-worst record (after agriculture) for health and safety. Improvements in safety have been a priority over the years, but now there is the realisation that there is much to be done in tackling health in construction. For although progress has been made and there is now an improved awareness of safety (see, for instance the Working Well Together campaign supported by Deputy Prime Minister John Prescott), the Civil Engineering Contractor's Association states (CECA Industry Issues, online 21/01/2005) that:

> **'little or no health screening is currently undertaken in construction'.**

OCCUPATIONAL HEALTH PROGRAMMES

The control of occupational health and hygiene problems can be achieved by:

- eliminating hazards at source through design and process engineering
- isolating hazardous processes and substances so that workers do not come into contact with them
- changing the processes or substances used to promote better protection or eliminate the risk
- providing protective equipment – but only if changes to the design, process or specification cannot completely remove the hazard
- training workers to avoid risk
- maintaining plant and equipment to eliminate the possibility of harmful emissions, controlling the use of toxic substances, and eliminating radiation hazards
- good housekeeping to keep premises and machinery clean and free from toxic substances
- regular inspections to ensure that potential health risks are identified in good time
- pre-employment medical examinations and regular checks on those exposed to risk
- ensuring that ergonomic considerations (ie the design and use of equipment, machines, processes and workstations) are taken into account in design specifications, establishing work routines and training – this is particularly important as a means of minimising the incidence of repetitive strain injury (RSI)
- maintaining preventive medicine programmes which develop health standards for each job and involve regular audits of potential health hazards and regular examinations for anyone at risk.

Particular attention must be paid to the control of noise, fatigue and stress. Control of stress should be regarded as a major part of any occupational health programme.

Managing stress

There are four main reasons why organisations should take account of stress and do something about it – first, because they have the social responsibility to provide a good quality of working life; second, because excessive stress causes illness; third, because it can result in inability to cope with the demands of the job which, of course, creates more stress; and finally, because excessive stress can reduce employee effectiveness and therefore organisational performance.

The ways in which stress can be managed by an organisation include:

- job design – clarifying roles, reducing the danger of role ambiguity and conflict and giving people more autonomy within a defined structure to manage their responsibilities
- targets and performance standards – setting reasonable and achievable targets which may stretch people but do not place impossible burdens on them
- placement – taking care to place people in jobs which are within their capabilities
- career development – planning careers and promoting staff in accordance with their capabilities; taking care not to over- or under-promote
- performance-management processes – allowing a dialogue to take place between managers and individuals about individuals' work problems and ambitions
- counselling – giving individuals the opportunity to talk about their problems with a member of the personnel department or the company medical officer, or through an employee-assistance programme
- management training – training in performance review and counselling techniques and in what managers can do to alleviate their own stress and reduce it in others.

EXERCISE 12.7 RECENT TRENDS

The article that constitutes the case study below is taken from *People Management*, November 2004, and looks at a new set of voluntary standards relating to the management of stress in the workplace. Read the article and reflect on the new standards so as to form your own personal opinion of them. Then answer the questions at the end.

Case study: 'The HSE stresses the standard'

by Julie Griffiths

Stress management standards and an accompanying toolkit were launched by the Health and Safety Executive (HSE) and Jane Kennedy, Minister for Work, last week. The standards, which are voluntary, enable employers to set their own goals to manage stress, with a focus on continuous improvement rather than meeting an HSE-set target. Firms will be required to carry out a risk assessment covering six areas of work that can cause stress: workload, control, support, relationships, role, and change management. An online toolkit will automatically benchmark employers against the top 20 per cent of companies in the country.

Ben Willmot, CIPD Adviser, Employee Relations, said the HSE had been pragmatic in choosing a flexible model. 'One concern of CIPD members was that the HSE would take a "one size fits all" approach. Most will be pleased with this because of the flexibility that it affords,' he said.

Liz Redway, HR manager at Borders UK, welcomed the standards but warned that they could be ignored by some employers. 'The standards will help responsible employers tackle stress in a more structured way. But because they are voluntary, they will do nothing for organisations who ignore the issue.'

Conversely, Willmott said that the HSE could take enforcement action against firms that failed to act, because stress was covered by existing legislation. 'The standards may be voluntary, but they are a benchmark of good practice, so employers either have to follow them or implement their own,' he said. 'Any enforcerment action would be issued not for breaching the standards but for breaching the Health and Safety at Work Act 1974.'

Kennedy said that a voluntary route was preferable to legislation because of the complex nature of stress, but acknowledged that enforcement was necessary. 'Enforcement is an important motivator for some employers. But stress is not necessarily work-related, so it's complicated to legislate for it at work because of all the other factors,' she said. She added that employers already had a legal duty to ensure, as far as possible, the mental health of employees.

According to HSE and Office of National Statistics figures, 13.4 million days were lost to stress, depression and anxiety in 2001–2. New figures are due out this month.

EXERCISE 12.7 QUESTIONS

In a mail-order company absence rates through illness have been increasing for key punch operators (who are expected to meet demanding targets for key depressions per hour). You have been asked to investigate the causes.

- How would you conduct the investigation?
- What causes might you possibly identify?
- What action would you recommend?

Consider your own job or any other job with which you are familiar. To what extent is it stressful, and what could the organisation do about it?

SUMMARY

- Health and safety management is vital: a systematic and concerted effort is needed to minimise suffering and loss from accidents and occupational health problems.
- A powerful legislative framework of health and safety regulations is in place, supported by codes of practice, and founded on the overarching Health and Safety at Work (etc) Act 1974.
- Risk assessment identifies hazards, estimates their severity and determines the likelihood or probability of the hazards' leading to accidents. The degree of risk can be expressed in the formula severity $\times$ probability. Risk assessment leads to action that must be monitored and evaluated.
- Health and safety audits provide for a comprehensive review of all safety policies, procedures and practices to ensure that they meet health and safety aims and objectives.

- Safety inspections examine a specific area or process to locate any constituent elements in the system of work which might be the source of accidents so that corrective action can be taken.
- Occupational health programmes aim to deal with health hazards at source, by changing or isolating hazardous substances or processes, by setting up regular inspections, and by attending to ergonomic considerations in the design of work processes and stations.
- Accident prevention programmes identify the causes of potential accidents (primarily factors within systems of work), ensure that safety is built into the system, and monitor the design of safety equipment and protective devices.
- Health and safety performance indicators are used to identify trends in the frequency and severity of accidents or absence through work-related illness so that corrective action can be taken.
- Training in safety procedures is essential, especially for new starters and when jobs or processes are changed.

REFERENCES

A Strategy of Workplace Health and Safety in Great Britain to 2010 and Beyond, available online from http:// www.hse.gov.uk/aboutus/plans/index.htm

CECA INDUSTRY ISSUES (online 21/01/2005): www.ceca.co.uk

GRIFFITHS J. (2004) 'The HSE stresses the standard', *People Management*, November, p16.

HOLT A. and ANDREWS H. (1993) *Principles of Health and Safety at Work*. London, IOSH Publishing.

HSC (2003) *Delivering Health and Safety in Great Britain: Health and safety targets: how are we doing 2002/3?*, available online from www.hse.gov.uk

HSE (1995) *Health Risk Management: A practical guide for managers in small and medium-sized enterprises*. London, HMSO.

IDS (1997) *Safety at Work*, IDS Study. London, Incomes Data Services.

SAUNDERS R. (1992) *The Safety Audit*. London, Pitman.

Tolley's Health and Safety at Work Handbook 2005 (2004; 17th edition). London, LexisNexis.

Useful websites

Health and Safety Executive (HSE): www.hse.gov.uk

For government (HSE) health and safety statistics: www.hse.gov.uk/statistics

RoSPA (Royal Society for the Prevention of Accidents): www.rospa.com

Croner's (for advice, guidance, literature, etc): www.croner.ac.uk

Working Well Together (construction industry health awareness campaign): http://wwt.uk.com

British Safety Council (membership, courses, qualifications, advice): http://www.britishsafetycouncil.co.uk

Information on stress: www.hse.gov.uk/stress

INTRODUCTION

When we talk of 'quality' we naturally tend to think of those factors which differentiate a product or service and elevate it above its rivals – that which makes it 'excellent'. Having said this we also need infrastructure (rules, procedures, codes of practice, organisational structure) in place for this to occur. Also, we do not always define 'quality' as meaning 'of the best'. So how *do* we define 'quality'?

Quality can be defined as the degree of excellence achieved by an organisation in delivering products or services to its customers. There are three aspects of quality:

- *quality of design* – the degree to which the design achieves its purpose
- *quality of conformance* – the extent to which the product conforms with the design specification
- *quality of customer satisfaction* – the level at which value is delivered to customers by satisfying their needs.

Of these three aspects, the last is by far the most important. Quality of design and quality of conformance serve the sole purpose of satisfying customers. Quality is essentially a customer-oriented concept. Customer satisfaction is obtained by product designs or service programmes which meet their needs, by achieving quality specifications which have been built into the design of the product or service, by attaining high standards of reliability and equally high levels of customer service, and by paying constant attention to customer care.

The level of quality reached by an organisation is thus measured in terms of the extent to which customer requirements are satisfied. However, the reputation of an organisation for quality products or services extends beyond individual customers to the community at large. And this reputation must be protected and enhanced.

Competitive advantage is achieved by businesses which provide goods or services to quality levels higher than those offered by competitors. But they will be striving equally hard to match or exceed those levels. This means that policies of continuous improvement have to be implemented to maintain competitive advantage. Quality is a race without a finish: it is a race against tough competitors to achieve and sustain world-class performance. Quality differentiates companies from these competitors.

There are clearly links between management focus on quality and the desired results of customer satisfaction. Key performance results relating to efficiency and effectiveness are also related to quality. The role of 'the reflective practitioner' is itself reflected later in this chapter, notably through Deming's plan-do-check-act cycle. The roles of 'strategic thinker' and 'leader/visionary' are much in evidence in the design of quality-related systems such as ISO 9000 and the EFQM model. The implementation of new ways of operating also means that the successful implementor of quality has to be an adept change facilitator.

Learning outcomes: quality management

Quality has to be managed. It is not achieved easily. And it cannot be left to chance. Everyone in an organisation has to play their part, but what they do must be planned, monitored, measured and controlled. In short, they have to be managed.

There are a number of approaches to managing quality as defined later in this chapter. The overarching concept is that of 'total quality', which is achieved when the quality of a product or service achieves customer satisfaction. This is often called 'total quality management' (TQM) – but quality can be managed well without calling it TQM, and this chapter is concerned with all aspects of managing quality, not just TQM.

On completing it, a reader will be able to:

- understand the various terms used in quality management – 'inspection', 'quality control', 'statistical quality control', 'quality assurance', 'total quality', 'total quality management', etc
- outline the contribution of the quality 'gurus' Deming, Juran and Crosby
- state the basic principles of quality management
- discuss the development and implementation of quality management processes
- measure and monitor quality
- identify who is responsible for quality
- analyse the processes of empowering and involving people to achieve quality
- refer to the quality standards available – 1S0 9000 and the EFQM model including the RADAR concept
- outline the Six Sigma Process.

The important subjects of continuous improvement and customer care are treated separately in the next two chapters. Readers may wish to link this chapter and the next under the broad heading of 'Quality' in that one clearly leads on to the other.

The first main subjects of this chapter, meanwhile, are:

- inspection
- quality control
- quality assurance
- total quality management.

Figure 13.1 depicts the hierarchical relationship between these types of quality management methods.

INSPECTION

Perhaps one of the simplest methods of influencing quality is to use the system of inspection. Inspection is an after-the-event activity concerned with locating faults when they have already occurred so that they can either be put right (for example, re-worked) or the defective item scrapped. From the point of view of the customer this is preferable to receiving faulty goods which have to be returned or which lead to complaints. Arguably, if mistakes are few and the inspection process is both thorough and inexpensive, this system would seem to be a good Idea. Traditionally, it has been the method of

Figure 13.1 *The hierarchy of the quality management methods inspection, quality control, quality assurance and Total Quality Management*

choice for many organisations where quality is concerned, largely because of the simplicity of the method. However, relying solely upon an inspection process can be both misleading and expensive.

Cost

Often re-working is not possible – and scrapping finished products can be very expensive in terms of both materials and time spent In production. The BBC film documentary *The People's Century*, part 6: *1924, On the Line* (1995) shows a clip featuring an old man who in the 1920s worked for a manufacturer of wireless sets (radios). It was his job to hook up each completed wireless set to the mains electricity. Inspection was simple: the wireless set was turned on and left on a 'soak test' for 24 hours. Sometimes, as he says, the wireless set didn't work or caught fire or blew up. If none of these scenarios occurred, the set was switched off at the end of the test and put into a box ready for dispatch to the customer. This 100-per-cent inspection certainly detected the faulty wireless sets, but at an obvious cost. Furthermore, it did not attempt to correct the real problems – it only fixed the symptoms.

Boredom

One of the biggest problems when relying solely upon inspection is the human tendency to become bored by having to repeat mundane checking tasks time and time again. Sometimes it is possible for the individual to work quite successfully 'on auto-pilot' and still carry out a conversation with a colleague, for instance. Other types of inspection require careful attention to detail and are thus difficult *and* monotonous.

Destructive tests

Sometimes inspection is simply not possible for all products. For instance, to test concrete structures for strength purposes it is necessary to subject the concrete to destruction. This cries out for some sort of sampling method (see the section on *Quality control* which follows).

However, for something as important as the blades of an aircraft jet turbine engine, inspection would be carried out (using non-destructive methods!) on each blade.

Final safety-net

Ideally, the quality control and quality assurance procedures which we outline below should eliminate the need for inspection. But we do not live in an ideal world, and inspection procedures are still used in many manufacturing organisations as the final safety-net.

QUALITY CONTROL

Quality control involves the application of data collection and analysis to monitor and measure the extent to which quality assurance requirements have been met in terms of product or service performance and reliability. As already discussed, the traditional approach to controlling quality is inspection. Control can be exercised more scientifically by means of statistical techniques. This means that we can often infer crucial quality parameters (for example, the acceptability of a large amount of material) by using sampling techniques. We can also build in inspections at various points in the process rather than leaving everything to end inspection.

Statistical process control (SPC)

Statistical process control uses sampling techniques and mathematical analysis to ensure that during design, manufacturing and servicing, work is carried out and material used within the specified limits required to produce the desired standards of quality, performance and reliability. The aim is to minimise defects, not only for the practical reason that defects lose business but also because, ethically, no self-respecting company deserves to survive on the sale of sub-standard products or the delivery of inferior services. But the approach to the reduction of defects must consider the cost of their minimisation, and statistical quality control techniques identify not only the scope for improvement but also the cost of achieving the desired result. The statistical theory for SPC was written in the 1930s, but it was not until after World War II that American consultants brought its use to Japan. Here, industry seized upon its techniques with such effect that the United States, later followed by Britain and other countries, took it to heart. These days the use of SPC is very common in manufacturing industry.

As Frank Price directly puts it in his book *Right First Time* (1984), we can use SPC to ask the following questions:

- Can we make it OK? (capability)
- Are we making it OK? (control)
- Have we made it OK? (quality assurance)
- Could we make it better? (improvement)

John Oakland poses the same questions in *Statistical Process Control* (2000).

Let us consider the first two of these questions in a little more detail.

Can we make it OK?

Given that variability of the process will inevitably exist, before we went into production it would be very wise to ask ourselves if our processes and equipment were capable of achieving the required specification and tolerances (in other words, the allowable deviation either side of the specification). We would consider both the precision (how closely bunched our results were) and accuracy (how close to the target) of the process. By considering test results from trying the process out, statistics can answer these questions; it can even predict the percentage of results that will be outside the acceptable range, even if none of our sample results was.

Are we making it OK?

There's an old saying, 'Rubbish in, rubbish out'. This is true from the moment raw materials arrive and right through each stage of the process. One technique used is that of *acceptance sampling*.

Acceptance sampling ensures that items do not pass to the next stage in the process if an unacceptably high proportion of the batch is outside the quality limit. Sampling consists of taking a representative number of examples from a population and drawing conclusions about the behaviour of the whole population from the behaviour of the sample. Sampling techniques are based on statistical theory, including probability theory.

One means by which operators in the process can monitor and control it is to use control charts on which the results of the inspection of samples are compared with the results expected from a stable situation. If they do not match, action may be necessary. These comparisons can be recorded graphically on control charts on which warning and action levels are marked. Control charts set out the control limits which either warn that a problem exists or indicate that action must be taken (warning and action limits). Control can be affected by consideration of either attributes or variables:

- *control by attributes* – There are only two attributes: acceptable or unacceptable, of which any article or unit must be one or the other. The information required for control purposes compares the number of defects and/or the number of defects per unit, which are compared with the desired level of quality – the acceptable quality level (AQL)
- *control by variables* – Variables can have any value on a continuous scale. Control by variables therefore takes place when a distribution of features is being measured

rather than where there is a go or no-go position as in control by attributes. Variables are therefore measured, in contrast to attributes, which are counted.

Three rules of quality control

Price (1984) also states that there are 'three rules of quality control', namely:

- No inspection or measurement without proper recording.
- No recording without analysis.
- No analysis without action.

Beyond quality control

Total quality control processes aim to organise quality into the product or service by pursuing policies of assuring and controlling quality. Total quality control takes a comprehensive view of all aspects of quality through techniques such as zero-defects programmes or the Taguchi methodology.

Zero-defects programmes

Zero-defects programmes aim to improve product quality beyond the level that might economically be achieved through statistical procedures. The ultimate aim is to eliminate defects so far as is conceivably possible.

The principal features of such programmes are:

- Agreement is reached with all concerned over the quality goals to be attained and the quality problems that might prevent their achievement.
- The participation of all those involved in establishing and running the quality programme is organised.
- Clear targets are set against which improvements can be measured.
- Procedures are established for providing prompt feedback for employees on their quality achievements.
- Rewards are offered for achieving high quality standards.
- Employees are encouraged to make suggestions on the causes of errors and the remedies, and ideas are then implemented jointly.
- Work is organised and jobs are designed to facilitate all of the above.

Taguchi methodology

This methodology was developed by the Japanese engineer Dr Genichi Taguchi during the 1980s (Bicheno, 2002). Its main features are to:

- push quality back to the design stage because quality control can never compensate for bad design
- emphasise design rather than inspection for control of production
- produce robust products with intrinsic quality and reliability characteristics
- prototype product designs and production processes
- concentrate on the practical engineering, not the statistical niceties of quality control theory.

Detailed consideration of the use of statistics is outside the scope of this book. However, it should be noted that the basic principles of statistics, including the use of control charts, are widely used by operators who have been trained to use them in their everyday work.

QUALITY ASSURANCE

Quality assurance is the next stage up in the hierarchy of quality processes. As its name implies, the main purpose is to assure those involved in the process – and as importantly, the customer – that quality processes and procedures are in place. In addition to finding quality-related problems as they occur, there is a bias towards actively hunting down possible defects and altering the process so that such mistakes do not occur in the future.

Quality assurance (QA) involves the use of documented procedures designed to ensure that the activities carried out in the organisation (design, development, manufacturing, service delivery) result in products or services that meet the requirements and needs of customers. Both inspection and quality control methods, examined above, may be a part of the QA process. The underpinning philosophy of quality assurance is that right methods will produce right results (quality products or services).

ISO 9000, discussed later in this chapter, is an example of a quality assurance process.

TOTAL QUALITY AND TOTAL QUALITY MANAGEMENT

Total quality

Total quality implies the use of a disciplined, structured and all-embracing approach to quality management. It incorporates quality assurance and quality control techniques but, as the name implies, it includes all aspects of an organisation's activities and concerns everyone in the organisation. It is thus focused on delivering quality services to internal as well as external customers.

The four basic principles of total quality are:

- customer satisfaction – The only real measure of the quality of a product or service is the extent to which it delivers customer satisfaction. The word 'satisfaction' can be defined as when all customers' wants, needs and expectations are met, whether or not they have been verbally expressed and whether or not any feedback is forthcoming
- continuous improvement – The concept of continuous improvement is based on the belief that continually striving to reach higher and higher standards in every part of the organisation will result in a series of incremental gains that will engender superior performance. It involves creating an environment in which all employees contribute to improving performance and quality as a normal part of their job
- the significance of internal customers – This relies on the concept that everyone who receives goods or services from a colleague within an organisation is a customer of that colleague. Suppliers of goods and services within an organisation have to be just as aware of the need to achieve high levels of quality for their colleagues as for their ultimate customers. The ultimate goal of complete customer satisfaction can only be guaranteed if attention is paid to quality in all the transactions and processes which take place within the organisation

■ an all-embracing approach – The concept of total quality focuses on the requirement for all employees in the organisation to be involved all the time in meeting all customer requirements.

The concept of total quality incorporates the notion of total quality control but goes even further in emphasising that quality should be managed into the system, and that quality management should always be oriented towards the achievement of complete customer satisfaction.

A total quality approach is a systematic way of ensuring that all activities within an organisation happen exactly as they have been planned in order to meet the defined needs of customers. The emphasis is on involving everyone in the organisation in activities which provide for continuous improvement and for achieving sustained high levels of performance.

The philosophy is about getting commitment to quality. Everyone at every level in the organisation has genuinely to believe in quality and to act on that belief. Total quality can be described as an attitude of mind which leads to appropriate behaviour and actions. It has to be, as at Nissan, the centre-piece of the company's philosophy, with commitment at every level to a zero-defects product.

Total Quality Management

Total Quality Management (TQM) can be defined as a systematic way of *guaranteeing* that all activities within an organisation happen exactly as they have been planned in order to meet the defined needs of customers. Put like this, it seems conceptually to be the same as total quality, the philosophy of which it essentially shares. TQM could be regarded as a method of systematising or packaging the notion of total quality so that it can act as a brand name which managements can identify with when introducing quality programmes. However, Hutchins (1992) suggests that TQM is a sub-set of total quality. In his opinion, the word 'management' means 'authoritative control over the affairs of others': its addition to the concept of total quality is unhelpful and 'does nothing to encourage the cascade of quality responsibility down through the workforce'.

This may be an extreme view which many TQM consultants would reject. They would claim that TQM is designed to encourage commitment to quality throughout the organisation and is not a top-down approach as Hutchins implies. TQM programmes can and generally do incorporate the principles of total quality as described above. But many organisations prefer to believe that what they are doing is managing total quality rather than TQM because TQM has in some quarters acquired the perhaps unjustified reputation of a management package or finite programme which, when introduced, solves every quality problem.

The contribution of the quality gurus

Much of the thinking behind total quality was based on the work of the three principal quality gurus: Deming, Juran and Crosby.

Figure 13.2 *Deming's model of the quality cycle*

W. Edwards Deming

Deming's (1986) greatest contribution – which was based on his work in Japan – was to emphasise the importance of customers, the significance of continuous improvement, and the fact that quality is determined by the system.

He believed that competitiveness depends upon customer satisfaction that is created by a combination of responsiveness to customers' views and needs, and the continuous improvement of products or services. Furthermore, in order to remain competitive, organisations must constantly seek ways of improving their operational systems and the customer appeal of their products or services. Improvement is not just the responsibility of operations and sales departments – it must be the aim in all areas of the organisation and at all levels. And it must be a major influence on short-, medium- and long-term plans. Finally, the system determines quality levels. It is defined as inputs and the manner in which they are processed.

Deming's model of the quality cycle is illustrated in Figure 13.2.

J. M. Juran

Juran's (1988) major contribution to the philosophy of total quality was his concept of managerial breakthrough. In the traditional control situation, the typical managerial attitude is that the present level of performance is good enough or cannot be improved. The aim is therefore to perpetuate performance at that level. Management attempts simply to identify and eliminate short-term deviations from the usual performance.

Juran stated that in the breakthrough situation, management adopts a completely different attitude. The belief is held strongly that change is desirable and possible in all aspects of operation. It is up to managers to make the 'breakthrough'. They must recognise and act on the need for what is, in effect, continuous improvement.

However, as Collard (1993) points out,

> **'One of the difficulties, of course, is that managers simply have no time for "breakthrough", because they cannot leave the treadmill of control. Few managers would argue against the merits of "breakthrough", but they do need respite from the never-ending emergencies and crises. Seldom are harassed managers able to work their way out without help from top management and assistance from other specialists.'**

Philip B. Crosby

Crosby (1978) emphasised that 'in discussing quality we are dealing with a people situation'. He suggested five factors which govern the management of quality:

- Quality means conformance, not elegance.
- There is no such thing as a quality problem.
- There is no such thing as the economics of quality. It is always cheaper to do the job right first time.
- The only performance measurement is the cost of quality.
- The only performance standard is zero defects.

THE PRINCIPLES OF QUALITY MANAGEMENT

Quality management principles are based on the philosophy of total quality. They can be summed up in the terms 'customer satisfaction', 'continuous improvement', 'involving everyone', 'creating commitment to quality' and 'looking at the system as a whole'. This approach provides for the effective management of the dynamic relationship between what organisations have to do to develop and sustain customer satisfaction and the ever-changing needs of consumers and the continuous pressure of competition. It is a means of ensuring that quality is achieved and improved but does not obviate the need for quality control. Achievements must be measured to ensure that corrective action can be taken, and this action must focus on the root causes of the problem, not the symptoms.

The basic principles

The six basic principles of total quality as defined by Collard (1993) are:

1   Top management commitment – Top management should continuously reinforce a total quality programme by what they do. They have to ensure that everyone knows how important total quality is and appreciates the long-term goals of the organisation's total quality processes.
2   Attitude change – Total quality requires a complete change in the attitude and culture prevailing in an organisation.
3   Continuous improvement – The need to create a climate of continuous improvement is linked to attitude change. As Collard states, 'Quality improvement should always be at the forefront of everything that is done.'

4 Supervision – The successful introduction of total quality gives a key role to supervision in ensuring that the quality message is carried down to grassroots level.

5 Training – If the key to success is supervision, then it is important to ensure that the selection, training and motivation of supervisors allows for the development of the skills that enable them to become a dynamic force for improving performance.

6 Recognition – Performance and achievement in improving quality should be recognised. The recognition of contribution can be made effectively through non-financial means – publicly for individual or team achievement, through competitions and prizes for teams.

EXERCISE 13.1

Consider your own organisation, or any organisation you know, and analyse the extent to which Collard's six principles have been applied. If they have been applied completely, or to a degree, what impact have they made on quality performance?

You have been asked by your managing director to explain the foundation upon which a total quality approach should be adopted in your organisation. How would you use Collard's six principles in making your proposals?

The development and implementation of quality management processes

Quality management is a process, a way of doing things. It is not a programme with a finite start and finish. The management of quality is a continuous process which may make use of a number of techniques – for example, statistical quality control – but it ultimately depends on the attitudes and behaviour of all concerned. Quality management has to be based on a clearly stated policy.

Total quality policy

The policy could include the following points:

- The goal of the organisation is to achieve customer satisfaction by meeting the requirements of both external and internal customers.
- The need is to establish customer requirements and to respond quickly and effectively to them.
- It is essential to concentrate on prevention rather than cure.
- Everyone is involved – all work done by company employees, suppliers and product outlets is part of a process which creates a product or service for a customer.
- Each employee is a customer for work done by other employees and has the right to expect good work from them and the obligation to contribute work of high calibre to them.
- The standard of quality is 'zero defects' or 'no failures' – everyone has to understand the standards required and the need to do it right first time.
- Sustained quality excellence requires continuous improvement.
- Quality performance and costs should be measured systematically.

- Continuous attention must be paid to satisfying educational and training needs.
- High-quality performance will be recognised and rewarded.
- Quality improvement is best achieved by the joint efforts of all stakeholders.

Planning for total quality

Planning for total quality involves:

- recording the series of events and activities that constitute the total process by flow-charting and other means of activity analysis
- analysing the existing processes and system flows to establish inconsistencies and potential sources of variations and defects
- specifying for each activity the necessary quality-related activities, including material and packaging specifications, quality control procedures, process control systems, and sampling and inspection procedures
- developing, as appropriate, just-in-time (JIT) systems which provide for the right quantities to be produced or delivered at the right time and which ensure that there is no waste
- determining how to achieve quality in the purchasing system, with particular reference to the development of long-term relationships with suppliers so that dependable product quality and delivery standards can be defined and maintained
- conducting failure mode, effect and criticality (FMEC) studies to determine possible modes of failure and their effects on the performance of the product or service, and to establish which features of product design, production or operation are critical to the various modes of failure
- developing planned maintenance systems to reduce the incidence of emergency maintenance
- designing quality into the product, making sure that standards and specifications meet customer needs and can be achieved by existing processes (or, if not, by improving these processes in particular ways)
- conducting process capability studies to ensure that it will be possible to achieve quality standards through existing processes or, if not, to ascertain what changes are required
- examining quality requirements in manufacturing to ensure that answers can be forthcoming to the following questions: Can we make it? Are we making it? Have we made it? Could we make it better?
- studying storage, distribution and delivery arrangements to ensure that they are capable of meeting customer demands
- examining after-sales service procedures and achievements to identify areas for improvement.

MEASURING AND MONITORING QUALITY

The process of managing quality as set out above aims to ensure that everyone is involved and committed to the continuous improvement of quality standards and to 'delighting' customers. But it is necessary to be explicit about the standards of quality required even if these are subject to continuous development. And it is equally important to measure and monitor quality performance against these standards. Only by doing this is it possible to identify where corrective action, aimed at the root causes of the problem, is required. Continuous improvement means doing everything better all the time, but it also means learning from problems and mistakes to ensure that they do not happen again. And this should be double- as well as single-loop learning – ie it is not a matter of simply correcting errors, it is much more about learning something new about what has to be achieved in the light of the changed circumstances and then deciding how it can be achieved. The emphasis is on using control information to initiate preventive as well as corrective action. In other words, it is not just about putting things right; it is truly about ensuring that things do not go wrong again.

The measurement and monitoring of quality can be carried out:

■ at the most basic level, by simply comparing outputs or actions against predetermined standards
■ by inspection – an after-the-event technique which does not address any real quality problems
■ by the various techniques of statistical quality control – acceptance sampling, control charts, control by attributes, control by variables
■ by statistical process control
■ by benchmarking
■ by customer and internal surveys.

EXERCISE 13.2

What do you think are the most important actions an organisation should take when introducing total quality?

Comparison of outputs and actions against standards

If standards, targets or indicators – for example, the proportion of rejects or the time taken to respond to a telephone call – have been established, results can be measured against them. This is a simple method of performance measurement but it can be somewhat crude. It may address only one or two aspects of performance and is not so comprehensive as the use of a battery of statistical control techniques, as described below. And, of course, it is only effective if standards are properly set and the information provides a reliable guide to preventive as well as to corrective action.

Inspection

Inspection of the finished product to establish the degree to which it conforms to specification is the traditional method of monitoring quality. But it is severely limited to after-the-event analysis. What it does not do is address the more fundamental aspects of quality – why things have gone wrong as well as what has gone wrong.

Statistical quality control

Statistical quality control, as described earlier in this chapter, is essentially a preventive measure. It is a before-the-event activity in that unlike inspection it does not wait until the end of the line, when the product has been manufactured or the process completed.

Instead, it identifies potential problems before they arise so that preventive rather than corrective actions can be taken.

Statistical process control

Statistical process control techniques detect and help to eliminate unacceptable variations as the process is operating. The statistical part is an analysis of what the process is capable of doing (process capability analysis) in order to establish the criteria by which it will be controlled. The question statistical process control is there to answer is 'What is going wrong with the process?' It assigns causes and points the way to preventive action.

Benchmarking

Benchmarking aims to establish 'best practice' by making inter-firm comparisons. Best practice is expressed in terms of what comparable firms are achieving in the shape of quality standards. Benchmarking is a means of setting standards, but it is also used to monitor company performance against what is being achieved elsewhere. If possible, benchmarking goes beyond simply collecting statistics on what other firms are achieving and tries to find out what methods are being used to get results. Clearly, the full amount of information will be limited or unavailable from some direct competitors and this may reduce the reliability and comprehensiveness of the data. But serious attempts at what is often called 'competitive benchmarking' are well worth making.

Customer service surveys

Surveys can be made of the reactions of customers to the company's products or services. These can take the form of direct enquiries after the event or more regular surveys. The level of customer service in retail organisations can also be monitored by 'mystery shopping' – market research personnel acting as shoppers or telephone enquirers who analyse the service they get (see also Chapter 15).

Internal surveys

Internal surveys can be conducted of the level of service provided by departments to their internal customers within the organisation. Employee-attitude surveys can be used to assess how quality is regarded, and what people are doing about it.

WHO IS RESPONSIBLE FOR ACHIEVING QUALITY?

The simple answer to this question is 'everybody in the organisation', but top management, line management and quality specialists have specific roles.

Top management

Top management set the direction and lead by example. They should ensure that a total quality strategy is developed and communicated to all employees. And they must provide the means for developing, implementing and monitoring the achievement of the strategy. Their role is to ensure that customer care and continuous improvement are in the forefront of everyone's minds as they go about their business.

Line managers

Line managers have the prime responsibility for achieving total quality. This is a matter of leadership, communication and involving people in developing and implementing total quality processes and in jointly taking action to improve performance. Line managers are closely involved in continuous improvement. Their role is to monitor quality against standards they have helped to create by using appropriate control techniques and ensuring that action is taken on the basis of the information they provide.

Total quality consultants and specialists

External and internal quality consultants provide advice on approaches to total quality and the particular techniques involved. These may be packaged in the form of a total quality management programme. Consultants may have an important part to play in communicating quality principles and methods, and in training managers and employees in how to apply them. Because quality achievements depend largely on attitudes, their activities can often focus on developing the right approach by organising various kinds of learning experiences.

INVOLVING AND EMPOWERING EMPLOYEES

Total quality will not work unless everyone is involved. This is the main challenge faced by anyone concerned with quality management – 'How can I get people committed to quality?' Clearly, communication and training help, but involvement in the development and application of the principles and practice of total quality achieves a deeper and longer-lasting effect. And empowering people to take control over their own quality practices can be just as important – if not more so.

Involvement

Involvement can be relatively unstructured in the sense that managers and their teams may get together from time to time to identify quality issues and agree methods of dealing with them. More structure can be provided by holding meetings regularly with agendas in the form of progress reports and lists of new issues and action plans.

A fully structured approach can take the form of quality circles, which consist of small groups of volunteers who hold regular meetings to discuss and propose ways of improving working methods or arrangements under a trained leader. They ordinarily concentrate on actions that will improve quality, but they may extend their remit to cover improvements to productivity or the scope for increasing efficiency or reducing costs. In this extended role they are often called improvement groups.

Empowerment

Empowerment is the process of giving people more scope or 'power' to exercise control over, and take responsibility for, their work. It provides greater 'space' for individuals to use their abilities by enabling them and encouraging them to take decisions close to the point of impact.

Empowered decisions are frequently concerned with the achievement of quality in production or service delivery. Empowered employees are encouraged to use their creative and innovative capabilities to identify and address quality problems by themselves and, more frequently, with their fellow team-members. They set quality standards in agreement with their team leaders and monitor their own performance to ensure that these standards are met. They are encouraged to 'manage their own quality' by monitoring their own perform-ance and taking corrective action themselves when a problem arises that is within their own control. When it is caused by a factor they cannot control, they refer the problem to their team leader or a colleague with, ideally, an analysis of the cause of the problem and sugges-tions on what might be done about it.

Empowerment is not something that happens overnight – it takes time to achieve and requires skilled and sympathetic leadership. Managers and team leaders have to learn how to delegate more and to allow individuals and teams greater scope to plan, act, monitor and review their own performance. But they still have to provide the guidance and support required. And they must in their turn be helped to develop the skills required to function effectively as leaders in an empowered environment.

QUALITY STANDARDS

ISO 9000

Quality standards provide a set of principles – a template or framework that constitutes a basis for developing and measuring the effectiveness of a quality system. In effect, quality standards provide a specification for the capability of a business to manage quality. The first UK standard for quality assurance was BS (British Standard) 5750, published in 1979. This largely formed the basis for the international standard ISO (International Organisation for Standardisation) 9000, which was introduced in 1987 to general acceptance. An update on the ISO standards emerged in 1994 to form the ISO 9000: 1994 series of documents. More recently, a further revision has taken place – the ISO 9000: 2000 family of standards. The term 'quality assurance system' has been replaced with 'quality management system' in the new standard because (EN ISO 9001: 2000, Foreword, Endorsement notice):

> **'the . . . requirements in this edition of ISO 9001, in addition to quality assurance of the product, also aim to satisfy customer satisfaction'.**

ISO 9000: 2000 family of standards

ISO 9000: 2000 describes the basics principles of quality management systems, including terminology.

ISO 9004: 2000 gives guidelines on quality management systems and has an emphasis on continuous improvement. This goes beyond the scope of the standard ISO 9001: 2000 (see below) and gives a framework for improvement: it is not assessed.

ISO 9001: 2000 details all of the requirements an organisation must meet in order to satisfy the requirements of the standard; this forms the backbone of the standards and is the only one against which certification can be gained. (For those who are familiar with the previous ISO 9000: 1987 and ISO 9004, this revision compacts Parts 1, 2 and 3 into one document.)

There are four major generic business practices (Tricker, 2001):

- management responsibility (policy, planning, system, review)
- resource management (human resources, information, facilities)
- product realisation (customer, design, purchasing, production, calibration)
- measurement, analysis and improvement (audit, process/product control, improvement).

These are covered by eight sections within the standard.

THE EIGHT SECTIONS OF THE STANDARD

- Section 1: Scope – this introduces the standard
- Section 2: Normative reference – details other, related, mandatory standards
- Section 3: Terms and definitions
- Section 4: Quality management system – outlines requirements, eg the need for a quality manual and documented procedures
- Section 5: Management responsibility
- Section 6: Resource management – people, equipment, facilities, etc
- Section 7: Product realisation – process control, design and development, purchasing, handling and storage, measuring equipment
- Section 8: Measurement, analysis and improvement – eg inspection, monitoring, system for non-conformity, internal audits, customer satisfaction

This and further information can be obtained from the British Standards Institute, or from http://bsonline.techindex.co.uk

Cutting through the terminology can be rather daunting for a first-time user, because the standards are written in such a general way that they can be interpreted by any organisation and applied to the management of their quality system. To really make sense of what the standard is trying to achieve, we must apply it to specific examples. Let us consider the following case to illustrate some of the key features of ISO 9001: 2000.

Case study: Enviricycle

Jim Seaton is the business development manager for Enviricycle, an organisation involved in the recycling of waste materials (paper, glass and metals). He reports to the managing director and his brief is to initiate all sorts of projects that will take the company forward in its plans for rapid growth.

At present there are 20 recycling plants spread throughout the country, each with its own manager and crew. More than half of these factories have been acquired over the last five years when rival companies were bought out, and they still retain much of their individuality (and staff) although they are slowly conforming to Enviricycle's way of doing things. Each plant collects waste materials and then sorts, grades and 'packages' (ie compresses) them into bales ready for sale. Managers have usually come through the ranks (some have been lorry drivers, others sales representatives) and have many years' experience or are part of a recent graduate recruitment (high-flyer) programme. Head Office is in Newcastle, where the sales and finance functions are carried out.

The company (ie the managing director!) has decided to go for registration to the quality management system ISO 9000: 2001. This requires assessment of the company by (in this case) the British Standards Institute, which is a government body. Holders of ISO 9000: 2001 must demonstrate that they have systems to measure quality at various stages of (in this particular case) the recycling process; that they can trace quality-related problems; that they listen to customer complaints (in this case the customers are the mills who buy Enviricycle's material and turn it back into usable paper, metal, etc); and that they have a system for regularly monitoring and reviewing the quality systems in place. Typical customer complaints are of contaminated or incorrect specification material, poorly packaged material and excessive water content in waste paper.

Commentary

Every organisation must interpret the standard according to its own particular set-up and mode of operation. Enviricycle must take stock of the ways in which it manages and operates its business. Activities which perhaps for years have been carried out and taken for granted must now be assessed against the requirements of the standard, and where deficient, new procedures introduced. It is essential that policies and procedures are documented clearly in the organisation's specifically tailored quality manual, which will take the standard as its framework.

The case outlined above is relatively simple in that the organisation does not actually design anything (admittedly, it repackages and sorts material, but it doesn't actually 'manufacture' them) and could be classed as a 'service operation'. So one area of the standard that is not relevant is design. However, other areas such as purchasing, handling and storage are still relevant (Section 7 of the standard). In this particular case, Section 8 will feature strongly, because operations centre on the need to inspect incoming waste material, check output for non-conformity, and strive for customer satisfaction at the mills.

The managing director has directed that the company should embark upon the ISO route, so it is clear that he is involved, but his responsibility (Section 5) and that of the other managers and other personnel must be clearly described in the quality manual (Section 4). Key people with specific mention may include each recycling plant manager, the sales director and the finance director, as well as internal auditors.

The standard does not usually prescribe a specific way to satisfy a given requirement, but the organisation's quality manual will. For instance, it is a requirement to monitor customer satisfaction, but the actual method by which it is done (customer complaints forms, surveys, etc) may differ between companies or between plants.

Typical problems in such a scenario would include:

- gaining the commitment of directors who might question the cost/ benefit
- gaining the commitment of the plant managers and their staff who might question the need for the ISO to improve quality
- training existing staff who might take this as an affront or meaningless
- educating managers in the system's requirements
- keeping documentation concise and workable so as not to swamp everybody with forms and checklists.

In some ways, however, the introduction of the ISO might serve to integrate the previously separate companies as people become accustomed to the more uniform approach dictated by the ISO requirements.

Another important development in quality standards has been produced by the European Foundation for Quality Management, the EFQM model, outlined below.

The EFQM model of quality

The European Foundation for Quality Management (EFQM) model, as shown in Figure 13.3, indicates that customer satisfaction, people (employee) satisfaction and impact on society are achieved through leadership. Leadership drives the policy and strategy, the people management, resources and processes required to produce excellence in business results.

The EFQM model provides a much more dynamic set of standards for developing and measuring the effectiveness of total quality approaches than ISO 9000. The emphasis is on people and customers as well as processes.

Currently the EFQM model is very popular with many organisations within the UK. It is regarded as inspirational. Many different sectors are using its principles even if not actually signing up to be EFQM members (Dale, 1999); the more ambitious companies present themselves for various EFQM awards. By 2003 there were some 800 organisations that were EFQM members and thousands of organisations which were partnered to the EFQM through similar national organisations in Europe (EFQM, 1999–2003). One such programme is the Investors in Excellence programme launched by the UK Excellence Federation in the northeast of England in October 2004 (Investors in Excellence, 2004).

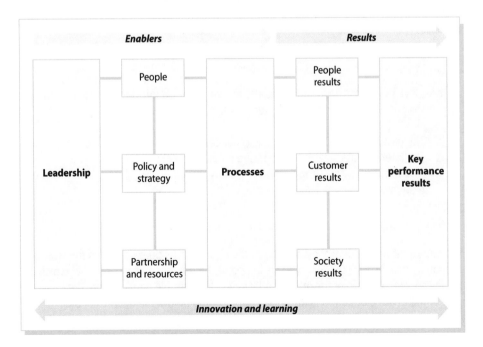

Figure 13.3 *The EFQM model of quality (1999)*
Source: European Foundation for Quality Management, 1999–2003

The NHS and the public sector

And it is not just manufacturing organisations that are favouring this approach. The CLDI (Centre of Learning Development and Innovation, run by the NHS), for instance, is a strong believer in EFQM principles. EFQM has a public sector version of its model (see www.efqm.org).

SMEs

Small and medium-sized enterprises are also catered for separately by the EFQM (again, see www.efqm.org).

Higher education institutions

Another important sector is education. Osseo-Asare and Longbottom (2002) reflect upon the need for higher education institutions (HEIs) to adopt the EFQM approach in response to new government-led (the Quality Assurance Agency, or QAA) quality guidelines. They state that 'government policies dictate that HEIs look to profit-making organisations for models for quality improvement' (ibid), although at that time only a small number of institutions had actually moved towards an explicit use of the EFQM framework. However, quality watchdogs (such as the QAA) continue to exert a great deal of influence throughout the higher education institutions – and for very good reasons: funding and reputation. Prospective students (and their parents) will scan any information on quality ratings they can find, and this often has a significant effect upon their choice of institution. It would appear reasonable to assume that the power of the QAA and the students and their parents will, if anything, increase as student fees increase in the future; the quality of the HEIs will come under ever greater scrutiny and stimulate an even greater push towards the adoption of the EFQM approach and perhaps the badging of EFQM-related certification for marketing purposes.

EFQM awards: three levels of excellence

All three levels of the EFQM awards demonstrate the organisation's focus on quality and can be used as promotional and marketing tools by their recipients.

- The basic award is 'Committed to Excellence'.
- The intermediate award is 'Recognised for Excellence'.
- And the top award is the European Quality Award (EQA), which is a highly prestigious award.

EFQM, ISO and Investors in People

It is important to note that the adoption of the EFQM model does not mean the scrapping of models such as ISO 9000 or Investors in People. Rather, it is a broader model which can readily encompass both of the other two. ISO 9000, for example, would fit into the Processes part of the EFQM model, and Investors in People would fit into the People enabler.

The RADAR concept and EFQM

The so-called RADAR concept (Sheffield Hallam, 2003) can be used with the EFQM framework. This a cyclical model which poses certain key questions related to the following factors:

- **R**esults
- **A**pproach
- **D**eployment
- **A**ssessment and **R**eview.

The first of these, Results, is clearly linked to the Results of the EFQM model. It forces the issue of which results the organisation wishes to focus on. It is interesting to note that the EFQM model considers a balance of results (People, Customers, Key performance indicators and one which most other systems omit, Society results).

The next element, Approach, refers to all of the ways though which the organisation intends to achieve the Results, and how well they are performing in this task.

Deployment considers the implementation of the plans and strategies – how effective and efficient this implementation is.

Assessment and Review are directly linked to the desired results and are the basis for corrective action.

RADAR can be used with the EFQM model when developing business plans or for benchmarking purposes to establish where an organisation is in terms of its quality against where it wishes to be, and also to compare against similar organisations or industry/sector norms.

EXERCISE 13.3

Compare and contrast the approach adopted by ISO 9000 and EFQM quality standards. What have they each got to offer organisations? Is one potentially more valuable than the other? If so, why?

Six Sigma

During the 1980s Motorola devised a quality management system which they called Six Sigma and which has been highly influential, particularly (though not exclusively) in the manufacturing sectors. Its name derives from the 'normal distribution' – the bell-shaped curve used in statistics which shows the natural variation of a given 'population'. The term 'standard deviation' (symbolised by the Greek letter sigma) is used to describe the degree of spread of the curve. The theory states that 99.7 per cent of all values on the normal distribution lie between +3 and –3 standard deviations of the mean – ie a total of six sigma.

Six Sigma has developed over time. At first it was very process-based. It sought to reduce process variation and thereby improve process capability. It uses a collection of existing analytical tools but provides a coherent framework in which to use them.

It has grown in stature, boosted by Motorola's winning the prestigious Malcolm Baldridge National Quality Award (the United States' premier prize for business excellence) in 1988. As Tennant states in *Six Sigma: SPC and TQM in Manufacturing Services* (2001),

> **'Six sigma can be seen as a vision; a philosophy; a symbol; a metric; a goal; a methodology.'**

There are even those who consider Six Sigma to be more 'hard-nosed' (Bicheno, 2002) because it is more bottom-line-oriented than, say, TQM and tackles projects one by one.

Six Sigma uses judo terminology (eg 'black belts') to describe staff who have been trained in its techniques. The accepted notion is that it is essential that those organisations that are considering using the process should educate and train their staff first. The reader is invited to investigate the websites at the end of this chapter as the first step.

EXERCISE 13.4: QUALITY ASSURANCE

Read the following case study and answer the questions at the end of it.

Case study: Rapid Concrete Products Ltd

Rapid Concrete Products Ltd (RCP) is one of a group of associated companies under one ownership. It manufactures concrete paving slabs, kerbstones and reinforced concrete door and window lintels (concrete beams placed above doors and windows to support brickwork above). It operates a batch process system in which a customer order is received for a given number of slabs or lintels and the relevant moulds are prepared to the required sizes and concrete mixed to the required strengths before being poured and left to 'cure'. Small test cubes of concrete (three per batch) are taken at the same time as the concrete is poured into the moulds, and these are tested by a special crushing machine on site so as to ensure that the concrete is reaching the required strengths. These tests are carried out after 24 hours and again after seven days (concrete gains about 50 per cent of its strength within this time although the chemical reactions which are part of this process go on for a very long time). It is essential throughout the curing process that the concrete is not allowed to dry out, and for this purpose it is covered with plastic sheeting and occasionally dowsed with water on hot days.

RCP's managing director (a grand title for what is quite a small operation!) is George Flanders. George handles sales, accounts and administration and is responsible for the overall running of the company.

Sam Dobson is in charge of site operations, a job he has held for the last three years. He is under intense pressure from George (himself under pressure from RCP's board) to hit monthly profit targets. Sam has a general building background, working his way up in the building trade from bricklayer to building foreman to his present position. He is in charge of

10 people on site, a figure made up of two steel reinforcement fixers, a technician responsible for carrying out tests (amongst other duties) , and seven general operatives. Wages are not that good, but a bonus system is in operation for meeting production targets.

Bill Small is Sam's technician – a recent civil engineering graduate who, if truth be told, has only accepted this job until something better comes up. He resents having to work under pressure and is not too happy with Sam's rather cavalier attitude to quality control. For instance, during a major rush job on a batch of concrete paving slabs he was told to 'make sure' that his test results were up to the mark. 'What difference does a few cracked paving slabs make?' were the words Sam used.

As it happened, the results were fine … but Bill wonders about the test equipment itself which seems rather old and without any form of documentation or certificate.

At present, whenever Sam requires a load of concrete he phones the company's sister company Quickmix, and it sends a concrete wagon over to him. Sometimes they need two or three deliveries a day. On occasion there have been mistakes which have resulted in the wrong grade of concrete being delivered. Bill has seen some rather erratic test results (some way too high, others too low) and suspects that at times this happens but is not noticed on site.

Recently, RPC has received complaints from Bettabuild (a small construction company) concerning a batch of reinforced concrete door lintels which they claim were delivered to their yard with a substantial number of defects, including chipped corners and with some lintels having the reinforcement bars showing through.

This is something which George Flanders (the MD) could do without, especially as he is bidding to supply a large order of reinforced concrete walkway panels for a motorway footbridge. However, he knows that quality is of paramount importance in securing this order and is thinking of introducing a quality assurance system.

EXERCISE 13.4 QUESTIONS

Which areas do you think such a quality assurance system could contribute towards in the running of this operation? Explain.

What do you think might be the major difficulties in communicating the relevant changes that have to be made?

EXERCISE 13.5: RADAR

Consider the RADAR concept introduced earlier in the chapter when looking at the EFQM framework. Prepare a list of what you regard as desirable results for your organisation (or, if relevant, you may wish to consider the university or college at which you are studying) in terms of

- people
- customers
- society
- key performance results.

Discuss with others.

EXERCISE 13.6: WEBSITE EXERCISE

With up to half of all public sector organisations in the country having an interest in the EFQM approach there is a wealth of information available on websites. Select an area of your choice and investigate the EFQM links.

EXERCISE 13.7: MANAGING FOR RESULTS MODEL AND QUALITY EXERCISE

Refer back to the Managing for Results model (see Introduction, Chapter 1). It was stated that:

There are clearly links between management focus on quality and the desired results of customer satsifaction. Key performance results relating to efficiency and effectiveness are also related to quality. The role of 'the reflective practitioner' is itself reflected later in this chapter, notably through Deming's plan-do-check-act cycle. The roles of 'strategic thinker' and 'leader/visionary' are much in evidence in the design of quality-related systems such as ISO 9000 and the EFQM model. The implementation of new ways of operating also means that the successful implementor of quality has to be an adept change facilitator.

Take an organisation of your choice. Now outline how the roles of 'reflective practitioner', 'strategic thinker' and 'leader/visionary' might apply in terms of quality within the organisation.

SUMMARY

- Quality can be defined as the degree of excellence achieved by an organisation in delivering products or services to its customers.

- Quality assurance involves the use of documented procedures designed to ensure that the activities carried out in the organisation result in products or services which meet the requirements and needs of customers.

- Quality control involves the application of data collection and analysis to monitor and measure the extent to which quality assurance requirements have been met in terms of product or service performance and reliability.

- Inspection is an after-the-event activity which is concerned with locating faults when they have already occurred so that they can be put right.

- Statistical quality control uses sampling techniques and mathematical analysis to ensure that during design, manufacturing and servicing, work is carried out and material used within the specified limits required to produce the desired standards of quality, performance and reliability.

- Total quality control processes aim to organise quality into the product or service by pursuing policies of assuring quality and continuous improvement in order to create an environment in which all employees can contribute to improving quality as a normal part of their job.

- Total quality embraces everything an organisation does to deliver value and high levels of satisfaction to its customers. It requires the use of a disciplined, structured and comprehensive approach to quality management. It incorporates quality assurance and quality control techniques but, as the name implies, it includes all aspects of an organisation's activities and concerns everyone in the organisation.

- Total Quality Management (TQM) can be defined as a systematic way of guaranteeing that all activities within an organisation happen exactly as they have been planned in order to meet the defined needs of customers. It may be regarded as a brand name given to an approach to total quality.

- The principles of quality management can be summed up in the words 'customer satisfaction', 'continuous improvement', 'involving everyone', 'creating commitment to quality' and 'looking at the system as a whole'.

- Quality management is a process, a way of doing things. It is not a programme with a finite start and finish. The management of quality is a continuous process which may make use of a number of techniques – for example, statistical quality control – but which ultimately depends on the attitudes and behaviour of all concerned. Quality management has to be based on a clearly stated policy.

- The measurement and monitoring of quality can be achieved by comparison of outputs with standards, inspection, statistical quality control, benchmarking and surveys.

- Total quality will only work if everyone is involved. It is important to empower employees so that they are committed to managing quality themselves.

- The major quality standards are ISO 9000 and the EFQM model. But these serve as a framework for designing quality control systems; they are not a substitute for total quality.

- Six Sigma is a powerful quality model pioneered by Motorola and now used in many organisations.

REFERENCES

BBC (1995) (video) *The People's Century*, part 6: *1924*. London, BBC.

BICHENO J. (2002) *The Quality 75: Towards Six Sigma performance in service and manufacturing*. Birmingham, UK, PICSIE Books.

COLLARD R. (1993; 2nd edition) *Total Quality: Success through people*. London, Institute of Personnel and Development.

CROSBY P. B. (1978) *Quality Is Free*. New York, McGraw-Hill.

DALE B. G. (1999; 3rd edition) *Managing Quality*. Oxford, Blackwell.

DEMING W. E. (1986) *Out of the Crisis*. Boston, MA, MIT Center for Advanced Engineering Study.

HUTCHINS D. (1992) *Achieve Total Quality*. Hemel Hempstead, Director Books.

INVESTORS IN EXCELLENCE (2004) *Investors in Excellence, the UK Excellence Recognition Programme: The standard*. Investors in Excellence Ltd.

JURAN J. M. (1988) *Quality Control Handbook*. Maidenhead, McGraw-Hill.

OAKLAND J. S. (2000) *Statistical Process Control*. Oxford, Butterworth-Heinemann.

OSSEO-ASARE A. E. and LONGBOTTOM D. (2002) 'The need for education and training in the use of the EFQM model for quality management in UK higher education institutions', *Quality Assurance in Education*, Vol. 10, No. 1, pp23–6.

PRICE F. (1984) *Right First Time: Using quality control for profit*. Wildwood House/Gower.

SHEFFIELD HALLAM UNIVERSITY (2003) *Embracing Excellence in Education: A summary of the learning gained from applying the EFQM Exellence Model in further and higher education*. Sheffield Hallam University, Centre for Integral Excellence.

TENNANT G. (2001) *Six Sigma: SPC and TQM in Manufacturing Services*. Aldershot, Gower.

TRICKER R. (2001) *ISO 9001: 2000 for Small Businesses*. Oxford, Butterworth-Heinemann.

Websites

Information on ISO 9000 can be found at the British Standards Institute or the website http://bsonline.techindex.co.uk

Information on EFQM can be found at www.efqm.org

Information on the Malcolm Baldridge National Quality Award can be found on the Motorola website at www.mot.com

Information on Six Sigma can be found on the Motorola website and also the General Electric website at www.ge.com

Continuous improvement

This chapter is closely linked to the previous chapter on the subject of quality. It focuses upon the philosophy of continuous improvement and shows some of the approaches now being adopted by leading organisations. The second part of the chapter reflects upon the nature of continuous improvement in terms of its links with how we learn. Recalling our model, we can see that the managerial development roles that are appropriate are those of 'reflective practitioner' and 'lifelong learner'. The focus is on 'continuous improvement' and the desired results are 'key performance results'.

Learning objectives

At the end of this chapter, the reader will understand and be able to explain:

- the significance of continuous improvement
- the process of continuous improvement
- how to assess the impact of continuous improvement teams
- the relevance of 'organisational learning' and 'the learning organisation'.

THE PHILOSOPHY OF CONTINUOUS IMPROVEMENT

The philosophy of continuous improvement is that organisations must constantly seek ways of improving their operational systems, the quality of their products and services, and the customer appeal of those products and services. Continuous improvement involves enlisting the ideas and efforts of everyone in the organisation to ensure that a steady stream of suggestions is obtained and acted upon to provide for incremental improvements to operational and quality performance.

'Incremental' is the key word in continuous improvement. It is not about making sudden quantum leaps in response to crisis situations. It is about adopting a steady step-by-step approach to improving the ways in which the organisation goes about doing things when carrying out the activities required to deliver value to its customers.

The importance of continuous improvement has been emphasised by Oakland (1989):

> **'Never-ending or continuous improvement is probably the most powerful concept to guide management. It is a term not well understood in many organisations, although that must begin to change if those organisations are to survive. To maintain a wave of interest in quality, it is necessary to develop generations of managers who not only understand but are dedicated to the pursuit of never-ending improvement in meeting external and internal customer needs.'**

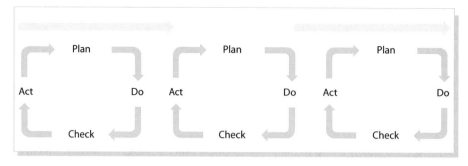

Figure 14.1 *The* kaizen *approach*
Source: courtesy of I. Green, Nissan NMUK, 2004

The significance of continuous improvement

In Japan the process of continuous improvement is called *kaizen*, which is a composite of the words *kai* meaning 'change', and *zen* meaning 'good' or 'for the better'. The *kaizen* management style relies on a foundation of gradual change, building up a culture of quality awareness and constant learning. It is almost the opposite of the Western culture of innovation which is based on sudden change and great leaps forward in business. It can be represented as a series of Deming cycles – see Figure 14.1.

The significance of continuous improvement is that it is a *day-to-day* process in which everyone is involved. As established at Courtelle (the acrylic manufacturers), continuous improvement changes the way people think about their work, and it is the process of change which is important as well as the results achieved.

Its significance also rests on the fact that continuous improvement uses the contributions of *all* employees. It encourages the production of a stream of suggestions for modest, incremental improvements, which can be translated into immediate changes in working practices. As IRS (1991) points out:

> **'Its main focus is customer satisfaction, although resource utilisation is just as important, since it enables an organisation to bring a product or service to a customer at the lowest possible cost.'**

IRS also states that continuous improvement is based on the belief that it is front-line employees who are best able to come up with the ideas necessary for improvement. Employees must therefore be involved in the process. (See Figure 14.2.)

The process of continuous improvement

Continuous improvement is part of the total quality philosophy but it can exist in its own right as a distinct process. Courtelle, for example, abandoned a formal TQM programme and replaced it with continuous improvement.

The Continuous Improvement Research for Competitive Advantage (CIRCA) unit at Brighton University, as reported by IRS (1997), states that the framework for successful continuous improvement consists of five elements:

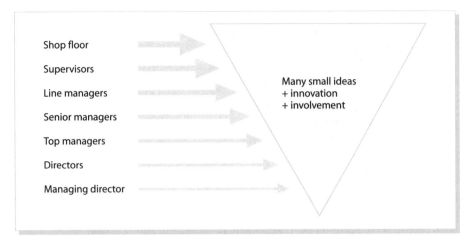

Shop floor

Supervisors

Line managers

Senior managers

Top managers

Directors

Managing director

Many small ideas
+ innovation
+ involvement

Figure 14.2 *The continuous improvement approach*
Source: courtesy of I. Green, Nissan NMUK, 2004

- *strategy* – Clear strategic goals have to be set for continuous improvement providing 'signposted destinations'. These goals should be communicated across the whole organisation and translated into specific targets for teams and individual workers
- *culture* – The culture of the organisation should be developed to support continuous improvement and develop quality awareness. This means defining and communicating values about the need to persist in making incremental improvements to quality as perceived by customers, and about autonomy and empowerment for those involved in improvement on a continuous basis
- *infrastructure* – As recommended by the CIRCA unit, the type of organisation-wide framework necessary for the successful development of continuous improvement includes open management systems, cross-functional management and structures, teamworking, two-way communication processes, joint decision-making, and employee autonomy and participation. This framework depends largely on trust:

'Managers have to trust their workers if they are going to grant them greater responsibility and authority. Empowered employees, similarly, have to trust those in senior positions not to take advantage of employees' ideas to cut jobs. Information is a key component of the creation of greater trust.'

- *process* – The processes used in continuous improvement include individual problem-seeking activities, problem-solving groups, suggestion schemes and company-wide campaigns to promote continuous improvement. Continuous improvement does not simply happen by itself. It has to be encouraged and facilitated by management action
- *tools* – Continuous improvement is enhanced by the use of the various problem-solving tools available for individuals and groups. These include Pareto diagrams, cause-and-effect diagrams and various statistical tools (Bicheno, 2002) such as

control charts and scatter diagrams. Benchmarking is another important tool to establish standards for continuous improvement. Groups can use brainstorming techniques to develop ideas.

INTRODUCING CONTINUOUS IMPROVEMENT PROCESSES

The introduction of continuous improvement is by means of communications, involvement, process development and training. Line managers play a key role in all these activities.

Communications

Top management takes the lead by communicating the values governing continuous improvement, emphasising the need for everyone to be involved, and setting out strategic goals. Line managers develop the top management message in association with their teams, translating it into their own departmental context and agreeing team goals.

The communications should emphasise that everyone is expected to operate proactively in the search for improvement rather than let problems arise and then react to them.

Continuous improvement goals may be set as in the examples given below (adapted from IRS *Employment Trends* No. 624, January 1997):

- to meet client needs at a realistic cost
- to ensure that the service operates efficiently
- to get things right first time
- to increase customer satisfaction and to improve partnership and teamworking internally
- to achieve the total involvement of the workforce towards continuous improvement
- to become a world-class leader
- to achieve full customer satisfaction
- to improve customer satisfaction and service delivery
- to achieve operational goals as part of the strategic plan
- to continuously improve
- to empower any and every employee to effect change if the result improves customer service
- to improve customer satisfaction while reducing organisational operating costs
- to achieve 800 points on the EFQM model
- to increase awareness and encourage involvement as widely as possible across the organisation.

Involvement

The achievement of continuous improvement should involve everyone in the organisation. The IRS survey of continuous improvement policies established that group activities were the most common employee-involvement strategy. Nearly 83 per cent of the organisations had introduced at least one method of involving employees in the continuous improvement process, and of those, 25 per cent had established teamworking or some form of improvement group.

The introduction of continuous improvement requires consideration of how involvement can take place either in the form of group activities or by getting individuals and teams to act as assessors or verifiers. Setting up improvement groups means that an intensive training programme has to be planned and implemented.

Involvement can be organised formally by means of:

- improvement groups – These act upon broad management-given directives and advice. They are often inter-departmental
- problem-solving teams – These are teams brought together to solve specific management-directed problems
- quality circles – These are teams made up from members of one department or work area, identifying their own projects to develop. They may be composed of volunteers and management. Alternatively, supervision may not be directly involved in the teams' deliberations although they will take part in evaluating proposals and ensuring that they are implemented.

Facilitators may be made available from within the organisation to act as educators, trainers and coaches to teams, not only on specific problem-solving techniques but also on the general philosophy of continuous improvement.

Examples of continuous improvement

The following examples are taken from Nissan NMUK's *Production Brief*, a regular news update for staff:

- Example 1: Transporting car body panels (NMUK *Production Brief* 12)
  Previous to the improvement, an operator had to load car body panels onto a 'dolly' (a wheeled carrier) and then manually push the dolly on a 40-metre round-trip. The '*kaizen* team' developed an alternative system whereby the car body panels were loaded onto a 'shuttle' (a carrier on steel line tracks) which could transport the panels at the touch of a button. The estimated savings from this improvement were £80 000 per year.

- Example 2: Pulley power (NMUK *Production Brief* 13)
  At one time operators had to carefully lower a 9-kilogram car hood onto the car body in such a way as to avoid contact with a freshly applied sealant. A new system was devised whereby most of the weight of the hood was taken by using counterbalanced pulleys, reducing the effective weight of the hood to 1 kilogram and thus allowing the operators much more control over this process. The method took only two months to design and install.

Process development

The development of continuous improvement is partly about creating an infrastructure of involvement processes including suggestion schemes and improvement groups, but it is also concerned with developing appropriate tools and assessment procedures.

At Nissan they use a 'QC Story Eight-Step Activity' (quality circle) process, as depicted in Figure 14.3.

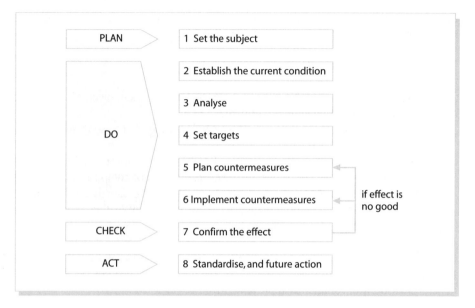

Figure 14.3 *Eight-step continuous improvement*

As reported in *Management Services* (October 1994), British Gas created a 'business improvement matrix' built round 'enablers' (leadership, policy and strategy, people management, resources and processes) and results (customer satisfaction, people satisfaction, impact on society, and business results). The matrix is used by teams to score their achievements against the EFQM categories.

At Courtelle – as reported in IRS *Employment Trends* (March 1991) – the development process emphasised teamworking and included the use of improvement groups directly supported by departmental managers.

At Lucas Electrical's Cannock factory – as reported in *Works Management* (September 1994) – improvement groups became a way of life. They are not voluntary (as was often the case in traditional quality circles). Employees are told that for one hour a week management wants them to think about nothing but developing improvements.

Developing and training

The purpose of education is to increase awareness of the need for continuous improvement. At Lucas Electrical, awareness and education courses were held to change people's perspective. These consisted of a half-day's appreciation course, a two-day course, and a lot of workshops to get everyone thinking and working in groups. This sort of education aims to change behaviour and by so doing encourage the right sort of attitude to improvement.

Training courses may be held to impart problem-solving and decision-making skills. The use of the various analytical and statistical tools can be demonstrated and practised. At Lucas Electrical the training was extended to the whole workforce and covered quality and maintenance techniques such as failure mode and effects analysis, statistical process control and total productive maintenance (TPM).

The role of line managers

Although continuous improvement involves the whole workforce, line managers still have a key role. Even if self-managed improvement groups or quality circles are in operation, it is up to managers to ensure that ideas are put into practice. Where improvement groups are not voluntary, line managers have an even more important leadership role – one of gaining participation and commitment and providing support, rather than issuing directives. Line managers in an active continuous-improvement environment act as enablers, consultants, facilitators and coaches to individual employees. As the IRS report comments:

> **'Middle-level managers no longer engage in their traditional per-formance-monitoring activities but become conduits for training needs and a source of help in implementing suggestions.'**

Evaluation

As Dale (1996) points out:

> **'If an improvement process is to progress in a continuous and incre-mental manner, it is necessary to evaluate it at regular intervals in order to identify the next steps, what else needs to be done, what has worked well and the reasons for this, and what has been unsuccessful; to focus people's efforts, highlight issues and problems and areas of concern or weakness which need to be addressed; and to recognise improvement opportunities.'**

This stage corresponds to the 'Check' phase of Nissan's QC Story (see Figure 14.3). Dale suggests that the progress of the improvement process can be measured and demonstrated in terms of:

- changes in behaviour and attitude (ie reduced industrial-relations conflicts, or the ease with which procedures crossing a variety of functions are changed)
- improvements in the key operational and business performance indicators (ie reduced internal defect rates, field failures and warranty claims; increased customer retention and savings from individual improvement projects)
- the degree to which quality improvement projects are aligned with the company's articulated strategies, policies and guidelines.

Holding the gains

Evaluation should lead to action – in Juran's (1988) phrase: 'holding the gains'. The gains may include better practices and processes, cost-savings and improved service to customers. (This stage corresponds to the 'Standardise, and future action' of Nissan's QC Story – see Figure 14.3.) Continuous effort is required to ensure that incremental gains are consolidated and become part of normal working practices to the benefit of customers and therefore of the organisation.

An example of Nissan's QC Story process

The following example shows a simple application of the QC Story (as featured in NMUK *Production Brief* 13).

1 Oil recycling success
2 The subject: oil overspill when filling car gearbox
3 The current condition: 3.7 litres of oil lost per shift
4 Analysis: this equates to 1,250 litres of oil lost per year
5 Target set: aim to recycle 95 per cent of lost oil
6 Countermeasures: can we recycle? Plan to install a pump to evacuate excess oil
7 Implementation of countermeasures: installation of oil pump and procedure
8 The effect: yes, it works. Savings confirmed
9 Standardise, and future action: incorporate oil recovery as part of the system for new models.

ORGANISATIONAL LEARNING AND THE LEARNING ORGANISATION

Continuous-improvement organisations are learning organisations. Those concerned with improvement need to know about how organisational learning takes place, about the principle of double-loop learning, and about how learning organisations function and develop.

Organisational learning

Organisations have been described by Harrison (1997) as continuous learning systems. Organisational learning can be defined as a process of analysing organisational events, experiences and developments to increase understanding of what must be done to improve performance. It is, or should be, happening all the time, and is therefore a means of enhancing continuous improvement.

Organisational learning aims to develop a firm's resource-based capability which, as defined by Harrison, is

'based on what the firm knows and can do, vested primarily in the legacy of knowledge, strategic assets, networks and reputation bestowed by its past human resources, and in the skills, values and performance of its current people'.

Argyris (1992) makes the point that:

> **'Learning is not simply having a new insight or a new idea. Learning occurs when we take effective action, when we detect and correct error. How do you know when you know something? When you can produce what it is you claim to know.'**

Single- and double-loop learning

[Note: We have mentioned the concept of double-loop learning previously, but it bears elaboration in the context of continuous improvement.]

Argyris suggests that learning occurs under two conditions: first, when an organisation achieves what is intended; and second, when a mismatch between intentions and outcomes is identified and corrected. But organisations do not perform the actions that produce the learning – it is individual members of the organisation who behave in ways that produce it, although organisations can create conditions which facilitate such learning.

Argyris distinguishes between single-loop and double-loop learning. Single-loop-learning organisations define the 'governing variables' – ie what they expect to achieve in terms of targets and standards. They then monitor and review achievements, and take corrective action as necessary, thus completing the loop. Double-loop learning occurs when the monitoring process initiates action to redefine the 'governing variables' to meet the new situation, which may be imposed by the external environment. The organisation has learned something new about what has to be achieved in the light of changed circumstances and can then decide how this should in turn be achieved. This learning is converted into action. The process is illustrated in Figure 14.4.

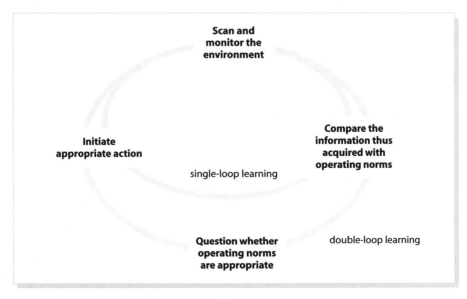

Figure 14.4 *Double-loop learning*
Adapted from Reid, Barrington and Brown, *Human Resource Development*, CIPD, 2004

Argyris believes that single-loop learning is appropriate for routine, repetitive issues – 'It helps get the everyday job done.' Double-loop learning is more relevant for complex, non-programmable issues. Double-loop learning questions why the problem occurred in the first place, and tackles its root causes rather than simply addressing its surface symptoms, as happens with single-loop learning. That is why double-loop learning is a necessary part of continuous improvement.

The learning organisation

A 'learning organisation' has been defined by Wick and Leon (1995) as one that:

> **'continually improves by rapidly creating and refining the capabilities required for future success'.**

As suggested by Garvin (1993), it is one which is

> **'skilled at creating, acquiring, and transferring knowledge, and at modifying its behaviour to reflect new knowledge and insights'.**

He has suggested that learning organisations are good at doing four things:

- systematic problem-solving which rests heavily on the philosophy and methods of the quality movement. Its underlying ideas include:
  - relying on scientific method, rather than guesswork, for diagnosing problems: what can be described as 'hypothesis-generating, hypothesis-testing' techniques
  - insisting on data rather than assumptions as the background to decision-making: what quality practitioners call 'fact-based management'
  - using simple statistical tools such as histograms, Pareto charts and cause-and-effect diagrams to organise data and draw inferences
- experimentation – This activity involves the systematic search for and testing of new knowledge. Continuous improvement programmes are an important feature in a learning organisation
- learning from past experience – Learning organisations review their successes and failures, assess them systematically and record the lessons learned in a way that employees find open and accessible
- transferring knowledge quickly and efficiently throughout the organisation by seconding people with new expertise, or by education and training programmes, as long as the latter are linked explicitly with implementation.

WHEN CONTINUOUS IMPROVEMENT IS MOST LIKELY TO WORK

The conditions under which continuous improvement is most likely to work well exist when

- top management provides the leadership and direction and ensures that the values underpinning continuous improvement are made clear to all concerned and are acted upon

- middle management supports the philosophy of continuous improvement and is prepared actively to support its introduction and to ensure that effort is sustained
- there is a high-involvement, high-commitment culture in the organisation
- there is trust between management and employees and vice versa. Management must trust employees to act independently, and employees must trust management not to exploit their ideas to their detriment. This trust must be earned. Management must deliver on their promises, and employees – with guidance, encouragement and help – must show that they can be trusted to get on with it
- continuous support is provided by management to the improvement process. This will include facilitating improvement groups and providing the education and training required
- action learning takes place – people learn from the actions they take. This means that processes of evaluation and action planning are required
- double-loop learning takes place
- the organisation functions as a learning organisation
- employees are rewarded for their contributions to continuous improvement, although such rewards are non-financial and take the form of various kinds of recognition, for teams and individuals, publicly and privately.

EXERCISE 14.1

1 The following three criticisms have been made about continuous improvement:
- Appropriating workers' ideas is just another form of managerial control.
- Improvement suggestions make employees party to their own exploitation because this invariably involves harder work.
- A successful suggestion may involve a reduction in the number of jobs.

What replies would you give to these comments?

2 Choose a topic for continuous improvement. Describe how the QC Story approach could be applied at each of the eight stages

SUMMARY

- The philosophy of continuous improvement is that organisations must constantly seek ways of improving their operational systems, the quality of their products and services, and the customer appeal of those products and services.
- Continuous improvement involves enlisting the ideas and efforts of everyone in the organisation to ensure that a steady stream of suggestions is obtained and acted upon to provide for incremental improvements to operational and quality performance.
- The significance of continuous improvement is that it is a day-to-day process in which everyone is involved.
- The framework for successful continuous improvement consists of five elements:

strategy; culture; infrastructure; processes such as individual problem-seeking activities, problem-solving groups and suggestion schemes; and problem-solving tools.

- The introduction of continuous improvement is by means of communications, involvement, process development and training. Line managers play a key role in these activities.
- The development of continuous improvement is partly about creating an infrastructure of involvement processes including suggestion schemes and improvement groups, but it is also concerned with developing appropriate tools and assessment procedures.
- If an improvement process is to progress in a continuous and incremental manner, it is necessary to evaluate achievements at regular intervals.
- Continuous effort is required to ensure that incremental gains are consolidated and become part of normal working practices to the benefit of customers and, therefore, of the organisation.
- Continuous improvement organisations are learning organisations.
- Continuous improvement is most likely to work well if there is firm top management leadership and direction, support from middle management, a high-involvement, high-commitment culture in the organisation, trust between management and employees and vice versa, and action learning (by which people learn from the actions they take).

REFERENCES

ARGYRIS C. (1992) *On Organisational Learning*. Cambridge, MA, Blackwell.

BICHENO J. (2002) *The Quality 75: Towards Six Sigma performance in service and manufacturing*. Birmingham, UK, PICSIE Books.

DALE B. G. (1996) 'Sustaining a process of continuous improvement', *The TQM Magazine*, Vol. 8, No. 2, pp49–51.

GARVIN D. A. (1993) 'Building a learning organisation', *Harvard Business Review*, July–August, pp78–91.

HARRISON R. (1997; 2nd edition) *Employee Development*. London, Institute of Personnel and Development.

INDUSTRIAL RELATIONS SERVICES (1991) 'Continuous improvement at Courtelle', IRS *Employment Trends* No. 484, pp11–15.

INDUSTRIAL RELATIONS SERVICES (1997) 'Variety through continuous improvement', IRS *Employment Trends* No. 624, pp8–16.

JURAN J. M. (ed.) (1988) *Quality Control Handbook*. Maidenhead, McGraw-Hill.

NMUK (2004) *Production Briefs* 13, 14.

OAKLAND J. S. (1989) *Total Quality Management*. Oxford, Butterworth-Heinemann.

REID M. A., BARRINGTON H. and BROWN M. (2004) *Human Resource Development: Beyond training interventions*. London, CIPD.

WICK C. W. and LEON L. S. (1995) 'Creating a learning organisation: from ideas to action', *Human Resource Management*, Summer, pp299–311.

INTRODUCTION

In profit-making businesses, the achievement of high standards of customer care is generally recognised as an essential element in gaining a competitive edge. In the public and not-for-profit sectors the delivery of satisfactory levels of service to the community in general or to clients and users in particular is one of the key performance indicators. Customers are the final arbiters of quality.

This chapter explores the processes required by organisations to develop, implement and, importantly, to sustain customer care initiatives.

Learning outcomes

On completing this chapter, the reader will be able to understand and explain:

- the basis and aims of customer care
- how to create a customer care culture
- the meaning of customer service
- the determinants of service quality
- establishing customer expectations
- auditing present customer service arrangements
- setting customer service standards
- measuring and monitoring customer service levels
- developing and implementing customer care strategies and initiatives.

THE BASIS OF CUSTOMER CARE

Customer care is concerned with looking after customers to ensure that their wants, needs and expectations are met or exceeded, thus creating customer satisfaction and loyalty. It is about everything an organisation does when it provides services for its customers. It is also about 'delighting' customers. The aim is not just to meet their needs but to go further – to give them something valuable which they did not expect, and which, perhaps, they did not even know they wanted.

The aims of customer care

The aims of customer care are:

1 to improve customer service by managing all customer contacts to mutual benefit
2 to persuade customers to purchase again – not to switch brands or change to another supplier, and
3 to increase the profitability of a business or the effectiveness of a service-provider organisation.

Ways in which customer care can increase profitability have been listed by Stone (1997):

- less lost business
- fewer lost customers
- repeat sales through increased customer loyalty
- better opportunities for communicating effectively with customers to increase sales
- more scope to identify the potential for increasing revenue from existing customers
- increased revenue and profit by targeting sales to customer needs
- more revenue due to the ability of sales staff to concentrate on calling on higher-revenue prospects
- better and more efficient arrangements for service delivery and therefore lower staff and administration costs.

Why customer care?

It was Jan Carlzon of Scandinavian Airlines System (SAS) who popularised the phrase 'moments of truth', pointing out that whenever customers came into contact with any part of the organisation, the whole was judged by the bit they had seen. Customer care can therefore enhance the organisation's reputation generally.

The need to improve levels of customer care also arises from competitive pressures. Companies compete on the quality of the goods and services they offer, and this extends not only to the products and services themselves but also to the ways in which the service is delivered.

Customer care initiatives can increase profitability, but they can also increase employee motivation and satisfaction by providing them with training to develop their skills and by recognising and rewarding customer care achievements. Research conducted by the Industrial Society (1995) showed that

'Managers see a strong, direct link between customer care programmes and financial performance. As well as tangible benefits such as increased business and higher profitability, customer care initiatives are also felt to deliver intangible advantages that include greater staff motivation and better work relationships.'

Customer care and total quality

Quality was defined in Chapter 13 as the degree of excellence achieved by an organisation in delivering products or services to its customers. Total quality embraces everything an organisation does to deliver value to those customers. Customer care is therefore an integral part of a total quality initiative, although the pursuit of higher standards of customer care can take place without being associated with formal total quality management processes, especially in service organisations. As Cullen and Hollingworth (1982) emphasise:

'A focus on customer satisfaction is the starting-point of quality.'

Total quality is concerned with both internal and external customers. The focus of customer care initiatives is usually on external customers but it is also important to pay attention to the levels of service provided internally.

Customer care and competitiveness

Hutchins (1992) points out that

> 'The customer does not know what is technically or organisationally feasible. So the key challenge to a competitive organisation is to raise the expectations of the marketplace by providing goods and services at quality levels higher than those offered by the competition. As the competition inevitably responds to these challenges, the total quality company will continue to change these expectations, usually in directions not predicted by the competitor.'

Creating a customer care culture

As the Industrial Society (1995) has stated:

> 'The continuity of customer care depends on establishing a pervasive culture of total customer focus by having continuous customer care conversations through the organisation. All activities must be open to re-examination to identify areas in which customer care can be improved.'

The creation of a customer care culture should be based on an understanding of the meaning of customer service, the determinants of service quality, research on customer expectations and an audit of current arrangements. These provide the foundation for the development of customer care strategies and initiatives. Customer care achievements need then to be continually measured and monitored to ensure that the initiatives are working and to provide the basis for remedial action as necessary. The rest of this chapter is devoted to describing each of these activities in turn.

THE MEANING OF CUSTOMER SERVICE

Customer service is to a certain degree intangible because it is about performance – the manner in which the service is delivered – as well as about outcomes – what the customer actually gets. Holberton (1991) has offered five different meanings for the term 'customer service':

- the activities involved in ensuring that a product or service is delivered to the customer on time, in the correct quantities

- the inter-personal working relationships between the staff of a supplier and a customer
- the provision of after-sales repair and maintenance
- the department of an organisation that handles customer complaints
- the order-taking department of an organisation.

DETERMINANTS OF SERVICE QUALITY

Ten determinants of service quality have been identified by Pasuram *et al* (1985):

- reliability – consistency of performance and dependability
- responsiveness – the willingness or readiness to provide service
- competence – having the required skills and knowledge to perform the service
- access – approachability and ease of contact
- courtesy – politeness, respect, consideration and friendliness of contact personnel
- communication – keeping the customers informed in language they can understand, and listening to them
- credibility – trustworthiness, believability, honesty
- security – freedom from danger, risk or doubt
- understanding/knowing the customer – making the effort to understand the customer's needs
- tangibles – the physical evidence of service.

System- *v* person-oriented

In recent years there has been a trend amongst companies to rationalise customer interaction through the use of set scripts and choice of product packages. There are clearly advantages for companies in terms of efficiency savings. A typical example of such rationalisation is that of the new call centres which process various customer transactions over the telephone (for instance, car insurance). These may be classed as 'system-oriented' approaches to customer service.

At the other extreme there are still companies who pride themselves upon offering a more personal or 'person-oriented' approach. Characteristics of these approaches are shown in Table 15.1.

Table 15.1 *System- v person-oriented characteristics of customer service*

System-oriented	Person-oriented
May be 'virtual' – ie computerised	Face-to-face
Economic in scale	Time-consuming, relatively expensive
Little training required	Requires experienced operators/individuals
Impersonal	Relationship-oriented
Scripted, standardised	Individual
Trust? Risk? Uncertainty?	Relies on personal advice

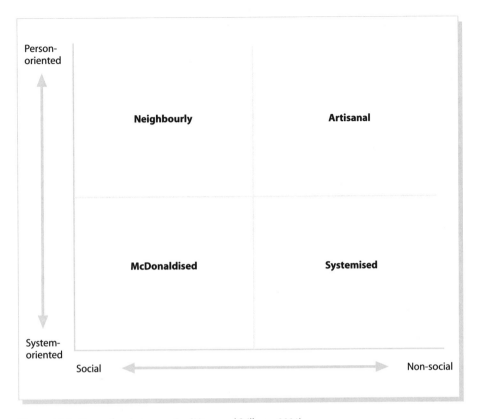

Figure 15.1   *Types of customer service (Ritzer and Stillman, 2001)*

The term 'McDonaldisation' has been used to describe a particular type of system-oriented system. This extends the scientific management approach (involving amongst other things careful and systematic analysis of the task and its constituent parts, careful training and selection of workers) to include customers within the system – for instance, by waiting for their 'number' in a queue, by adopting the specific jargon when making an order, by clearing away their own tables.

Ritzer and Stillman (2001) have categorised four types of customer service in terms of the variables of person-oriented and system-oriented service: see Figure 15.1.

Here we note that McDonaldisation is system-oriented but also has a social element ('Have a nice day!', and accompanying smile). The non-social/system-oriented service is termed 'systemised' (an example of this might be the impersonal completion of an insurance form on the Internet). The person-/social-oriented serviced is described as 'neighbourly' (an example of this might be the local milkman who stops for a chat on his round and enquires about your holidays). And the person-/non-social-oriented system is represented as 'artisanal' (for instance, the librarian who shows you how to access a particular class of journal).

Developing a customer care strategy

At the top level of the strategy process the term 'corporate strategy' is often used. This describes what sort of business(es) the organisation should be involved with. (For instance, an organisation that runs paper mills may decide to go into forestry, packaging, or even consider setting up a plastic films division.) Through its corporate mission statement it defines the reason for its existence, its prime purpose.

The next level of strategy concerns each of the businesses that the organisation is operating – its 'business strategy'. One way in which organisations do this is to consider their internal strengths and weaknesses and to match these to external opportunities and threats, bearing in mind the business objectives of what it would like to achieve. There are dynamic factors at work here if we consider that the organisation is operating in an 'open' rather than a 'closed' system. Also, we should note that strategy is not always determined rationally but is often influenced by political factors (eg the power and internal agendas of those who work within it). Advanced discussion of strategy is outside the scope of this text. However, for our purposes we may consider customer care strategy to be one of the inter-related functional strategies within the business strategy. (Others might include strategies on marketing, production, quality, human resources and/or finance.)

Customer care strategy concerns the long-term plans in respect of customer care, and has implications for every department in the organisation. Adopting a rational approach to the process of developing a customer care strategy, an organisation might follow the sort of process outlined below:

1 Develop customer care mission and value statements consistent with business mission and objectives.
2 Assess customer expectations and reactions (which has the effect of asking 'Where do we want to be?').
3 Analyse present customer care arrangements (this asks the question 'Where are we now?' in terms of satisfying the customer), including benchmarking.

Clearly, if there is a performance gap between the first two of these steps, the organisational strategy should address how to reduce this gap. However, even if the gap is negligible we must bear in mind the dynamic aspects of customer expectations which can change (eg with the advent of new technology or competition from other companies) and should not be complacent.

4 Develop standards and measures.
5 Involve staff.
6 Formulate and implement a communication strategy.
7 Identify and meet training needs.
8 Implement customer care processes.
9 Monitor.
10 Analyse results.
11 Take corrective action.

In the next section we consider each of these areas.

Customer care mission and value statements

Customer care strategies indicate the intentions of the organisation concerning the maintenance and improvement of customer service levels. They emphasise the customer orientation of the business and the part everyone is expected to play. The point may be made in the words of Furnham and Gunter (1993) that:

> **'Customer service ... depends crucially on the people who work for the organisation. Good service stems from an organisation's ability, through skilled and knowledgeable staff, to fulfil the obligations it undertakes in its service strategy.'**

Customer care strategies emanate from top management and set the direction. They may well be summarised in a mission statement such as the Xerox statement reported by Furnham and Gunter:

> **'Xerox is a quality company. Quality is a basic business principle for Xerox. Quality means providing our external and internal customers with innovation products and services to fully satisfy their require- ment. Quality improvement is the job of every Xerox employee.'**

The mission statement can be supported by value statements which spell out the import- ance attached to service quality and provide a basis for measuring customer care performance for the organisation, teams and individuals. The statement might refer to such values as:

- putting the customer first
- understanding the product or service
- meeting customers' needs and expectations
- the importance of customer care to the organisation.

Mission and value statements underpin the customer care strategy, which will itself reflect the organisation's intentions with regard to:

- the analysis of customer expectations and reactions
- setting standards
- measuring and monitoring performance against the standards
- providing staff with information on the importance of customer care (a communi- cation strategy)
- providing staff with leadership
- training staff
- rewarding teams and individuals for good performance
- helping and supporting people to improve performance
- attending to the needs of both internal and external customers
- generally developing a customer care culture which includes managing change, especially the transition from the existing to the desired state.

EXERCISE 15.1

Company 'A' and Company 'B' both make and sell light trailers of the sort towed by the average family saloon car or modern 4x4 vehicle. Company 'A' is a small family business which only makes trailers. It produces a range of trailers and will also take customers' orders and build custom-made trailers. Company 'B' is a large multi-site car accessory business selling everything from car parts to driver's gloves. It produces a set range of trailers. It does not custom-build any trailers.

Construct a possible mission statement for Company 'A' and also one for Company 'B'.

ESTABLISHING CUSTOMER EXPECTATIONS

When developing customer care initiatives, it is necessary to establish what the customer expects in terms of 'deliverables': conformity to specifications, quality, price, and reliability in service, in delivery dates, in price and in after-sales service. The two fundamental questions to be answered are:

1   What services do existing and potential customers want? and
2   What service is provided by competitors?

Establishing customer expectations can be done by surveying customers. Abbey Life sent out questionnaires to 1,000 clients in each of its business sections. On the credit side, this revealed that customers were satisfied with the time it took for their letters to be answered. But there was dissatisfaction with replies that customers felt did not fully answer their questions. The company now believes it has solved this problem.

Customer expectations can also be assessed by using market research techniques such as opinion surveys and focus groups. Further information can be obtained from data the organisation may already have in the form of analyses of customer complaints and questions. The opinion of staff about what their customers want is worth having. Industry data published by trade associations and in journals is another source.

EXERCISE 15.2

Recent developments in call centre technology now means that some large companies such as banks classify customers on their potential profitability by sophisticated use of computers that can analyse the postcode of the caller. 'Intelligent' call-routing is then made to appropriate operators who have more scope to negotiate with and offer better service to 'rich' customers whom they wish to retain (Winnett and Thomas, 2003).

Discuss what you regard as the advantages and disadvantages of such 'intelligent' call-routing.

ANALYSING PRESENT CUSTOMER CARE ARRANGEMENTS

It is important to find out what customers want. It is equally important to establish what they get. If the level of service delivery falls below expectations, a customer care gap will be revealed which must be filled.

Walker (1990) suggests that a customer service audit has to address both material service and personal service. Material service is what is actually delivered. Customers want value for money, products or services which function properly in the way they are supposed to do, efficient delivery systems, and responsive after-sales. Personal service can make a greater impact on customer attitudes than material service. Customers want to be dealt with by staff who have the knowledge, skills and competences required. These will include technical and product knowledge, the inter-personal skills needed to handle customers, being able to deal with complaints, and generally being helpful, polite and courteous.

The audit aims to establish what is happening now in order to identify gaps in customer care provision and to indicate what must be done to develop customer care strategies, policies and initiatives. The audit is concerned mainly with internal procedures to find out the extent to which they are capable of meeting customer expectations.

However, an analysis of customer expectations carried out by means of questionnaires and market research will provide criteria against which present arrangements can be assessed.

Benchmarking

It is at this stage that benchmarking should be carried out to find out, as far as possible, what competitors are doing. This will provide a further check on the extent to which present arrangements are satisfactory, and a basis for developing customer service standards for the organisation.

DEVELOPING CUSTOMER SERVICE STANDARDS AND MEASURES

Customer service standards are related to the key aspects of customer service revealed by surveys of customer expectations and present arrangements. The aim is to distil the information to identify critical customer service success factors. These are likely to fall into main categories:

- speed of response and processing of orders, enquiries, complaints, requests for service or spare parts
- quality of response to enquiries or complaints
- backlog of enquiries or complaints
- in call centres, call pick-up and lost-call rate
- number of complaints (as a proportion of total orders)
- time taken between order and delivery
- the extent to which customer expectations have been met in service delivery
- customer reactions to service and perceptions of service quality.

Examples of how qualitative standards might be expressed are:

- response rates – percentage of letters or calls answered in *n* days

- call pick-up – percentage of calls answered in *n* seconds or within a certain number of rings (six at Hertz, for example)
- lost-call rates – percentage of inbound calls lost
- backlog – no more than *n* items to be processed at end of day/week
- field servicing – time to complete service.

More qualitative standards can be developed – for example, on how customers should be approached and be responded to, how complaints should be dealt with, and what information should be provided in response to enquiries. These qualitative standards can be set out under the headings for service quality given earlier in this chapter: 'reliability', 'responsiveness', 'competence', 'access', 'courtesy', 'communication', 'credibility', 'security', 'understanding/knowing the customer' and 'the physical evidence of service'.

EXERCISE 15.3

Refer back to the 'mini case' scenario outlined in Exercise 15.1.

Make lists of what Company 'A' and Company 'B' might describe as 'critical success factors'.

Involving staff

Staff should be involved throughout the process. They should certainly participate in developing standards and measures, and should take part in monitoring performance and in deciding on any actions they need to take.

Communications

It is essential to take the trouble to develop and implement a communications strategy. Employees must be informed of the customer care strategies, policies and values of the business. They should be aware of the standards they have to achieve and why they are important – to their own future and security as well as to the prosperity or success of the organisation. They should understand how their performance will be measured and rewarded, and be fully aware of the benefits of the training they will be given in customer care.

IDENTIFYING AND MEETING TRAINING NEEDS

Training is the key to successful customer care. The needs for training are identified by defining the gap between what is being done and what should be being done. The training will be concentrated on the development and practice of inter-personal skills and the provision of information on the organisation's customer care policies and procedures.

Companies, as reported by IDS (1992), place considerable emphasis on the importance of including a strong customer care context in induction training. Customer service information is included in training packs at B&Q, Kent's Art and Libraries Department, and Hertz.

Customer service levels must be continuously improved. All the companies in the IDS survey spent considerable time and resources in stressing the importance of the customer to their employees and in developing their skills.

NVQs in customer service

National Vocational Qualifications (NVQs), and in Scotland SVQs, are well established as measures of competence at various levels in a great number of practical and technical disciplines. As with all educational endeavours, their standards have to be rigorously maintained and occasionally updated by the authorities licensed to award the qualifications.

National standards for NVQs in customer service were originally developed by the Customer Service Lead Body. Current standards have been described by the Department for Education and Skills (DfES) NVQ website (2004) in the following terms:

> **'The central feature of NVQs is the National Occupational Standards (NOS) on which they are based. NOS are statements of performance standards which describe what competent people in a particular occupation are expected to be able to do. They cover all the main aspects of an occupation, including current best practice, the ability to adapt to future requirements and the knowledge and understanding which underpins competent performance. The standards are developed by Standards Setting Bodies . . .'**

Staff can be encouraged to take NVQs and given support by their organisations and their managers.

NVQs are arranged in five levels of ascending competence. There are various awarding bodies. If we look at City & Guilds (openQuals website, 2004) NVQs in customer service, we note the units at levels 1, 2, 3, and 4 shown in Table 15.2.

Table 15.2 *NVQs in customer service, levels 1–4*

LEVEL 1	LEVEL 2	LEVEL 3	LEVEL 4
Unit 01 Prepare yourself to give good customer service	Unit CS01 (Mandatory) Give customers a positive impression of yourself and your organisation	Unit CS001 (Mandatory) Organise, deliver and maintain reliable customer service	Unit 01 (Mandatory) Build and maintain effective customer relations
Unit 02 Maintain a positive and friendly attitude	Unit CS02 (Mandatory) Deliver reliable customer service	Unit CS002 (Mandatory) Improve the customer relationship	Unit 02 (Mandatory) Promote and support customer service
Unit 03 Communicate effectively with customers	Unit CS03 (Mandatory) Develop customer relationships	Unit CS003 (Mandatory) Work with others to improve customer service	Unit 03 (Mandatory) Work as a member of a team to enhance customer service
Unit 04 Do your job in a customer-friendly way	Unit CS04 (Mandatory) Resolve customer service problems	Unit CS004 (Mandatory) Monitor and solve customer service problems	Unit B2 (optional) Manage the use of physical resources
Unit 05 Provide customer service with the rules	Unit CS05 (optional) Support customer service improvements	Unit CS005 (Mandatory) Promote continuous improvement	Unit C2 (optional) Develop your own resources
Unit 06 Recognise and deal with customer queries, requests and problems	Unit CS06 (optional) Develop personal competence through delivering customer service	Unit CS006 (optional) Develop your own and others' customer service skills	Unit 04 (optional) Contribute to the development of customer service staff
	Unit CS07 (optional) Promote additional products or services to customers	Unit CS007 (optional) Organise and promote products or services to customers	Unit 05 (optional) Evaluate the quality of customer service
	Unit CS08 (optional) Process customer service information	Unit CS008 (optional) Lead the work of teams and individuals to improve customer service	Unit 06 (optional) Contribute to developing a customer service strategy for a specific area

Table 15.2 *continued*

LEVEL 1	LEVEL 2	LEVEL 3	LEVEL 4
			Unit 07 (optional) Contribute to designing quality improvements to customer service
			Unit 08 (optional) Contribute to implementing quality improvements to customer service
			Unit 09 (optional) Plan, organise and control customer service
			Unit 10 (optional) Lead and improve the work of customer service staff
			Unit 11 (optional) Handle referred customer complaints
			Unit 12 (optional) Maintain and develop a healthy and safe customer service environment
			Unit 15 (optional) Manage the operation of telecommunication facilities for call handling activities

Source: City & Guilds. The City and Guilds of London Institute accepts no liability for the contents of this book.

The NVQ units can be used as the framework for ongoing customer care training within the organisation.

Implementation

Implementation involves putting customer care procedures in place and ensuring that they work. It is aided by communication and training, but the main responsibility rests with line management and supervision. Implementation covers such activities as:

- applying turnaround standards for replying to letters
- collecting and analysing samples of work – as at Abbey Life, where records are kept of errors which are fed back to employees who are given quality standards to meet
- installing equipment such as that required to measure performance in call centres which displays the number of calls to be answered or to monitor telephone calls
- developing performance-management processes which involve agreeing targets for customer care performance, reviewing results and preparing personal development plans to improve performance
- regularly holding customer service audits and consumer surveys.

MEASURING AND MONITORING CUSTOMER SERVICE LEVELS

The measurement of quality service levels is the basis for monitoring and managing customer care. The starting-point is to define standards as described above. The next step is to decide how to measure and monitor the achievement of those standards so that corrective action can be taken. In the formative stages of developing a customer care strategy, measurements indicate where the priorities lie by highlighting areas for concern. The main measurement and monitoring techniques are described below.

Customer questionnaires

Customer questionnaires are probably the most common method of measuring satisfaction. They are presented immediately after a service comes to an end – for example, when leaving a hotel or on completion of a car service. Questionnaires ask customers to rate the service provided from 'excellent' to 'poor' in such categories as 'politeness/courtesy', 'willingness to help', 'attention to requirements', 'speed of response', 'overall quality'. The responses are analysed and the analysis is fed back to staff. Customer questionnaires provide immediate reactions – but they may be completed only by an unrepresentative sample of customers – for example, those who were highly satisfied or dissatisfied.

Customer surveys

Customer surveys, often conducted by market research companies or specialised consumer research firms, cover a much wider and more balanced sample of customers. They ask questions or get customers to respond on a scale (eg 'fully agree', 'generally agree', 'disagree') to such statements as:

- *Staff respond to customer requests promptly.*
- *Staff are polite.*
- *Staff are not always willing to help customers.*
- *Staff keep their promises to customers.*
- *Staff do not give you individual attention.*
- *You have to wait ages to get through to the company by telephone.*
- *Staff return your calls quickly.*

Customer surveys can be comprehensive and illuminating if properly constructed and run. It is best to conduct them regularly in order to analyse trends. Results should be fed back to staff so that action can be taken. But surveys, like questionnaires, cover only shoppers who buy, and they therefore do not identify any aspects of staff behaviour which may cause some shoppers to leave before buying. And customers may find it hard to remember the details of their treatment some time after the event.

An alternative approach which overcomes at least the first of these objections (although it may create other problems) is mystery shopping.

Mystery shopping

Mystery shopping enables the quality of customer service to be assessed at the critical point at which customers come into contact with sales staff – in a retail or service outlet or over the telephone. People (usually from market research firms) are sent into a retail outlet to see how they are treated. Or they may make a telephone enquiry. They then record their observations of how well or badly they were handled against a set of basic standards covering such aspects of service as friendly reception, paying attention to the shopper's wants, helpfulness, knowledge of the product, willingness to listen to and respond to the customer's requests and queries, and avoiding pressurised sales techniques.

At Allied Carpets Group, as reported by IRS (1995), mystery shopping research, together with new technology recording the stores' busiest sales times, was used as a basis for identifying customer needs and restructuring the organisation accordingly. The researchers found that in busy periods there could be long delays before a salesperson approached a customer simply because staff were fully occupied. Allied Carpets dealt with this problem by introducing more flexible staffing arrangements, including raising the proportion of part-time staff.

Mystery shopping could be regarded as a process of spying on staff – catching them unawares and keeping them on their toes by subterfuge rather than effective supervision. However, specialised mystery shopping consultants claim that the ethics of mystery shopping should be to reward staff for good performance, not to castigate them for poor performance. Those companies which adopt an ethical approach to mystery shopping do not request reports that identify individual staff but rely on general reports setting out strengths and weaknesses in various areas.

Mystery shopping can be extended to call centres and telephone contacts with companies. The same approach is used, but speed of response, helpfulness and understanding are particularly important.

EXERCISE 15.4

Describe and evaluate the various methods of measuring customer service levels.

Do you think mystery shopping is a legitimate approach to measurement? If so, why? If not, why not?

Analysing results: company analysis

A company can undertake its own analysis of the quality of the service provided for both external and internal customers. At AA Insurance and Abbey Life, equipment has been installed in their telephone call centres which displays the number of calls waiting to be answered. As reported by IDS (1992), Abbey Life also uses its Customer-Focused Quality Initiative to sample and check its employees' work. Errors in policies due to be sent out to clients are analysed and fed back to employees who are given quality targets to attain. Errors are classified as being of presentation, accuracy or completeness. The errors are listed on the employees' own scorecards, at the bottom of which there is space for managers to enter a prescription to rectify any problems.

Some organisations monitor telephone conversations between staff and customers as a basis for feedback.

Benchmarking

Benchmarking – comparing the standards achieved by comparable organisations with those achieved in one's own organisation – is a valuable way of assessing how the organisation is doing.

Supervisors

Supervisors are in the best position to observe from day to day the quality of customer care delivered by their staff. Supervisors should be made aware of the standards they are looking for and they should share this knowledge with their team. In a retail organisation, they can walk around the store and check on how things are going. They can praise good work and discuss how weaknesses can be overcome.

TAKING CORRECTIVE ACTION

Customer care standards and levels of service have to be continually monitored, and the results analysed and fed back to employees. Feedback has to point the way to specific improvements in the service quality and/or the introduction of new processes to improve service levels, including training.

Assessing team and individual performance

Monitoring and feedback should generate the information required to assess team and individual performance. This should be done systematically and at regular intervals. It should not wait until an annual performance appraisal meeting is held.

Feedback and performance assessments should be constructive. Good performance should be recognised, and areas for further improvement – and how it is to be achieved – agreed.

EXERCISE 15.5

Read the case study below and answer the questions at the end.

Case study: 'after sales' at Berghaus

Berghaus, based in the north-east of England, is a leading company in the design and manufacture of outdoor clothing and equipment. Its products are instantly recognisable to a whole generation of climbers, walkers and skiers. Their motto, *Trust is earned*, reflects not only the quality of their products but an attitude towards the customer.

Berghaus operates an after-sales department which has close links with the sales, quality assurance and design departments, and with product managers. It is thus in a position to feed back information from customers to all parts of the company. The after-sales department talks about the 'whole package' which the customer purchases and of which it considers itself an important part.

The company prides itself on being responsive to customer suggestions and complaints, and on giving reliable advice to end-users. It rarely uses computerised telephone queuing, much preferring customers to speak directly to a 'human voice'. Many members of staff have an interest (if not a passion!) for the outdoors; this and product training enables staff to speak knowledgeably about the products. Berghaus's chairman is the well-known mountaineer Sir Chris Bonington. Alan Hinkes – well on the way to achieving his quest to climb all 14 of the world's 8,000-metre mountains – is among several high-profile figures who belong to the Berghaus team.

Berghaus has two sets of external customers – the various independent retail outlets (climbing and walking shops, for instance), and groups and individuals who are end-users of the equipment. It strives to maintain a close partnership with the retailers, to the extent that it offers training and technical advice on products; it will work with retailers to offer advice and solutions for the more unusual problems or more demanding end-users. The emphasis is on retaining customer and end-user loyalty to the brand. For instance, Berghaus has links with a specialist company which will advise upon and repair items of clothing (bear in mind that specialist mountain jackets can typically cost £200–£300). This might seem to some to be a strange stance to adopt in today's throw-away convenience society. However, the focus is on providing a service for the customer who is therefore more likely to begin to trust the company. Customer service thus adds to the overall product package – the customer goes away happy and the company has gained a measure of loyalty and credibility for that customer's next purchase.

The company also cares for the customer in a much wider sense, through its support for various community ventures, to which it donates clothing and equipment. (Berghaus is a backer of 'Action in Nepal', for instance, which assists the Sherpa community, of the Durham/Lesotho link which helps the tiny mountain kingdom of Lesotho, and more locally of the Uphill Ski Club based in Aviemore, which caters for people with various disabilities who wish to enjoy the sport.) The company strives to maintain a positive environmental stance as well.

Feedback on the products comes in different ways. Every month a summary of all customer complaints and queries is presented at senior level. A variety of product testers (some are very well known in the outdoors field, others are people who work outdoors for their livelihood) report back on various products which they have used. This wealth of knowledge and experience from the department is fed back into the design of new and improved products.

EXERCISE 15.5 QUESTIONS

Which factors in the case study do you think assist or are consistent with the motto *Trust is earned?*

Referring to Figure 15.1 *Types of customer service,* which type(s) of service do you think Berghaus provides for a) retailers, and b) individuals and groups who are end-users of the products? List potential benefits and drawbacks of this service as you see relevant for this type of company.

EXERCISE 15.6

Consider low-touch organisations (eg telephone directory enquiries). List benefits and drawbacks for you, the customer.

SUMMARY

- Customer care is concerned with looking after customers to ensure that their wants, needs and expectations are met or exceeded, thus creating customer satisfaction and loyalty.
- The aims of customer care are 1) to improve customer service by managing all customer contacts to mutual benefit, 2) to persuade customers to purchase again – not to switch brands or change to another supplier, and 3) to increase the profitability of a business or the effectiveness of a service-provider organisation.
- Customer care is an integral part of a total quality initiative, although the pursuit of higher standards of customer care can take place without being associated with formal total quality management processes, especially in service organisations.
- The term 'customer service' can involve delivery, inter-personal relationships, after-sales service, handling complaints and taking orders.
- It is necessary to establish what the customer expects in terms of 'deliverables': conformity to specifications, quality, price, and reliability in service, in delivery dates, in price and in after-sales service.
- It is equally important to establish what customers get. If the level of service delivery falls below expectations – then a customer care gap will be revealed that must be filled.
- A customer service audit is required which addresses both material service (what is delivered) and personal service.
- Standards are related to the key aspects of customer service revealed by surveys of customer expectations and present arrangements. The aim is to distil the information to identify critical customer service success factors. These are likely to fall into such categories as speed of response and processing, quality of response, backlogs, complaints, customer reactions.
- The main methods of monitoring levels of service are customer questionnaires, customer surveys, mystery shopping, company analysis, observations by supervisors and benchmarking.

■ Customer care strategies reflect the intentions of the organisation concerning the maintenance and improvement of customer service levels. They emphasise the customer orientation of the business and the part everyone is expected to play. Customer care strategies emanate from top management and set the direction. They may well be summarised in a mission statement supported by a statement of core values.

■ The key elements in a customer care programme are involving staff, communicating to them, and providing training.

REFERENCES

CULLEN J. and HOLLINGWORTH J. (1982) *Implementing Total Quality*. Bedford, Jfs Publications.

DfES (2004) NVQ on www.dfes.gov.uk/nvq (accessed 6/12/04).

FURNHAM A. and GUNTER B. (1993) *Corporate Assessment*. London, Routledge.

GRONROOS C. (2000) *Service Management and Marketing: A customer relationship management approach*. Chichester, Wiley.

HOLBERTON S. (1991) 'An idea whose time has not only come but will prevail', *Financial Times*, 30 March, p10.

HUTCHINS D. (1992) *Achieve Total Quality*. Hemel Hempstead, Director Books.

INCOMES DATA SERVICES (1992) IDS Study, *Customer Care*. London, IDS.

INDUSTRIAL RELATIONS SERVICES (1995) 'The customer is boss: matching employee performance to customer service needs', IRS *Employment Trends* No. 585, pp7–10.

INDUSTRIAL SOCIETY (1995) 'Managing best practice', *Customer Care*, No. 9.

JOHNSON G. and SCHOLES K. (1989) *Exploring Corporate Strategy: Text and cases*. London, Prentice Hall.

OPENQUALS (2004) QCA's database of accredited qualifications, on www.openquals.org.uk/openquals/qualification (accessed 6/12/04).

PASURAM A., ZEITHAMI W. and BERRY I. (1985) 'A conceptual model of service quality and its implications for future research', *Journal of Retailing*, 44, pp12–40.

RITZER G. and STILLMAN T. (2001) 'From person- to system-oriented service', in STURDY A., GRUGULIS I. and WILMOTT H. (eds) *Customer Service: Empowerment and entrapment*. Basingstoke, Palgrave (formerly Macmillan Press).

STONE M. (1997) 'Evaluating the profitability of customer service', in MARLEY P. (ed.) *The Gower Handbook of Customer Service*. Aldershot, Gower.

WALKER D. (1990) *Customer First: A strategy for quality service*. Aldershot, Gower.

WINNETT R. and THOMAS Z. (2003) 'Are you a second-class consumer?', *Sunday Times*, 19 October.

Future directions: managing change

CHAPTER 16

INTRODUCTION

Organisations are in a perpetual state of change. This is because of constant external pressures and the need to innovate and adapt to new demands and circumstances. To survive and thrive, businesses have to grow. They must develop new products, expand into new markets, re-organise, re-engineer, introduce new technology and change working methods and practices. Even if this does not happen voluntarily, change may be forced upon them by competition and developments in the business, or by the political and social environment. Managers have to be able to introduce and to manage change, and gain the commitment of their teams to implementing and living with the change.

Change, as Rosabeth Moss Kanter (1984) has suggested, can be regarded as the process of 'analysing the past to elicit the present actions required for the future'. It involves moving from a present state, through a transition state, to a future desired state.

In terms of the book schema (Figure 16.1), we are focusing on the need to 'Provide direction', 'Gain commitment' and 'Facilitate change'. We might include all of the Desired results (depending upon the change). In terms of 'Managerial development' those of 'Leader/visionary', 'Change facilitator' and 'Strategic thinker' are, perhaps, the most relevant. However, we may need to draw on any or all of the elements of the model for a given change situation.

In the first part of this chapter we note that 'change' is an extremely broad term, and we consider it in terms of both operational and strategic change, 'hard' and 'soft' changes, and internal change. The well-known (early) work of Kurt Lewin (iceblock three-phase model and

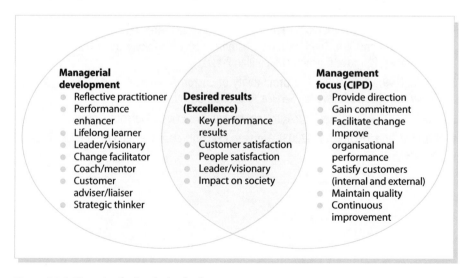

Figure 16.1 *Managing for Results: book schema*

forcefield analysis) is outlined and introduces the reader to the concept of managing change. Barriers to change and associated approaches by management to reduce of overcome these barriers feature strongly. However, Lewin's ideas and the work of other early theorists have been challenged as being too simplistic and offering a 'recipe' approach to change that does not fully reflect the complex nature of the environment in which change occurs. The reader is thus directed at other points in this chapter to consider change as something which managers have limited ability to analyse and control, depending upon the nature of change itself and the complex environment in which change is occurring.

Perhaps the question we must ask ourselves if we are 'managing for results' is the extent to which our attempts to analyse (and possibly influence) change may benefit from a consideration of the theoretical models presently available, flawed though they may be. Certainly a 'contingency' approach, which attempts to take into account the specific variables operating at the time, would seem to offer a reasonable compromise in that it recognises the uniqueness of every situation while still allowing the use of certain key guidelines on managing change. The positioning of this chapter, at the end of the book, allows for reflection on earlier chapters and the incorporation of theories and concepts in such a contingency approach – for instance, the effects of power and politics, which can often override the rational approach to change management; organisational culture, which is clearly linked to internal change; the role of the manager in the change process as change facilitator.

Learning outcomes

On completing this chapter, the reader will:

- have an understanding of the nature of change
- be able to identify typical triggers for change
- be able to outline various early change management models such as those of Lewin
- be aware of the emergent approaches for managing change
- be able to propose ways to implement change in the work situation.

WHAT DO WE MEAN BY 'CHANGE'?

The term 'change' is extremely broad. At the one extreme it means something that has a significant impact upon the organisation; at the other extreme it may mean something that hardly raises a ripple in the organisation's environment. Boddy (2002) analyses changes on two dimensions: *familiar* versus *novel*; *margin* versus *core*. As might be expected, it is usually more difficult to implement a completely novel change than a familiar change which has been enacted many times over. By the same token it is usually much more difficult to elicit a change that is 'core' to the organisation than a change which only affects it at the 'margin' (ie the periphery of its main operations).

EXERCISE 16.1

List changes in an organisation with which you are familiar which correspond to each of Boddy's four types of change.

Change as part of the work process

Not all changes come as a surprise. Research would not be 'research' if the answers to the questions were known in advance; part of the process is to proceed tentatively from one step to another, being alert to new knowledge, ideas, revelations on the way. In the same way, a computer software development project may be considered an 'incremental development process in which people learn from their mistakes' (Cockburn, 2002).

Again, if we consider any major construction project, we expect changes to happen and actually build in periodic reviews to keep the project on track (Briner, Hastings and Geddes, 1999) so that the planning cycle is one of plan-do-check/review by the project team, and discussion with the stakeholders, before action on revising the plans.

'Hard' and 'soft' changes

The sort of changes that are enacted during the typical construction project mentioned just above are very often ones which affect architect's drawings and engineering plans when there is a specification change or an addition or deletion. Very often these are purely technical changes: we could call them 'hard' changes.

'Soft' changes impact upon people; they are much less well defined and often demand a more intuitive approach. These changes may be forced upon the organisation or may result from the introduction of some 'hard change' (for instance, the introduction of a new computerised records system in a hospital).

Internal change projects

Sometimes the purpose of the change is to influence the behaviour of those within the organisation. Many quality initiatives (ISO 9000, Business Excellence) are essentially internal change projects – these inevitably have a high proportion of soft change in addition to the infrastructure of the quality assurance processes.

TRIGGERS FOR CHANGE

The change process often starts with an awareness of the need for change to meet internal requirements or to respond to external pressures. Typical events and factors which trigger an awareness of the need for change include:

- organisational growth or contraction
- an alteration to the business environment
- a perceived need to diversify
- the arrival of new personnel or the emergence of a new outlook
- the introduction of new technology.

Organisational growth or contraction

A consideration of growth or contraction must address the size and structure of the organisation and whether there will be greater centralisation or more delegation to local 'cost centres'. The environment, any diversification of products or services, the human resource factors or emerging technologies will influence a strategic evaluation that responds to the growth and contraction debate.

The business environment

This includes all aspects of the external environment that may have some impact on the organisation and its employees. For example, change might occur in:

- consumer behaviour – Customers might change their buying and spending habits (this could also be linked to social attitudes)
- the competition – Competitors could develop a new product that impinges on your organisation's profit margins, or conversely, your organisation might be expanding and taking over the competitors' markets
- social attitudes – Topical or health factors could affect the way a product or the company itself is perceived by the public. For example, many companies today want their products to be seen as 'environmentally friendly'
- economics – Government/EU/global actions have an impact on the macro scale … and a person's take-home pay at the micro level
- legislation – Changes to the law can have a wide-ranging effect on the policies and procedures an organisation adopts.

Diversification

As suggested above, any form of diversification will have significance. The diversification may be necessary for a number of reasons – eg failing products, changes in consumer needs, the need to introduce new technologies, pressure from competitors, changes to the workforce, and so forth.

Human resources

Factors that affect the human resource are numerous. Such changes include:

- change at the top – a new CEO may precipitate a culture change, re-organisation, or similar
- change to work functions, products, procedures, and technologies, which in turn may herald the need to change recruitment patterns and also alter the organisation's training and development programme (perhaps to move towards a knowledge management perspective)
- changes to any form of employment legislation that prompt a review of HR policies and procedures
- changes in work relationships due to issues of personality, capability or communication.

Technology

New technology is a major cause of change in organisations. We continue to develop more computerised technology-led functions, which in turn change products and work practices. A decision is then necessary on how to get from here to there. Managing change during this transition state is a critical phase in the change process. It is here that the problems of introducing change emerge and have to be managed. These problems can include resistance to change, low stability, high levels of stress, misdirected energy, conflict, and loss of momentum – hence the need to do everything possible to anticipate reactions and likely impediments to the introduction of change.

The installation stage can also be painful. When planning change there is a tendency for people to think that it will be an entirely logical and linear process of going from A to B. It is generally not like that at all. As Pettigrew and Whipp (1991) describe, the implementation of change is an 'iterative, cumulative and reformulation-in-use process'.

To attempt to manage change (or at least to be aware of the problems of managing change), it is first necessary to understand the various mechanisms for change as have been described in a number of change models briefly outlined below.

CHANGE MODELS

Many of the early theorists set out to identify a framework for the change process. The emphasis was upon a rationally based understanding of the process and thus a mechanism that managers could employ in managing change in a planned and systematic way. Two of the best-known change models of this genre are the three-phase model of change and force-field analysis, both developed by Kurt Lewin in the 1950s.

These models are outlined below because they are useful in the introduction of change terminology and concepts (such as barriers to change). They still feature in modern textbooks and in training courses.

Lewin's three-phase model

The three phases that represent basic mechanisms for managing change, as described by Lewin (1951), are:

1 'unfreezing' – altering the present stable equilibrium which supports existing behaviours and attitudes: this process must take account of the inherent threats to people that change represents and the need to motivate those affected to attain a new natural state of equilibrium by accepting change
2 changing – developing new responses based on new information
3 're-freezing' – stabilising the change by introducing the new responses into the personalities of those concerned.

Kanter *et al* (1992) have severely criticised this model, describing it as being 'quaintly linear and static' and 'wildly inappropriate'. They argue that rarely are mechanisms fixed in place, and that rather than occurring in stages, elements of the change process overlap.

EXERCISE 16.2

Think of an example of organisational change with which you are familiar. Was it a case of changing from one relatively fixed way of doing things to another? To what extent were the elements of the change process sequential?

Force-field analysis

Lewin also suggested a methodology for analysing change which he called 'force-field analysis'. This involves:

- analysing the driving and restraining forces that will affect the change: restraining forces typically include factors such as cost but also the reactions of those who see change as unnecessary or as constituting a threat (see *Resistance to change* below), whereas driving forces clearly include the benefits of the change
- assessing which of the driving and restraining forces are critical
- taking steps both to increase the critical driving forces and to decrease the critical restraining forces.

(See *Force-field analysis case study* and Figure 16.2 below.)

This is a timely point at which to examine people's resistance to change.

Resistance to change

People resist change because it is perceived as a threat to familiar patterns of behaviour as well as to status and financial rewards. Joan Woodward (1968) made this point clearly:

'When we talk about resistance to change we tend to imply that management is always rational in changing its direction, and that employees are stupid, emotional or irrational in not responding in the way they should. But if an individual is going to be worse off, explicitly or implicitly, when the proposed changes have been made, any resistance is entirely rational in terms of his or her own best interest. The interests of the organisation and the individual do not always coincide.'

The ways in which people change were described by Bandura (1986):

- People make conscious choices about their behaviours.
- The information people use to make their choices comes from their environment.
- Their choices are based upon the things that are important to them, the views they have about their own abilities to behave in certain ways, and the consequences they think will accrue to whatever behaviour they decide to engage in.

For those concerned in change management, the implications of the Bandura theory are that firstly, the tighter the link between a particular behaviour and a particular outcome, the more likely it is that we will engage in that behaviour; secondly, the more desirable the outcome, the more likely it is that we will engage in behaviour that we believe will lead to it; and finally, the more confident we are that we can actually assume a new behaviour, the more likely we are to try it.

However, we should not be totally negative – we should also note that change from an employee's point of view can be viewed as a positive experience. Staff will have their own reasons for embracing or rejecting the proposed changes based on their own beliefs, attitudes and values.

Some of the the main reasons for people's resisting change are:

- the shock of the new – people are suspicious of anything that they perceive will upset their established routines, methods of working or conditions of employment – they do not want to lose the security of what is familiar to them; they may not believe statements by management that the change is for their benefit as well as that of the organisation – sometimes with good reason; they may feel that management has ulterior motives; on occasion, the louder the protestations of management are, the less they are believed
- economic fears – loss of money, threats to job security
- inconvenience – the change will make life altogether more difficult
- symbolic fears – a small change that may affect some treasured symbol, such as a separate office or a reserved parking-space, may suggest that bigger changes are on the way, especially when employees are uncertain about how extensive the programme of change will be
- lack of respect for the proposer of the change
- feelings of having been excluded from participating in the changes
- general dislike of the idea and/or disappointment with the way change has been communicated; the importance of good communication cannot be overemphasised – it is essential throughout the change process
- the threat to inter-personal relationships – to anything that disrupts the customary social relationships and standards of the group
- the threat to status or skills, if the change is perceived as reducing the status of individuals or as de-skilling them
- competence fears – concern about the ability to cope with new demands or to acquire new skills.

Embracing change

Typical reasons for people to embrace change include:

- Change can provide people with a new challenge.
- Change can enliven work and reduce stress.
- The individual or group respects, agrees with or has an alliance with the proposer of the change.
- The individual or group expects some personal advantage/promotion/gain.
- The individual or group agrees with the idea or appreciates the way the change process has been communicated.
- Change may improve personal/professional prospects (this could include pay).
- The individual or group feels ownership of the changes, feels part of the change process.

Returning now to the use of force-field analysis, we can see how the forces against change (the restraining forces) may be represented on one side of the diagram. Those who advocate the method (eg Pedler, Boydell and Burgoyne, 1998) see this as a useful method because it allows those planning the change to analyse possible problems, ideally in advance of the change, thus assisting the 'unfreezing' process. It can form the basis of either individual or group consideration of a change situation. The following case study illustrates how we might use the method.

Force-field analysis case study: Printworthy Ltd

Printworthy Ltd is a medium-sized printing company, employing 30 employees. Its present factory is located in a run-down industrial estate. The factory itself is old and access to the site is difficult for large delivery lorries to negotiate. Mrs Jones, the managing director, has recently thought it would be a good idea to relocate the factory, taking advantage of a regional development grant to assist the funding (which she knows will stretch the finances of the company). The market for the company's products is growing but the present factory has reached maximum capacity. The site she has in mind is near to a newly built housing estate with an excellent road infrastructure and is 10 miles away from the present site. This will also be her opportunity to buy some new, more efficient machinery (some of it auto-mated) to replace some of their old-fashioned equipment.

Mrs Jones decides to hold a meeting with her management team to discuss her plans and to investigate some of the issues using force-field analysis. Figure 16.2, saved for record pur-poses on the flip-chart she used, shows the working of the group.

You will note that the group has decided upon the likely importance of the forces – however, you should note that this is subjective and not absolute. Also note that the diagram can include named individuals, groups, and various issues (eg the regional devel-opment grant, better access roads) – in fact, whatever force the group thinks is important and relevant.

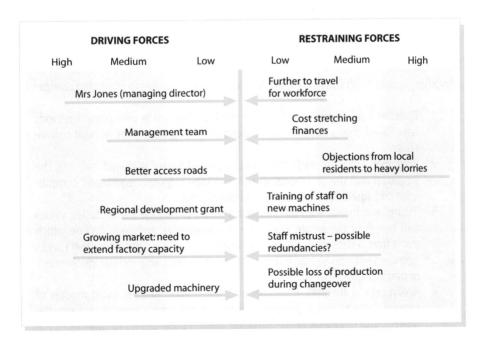

Figure 16.2 *Force-field diagram: proposed relocation of factory to new site*

Analysis of the diagram would be the next stage. In some cases it might be apparent that the driving forces will easily deliver the change because the restraining forces are not significant enough to worry about. In such cases the manager can carry out the plan without any special intervention. However, in the case shown, Mrs Jones might well feel that she needs to address the problems of objections from local residents rather than ignore the problem (it is often a better strategy to reduce restraining forces than to try to bulldoze them with increased driving forces) as well as to allay (possibly unfounded) fears of staff redundancies.

Other 'recipe' theories

David Collins (1998) is another writer who has been highly critical of Lewin and those other theories which put forward what he terms a 'recipe' approach to managing change. Under this 'recipe' approach we might include examples such as Richard Beckhard.

Beckhard

According to Beckhard (1969), a change programme should incorporate specific processes:

- setting goals and defining the future state or organisational conditions desired after the change
- diagnosing the present condition in relation to these goals
- defining the transition state activities and commitments required to meet the future state
- developing strategies and action plans for managing this transition in the light of an analysis of the factors likely to affect the introduction of change.

EXERCISE 16.3

Another theorist, Keith Thurley (1979), described five approaches to managing change:

1 Directive – the imposition of change in crisis situations or when other methods have failed: this is done by the exercise of managerial power without consultation
2 Bargained – an approach that recognises that power is shared between the employer and the employed, and that change requires negotiation, compromise and agreement before being implemented
3 'Hearts and minds' – an all-embracing thrust to change the attitudes, values and beliefs of the whole workforce: this 'normative' approach (ie one which starts from a definition of what management thinks is right or 'normal') seeks 'commitment' and 'shared vision' but does not necessarily include involvement or participation
4 Analytical – a theoretical approach to the change process using models of change such as those described above. It proceeds sequentially from the analysis and diagnosis of the situation, through the setting of objectives, the design of the change process, the evaluation of the results, finally to the deter-

mination of the objectives for the next stage in the change process. This is the rational and logical approach much favoured by consultants – external and internal. But change seldom proceeds as smoothly as this model would suggest. Emotions, power-politics and external pressures mean that the rational approach, although it might be the right way to start, is difficult to sustain

5 Action-based – an approach that recognises that the way managers behave in practice bears little resemblance to the analytical, theoretical model. The distinction between managerial thought and managerial action blurs in practice to the point of invisibility. What managers think is what they do. Real life therefore often results in a 'Ready – aim – fire!' outlook on change management. This typical approach to change starts with a broad belief that some sort of problem exists, although it may not be well-defined. The identification of possible solutions, often on a trial-and-error basis, leads to a clarification of the nature of the problem and a shared understanding of a possible optimal solution, or at least a framework within which solutions can be discovered.

Which of these five approaches can be clearly be identified as a 'recipe' approach?

EXERCISE 16.4

Consider the Printworthy Ltd case study outlined earlier. One of the issues raised by the force-field analysis was the likely resistance of staff to the proposed move. For this particular situation, briefly list and compare the advantages and disadvantages for Mrs Jones (the managing director) in relation to the first two of Thurley's approaches (listed in Exercise 16.3).

EXERCISE 16.5

Consider the Printworthy Ltd case study once more, and the likely resistance of staff to the proposed move. Let us assume that the staff's behaviour tends towards accepting the move to the new factory and all that that entails. What do you think are possible outcomes for the staff if they do this? How desirable do you think these outcomes might be? Make a list – and then compare your answers with the suggested ones given below.

Suggested answers
Going along with the change could enable the staff to be regarded in a positive light by management. This might be reflected by more positive appraisals or even promotion in

some cases. Another possible outcome is that the new efficiencies introduced would ulti-mately lead to redundancies.

Staff ought then to consider how tight the link is between accepting the changes and the possible outcomes listed above.

Our immediate reaction to the desirability of the outcomes for staff would be that pro-motion is desirable and redundancy undesirable. However, this may not always be the case: some staff may not wish for promotion; others may welcome the opportunity to take redundancy if the terms are favourable.

Emergent change

Since the 1980s there has been a loosely gathered school of thought that can be classified as the 'emergent approach to change'. The emergent approach does not have a simple defi-nition because it embodies a number of different views. However, what is common amongst these views is that the planned approach to change is too simplistic: these writers see change instead as 'an *emerging* and ongoing process of organisational adaptation and transformation' (Burnes, 2004; p291). Additionally, they view the organisation as existing in an 'open system' in which interactions can take place between it and the external environ-ment.

Within the organisation there are variables at play which impact upon change. Five of the most important of these are:

- power and politics in the organisation
- organisational structure
- organisational culture
- managerial behaviour
- organisational learning.

Each of these is addressed below.

Power and politics

Dawson (2000) states that managers often seek to legitimise their proposals for change by suggesting a rational reason for the change whereas they are often driven by ulterior motives of their own. Even after the change they will construct a story that emphasises this rational approach to decision-making. In this sense change is essentially political. He goes on to conclude that other groups in the organisation may 'recount stories' that are different in terms of how the change occurred and their part in it according to their own interests.

Thus, referring back to the Printworthy Ltd case study we might look more deeply at the motives of Mrs Jones and how she views the change process. We can only guess her inner-most reasons for wanting to relocate – indeed, she may be a very task-driven, company-oriented person whose only consideration is for the success of the organisation, rather than herself. Such a selfless attitude may be considered by some as admirable and the 'correct' way for managers to approach such a decision.

What do you think? Is it permissible for senior managers to consider their own interests? To what extent?

Reflection on the Exercise

If you have views on this which differ from those of your colleagues, or if you have contrasting views of your own, then you are not alone! We have already touched upon this in the Power and politics chapter (Chapter 11) when considering the work of Verma (1996) who advocates what he calls the 'sensible' approach rather than the 'submissive' or the 'shark' – in other words, to be aware that politics is part of organisational life and to be prepared to take part in the 'game' at the risk of being a victim of the process. If you wish to read further you may consider the work of Knights and Murray (1998) who talks of a 'critical processual perspective' in which he does not attempt to label political actions and motives as good or bad, questions the idea of rationality in decision-making, and declares that we should understand the political processes if we are to make sense of change. The work of Buchanan and Badham (1999) goes further in that it suggests that those who are attempting to bring about change will fail if they ignore the politics of the situation. The authors go on to provide some guidelines for would-be change agents. Pfeffer (1981, 1992) talks about power as being more important than rational decision-making.

Referring once more to the Printworthy Ltd case study and Mrs Jones: regardless of her own personal interests in the proposed relocation, there remains the issue of how she views the change process itself. If we take note of the theorists just mentioned, then for success, she should adopt a political perspective (as well as rational) if the change is to be successful. She must consider the perspectives and interests of the key players and be aware of their likely moves while at the same time considering how she can bring influence to bear upon the situation.

Organisational structure

From a basic structural point of view the allocation of duties, responsibilities and accountabilities is enacted through the organisational form. Kotter (1996a) maintains that a flat hierarchy in which people are empowered to make decisions quickly at their level is an advantage for the organisation's ability to manage change.

Taking a more radical view, Michael Beer and colleagues (1990) have suggested that individual behaviour is powerfully shaped by the organisational roles people play, and that the most effective way to change behaviour, therefore, is to put people into a new organisational context which imposes new roles, responsibilities and relationships on them – ie to change the structure. This creates a situation that in a sense 'forces' new attitudes and behaviour on people.

If we consider the Printworthy Ltd case study, the proposed move presents an opportunity for modernising the production process and the reconsideration of staff roles which without the move might have been more difficult to implement.

Organisational culture – readiness for change – reshaping capabilities

Organisational culture is clearly an important factor in organisational change. As discussed in the chapter on culture (Chapter 10), views range from those who believe culture can be managed to those who state that to do so is a futile task. Some writers go so far as to say that the culture *is* the organisation, and not some 'bolt-on', and therefore to change the culture is to change the organisation and vice versa.

Jones *et al* (2005) consider the 'readiness for change' of an organisation in relation to its culture and reshaping capabilities. They refer to four types of culture – human relations, open systems, internal process and rational goal cultures – which originate from Quinn's (1988) 'competing values' organisational framework.

The *human relations culture* focuses on cohesion and morale amongst staff and aims to achieve this through training and development, open communication and participative decision-making. The *open systems culture* focuses on innovation and development and aims to achieve this through adaptability and readiness, visionary communication, and adaptable decision-making. The *internal process culture* focuses on stability and control and aims to achieve this by information management, precise communication, and data-based decision-making. Finally, the *rational goal culture* focuses on efficiency and productivity and aims to achieve this by goal-setting and planning, instructional communication, and centralised decision-making.

Of these the researchers found that a human relations culture was linked to higher levels of readiness for change. (Note that all four types of organisational culture can co-exist in the same organisation.)

Apart from these motivational aspects, Jones *et al* (2005) raise the concept of the 'reshaping capabilities' of the organisation. It is not sufficient just to want to change – the organisation must have the requisite competences to make the change, and these competences are different from the competences required for the everyday running of the business. These competences are those of encouraging commitment from staff, developing the systems required for the changes, and proactively managing the change – what Turner and Crawford (1998) refer to as 'engagement, development and performance management'. Not surprisingly, there are links between the human relations culture and this framework.

Managerial behaviour

Managers v leaders, and change

Kotter (1996b) separates leadership from management and argues that what is needed in today's fast-moving environment with its demands for continuous improvements in quality and efficiencies is good leadership. He states that:

> **'successful transformation is 70 to 90 per cent leadership and only 10 to 30 per cent management'.**

He says that historically this was not always so – in the 1960s, for instance, the planning, organising and controlling functions of management were well suited to the much more stable market environment. However, successful organisations may reach a stage in their life cycle when increased bureaucracy (brought about to handle this very success) begins to stifle initiative and encourages management at the expense of leadership. The other point he raises is that management competence is more readily defined than leadership and is often the focus of managerial development.

Credibility and trust

Leadership is concerned with giving direction, motivating and developing others, and is essential to the change process. As we will see shortly, this does not have to be the sole preserve of the 'change agent'. However, it is important for change to succeed that leaders are seen as credible and trustworthy. Kouzes and Posner (1995) stated that these characteristics were what most employees wanted from their managers – but also the same traits that were perceived to be most lacking. Credibility was linked to a number of factors: honesty, integrity, and technical competence.

Morgan and Zeffane (2003) go further and say that *any* change diminishes trust in management because it decreases stability, and that this is only overcome by a direct form of consultation between management and staff. The lack of such consultation implies that employees cannot be trusted to make important decisions.

They go on to say that declining trust is associated with downsizing and major structural change, 'especially where it is frequent'. In their eyes honesty is a matter of consistency of word and deed.

The power of emotional appeal and the use of language

The ability to appeal to people's emotions can win many an argument and be a prime motivating factor for change. On a personal level we are all aware of this: the newspapers and media play on it. When some disaster is reported, it is not merely the facts that we are given – we also see and hear the plight of individuals. The facts themselves may prompt us to donate for such a disaster appeal on the basis that we might expect the same in their situation, but if we identify with the grief of individuals, we are far more likely to help. We relate to our own experiences too and our personal values: at the sight of a suffering child we might think of our own child, and that is the feeling that motivates. Actions based upon emotion are thus not always rational to the outsider. We might prefer to be seen to act 'rationally' as managers, but we should be aware that even in the work situation emotions must be considered, none more so than in the event of controversial change when people might feel that their interests are threatened.

Fox and Amichai-Hamburger (2001) offer practical methods on how to appeal to people's emotions in promoting organisational change programmes, under the following headings:

- The core messages – for instance using words such as 'danger' or 'loss' in respect to the existing situation, and words such as 'progress' and 'relief' for the proposed situation; using metaphors which appeal emotionally
- The packaging of the messages – using a variety of the audience's senses. Managers should show their own emotions to emphasise key points and should listen to their audience, letting them express their fears and aspirations
- The characteristics of change leaders – credibility, likeableness and attractiveness are cited as the 'essential ingredients in building trust'. Also, the trust of managers in their audience

- The behaviour of change managers towards their audience – listen to their audience, respect their views and opinions
- The setting in which the interaction takes place – consideration of who to involve for group dynamics; the use of ceremonies to mark the beginning or end of a change action.

EXERCISE 16.7

Listen to a famous speech which has changed people's lives (for instance, JFK's speech about putting a man on the moon, any of Churchill's wartime speeches, or Martin Luther King's 'I have a dream' speech). Now analyse that speech in terms of the five headings in the bullet-list above.

To what extent do you regard appealing to people's emotions as something that is legitimate?

Organisational learning

EXERCISE 16.8

To what extent do you think that change is linked to the learning of individuals and groups in the organisation? Do you think that an organisation in itself exists as a thinking entity, with its own repository of knowledge, skills and behaviour, its own ability to learn and develop?

Change in the organisation does not automatically mean that it has to learn a new system (it might, for instance, be reverting to a former system, or to one with which it is already familiar). However, it is probably safe to assume that for a large number of situations, the change will involve individuals, groups and the organisation in something which they are not totally familiar with (and, in some cases, completely new to). The ability to react to and readily assimilate new ways of thinking and doing (ie change) is clearly an advantage in today's highly competitive business environment – in other words, the ability to *learn*.

We have already discussed the concepts of 'single-loop' and 'double-loop' learning in an earlier chapter with relation to the role of the manager and thus are already aware that learning in this context is important. What we have not yet discussed is the broader implications of learning for the organisation itself. Let us consider one definition of organisational learning, as given by Probst and Buchel (1997):

> **'Organisational learning is the process by which the organisation's knowledge and value base changes, leading to improved problem-solving and capacity for action.'**

With reference back to Exercise 16.8, this definition asserts that organisations can of themselves be entities with a capacity to retain information and hold their own set of values. In other words, although an organisation may be regarded as being its people, the collective sum of their knowledge and experience can somehow be held within the organisation to exist semi-autonomously (and thus be retained even after one or more individuals have departed) and in a synergistic way.

For example, a construction company has the opportunity to learn from every project it is involved with because, by definition, every project (even if similar) is unique. This learning is not just on the part of individuals but concerns the integration of every part of the organisation in carrying out the activity. Learning is thus also to do with the systems of the organisation: how it goes about its planning, organising and controlling; how it leads and develops its staff. The successful organisation will retain the knowledge from its experiences for later projects and will hone its skills upon reflection on them. Internal change is also accommodated through this interaction of individual, group and organisational structure, values and systems. Senge in his book *The Fifth Discipline* (1990) lists the following set of inter-related factors as conducive to [organisational] learning:

- personal mastery – This goes beyond competence and skills (for instance, it includes personal vision which allows individuals to see room for development) although it is grounded in them; Senge goes on to say that 'People with a high level of mastery live in a continual learning mode'
- mental models – Assumptions held by individuals can tie them to the past way of doing things; to move forward, people must see that their mental models are always incomplete and are often based upon generalisations of truth (eg employees are lower in the hierarchy than management and so have nothing creative to offer) and frequently do not take into account the whole situation. Having a mental model can/will create a reality
- shared visions – Senge says that this goes beyond a shared idea: it is a 'force in people's hearts'
- team learning – The team must be aligned in its thinking, to enter into dialogue and discussion, to be able to unlock the routines and protocol that appear to protect us but which block learning
- systems thinking – This shows that it is not always possible to reduce complex interactions into simple models; we must be aware of the inter-relationships that exist.

According to this viewpoint effective organisational change is thus coupled with organisational learning.

GUIDELINES FOR CHANGE MANAGEMENT

What guidance can we give to the manager, given that – as we have seen from this brief coverage – change is often a complex business? Can the early ideas of Lewin still be used? If change is as complex as the emergent thinkers believe it is, and if 'recipe' approaches are to be regarded as too simplistic, can there be any practical advice from this front?

To answer the first question is problematic. In order to give some guidance here the suggestion is that the pragmatic manager may well use force-field analysis in the first instance as one method in the process of change management – although it is important to accept that it will be a simplification of the situation (which some emergent thinkers would, therefore, state invalidates it) – while being prepared to consider such variables as power and culture at the same time.

To consider the process in more detail, the eight stages of the change process as described by Kotter (1996) could also be used.

But wait a minute! Wasn't Kotter, as one of the writers advocating emergent change, someone who railed against 'recipe' methods for change? The response to this is that what Kotter is advocating here are processes, the precise nature of which will vary according to the situation. The suggestion here is that although this approach still has echoes of a 'top-down' approach and is still prescriptive to some extent, it does give some meaningful advice to the manager while still encompassing emergent thinking. Kotter's eight stages (1996) are:

1 Establish a sense of urgency.
2 Create the guiding coalition.
3 Develop a vision and strategy.
4 Communicate the change vision.
5 Empower broad-based action: get rid of obstacles
6 Generate short-term gains.
7 Consolidate gains and produce more change.
8 Institutionalise new approaches in the culture.

It is interesting to note what Kotter (1996) goes on to say about all this:

> **'The four steps in the transformation process help defrost a hardened status quo. If change were easy, you wouldn't need all that effort. Phases 5 to 7 then introduce new practices. The last stage grounds the changes in the corporate culture and helps make them stick.'**

A different approach is offered by Beer et al (1990), who focus at first on the task rather than on values. They suggest six steps to effective change which concentrate on what they call 'task alignment' – reorganising employees' roles, responsibilities and relationships to solve specific business problems in small units where goals and tasks can be clearly defined. The aim of following the overlapping steps is to build a self-reinforcing cycle of commitment, co-ordination and competence. The steps are:

1 Mobilise commitment to change through the joint analysis of problems.
2 Develop a shared vision of how to organise and manage to achieve goals such as competitiveness.

3   Foster consensus for the new vision, competence to enact it, and cohesion to move it along.
4   Spread revitalisation to all departments without pushing it from the top – don't force the issue: let each department find its own way to the new organisation.
5   Institutionalise revitalisation through formal policies, systems and structures.
6   Monitor and adjust strategies in response to problems in the revitalisation process.

According to Beer and colleagues, this approach is fundamental to the effective management of change. Nonetheless, account should be taken of the likelihood of resistance to change and what can be done about it.

We should note that although there may be an overall strategy for change, writers such as Pettigrew and Whipp (1991) would suggest that it is best tackled incrementally (except in crisis conditions). The change programme should be broken down into actionable segments for which people can be held accountable. Change implies streams of activity across time and (Pettigrew and Whipp, 1991):

> **'may require the enduring of abortive efforts or the build-up of slow incremental phases of adjustment which then allow short bursts of incremental action to take place'.**

Finally, Kotter (1996) also considers the way in which major projects are structured. In many situations there is not one project going on but a number of them which depend upon each other, sometimes concurrently, sometimes sequentially. The first of these might be what he terms 'save-the-ship', the second 're-engineering', and the third 'major structural and cultural change'.

EXERCISE 16.9

To what extent do you think the changes in the Printworthy Ltd case study could be implemented incrementally?

Now imagine that Mrs Jones decides against the factory relocation but still wants to modernise the factory's operations. To what extent do you think the changes could be introduced incrementally, and what would be the benefits of such incremental change?

Change agents

The role of the change agent (the person or persons introducing the change) has been identified in the change process from the early theories of Lewin onwards. The advocated nature of this role, however, varies according to the perspective taken on change. For instance, the role is different for a top-down approach to change (still much in favour with management today) from a bottom-up approach (in line with some of the emergent thinking just discussed). The top-down approach often regards the change agent as a visionary figure and the main driver of the change. The bottom-up approach, by which people at different levels in the organisation also drive the change, suggests a role that is more facilitative in nature. The role of the specialist change consultant also comes into play, and here the tension is between the organisation's capabilities for managing change versus the expertise the consultant can offer and the extent to which the organisation wishes to involve its staff in developing and owning the changes.

In the Printworthy Ltd case study, the change agent corresponds to Mrs Jones, the managing director. But the boss is not always the prime mover, let alone the change agent. Sometimes a change project will have a 'project manager' whose job it is to introduce the change. This person may not have formal or direct authority over others, so will be unable to use Thurley's Directive approach (see Exercise 16.3) and will therefore have to behave in a more facilitative way.

Involvement in the change process gives people the chance to raise and resolve their concerns and make suggestions about the form of the change and how it should be introduced. The aim is to transfer 'ownership' – a feeling amongst people that the change is something that they are happy to live with because they have been involved in its planning and introduction – it has become *their* change.

Communications about the proposed change should be carefully prepared and worded so that unnecessary fears are allayed. All the available channels should be used, but face-to-face communications direct from managers to individuals or through a team-briefing system are best.

EXERCISE 16.10

Read the case study below and carry out the tasks at the end.

Case study: the Centre for Learning Development and Innovation

The Tees and North-East Yorkshire (TNEY) Trust has over recent years become nationally recognised as an organisation which provides high-quality specialist mental health and learning disability services for 80,000 people across Teesside, North-East Yorkshire and East Durham. The Trust has been very successful in both service delivery and managing organisational change, and consequently has established a high national and local profile.

TNEY is a relatively small but complex organisation, covering a large geographical area with both rural and urban populations. Structurally it is divided into three localities with different ranges of services. This area incorporates two strategic health authorities, six local authorities and social service departments, together with several different Primary Care Trusts all in various stages of development, organisation maturity and partnership development.

A dedicated support function for these services is the recently launched (2002) Centre for Learning Development and Innovation, the aims of which are (CLDI Strategy 2003–2006) to:

'foster the innovation and promote the identification and dissemination of good practice and learning across mental health and learning disability services within the Trust and with external organisations'.

Acting as a forum for the 'dissemination of good practice', part of this role is to assist in the support of training and development within the existing organisational structure of the various Trust-based services. However, its wider role is to promote the establishment and operation of 'virtual teams' which involve not just the National Health Service but also other services such as local authorities (eg the social services), nursing and care homes, other Trusts, and teaching institutions. The CLDI's activities are shown in Figure 16.3.

The concept of the 'patient pathway' is central to this approach. Take, for instance – a fairly common disorder – the case of a person who is diagnosed with severe clinical depression,

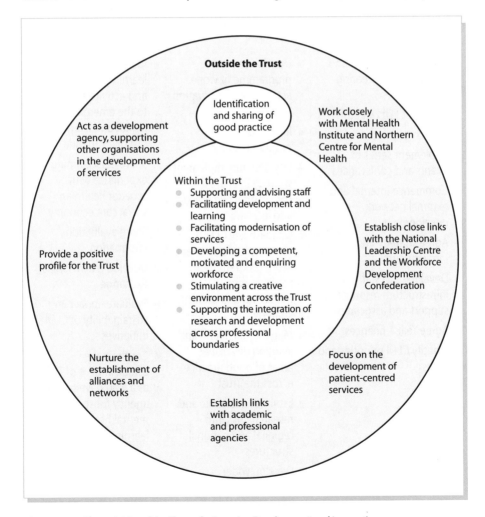

Figure 16.3 *The activities of the Centre for Learning Development and Innovation*

the long-term symptoms of which include complete lack of purpose, loss of energy, and deep despair. Treatment of such an illness can take a number of months or more – during which the patient may require the assistance and understanding of a number of services – from the initial acute stage (which may require close medical supervision in a hospital) to out-patient clinic (eg counselling and behavioural therapy) and then to general practioner's surgery (eg for drugs) as the patient recovers. The stigma of mental illness is still strong in society and the individual may find himself or herself out of a job. Perhaps the job was itself one of the precipitating factors into illness and a new one is needed, which may involve additional training. In either case, help may be sought. If it is felt that the person may require additional help to care for others (for instance, he or she may be a parent or guardian), the social services may become involved. The concept of 'patient pathway' treats the individual from beginning to end of this process, so as to provide 'joined-up' care.

As previously stated, the CLDI is in its early years of development as an organisation. Table 16.1 charts its progress to early 2004, and shows further development.

Table 16.1 *The process of development for the CLDI*

2002–2003	2003–2004	2004–2005
■ Agree CLDI concept and establish local steering group ■ Appoint CLDI Director ■ Launch event ■ Implement series of events and conferences ■ Commence internal and external network development ■ Agree strategy and infrastructure ■ Develop CLDI staff infrastructure resource support and associates ■ Agree Year 1 finances ■ Identify CLDI priorities and plans	■ Develop annual programme of work activities and evaluation strategies ■ Implement work programmes ■ Develop and implement strategy to share and spread effective practice and learning ■ Establish key CLDI services, conference and event programme together with marketing and publicity strategy ■ Map mental health and learning disabilities areas of good practice across the Trust ■ Establish academic and research links into regional and national structures ■ Develop wider relationships with other key organisations/ groups	■ Identify the broader learning opportunities and activities in relation to the emerging mental health and learning disability agenda ■ Share CLDI learning experience with broader health and social care economy ■ Share evaluation information ■ Develop partnerships exchange ■ Evaluate impact and sustainability of CLDI initiatives ■ Continue the establishment of TNEY as a lead development agency for specialist mental health and learning disabilities

EXERCISE 16.11 TASKS

List what you consider to be the important (emerging) values of the Centre for Learning Development and Innovation (CLDI).

List potential barriers to changing the culture of those involved in the 'patient pathway'.

SUMMARY

- This chapter has considered some of the complexities of managing change. The positioning of the chapter, as the last in the book, signifies the integrative nature of all of the elements of 'managing for results'.
- The wide-spanning nature of change has been considered: 'hard' and 'soft' changes; change as an integral process in the operational process; change as internal change in the organisation.
- The early ideas of theorists such as Kurt Lewin have been explored and other change theories which belong to a top-down, generally prescriptive, approach have been introduced as models for change.
- Attention has been drawn to the concept of 'resistance to change' by those opposed to change for a number of reasons, including their perspective to the change and self-interests.
- The emergent theories of change of the last 20 years have been discussed. These broadened the context in which change takes place and point to the interaction of other factors which can influence the change process. In particular, the work of Pfeffer and Dawson (politics) has been cited, and the role of culture (Schein, Jones) has been emphasised. The simplistic nature of some of the early theories and the extent to which change can be managed has been challenged. The nature of change in terms of its time-frame and continuity has been raised. The work of Beer has questioned whether the main emphasis should be on changing people's values first or (as he proposes) whether if the organisational context is changed values will follow.
- Finally, the chapter has attempted to provide some meaningful guidelines for the would-be change agent to consider when faced with change. The suggestions of Kotter, Beer, and the earlier ideas of Lewin and others are featured here. However, the overall thrust of the chapter is to offer the reader food for thought and some tips for methodologies which best suit their own particular situation.

REFERENCES

BANDURA A. (1986) *Social Boundaries of Thought and Action.* Englewood Cliffs, NJ, Prentice Hall.

BECKHARD R. (1969) *Organisation Development: Strategy and Models.* Reading MA, Addison-Wesley.

BEER M., EISENSTAT R. and SPECTOR B. (1990) 'Why change programs don't produce change', *Harvard Business Review*, November–December, pp158–66.

BODDY D. (2002) *Management: An introduction.* London, Pearson Education.

BRINER W., HASTINGS C. and GEDDES M. (1999; 2nd edition) *Project Leadership.* Aldershot, Gower.

BUCHANAN D. and BADHAM R. (1999) *Power, Politics and Organisation Change: Winning the turf game.* London, Sage.

BURNES B. (2004; 4th edition) *Managing Change.* Harlow, Essex, FT/Prentice Hall.

COCKBURN A. (2002) *Agile Software Development.* Reading, MA, Addison-Wesley.

COLLINS D. (1998) *Organizational Change: Sociological perspectives.* London, Routledge.

DAWSON P. (2000) 'Technology, work restructuring and the orchestration of a rational narrative in the pursuit of "management objectives": the political process of plant-level change', *Technology Analysis and Strategic Management,* Vol. 12, No. 1, March.

FOX S. and AMICHAI-HAMBURGER Y. (2001) 'The power of emotional appeals in promoting organizational change programs', *Academy of Management Executive,* Vol. 15, No. 4, November.

JONES R. A., JIMMIESON N. L. and GRIFFITHS A. (2005) 'The impact of organizational culture and reshaping capabilities on change implementation success: the mediating role of readiness for change', *Journal of Management Studies,* Vol. 42, No. 2, pp361–86.

KANTER R. M. (1984) *The Change Masters.* London, Allen & Unwin.

KANTER R. M., STEIN B. A. and JICK T. D. (1992) *The Challenge of Organisational Change.* New York, Free Press – as quoted in BURNES B. (2004; 4th edition) *Managing Change.* Harlow, Essex, FT/Prentice Hall.

KNIGHTS D. and MURRAY F. (1998) *Managers Divided: Organisation politics and Information Technology management.* Chichester, John Wiley.

KOTTER J. P. (1996a) *Leading Change.* Boston, MA, Harvard Business School Press.

KOTTER J. P. (1996b) 'Successful change and the force that drives it', *Canadian Manager,* Vol. 21, No. 3, Fall, pp 20–3.

KOUZES J. M. and POSNER B. Z. (1995) *The Leadership Challenge.* San Francisco, Jossey-Bass.

LEWIN K. (1951) *Field Theory in Social Science.* New York, Harper & Row.

MORGAN D. E. and ZEFFANE R. (2003) 'Employee Involvement, organizational change and trust in management', *International Journal of Human Resource Management,* Vol. 14, No. 1, February, pp55–75.

PEDLER M., BOYDELL T. and BURGOYNE J. G. (1998; 3rd edition) *A Manager's Guide to Self-Development.* Maidenhead, McGraw-Hill.

PETTIGREW A. and WHIPP R. (1991) *Managing Change for Competitive Success.* Oxford, Blackwell.

PFEFFER J. (1981) *Power in Organizations.* Cambridge, MA, Pitman.

PFEFFER J. (1992) *Managing Power: Politics and influence in organizations.* Boston, MA, Harvard Business School Press.

PROBST G. and BUCHEL B. (1997) *Organisational Learning.* London, Prentice Hall.

QUINN R. E. (1988) *Beyond Rational Management: Mastering the paradoxes and competing demands of high performance.* San Francisco, Jossey-Bass.

SCHEIN E.H. (1968) 'Organizational Socialization and the Profession of Management', *Industrial Management Review,* Winter pp1–16.

SENGE P. M. (1990) *The Fifth Discipline: The art and practice of the learning organization.* London, Century Business.

THURLEY K. (1979) *Supervision: A reappraisal.* London, Heinemann.

TURNER D. and CRAWFORD M. (1998) *Change Power: Capabilities that drive corporate renewal.* Warriewood, NSW, Business and Professional Publishing.

VERMA K. (1996) *Human Resource Skills for the Project Manager* (Vol. 2 of *The Human Aspects of Project Management*). Project Management Institute.

WOODWARD J. (1968) 'Resistance to change', *Management Review*, Vol. 8.

Index

Also from CIPD Publishing . . .

Business Environment:

Managing in a strategic context

John Kew and John Stredwick

Business environment has become an established and growing part of most business courses. Having knowledge of the key environmental influences – economic, social, and legal – is essential to developing an understanding of business strategy at every level.

Written in an easy to use format, for students with little or no prior knowledge of the subject area, practical implications of theories are emphasised and examples clearly set out.

The text also includes chapter objectives, student activities, definitions, case studies, lists of further reading and a tutor support site.

Order your copy now online at www.cipd.co.uk/bookstore or call us on 0870 800 3366

John Kew was Principal Lecturer in Management Studies and Head of the Business School at Harlow College until 1993, teaching Business Environment and Strategic Management on CIPD and DMS programmes. Since 1993 he has been an educational consultant, and has also written Flexible Learning material for the CIPD's Professional Development Scheme.

John Stredwick spent 25 years as a Human Resource Practitioner in publishing and shipbuilding before joining Everest Double Glazing for 11 years as Head of Personnel. In 1992, he joined Luton University as Senior Lecturer and has directed the CIPD programmes since that time. *Business Environment* is his sixth with the CIPD. He is a national moderator for the CIPD and has run several CIPD short courses on reward management.

Published 2005	1 84398 079 7	Paperback	304 pages

The Chartered Institute of Personnel and Development is the leading publisher of books and reports for personnel and training professionals, students and all those concerned with the effective management and development of people at work.

Also from CIPD Publishing . . .

Managing and Leading People

Charlotte Rayner and Derek Adam-Smith

The text is aimed specifically at students taking the CIPD qualification in Managing and Leading People, taking into account the new Standards coming into effect September 2005.

The text will encompass the following approach that the authors feel is synergetic with the CIPD aims:

- a critical approach commensurate to 'Masters' level courses of study.
- an appropriate theory base that one would expect at 'Masters' level.
- an evidenced-based approach. This will draw on academic evidence from theory and research as well as practical evidence through case studies.
- an appropriateness to many workplace settings. Included are a wide spread of examples and comment so that public, private and voluntary sectors are encompassed. Small, medium and large organisations are used both for evidence and also in discussing application of theory and research.
- attention is drawn to the need for context-fit for any application of theory and practice. A variety of examples and resources are provided, so that ultimately students are equipped with the tools to extend their enquiry to find the best fit for their own organisation.

Order your copy now online at www.cipd.co.uk/bookstore or call us on 0870 800 3366

Charlotte Rayner is Professor of Human Resource Management at Portsmouth Business School.

Derek Adam-Smith is Head of the Human Resource and Marketing Management department at Portsmouth Business School.

Published 2005	1 84398 115 7	Paperback	256 pages

The Chartered Institute of Personnel and Development is the leading publisher of books and reports for personnel and training professionals, students and all those concerned with the effective management and development of people at work.

Also from CIPD Publishing . . .

Managing Information and Statistics

2nd edition

Roland and Frances Bee

This edition has been written specifically for the new Managing Information for Competitive Advantage module, which forms part of the core Leadership and Management section of the CIPD professional qualifications. It covers both information systems and statistics and offers a clear and comprehensive view of these subject areas.

The new edition includes:

- a wide range of case studies and worked examples
- exercises to review and reinforce learning
- chapter objectives to signpost the reader through the text
- new chapters on knowledge management systems and the e-organisation (including e-commerce).

All these combine to make this traditionally daunting subject more accessible and provide an updated source of relevant material.

'I strongly recommend Managing Information and Statistics as essential reading for all students aspiring to meet the new CIPD Thinking Performer standards, as well as for the continuous development of existing CIPD members.'
David Allen, CIPD Chief Examiner, Managing Information for Competitive Advantage.

Order your copy now online at www.cipd.co.uk/bookstore or call us on 0870 800 3366

Roland and Frances Bee are Managing Consultants with Time for People, a learning consultancy specialising in information management, and learning needs analysis and evaluation. They have worked with a wide variety of public and private sector organisations and are authors of several books published by the CIPD. Their practical experience as statisticians, HR professionals, finance and line managers give them a unique perspective on the area.

| Published 2005 | 0 85292 995 1 | Paperback | 320 pages |

The Chartered Institute of Personnel and Development is the leading publisher of books and reports for personnel and training professionals, students and all those concerned with the effective management and development of people at work.

Also from CIPD Publishing . . .

Personal Effectiveness

Diana Winstanley

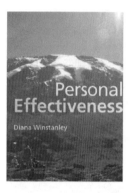

Written by a leading author in this field, this new text on Personal Effectiveness is designed to give students a basic understanding of study skills and management skills, and to give context to other studies.

Suitable for use on a range of undergraduate and postgraduate modules, including those relating to self development, personal skills, learning and development, management skills, study skills and coaching modules, and as part of general business or HR degrees, this text seeks to be both comprehensive and accessible through the use of learning aids.

Each chapter includes:
- learning objectives and a synopsis of content;
- vignette examples to illustrate key points;
- exercises with feedback;
- a self-check exercise and synopsis at the end of the chapter; and
- references and further sources of information.

Order your copy now online at www.cipd.co.uk/bookstore or call us on 0870 800 3366

Diana Winstanley has over 15 years experience of training staff, students and managers in personal effectiveness, as well as in human resource management, and is already a well respected author of a number of books and articles. She has also led, designed and supported a number of PhD and postgraduate programmes in transferable skills and personal effectiveness, and is currently Professor of Management and Director of Postgraduate Programmes at Kingston Business School. Previously she has been Senior Lecturer in Management and Personal Development, Deputy Director of the full-time MBA programme and Senior Tutor at Tanaka Business School, Imperial College London. She also has professional qualifications as a humanistic counsellor.

| Published 2005 | 1 84398 002 9 | Paperback | 256 pages |

The Chartered Institute of Personnel and Development is the leading publisher of books and reports for personnel and training professionals, students and all those concerned with the effective management and development of people at work.

Also from CIPD Publishing . . .

Personnel Practice

4th edition

Malcolm Martin and Tricia Jackson

Personnel Practice is widely acclaimed as the definitive introduction to human resource management. It is designed specifically to cater for the CIPD Certificate in Personnel Practice and is invaluable for all students taking the Certificate as well as anyone seeking an overview of the subject area.

This new edition offers an updated look at the subject area, with coverage of up-to-date legislation and information management. Each chapter has a clear overview and concise summary, providing ideal points for revision and reference. The text also contains detailed sources of further information, alongside activities and case studies to test knowledge and link knowledge to practice.

'Personnel Practice should be the standard reference text for all line managers, HR practitioners and undergraduate HR and personnel students developing an interest in and/or responsibility for HR issues who need an understanding of maximising people performance in today's competitive environment.' Alan Lund MCIPD, Programme Manager, East Lancashire Business School

Order your copy now online at www.cipd.co.uk/bookstore or call us on 0870 800 3366

Malcolm Martin BSc, MCMI, FCIPD has been involved in the design and delivery of the Certificate in Personnel Practice programmes for many years, primarily at the training provider, MOL. He has worked for British Steel, Dunlop, Guthrie and the BBA Group, where he held managerial positions in industrial relations, project management and personnel. Since then he has directed numerous CPP courses for corporate clients and for public programmes.

Tricia Jackson BA, MSc (Personnel Management), MInstAM, Chartered FCIPD is a freelance training and personnel consultant, specialising in employment law. Tricia has many years' experience as a generalist practitioner in both the public and private sectors. She is currently involved in tutoring on open-learning and college-based CIPD programmes, competence assessment, identifying and providing training solutions, personnel consultancy and representing clients at employment tribunals.

Published 2004	1 84398 102 5	Paperback	240 pages

The Chartered Institute of Personnel and Development is the leading publisher of books and reports for personnel and training professionals, students and all those concerned with the effective management and development of people at work.

Also from CIPD Publishing . . .

Equality, Diversity and Discrimination

Kathy Daniels and Lynda Macdonald

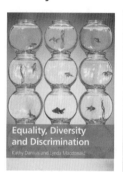

This text is designed specifically for the increasing number of students taking a module in Equality and Diversity, including those students taking the CIPD specialist elective, Managing Diversity and Equal Opportunities. It will also be relevant on many equality, diversity and equal opportunities modules that are part of general business or HR degrees.

The text contains a range of features, including:
- learning objectives – at the beginning of each chapter summarising the content
- interactive tasks to encourage students to research around the subject
- case studies
- legal cases
- key points and summary at the end of each chapter
- examples to work through at the end of each chapter.

Order your copy now online at www.cipd.co.uk/bookstore or call us on 0870 800 3366

Kathy Daniels teaches at Aston Business School and is a tutor for ICS Ltd in Employment Law and related topics. She is also a tutor on the Advanced Certificate in Employment Law for the Chartered Institute of Personnel and Development. A Fellow of the CIPD, she is a lay member of the Employment Tribunals sitting in Birmingham. Prior to these appointments she was a senior personnel manager in the manufacturing sector.

Lynda Macdonald is a freelance employment law trainer, adviser and writer. For fifteen years prior to setting up her own business, she gained substantial practical experience of employee relations, recruitment and selection, dismissal procedures, employment law and other aspects of human resource management through working in industry. With this solid background in human resource management, she successfully established, and currently runs, her own business in employment law and management training/consultancy.

| Published 2005 | 1 84398 112 2 | Paperback | 272 pages |

The Chartered Institute of Personnel and Development is the leading publisher of books and reports for personnel and training professionals, students and all those concerned with the effective management and development of people at work.

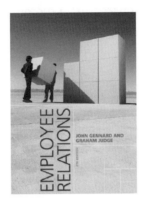

Membership has its rewards

Join us online today as an Affiliate member and get immediate access to our member services. As a member you'll also be entitled to special discounts on our range of courses, conferences, books and training resources.

To find out more, visit www.cipd.co.uk/affiliate or call us on 020 8612 6208.